Queenship and Power

Series Editors

Charles Beem
University of North Carolina, Pembroke
Pembroke, USA

Carole Levin
University of Nebraska-Lincoln
Lincoln, USA

Aims of the Series

This series focuses on works specializing in gender analysis, women's studies, literary interpretation, and cultural, political, constitutional, and diplomatic history. It aims to broaden our understanding of the strategies that queens-both consorts and regnants, as well as female regents-pursued in order to wield political power within the structures of male-dominant societies. The works describe queenship in Europe as well as many other parts of the world, including East Asia, Sub-Saharan Africa, and Islamic civilization.

More information about this series at
http://www.springer.com/series/14523

Cinzia Recca

The Diary of Queen Maria Carolina of Naples, 1781–1785

New Evidence of Queenship at Court

palgrave
macmillan

Cinzia Recca
University of Catania
Catania, Italy

Queenship and Power
ISBN 978-3-319-31986-5   ISBN 978-3-319-31987-2   (eBook)
DOI 10.1007/978-3-319-31987-2

Library of Congress Control Number: 2016947974

Cover image © Peter Horree / Alamy Stock Photo

Printed on acid-free paper

This Palgrave Macmillan imprint is published by Springer Nature
The registered company is Springer International Publishing AG Switzerland

PREFACE

This study focuses on the presentation and examination of the Journal of Queen Maria Carolina which recounts private events that occurred between the years 1781 and 1785. It is housed at the State Archives of Naples, Bourbon Archives, Folder 96. With the purpose of highlighting little-known aspects of the Queen's personality, we conducted a thorough survey of her diary and took into account the following components: content, historical and topographical indications (place and date of writing) and peculiarities of rhetorical and formal order (language used in writing, the way she opened and closed her entries as well as the length, and the hierarchical arrangement of topics).

We focused on the analysis and enhancement of the Queen's public, political, social and cultural roles, while at the same time discussing the many aspects of her intimate life. In the pursuit of this goal, we focused on the moments in which the Queen's public and private sectors are discussed, in which her social–political commitments are connected to those of her familial setting. In this regard, we have revealed numerous references in the Journal to be particularly interesting: hearings, meetings with prominent members of the political world, the diplomatic environment, the clergy and the scientific and artistic milieux.

We have therefore correlated the specific theme of our analysis in a historical context for reference, connected directly to the Kingdom of Naples and including a chronological arc between 1776 (the year Maria Carolina joined the State Council) and 1785 (when the current pro-Spanish diplomats, led by the Marquis of Sambuca, conspired against the Royal couple and Mr Acton). There is no hint in the Journal about this event, which takes on crucial importance in relation to the public image and the regency of Maria Carolina. Instead, in the correspondence between the Queen of Naples and her brother, Grand Duke of Tuscany Peter Leopold, in epistolary material housed at the State Archives of Vienna, we found testimonies by the two corresponding relatives which discuss the attempt to sabotage the reform policy pursued by various rulers and Acton. The year 1785 is also the last year in which the diary pages were currently available to us and thus examined at the State Archive of Naples.

Comparing the testimony found in the diary with musings that Maria Carolina elaborated elsewhere, and looking at the broad picture of the political situation of the 1780s, we tried to reconsider some issues taken for granted in historiography. In this regard, the ability to correlate the diary to the letters written in the same period, which the Queen sent to her beloved Peter Leopold, appears to be of great importance. In fact, the cross-comparison of two handwritten sources (both poorly studied, even today) allows one to shed new light on the dramatic circumstances surrounding the ongoing political struggle at Court in those years. Therefore, one must ask the age-old question of the role played by Maria Carolina in the political involvement of the Bourbon dynasty.

Catania, Italy   Cinzia Recca

ACKNOWLEDGEMENTS

While preparing the edition for publication, I would like to express my sincere and heartfelt gratitude towards many persons, institutions, and to all those who extended their helping hands towards me in various ways during the completion of this work.

First, my sincere thanks to the Staff at the Archive of State of Vienna and Naples who provided an efficient support throughout, in particular in Naples, I am very grateful to the Director, Dr. Imma Ascione, and Dr. Barbara Orciouli.

It was in March 2012 that, during an International Conference "The Royal Body" at the Royal Holloway University, I met for the first time Elena Woodacre who, curious and fascinated by my research, suggested writing this work in English. Since that time we started to collaborate together in the Royal Studies Network and Journal that Ellie has greatly created. So I am deeply grateful to Ellie for much moral support and for many years of intellectual exchange and friendship.

I am also especially grateful to Prof. Andrew Brayley for his corrections and suggestions, which helped in overcoming the hurdles in the completion of the translation of Maria Carolina's diary.

In addition, I am greatly thankful to the team of Palgrave Macmillan for their professionalism and support, especially Charles Beem and Carole Levin for having believed in my early proposal for the Queenship and Power series. My sincere thanks to the commitments, patience and astute comments of my editors Kristin Purdy and Michelle Smith.

The insightful and anonymous reviewers have proved invaluable in producing the final work.

Last, but most important, thanks to my family and friends for their unfailing love, sacrifice, support and encouragement and, above all, to my husband Francesco and my sons, Antonio and Emilio.

Any omission in this brief acknowledgement does not mean lack of gratitude.

Contents

CHAPTER 1

Maria Carolina: Sovereign and Mother

Writing about Queen Maria Carolina implicitly involves writing about the history of the Kingdom of Naples during the turbulent revolutionary period and the Napoleonic wars. The reason for this is given by the overwhelming influence that the Queen had over the affairs of her husband's reign, in controlling the fate of the Two Sicilies for almost half a century. It was an era in which women had a dominant role in the affairs of many nations, but few possessed a power as real and as vast as that of the Queen of Naples.[1]

Maria Carolina of Habsburg-Lorraine was born in Vienna on 13 August 1752 in Schönbrunn castle.[2] She was the 13th daughter of Franz Joseph I, Emperor of the Holy Roman Empire, and of Maria Theresa, Archduchess of Austria and Queen of Hungary, Croatia and Bohemia.[3] Among all the sisters, she was especially close to Marie Antoinette, the future Queen of France, with whom she shared her childhood and early education under the aegis of the same governess, Countess Lerchenfeld. Their bond was so strong that when one of them was sick the other also fell ill immediately. But the idyllic situation between the two girls soon ended. By August 1767, they had been separated by their mother, for when the two princesses were together they became so unruly and restless that they behaved below their rank. Despite their separation, their bond remained strong throughout their lives.

Growing up in an austere Viennese Court, Archduchess Maria Carolina showed an aptitude for science. Her lack of interest in children's games

© The Author(s) 2017
C. Recca, *The Diary of Queen Maria Carolina of Naples, 1781–1785*,
Queenship and Power, DOI 10.1007/978-3-319-31987-2_1

and her intelligence, along with her comeliness, resulted in the particular tenderness her parents showed her. She was affectionately nicknamed Charlotte, a name which her mother, the Empress, had always loved.

Maria Carolina's personality was most similar to that of her mother's, from whom she inherited her strong character and passion for reforms, many of which were carried out, in fact, by Maria Theresa during her long reign. The Empress personally dealt with her daughter's development regarding roles which she was called to perform: Austrian ambassador and submissive wife. The contrast between these two aspects is obvious. On the one hand, Maria Theresa asked her daughter to be Austrian in heart and mind (i.e. not to forget the close relationship which tied her to her motherland) while, on the other hand, she suggested, with explicit clarity, submission and obedience to her husband, at least in the family sphere.[4] Therefore, in a letter written by Maria Theresa, she wrote, "Do not always speak of our country and do not make comparisons between our habits and theirs ... be a German in your heart and in uprightness of mind; in everything that does not matter, however, but not in things which are improper, you have to appear Neapolitan."[5]

Therefore, as a result of her mother's precise political plan, which was to extend her influence over Italy at the expense of the Bourbons, Maria Carolina, just 16, married Ferdinand IV, son of Charles III of Spain and Maria Amalia of Saxony. The marriage between Ferdinand and Maria Carolina slowly diminished the Spanish influence in Naples. As Vincenzo Cuoco wrote, "We became loyal to Austria, a distant power, from which our nation had nothing to hope and everything to fear."[6]

When the young Maria Carolina came to the Bourbon capital on 12 May 1768,[7] she immediately grasped the extraordinary beauty of the place and the climate. Proud of her origins, the daughter of a sovereign reformer, after her arrival in Naples she met with the Neapolitan Enlightenment. Maria Carolina was certainly struck by the apparent immaturity and excessive impetuosity of her husband. She soon realized that he was not inclined to handle the leadership of the Kingdom. Following the instructions that her mother had written,[8] she showed kindness towards her husband and immediately sought to identify the strategies aimed at implementing her mother's instructions. Therefore, from her mother she inherited the ability to administer power and *manoeuvre* between political skirmishes. Based on the Theresian model, the young Queen aimed at putting in place, with prudent vision, a modern economic policy and was attentive to the events that occurred in the areas of trade and finance in Europe and the

Kingdom of the Two Sicilies.[9] As the Empress of Austria, Maria Carolina looked towards the new frontiers of progress and aimed at restructuring her Kingdom into something more modern: "I was educated imperially, that is, with contempt for mankind. Everyone I saw at my feet was there to trample. Nature gave me beauty and intelligence[…] I learned many languages, including Greek and Latin; I studied literature and philosophy with my German siblings, Joseph and Peter Leopold; and I became open-minded, strong spirited, and desired like my brothers those reforms that put an end to the usurpations of the priesthood and increased the power of the principality. Freedom, progress, people's rights, were always for me words without meaning. I envisioned from a young age men destined to obey principles and nothing else."[10]

The relationship between the two spouses, as well as their character traits, influenced in a crucial way the premarital "instructions" provided by Maria Theresa to her daughter as well as the presence of "influential" figures, some of whom performed institutional roles, while others gravitated around the Court of Naples. Coming from a strict Court and under the iron yoke of her mother, Maria Carolina "impetuous, ardent, impressionable, intelligent, suddenly came to rule for herself and for her husband".[11] Described by various sources as distracted, lacking talent and lazy, Ferdinand could not be blamed for his inadequate education since, as was usual for a third child, he was intended for an ecclesiastical career. Only through a fortuitous circumstance was he crowned the new King of the Two Sicilies. In fact, in 1759 his father, Charles, became King of Spain due to the death of his brother Ferdinand VI, who died without direct heirs. At this point, it was necessary to deal with the succession in Naples, and since the eldest son Philip was excluded from the succession to the throne because of his mental disability, and because the second was assigned to the Spanish succession, Ferdinand was elected King of Naples at just eight years old. The King was instructed by the Prince of San Nicandro, Domenico Cattaneo, who cared little about the political and civil preparation of the King. He had been brought in the grossest ignorance, knew scarcely anything of any foreign tongue, and could not speak Italian; the jargon of the *lazzaroni* was what he used both in conversation and his letter. He was primarily instructed in hunting, shooting and fishing, occupations by which his daily routine was[12] wasted. An insatiable delight in practical joke was one of King's characteristic. So not having been prepared for the role which Ferdinand had to play,[13] during his youth he never participated in any government activities, which remained in the hands of Minister Bernardo Tanucci.[14] On 12 January 1767, when he became an adult, Ferdinand gave his seal to Tanucci to spare himself the effort of signing various documents, preferring other more pleasant commitments. Ferdinand's lazy nature, with interests in hunting, fishing and various pastimes, left Maria Carolina with a margin of independence, which in time would turn into real political influence. To rule was what Maria Carolina wanted more than anything else in the world. Therefore, after his marriage to Maria Carolina, the King delegated the management of power and the responsibility of policy-making and governance to his wife.[15]

Maria Carolina was conscious of the environment that she found, but since she had clear ideas about her goals, she never had a problem, immediately taking advantage of her husband's lack of interest in the affairs of State, managing to take control of the actual conduct of the government in order to withdraw the Kingdom from the Spanish alliance and submit it to Austrian influence.

The Queen was careful to direct the consort's opinion as she desired; she always made him to think they were originated by himself. Her goal of ruling could be achieved with the birth of an heir to the throne. In 1775, with the birth of her first son,[16] the Queen was allowed actual entry into the State Council (in compliance with the terms of her marriage contract strongly supported by Maria Theresa of Austria, who was aware of her daughter's political skills).[17] This was followed by the gradual expulsion of Bernardo Tanucci, guilty of excessive loyalty to the King of Spain.[18]

In reality, Maria Carolina's ideas were in line with the politics of the Enlightenment, until then followed by the Kingdom of Naples, but what she hoped for was a greater autonomy in relation to Spain and Minister Tanucci, a problem which Charles III had already faced in the past. But for Ferdinand, to rule under protection was not a problem; indeed, it was quite the opposite since he managed to assert himself every time a topic interested him directly and delegated other responsibilities to Tanucci. For Maria Carolina, on the contrary, it was humiliating to compete constantly with the Ministers. Thus, her entry into the State Council was an opportunity to oppose the Pisan Minister and upset the internal balance. It should be noted that the sovereign's marriage had been devised by the Habsburg diplomacy to ensure the Austrian presence in the Mediterranean and to reduce the effects of the Family Pact signed by the Bourbon sovereigns.[19]

As Charles III and the elderly Minister knew, it would not be easy to handle the political activism of the young Queen. Among other things, by deftly using her persuasive abilities, she cleverly induced her husband to go along with her. This was easily implementable since Ferdinand, besides having a weak and submissive character, shared the need for emancipation from Madrid.[20]

As the pretext to dismiss the troublesome Minister Tanucci, Maria Carolina was approached by the issue of the Freemasons. The presence of the lodge in the Kingdom of Naples had created many problems during Charles's reign.[21] In fact, as a result of Pope Benedict XIV's insistence, along with Tanucci's, on 10 July 1751, Charles of Bourbon issued an edict against the presence of Masonic lodges. As a result, many Masons publicly renounced their affiliation. Only a few of the weaker ones were punished.

In subsequent years, the number of lodges became increasingly widespread and intensified between 1770 and 1775 due to the circulation of new European intellectual trends in the Kingdom of Naples, thereby becoming a cultural salon in the south due to Maria Carolina's presence. Coming from Vienna, the city where the Masonic presence was one of the most remarkable in Europe, the Queen emphasized the worldly appearance and secular aspect of Freemasonry, making it a fashionable phenomenon, an expression of social life and likewise encouraging new affiliations.

In 1776, the Masonic problem had taken on an important political role. In fact, the legitimacy conferred by the Queen was in sharp contrast to the veto imposed by Charles of Bourbon in July 1751. Furthermore, since adepts (belonging mostly to the Court and the army) were part of high society, Freemasonry had become dangerous due to the location of its branches within the central power structure. This predicament was intertwined with a removal policy from Madrid.

It was urgent, therefore, to address the issue since the existence of the lodges contrasted with the moral principles of the Pisan Minister: "Always contrary to discipline, it is the union of the private lodges which deserved and deserves the censorship and prohibition of well-regulated governments."[22] Thus, on 12 September 1775, the able Minister Tanucci, in line with King Carlo, had promulgated an edict more incisive than that of 1751. Tanucci declared all Freemasons guilty of the crime of "lese-Majesty" and punishable. But his edict had gone unnoticed since the Queen was affiliated with the Freemasons and they were thus protected.

The Masonic issue facilitated and initiated the fulfilment of the Queen's dream: to govern independently, removing herself from Spanish protection. Within this process, a major role was played by Maria Carolina. The surprise in Capodimonte had important political consequences since

Tanucci's fall resulted from it (25 October 1776). It was, however, the chance result of a process with a wider scope, which was influenced only marginally by the Queen's grudges and the climate of opposition that was created around the Minister. His departure must be regarded as a natural consequence of the growth of the country crying out for autonomy from Spanish protection.[23]

Already by the summer of 1775, Ferdinand IV had complained to his father about Tanucci's interference, of the latter's reluctance to deliver the required documents from time to time and of the Minister's decisions which were independently made: "The others are the King and I'm the statue of the King of Naples."[24]

In May 1776, Ferdinand wrote to Charles III to relieve Tanucci from the serious charges which had occupied and preoccupied him. But the Spanish monarch had always responded with a refusal, reminding his son of Tanucci's long and faithful years of service and of the integrity of the faithful Minister. On 25 October, on his own initiative, Ferdinand fired Tanucci with a Royal note:

> Considerando io che la continuazione della Direzione immediata degli affari debba, malgrado il vostro zelo, pesare alla vostra età, e ricordando che varie volte avete desiderato di esserne discaricato, ho pensato combinare il mio servizio col minor danno della vostra salute, e per questo, col discaricarvi del Dipartimento della vostra Segreteria di Stato e delle altre incombenze affidate alla vostra direzione, riserbandomi di consultarvi nella vostra qualità di Consigliere di Stato sopra tutti gli affari che chiederanno i vostri lumi.[25]

This note was followed by a long interview with the King. Tanucci left the scene, embittered and without comment. He remained in Naples, despite his desire to return to his beloved Tuscany, due to his attachment to the city and at the insistence of Charles III. This, in fact, would have been troubling if the Minister had not continued to support Ferdinand.[26] Maria Carolina had taken full responsibility for the break with Minister Tanucci following a clear-cut strategy that, in case of failure, would not damage the Crown, finding even a justification in the young wife's impulsive and impetuous character.

On 29 October 1776, Tanucci handed over responsibility to the new Minister, Giuseppe Beccadelli Bologna, Marquis of Sambuca, Ambassador of the Two Sicilies in Vienna and therefore a welcome personality for the Habsburgs.[27] From that point on, Tanucci testified that he would move in a new political direction, although relations with Spain would be maintained with marriage contracts. But now the Kingdom of the Two Sicilies would demonstrate to Europe its autonomy. Sambuca's first act was to restore the honour of the Chinea to the Pope,[28] at the behest of Maria Carolina, which was meant to show the improvement via Roman approval to silence the pro-Tanucci party. In this way, a homage to Chinea was paid but only for one year (1777). This did not mean that the Queen wanted to abandon the anticlerical policy previously undertaken by the former Minister, but it was only an act of force to prove that any decision was now only up to the sovereigns. In fact, the previous policy regarding the Church–State relationship was quickly revived, and in 1779, a series of rules aimed at reducing Papal intrusiveness was developed, which abolished the Court of the Inquisition, reduced the number of monasteries and abolished ecclesiastical prisons. To develop relevant legislation, the Queen used the same man who had served years before for Tanucci[29]: the priest from Puglia, Ciro Saverio Minervino.

With the fall of Minister Bernardo Tanucci, the sovereigns began a golden decade. Taking advantage of the precious collaboration with the English Admiral John Acton and by surrounding herself with loyal allies, Maria Carolina carried out her coveted "Pro-Habsburg veer".[30] The Kingdom of Naples was then characterized by a series of reforms which would allow an organization to be considered among the most modern in the Mediterranean area.[31] As Pietro Colletta wrote, "The power of the Queen strengthened in the opinions of subjects and the councils of the State, which at the age of 25, wanting children, beautiful, superb by nature and size of the house, could easily subdue her husband, who was only intended for bodily pleasures. Thus she became the hope of the great, the ambitious, the honest, the people, and she felt her majesty and she was pleased."[32]

At the cultural level, the Queen proceeded by reforming education, which predicted an increase in university teaching posts and coordinated periods of teaching. In 1778, she founded the Royal Academy of Sciences and Humane Letters, which devoted more space to the field of science than humanities. This establishment was an important attempt in the direction of bringing together intellectual and cultural life.[33] Before that time, education was controlled by the Jesuits, so it was in the hands of the clergy. It lacked basic education while secondary education was reduced to teaching Latin; physical and natural sciences were neglected while the University gave importance to ecclesiastical censorship. New institutions, encouraged by the Masonic culture, began a fruitful work against igno-rance and oppression, reclaiming the cultural identity of the Kingdom.[34]

The Bourbon initiative was impressive, particularly regarding the insti-tutions, facilities and services that were essential to the tasks of a modern State. They improved what already existed and created what they lacked: a botanical garden, a naval observatory, various museums and university laboratories, a laboratory of mosaics. In addition, the streets were cared for, proving that the Bourbon government pursued a policy of develop-ment and improvement of both services and the infrastructures of the Kingdom.[35]

The Kingdom of Ferdinand and Maria Carolina in the period between 1768 and 1789 was characterized by and distinguished for its work of modernization as well as for its economic, cultural and institutional devel-opment. In this regard, one should remember that during that period, the Kingdom was among the major cultural centres of Europe and was home to the best minds of eighteenth-century Enlightenment. This lasted until the French Revolution, due to the disasters that occurred in Paris, such as the arrest of Louis XVI and his beloved Marie Antoinette. Even in the Neapolitan Kingdom, there was a reversal in the trend regarding the pro-gressive ideas which had found widespread use in Masonic lodges, which the Queen had once openly defended but now pursued with ferocity.

After the French Revolution and the subsequent rise of the Jacobin tide throughout the rest of Europe, Maria Carolina's relationship with her husband changed. In an effort to save her throne as well as those of her children, and also to punish the French who were guilty of the death of her beloved sister Marie Antoinette, the Queen hazarded strate-gic moves—first of hostilities and after—of undisguised neutrality towards France.[36] Among the consequences which followed we must include, among other things, the fall of the Kingdom and the proclamation of the Neapolitan Republic,[37] and the beginning of Ferdinand IV's hostility towards Maria Carolina. Until that moment, Sicily had remained sidelined to these events, after which it played a central role, offering refuge to the Court of Ferdinand of Bourbon as well as a base for military operations in the Bourbonic south which was occupied by the French. The Royal fam-ily withdrew, therefore, in temporary exile to the island, arriving aboard Nelson's HMS *Vanguard*.

Once when the Royal couple was forced into exile in Sicily, Maria Carolina was continually accused by her husband of being the cause of all the ills of the Kingdom.

She was insulted and vilified at every opportunity by her husband. This attitude also encouraged attacks and polemical pamphlets from Naples, which were hurled against him and, above all, against the Queen.[38] In a letter of March 1800, addressed to the Marquis De Gallo, the sovereign, noting that the relationship with the King was now irrecoverable, the Queen wrote that the recent revolution had, as a victim, only her and she complained about not being able anymore to interfere with the decisions of her spouse.[39] Things were not exactly in these terms: in 1806, when Napoleon invaded the Kingdom of Naples and forced the two sovereigns to flee again to Sicily, his intent was precisely to liquidate the politics of Maria Carolina, always ready to re-establish relations with the Court of Vienna against France. The second stay of the Royal couple on the island, still under British protection, lasted long and in those years the role of the Queen was much reduced.[40] The circumstance that the island was a British protectorate and depended on the British fleet for its survival against the French threat put Ferdinand in the hands of London's envoys and in vain Maria Carolina would try to suggest an independent policy.[41] Not only did her efforts prove to be useless, but the British, as they were intended to transform Sicily into a constitutional monarchy to oppose the absolutism of the Napoleonic Empire, found it as an expedient to get the Queen away from the Kingdom. So in 1813, King Ferdinand forced Maria Carolina to leave for Vienna. The trip to the Habsburg capital lasted eight months. The Queen arrived in the country on 14 February 1814. She retired to Hatzendorf castle, where she grew up, and died in solitude on 10 September of the same year.[42]

From a careful examination of documentary sources (The Journal, the exchange of letters with family members and those she trusted), it can be deduced that the Queen was undoubtedly a remarkable mother, very proactive about the health and education of her children.[43] Driven by an indefatigable solicitude, she knew each of their strengths, weaknesses, pleasures, and personally took care of their food, games, clothing and their education. A recurring phrase in her diary: "All the dear children are doing well."

After four years of marriage, Maria Carolina became already a mother for the first time on 6 June 1772. The eldest daughter was named Maria Teresa. Shortly after, in the following year, another child was born, Luisa Amalia. Pregnancies alternated with periods of rest, which lasted almost always the same length of time. The Queen was pregnant 18 times, of which 16 children were born between 1772 and 1793. On 4 January

1775, Naples greeted with a great celebration the long-awaited heir to the throne, Carlo Tito, whose arrival opened to the sovereign, as we previously remembered, the doors of the State Council. Since that time the political rise of the Queen would go hand in hand with her pregnancies.

Fatigued by the arrival of warm weather, shortly after the previous birth, Maria Carolina became pregnant again. She was plagued by persistent headaches that made her become aggressive towards those who contradicted her. Suffering from the pregnancy, she accused her husband of continuously getting her pregnant, and she became hostile towards their intimate marital relationship. On 24 June 1775, Princess Maria Anna was born, and on 19 August 1777 the Queen gave birth to another son, Francis, who was also received with endless rejoicing.[44]

At that time, the Royal family was living in Caserta to escape the contagion of smallpox contracted by Prince Philip, who was to die shortly thereafter. Fearing that her children could be affected by the disease, Maria Carolina asked her brother, Leopold, to send for Florence's famous Dr. Angelo Maria Gatti,[45] a specialist in vaccinations. He was sent to immunize Carlo, Teresa and Luisa. Fortunately, the inoculations worked. Antonio Genovesi, Ferdinando Galiani, Domenico Cotugno and subsequently Gatti were important for the development of the inoculation in Naples. Contrary to what had happened in other parts of Italy, the method of smallpox vaccination was immediately welcomed and encouraged by the rulers.[46]

In those years, the Royal family was expanding. On 17 January 1779, Maria Cristina was born. The joyous event, however, was preceded by mourning. On 17 December 1778, Carlo Tito had died at the age of 3. Unfortunately another tragedy was to hit Maria Carolina's family. On 21 February 1780, she found herself saying goodbye to little Marianna.[47] Since the Queen was pregnant again, she wanted to be convinced that the vital spirit of her daughter had relocated itself into Gennaro,[48] born shortly afterwards on 12 April. She felt she had to live with resignation, like many other women, the inevitable alternation of life and death.[49]

Pregnant again, on 18 June 1781, the Queen gave birth to Prince Joseph, and, on 26 April of the following year, Princess Amalia was born in Caserta. A new loss struck the Royal family on 19 February 1783, when at just two, the frail and sickly Joseph died.[50] On 14 December 1784, the sovereigns were comforted and cheered up by the birth of Princess Marie Antoinette.[51] Meanwhile, the eldest daughters, Maria Teresa and Luisa, had grown up and it was necessary to marry them off, planning their weddings in various European Courts. The Queen threw out any ideas regarding a union with the house of Spain due to grudges against Charles III. Likewise, the house of France was set aside because the Bourbons were intolerable. Therefore, she turned her sights to the Habsburg dynasty, to Leopold's sons, who could aspire to the succession of the throne of Austria and Hungary, since Emperor Joseph II was childless and in poor health. With that move, where the Queen began to play the card of their motherhood to reaffirm the close cooperation with Vienna, she annoyed the Spanish diplomacy, which would respond with the demand for speedy resignation of Acton, accused of being the lover of the Queen and the true promoter of the pro-Habsburg strategy.

Marzio Mastrilli, the Marquis de Gallo, was appointed ambassador to Vienna, and with continuous insistence Maria Carolina invited him to sponsor the negotiations for three good marriages with the sons of her brother, dreaming of giving the eldest, Maria Teresa, to Grand Duke Francesco who was already widowed; Luisa, the second, to Ferdinand; and asking the 16-year-old heir Francesco, Duke of Calabria, for the hand of little Clementina of Habsburg-Lorraine.

There were several anxious proposals. The Queen's insistence towards the Marquis de Gallo was strong, with constant letters urging him to work, full of details about her daughters' education as well as their aptitude, habits at Court, qualities, morals and physical qualities as well as their flaws. For Luisa, the Queen was worried because she was considered temperamentally closed, lazy and a bit simple. Teresa was feared to be excessively sensitive. Prince Francis was described as lazy, weak, indifferent and unwilling to study and concentrate. The ambassador was recommended by Maria Carolina because he had done a good job supervising the education of young Clementina, who grew up in the Cult of Supreme Truth and far from Court intrigues.[52]

On 18 February 1786, the Queen gave birth to Maria Clotilde and to Maria Errichetta the following year. On 27 August 1788, Prince Charles was born, but he unfortunately died the following year. Pregnant again, Maria Carolina gave birth to Prince Leopold on 2 July 1790.[53] In the same year, after endless negotiations, King Ferdinand and his wife went to Vienna with the two princesses and the heir to the throne to celebrate the marriages of the girls and to plan the wedding of their son who was just 13 years old.[54] Two years later, Prince Albert was born on 2 May, while the princesses Mary Clotilde and Maria Errichetta died the same year. On 2 December 1793, Princess Elizabeth was born.[55]

This detailed list of the maternity of the Queen shows how her political rise was closely linked to them: this is not only because the birth of Charles Titus had allowed her to enter the Council of State, but mainly because the many pregnancies became the constant test of her Queenship, and turned at the time into an important opportunity to develop her own political line. It was not a sudden rise, but a gradual affirmation, that—after the fall of Tanucci—found a way to extend around the first half of the 1780s. And with the nomination of Acton to guide the affairs of the Navy started the process of emancipation from Spain, which was sealed in 1785 by Ferdinand's resistance to the claims of his father Charles III to continue to dictate the choices of government. It is not a coincidence that after the removal of Tanucci, which marked the turning point in the political fortunes of Maria Carolina. And in the personal image of the Queen, at that time insinuations about her marital infidelity began to thicken.

The sources we used, therefore, attest that Maria Carolina had without a doubt a multi-faceted personality: loving and caring, affectionately exercising her role as mother, the Queen also showed an unprejudiced cynicism with stubborn tenacity in pursuing her political objectives. And it is precisely this intersection between private life and Court life, including marital duties and obligations of the government, that is one of the most interesting aspects of the diary of Queen Maria Carolina, from which we can take—such is our hope—an indication of some interest both on the side of social history and on that of the political history of the Kingdom of Naples in the difficult balance between reforming impulses and resistance of the ancien régime.

NOTES

1. See in this regard the introduction of the recent contribution edited by M. Mafrici, *All'Ombra della Corte. Donne e potere nella Napoli borbonica (1734–1860)*, (Napoli: Fridericiana Editrice Universitaria, 2010).
2. Her full name was Maria Carolina, Louise, Josephine, Jane, Antonia of Austria.
3. Maria Theresa of Austria was commonly recognized as the great enlightened sovereign: a promoter of reforms (such as the introduction of compulsory primary school, the separation of powers, the abolition of the Inquisition) which demonstrated her modernity compared with other rulers of the time. See, among others, J. P. Bled, *Maria Teresa d'Austria*, (Bologna: Il Mulino, 2003).

4. The young Archduchess was subjected to the strict upbringing that the Empress had chosen for their offspring, taking care to differentiate according to whether it was given to the sons or daughters. The archduchesses were educated to respect certain values, often ignored by the same mother, such as submission and acceptance of a marriage of convenience. The need to know how to perform in public, docility and obedience represented the other pillars of the education of daughters. See, H. Acton, *I Borboni di Napoli*, (Milano:Aldo Martello Editore, 1968), 147.

5. Maria Carolina did not intend to marry the young Ferdinand both because she had learned of his frivolous character, and because she did not want to go into a realm so far from Vienna, but agreed not to displease her mother, just as she had done her sister Maria Amalia. A. Frugoni, *Consigli matrimoniali alle figlie sovrane, di Maria Teresa d'Austria*, (Firenze: Passigli Editori, 2000), 55–56.

6. According to this, see the recent volume edited by A. De Francesco, V. Cuoco, *Saggio storico sulla Rivoluzione di Napoli*, (Manduria-Bari-Roma: Lacaita, 1998), 22.

7. Maria Carolina had already married King Ferdinand by proxy in Vienna, on 7 April 1768 at the Church of the Augustinian Friars. On the same day, she left Austria to live in Naples facing a journey that shocked, especially when he crossed the border of Habsburg domains in Italy. See, M. Schipa, *Nel Regno di Ferdinando IV*, (Firenze: Vallecchi, 1938), 35–76.

8. According to the two rulers, initially, there was talk of marital problems related mainly to the vagaries of the King and confidentiality and pride of the Queen. But her brother Peter Leopold, Grand Duke of Tuscany, intervened and informed the Empress mother who was able to advise her daughter about the success of the marriage. The Empress also sent her son Joseph to Naples. He was also entrusted with the task of "supervisor" of the marital relations of the sisters. Coming to Naples (1769) Joseph II obtained Ferdinand's helpfulness and reverence and was able to give useful advice to his sister, who was increasingly annoyed by having to follow the King in his hunting. See Giuseppe II d'Asburgo, *Cortelazzara. Relazione a Maria Teresa sui Reali di Napoli*, E. Garms Cornides (ed.), (Napoli: Di Mauro editore, 1992), 38–42.

9. In this regard, see especially G. Galasso, Il *Regno di Napoli. Il Mezzogiorno borbonico e napoleonico (1734–1815)*,(Torino: Utet, 2007), 580–613.

10. G. La Cecilia, "Confessioni di Maria Carolina. Da lei personalmente scritte in punto di morte" in *Storie segrete dei Borboni di Napoli e Sicilia*, (Palermo: di Marzo), 1860, 170.

11. T. Whitaker Scalia, "Studi sulla Regina Maria Carolina : considerazioni sopra due nuove biografie della medesima" in *Rassegna contemporanea*, G. Cesareo – V. Picarde (eds),Vol. I, ottobre, 1908, 275.

12. The daily notes written by King Ferdinand reveal his incompetence in ruling, preferring more amusing activities. The personal diary of the King has been published by U. Caldora (ed.), *Diario di Ferdinando IV di Borbone*, (Napoli: Edizioni scientifiche italiane, 1965).

13. Peter Leopold wrote to his mother: "those who have been responsible for the education of the King will have a lot to answer to God for having neglected the talents of a prince who could have become perfect, if he had been cultivated" in A. Wandruska, "Il Principe filosofo e il Re Lazzarone. Le lettere del granduca Pietro Leopoldo sul suo soggiorno a Napoli", in *Rivista storica italiana*, LXXII (1960), 508.

14. On Prime Minister Bernardo Tanucci see, E. Viviani della Robbia, *Bernardo Tanucci ed il suo più importante carteggio*, (Firenze: Sansoni, 1942), as well as R. Mincuzzi, *Bernardo Tanucci, ministro di Ferdinando di Borbone, 1759–1776*, Dedalo, Bari 1967 e F. Renda, "Dalle riforme al periodo costituzionale (1734–1816)", in *Storia della Sicilia*, diretta da R. Romeo, vol. VI, (Napoli: Società editrice Storia di Napoli e della Sicilia, 1978), 253–290; as well as more recently R. Tufano, *La Francia e le Sicilie, Stato e disgregazione sociale nel mezzogiorno d'Italia da Luigi XIV alla rivoluzione*, (Napoli:Arte tipografica editrice), 251–268.

15. The nature and the consequent behaviour of the consort facilitated the Queen in promoting the administration of the Kingdom. "Do you and then tell me": this phrase, usually uttered by King Ferdinand IV to his wife on the occasion of the sessions of the Council of State, may be regarded as the emblematic attention to the type of relationship existing between the two real until 1799 and the indicator of the completeness of the diplomatic and political role played by the queen until the exile in Sicily.

16. In 1775, the heir presumptive, Charles Titus was born, who died in 1778, so the second son, Francis, born in 1777, became heir to the throne. On the occasion of prenuptial agreements, Maria Teresa was able to obtain for their daughter the legal recognition of the right to vote and the presence of the Council of State in the case of the birth of a son as heir to the Crown. E. Caesar Corti, *Ich, eine Maria Theresias Tochter: ein Lebensbild der Königin Marie Karoline von Neapel*, 96–97, 107–108.

17. Archivio di Stato di Napoli, *Esteri*, f. 3923–3924, 3925–3929.

18. The letters Charles III and Ferdinand IV exchanged at that time have been published in part by L. Barreca, *Il tramonto di Bernardo Tanucci nella corrispondenza con Carlo III di Spagna*, (Palermo:Manfredi, 1976), VI–IX.

19. On 25 July 1731, in Seville, the Family Pact between the two branches of the Bourbons was signed; it stated the agreement between the two Royal houses of France and Spain and declared that the son of Elisabetta Farnese, Don Carlo, was assigned the duchies of Parma and Piacenza; therefore, Cosimo III de 'Medici recognized as his natural and legitimate successor

Infante Charles of Bourbon. On this subject, see R. Tufano, *La Francia e le Sicilie. Stato e disgregazione sociale nel Mezzogiorno d' Italia da Luigi XIV alla Rivoluzione*, 217–283.

20. See in this regard, G. Galasso, *Il Regno di Napoli. Il mezzogiorno borbonico e napoleonico (1734–1815)*, 474.

21. On Freemasonry's events in the Kingdom of Naples, with particular reference to the circumstances that led to the fall of Bernardo Tanucci, see the considerations of G. Giarrizzo, *Massoneria e Illuminismo nell' Europa del Setecento*, (Venezia: Marsilio, 1994), 383–404 as well as A.M. Rao, "La massoneria nel Regno di Napoli", in *Storia d' Italia, Annali, La Massoneria*, G.M. Cazzaniga, (ed), vol. 21, (Torino: Einaudi, 2006), 526–532.

22. See, G. Galasso, *Il Regno di Napoli. Il mezzogiorno borbonico e napoleonico (1734–1815)*, 178

23. Ibid., 488.

24. H. Acton, *I Borboni di Napoli* (1734–1825), 193.

25. "I consider that the continuation of the immediate Direction of the business must be, despite your zeal, a weight on your age, and remembering that several times you desired to be discharged, I thought about combining my service with minor damage to your health, and for this reason, to discharge you from the Department of your Secretary of State and of other responsibilities entrusted to you, to set aside for myself to consult you on the quality of your State Advisor above all the deals that we asked from your enlightenment". This extract of the Royal message signed by Ferdinand is transcribed in full in E. Viviani Della Robbia, *Bernardo Tanucci ed il suo importante carteggio*, 219.

26. The Minister spent the last years of his life in Naples, and his country of residence in S. Jorio (S. Giorgio a Cremano) at the foot of Vesuvius, taking refuge in otium and having long walks in the countryside. See E. Viviani Della Robbia, *Bernardo Tanucci ed il suo importante carteggio*, Firenze, 232; L. Barreca, *Il tramonto di Bernardo Tanucci nella corrispondenza con Carlo III di Spagna 1776–1783*, 459.

27. G. Galasso, *Il Regno di Napoli. Il mezzogiorno borbonico e napoleonico*, 493.

28. The Chinea (from the French *haquennée*) was a white mule (or horse of Asturias) that was offered annually to the Pope, in solemn form, for a tribute that the King of Naples paid to the Papal States for the privilege that the pope possessed as holder of the feudal rights over the Kingdom of Naples. The animal was properly trained to knell before the Pope and gave him a sum of money, 7000 ducats, contained in a silver vase attached to the saddle. See V. Cuoco. *Saggio storico sulla Rivoluzione di Napoli*, 73.

29. See R. Ajello, "I filosofi e la regina. Il governo delle due Sicilie da Tanucci a Caracciolo", in *Rivista Storica Italiana*, CII , Edizioni Scientifiche Italiane, 1991, 429.

30. A.M. Rao, "Corte e Paese: Il Regno di Napoli dal 1734 al 1806", in M. Mafrici, (ed.), *All'Ombra della Corte. Donne e potere nella Napoli borbonica (1734–1860)*, 22.

31. On this issue, see the notes of M. Mafrici, "Il Mezzogiorno d'Italia e il mare: problemi difensivi nel Settecento"in R. Cancila, (ed), Mediterraneo in armi (secc. XV–XVIII), in *Mediterranea. Ricerche storiche*, 4, (2007), t. II, 637–663; A.M. Rao, "Napoli e il Mediterraneo nel Settecento: frontiera d'Europa?", as well as the essays collected in E. Iachello, Militello P. (eds), *Il Mediterraneo delle città*, (Milano:Franco Angeli), 2011.

32. On the visit of Emperor Joseph II, see Giuseppe II d'Asburgo, *Corte Lazzara. Relazione a Maria Teresa sui Reali di Napoli.*

33. E. Caesar Corti, *Ich, eine Maria Theresias Tochter: ein Lebensbild der Königin Marie Karoline von Neapel*, 73–76.

34. G. Astuto, "Dalle riforme alle rivoluzioni. Maria Carolina d'Asburgo: una regina «austriaca» nel Regno di Napoli e di Sicilia", *Quaderni del dipartimento di studi politici*, n. 1, 2007, 34.

35. G. Galasso, *Storia del Regno di Napoli*, 583.

36. The negative influence of some aspects of Maria Carolina's character on the achievement of her political objectives that she intended to pursue is notorious. For example, she was influenced by her impulsivity, nervousness, restlessness, stubbornness and lack of reflective capacity. Cfr. E. Caesar Corti, *Ich, eine Maria Theresias Tochter: ein Lebensbild der Königin Marie Karoline von Neapel*, 106.

37. On 22 January 1799, while still *lazzari* fought against the French, the Jacobins proclaimed the Neapolitan Republic.

38. The pamphlets reported news concerning, mainly, the alleged romantic relationships of Queen Maria Carolina with General Acton and Lady Emma Hamilton. See on this regard R. Palumbo, *Carteggio di Maria Carolina con Lady Emma Hamilton*, (Bologna:Arnaldo Forni Editore, 1969).

39. M.H. Weil (ed.), *Correspondence inèdite de Marie Caroline, reine de Naples et de Sicile avec le Marquis de Gallo*, vol. I, Paul, Paris 1911, 140–141.

40. R. De Lorenzo, "Maria Carolina d'Austria e i napoleonidi: l'esercizio residuale della sovranità", in *Archivio storico per le provincie napoletane*, vol. 27 (2009), 185–200.

41. J. Rosselli, *Lord William Bentinck e l'occupazione britannica in Sicilia 1811–1814*, (Palermo: Sellerio, 2001), 207–232.

42. E. Caesar Corti, *Ich, eine Maria Theresias Tochter: ein Lebensbild der Königin Marie Karoline von Neapel*, 706.

43. Ibid., 114–115.

44. Ibid., 107.

45. See in this regard, ASN, *Archivio Borbone*, (3 novembre 1781).

46. On the debate about inoculation of the smallpox vaccine ramped in Europe in the eighteenth century, see interesting pages of «*Manoscritto per Teresa*» by Pietro Verri, as well as some artiche of «Il *Caffè*» (on the«*Manoscritto*» see the interesting study of G. Padovani, *La modellizzazione della femminilità da Alberti a Verri*, (Catania: Cuecm, 2002.) The vaccine represented the Enlightened evolution, which clashed with the theories of the *ancien régime* . On the issue, see the precious studies of B. Fadda, *L'innesto del vaiolo: un dibattito scientifico e culturale nell'Italia del Settecento*, (Franco Angeli: Milano, 1983); B. M. Assael, *Il favoloso innesto. Storia sociale della vaccinazione*, (Roma-Bari: Laterza, 1995). A. Borrelli, *Dall'innesto del vaiolo alla vaccinazione jenneriana: il dibattito scientifico napoletano*, (Firenze: Olschki, 1997); Id, "Editoria scientifica e professione medica nel Settecento" in A.M. Rao (ed.), *Editoria e cultura a Napoli nel XVIII secolo*, (Napoli: Liguori, 2001), 737–761.
47. ASN, *Archivio Borbone*, 96, (17 decembre mardy 1782).
48. Ibid., (21 novembre1781).
49. Ibid., 72, 77.
50. E. Caesar Corti, *Ich, eine Maria Theresias Tochter: ein Lebensbild der Königin Marie Karoline von Neapel*, 119.
51. L. Del Pozzo, *Cronaca civile e militare delle due Sicilie dall'anno 1734 in poi*, (Napoli:Stamperia Reale), 1857, 115,117,125.
52. In this regard, we would like to suggest the reading of the paper of C. Recca "Queenship and Family Dynamics through the Correspondence of Queen Maria Carolina of Naples" in *Queenship in the Mediterranean. Negotiating the Role of the Queen in the Medieval and* early Modern eras, edited by E. Woodacre, London-New York: Palgrave Macmillan, 2013, 263–284.
53. L. Del Pozzo, *Cronaca civile e militare delle due Sicilie dall'anno 1734 in poi*, 128, 132, 134, 136, 140.
54. E. Caesar Corti, *Ich, eine Maria Theresias Tochter: ein Lebensbild der Königin Marie Karoline von Neapel*, 173.
55. L. Del Pozzo, *Cronaca civile e militare delle due Sicilie dall'anno 1734 in poi*, 148–149.

CHAPTER 2

Structural Physiognomy, Historical Value of Diaries and the Daily Routine of the Queen

The diary of Queen Maria Carolina, kept in the State Archives of Naples, is certainly not unknown to scholars, particularly since Benedetto Croce mentioned it in 1934. However, his reading of those pages was dismissed with a few words.[1] Croce's judgement on the possibilities of gaining broad historical benefit was somewhat simplistic. However, in the first far-reaching biography dedicated to Maria Carolina, Egon Caesar Corti often referred to the diary in order to illustrate certain aspects related to the political action of the Queen regnant.[2]

Our recovery work and transcription of the diary have made it possible to rewrite the story of the Queen, including aspects of her life previously overlooked by historians. There are many intellectuals of her time, as well as contemporary scholars, who have recounted her life, while there are only a few historians who have given her space in their work. Maria Carolina is little more than a ghost, useful if anything to blame her for the searing, widespread attitudes which culminated in the revolution of 1799.

The Queen of Naples, however, was equipped with a very strong personality. Embodied within it were qualities and "virtues" typical of eighteenth-century civilization: grace, kindness, intelligence, elegance, and love of the arts. But her character traits and behaviour revealed strong contradictions.

The original manuscript contained, in the right-hand margin, personal memos concerning the health of Ferdinand IV and the children in the year 1872, which have been set here as boxed text.

© The Author(s) 2017
C. Recca, *The Diary of Queen Maria Carolina of Naples, 1781–1785,*
Queenship and Power, DOI 10.1007/978-3-319-31987-2_2

19

A passionate, dominatrix and energetic woman, Maria Carolina was also a loving mother and a loving sister. Capable of magnanimous gestures and generous impulses, she was, however, considered to be intriguing, blinded by hate, stubborn and a treacherous persecutor of those new ideals which during her reign found proponents and martyrs. Certainly, Maria Carolina's life was marked by a constant emotional struggle. Owing to her restless and fickle nature, the sovereign could be both a loving friend and a relentless enemy, merciful or vengeful, pious or frivolous.

Historians are often "prisoners" of their sources, and for a long time women's voices were put to rest in memories of the past. Women have left fewer historical traces than men.[3]

One of the most exciting events for us while in the archives was finding and combining the personal writings, family letters, diaries and memoirs, or the so-called auto-narrative sources, according to the definition generally used by intellectuals and historians. Personal documents are the primary source for the history of women; they are a channel, a way of transmitting their voices.[4] Family papers and letters, according to Joan Scott, reveal information about the texture of life and family relationships of women. Women represent real "family scribes" and their letters are full of news about public and private events.[5] Diaries, having had generally little attention paid to them for many years and sometimes "snobbishly" referred to as subliterature, are testimonials, "self-expressive" outpourings of life.[6] The ink was often entrusted with their thoughts, their innermost dreams, the reconstruction of daily events as well as the most dramatic events. Although the terms are often used interchangeably, there is a difference between journals and personal diaries: journals register events and activities experienced by the author, including information about the weather or transactions and negotiations; personal diaries contain feelings and self-examination. The difference of the terms is linked to the historical period in which these fine habits of recording the daily routine were practised. It is not an accident that a diary can be a witness to the author's life, but also to the times in which he or she lived. So the historical value of diaries is contained in the truth about individual lives not found in other places.[7]

French historiography has widely discussed the seductive charms of correspondence, of *journal intime* and autobiographical pages, as well as the theoretical and methodological issues raised by their reading and their use as a source.[8]

Starting with an analysis of diaries according to Philippe Lejeune, they are the junction where tales of life meet literature.[9] The French scholar is famous among academics for his much-discussed *Le pacte autobiographique* which, in the mid-1970s, began a large and productive debate on the autobiographical genre. For a long time, his studies focused on memoirs, autobiographies, auto-fiction, excluding the diary. By Lejeune's own admission, he had chosen, as an adult, to distance himself from his own personal diary written during adolescence. However, by 1986, Lejeune had opened a new chapter of his studies and considered, with increasing interest and a certain scientific rigour, diaries as the result of a mixture of anecdotal and personal facts. The analysis conducted by Lejeune remains, as he himself stated, francocentric and focuses on the use of diaries between the nineteenth and eighteenth centuries. In reality, the origins and development of the genre are in accordance with its contemporary definition, or as a "personal diary", and are quite complex and vary from country to country.

Assuming that the matter of a diary concerns the life of an individual, it could be said that daily records written in a journal are a form of autobiography.[10] But the main purpose of the diary changed during epochs. Many eighteenth- and nineteenth-century diaries, especially those kept by men, were a sort of semi-public documents intended to be read by an audience. The intent of the chronicle notes of that age was mostly to accumulate traces, a chronicle of an author's experience and, only subsequently, to move a reader.[11] In this way, the function of the diary is not the same for those who write (almost always with self-referencing intent[12]) and those who read (it could be the writer himself or others). The problem stems from the very nature of this textual typology. A diary, in fact, is the recording of events and episodes which mark segments of life, which are more or less expansive. It is only secondarily a creative act. It is above all a practice: on the one hand, it is a habit of handwriting and, on the other, the need to archive life's moments. The product of the diary would be, in a sense, the physiognomy of its author, which is beyond our knowledge. Therefore, reading notes in a diary is not like reading just any work, but it means venturing into a puzzle where overall there are huge gaps.[13]

Most of the diaries of the time lack any context, because they present themselves not only as repetitive and monotonous, but as mostly incoherent, as they are devoid of any consequentiality that does not refer to the passing of the day. Women diarists in particular wrote as family and community historians. They recorded in precise detail the births, deaths, illnesses, visits, travels, marriages, work and unusual circumstances that made up their lives.

The diary which President George Washington, for example, had begun to write before he was elected President, and which he gradually updated, is emblematic:

> Tuesday 1st. Thermometer at 52 in the Morning–65 at Noon And 64 at Night. Morning heavy with the Wind at South. Clear afterwards & very warm.
> Went with Mrs. Washington and Colo. Humphreys to visit Mr. & Mrs. Rogr. West. Dined there & returned in the afternoon.
> Previous to this I visited all my Plantations.[14]

A combination of personal and public notes, the text could be read as a State diary, as a register to record daily events but also as a sort of *hypomnenmata* of the ancient Greeks,[15] which is a kind of notebook to jot down personal memories and formulate opinions on personal experiences.

Therefore, the writer is referring to his or her own unique life, chronicling private events but sometimes indirectly witnessing a succession of complex sociopolitical situations, facts of institutional collective interest, meetings, natural disasters. Particularly during periods of crisis, there are many people who rely on their feelings and write a narrative of the most dramatic events. Examples are war diaries written by women, soldiers on the front, but also diaries of Heads of State. Penny Summerfield, with her enormous contribution to the British history relating the Second World War, highlighted the personal feelings and reaction of women to war through stories contained in diaries, memoirs and letters.[16]

A part of Italian historiography has focused on the reconstruction of experience, as it is lived, on mental processes and the imagination of their authors. Along these lines, we can include Antonio Gibelli's research on the Great War and the consequent transformations of the mental world, Fabio Caffarena on daily writings, and Giovanna Procacci on soldiers and Italian prisoners.[17] It is no coincidence that in Italy Gabriele De Rosa, in order to shed light on some of the most dramatic events in the history of the twentieth century—such as the world wars—often invited historians to consider other sources such as diaries and to initiate investigations that differed greatly from traditional ones. In 1966, De Rosa himself had published Federico Martini's diary as a response, at least in part, to the questions which had stranded diplomatic historiography: "What took place from 14 March to 15 May that was so serious … to produce a reversal so disastrous?"[18]

In the course of the eighteenth century, the changing of ideas brought by the arrival of Romanticism strongly influenced the lives of women and men, though there was a split between the public and private sphere.[19] The diaries changed in their content, function and form, becoming a record of individual consciousness to be kept from others' eyes.[20]

Before starting to analyse in detail Maria Carolina's diary, however, we must clarify the nature of its traditional entries, which in their structure do not differ much from those of a midwife of Maine. The great subtlety of interpretation of Laurel Thatcher Ulrich has allowed us to demonstrate its profound value in terms of social and cultural history. This substantial similarity in the structure of the source allows us to have such an essential guide in navigation through the pages of a diary, which otherwise would be insensitive and unreadable. The diary of Martha Ballard, as in the case of the one of Queen Maria Carolina, was known but was generally underestimated because it was considered of little significance for historical studies.[21] But it is the dailiness that characterizes the powerful component of the diary because of the difficulty of its use.[22] A scholar who wants to present a source of this kind must prepare an extensive introduction—such as the one here that we intended to present—so that readers can possibly be aware of the significance of the allusive references and develop interpretive perspectives that those pages contain.[23]

The plot of the study of Ulrich allows us to fix, in fact, the coordinates of the diary in its dimension as a source for the story. It highlighted the complexity and the subjectivity of historical reconstruction to give them some sense of both affinity and the distance between history and source. As we will see for Maria Carolina, Martha Ballard also rarely used punctuation. Like most of eighteenth-century diarists, she capitalizes randomly, abbreviates freely and spells even proper names:

> I sett out to visit Joseph Fosters Children. Met Ephraim Cowen by Brooks'Barn. Calld me to see his Dafters Polly & Nabby who are sick with the rash. Find them very ill. Gave directions. Was then Calld to Mrs Shaw who has been ill some time. Put her safe to Bed with daughter at 10 o clock this Evining. She is finely. Birth Mr Shaws Dafter.[24]

Diaries are a source that requires a detailed explanatory apparatus so that they can be useful, as the author, even when he quotes names and circumstances, does not aim at identifying them, because it is just a note, a kind of reminder, intended only for its own and personal use. This aspect, in fact, represents a serious problem for those who wish to examine this source. It must therefore identify each of the people present in the entry of the day, and sometimes it is also necessary to decode the involuntary allusions which could also appear in the text. As the work of Ulrich shows, the individual fragments scattered throughout daily entries suggest environmental atmospheres and moods. Therefore, they provide an interpretive key, which allows us to grasp the real meaning of actions which are almost never described in depth in the pages of the diary.

The personal diary of Maria Carolina consists of 25 volumes of manuscripts that sum up the annotations from 1781 to 1811. For more than 30 years, 10,905 days to be exact, the Queen faithfully kept her record. But unfortunately most of the manuscripts were lost during the Second World War. Housed at the State Archives of Munich until the third decade of the twentieth century, the diary was later transferred to the State Archives of Naples.[25] At the time of the Second World War, it was transported to San Paolo Belsito in the Nola countryside, along with other valuable material that was preserved from any damage caused by the bombing. But this did not make any difference since German soldiers set fire to the depository. As a result, surviving volumes, still in Naples, include the "Journal de November 1, 1781 jusqu'au December 1781" and the "Journal du September 1782 jusqu'au 31 December 1785".[26]

Using the policy which underlies the methodological approach proposed by contemporary scholars,[27] and by analysing the source, we have identified two major aspects: formal and thematic.

The first includes the following informative segments:

- text extension
- opening and closing pattern
- language and vocabulary

The second consists of the following categories:

- topics regarding daily news
- meetings with institutional figures: periodicity/frequency

The relationships between the aspects, resulting from a continuous comparison with the information gathered from the source, favour interpretation with respect to suspension of judgement. Therefore, through the analysis of manifest and latent structures of discourse (e.g. word associations, length of text, lexical and syntactic constructions, structural rigour, etc.) and the comparison of various aspects encountered within the diary, we tried *in primis* to grasp similarities, consistencies, differences, oppositions and afterwards, to understand them in the light of relevant historical facts also about the private life of the Queen.

As is well known, keeping a diary implies a selective and interpretative activity which links events and establishes relationships and hierarchies between individual facts.[28] Take as an example an excerpt from Maria Carolina's diary on 1 November 1781:
This November 1, 1781

> I got up at about 8 – saw my little ones – made my toilette – dressed – then talked with Ci. and M. – listened to two Masses – afterwards +++ read – afterwards saw my children – read the letters received in the mail – saw the King, who was returning from the pheasant farm where he had killed 24 pheasants – later dined with the King – then read – took care of little baby – of the toilette of Mimi, – afterwards read – later conversed with the King – afterwards prayed the rosary – vespers of the dead – said my prayers – afterwards the Council of Finance – so wrote my diary and saw Count Lamberg and went to bed – my health was the health of a pregnant woman – I was beginning to feel a toothache – in particular the last molar that was broken and I went to bed at ten o'clock.[29]

The diary is written in French. However, the vocabulary is misleading, as is characterized by terms which appear to come from an arbitrary translation of Italian, Neapolitan or even French. For example:

> On Wednesday June the 9th, I got up at 7 o'clock – had breakfast – combed my hair – dressed – heard holy Mass – stayed a long time with my beloved Mimi – then saw Sambuca – lunched with the children – took care of them – read + – wrote – kept myself busy – walked on the terrace – talked with Castelpagano – Belmonte – then got ready – to confess and went to bed – the children well – my dear Mimi was better but with fever – she asked for macaroni and ate them with appetite – in the morning the King went to Caserta and returned in the evening.[30]

As one can see, daily events are transcribed in the diary, events which are classified with the help of a secret symbology. In the beginning, Maria Carolina reported daily large fragments of letters sent and received. But soon, with the enormous increase of correspondence, this habit could no longer be maintained.[31] A consistent element in the Queen's diary is a scanning of the daily activities, which are sorted according to their importance ("je me suis levé [...] vus mon petit [...] toilettes [...], habillés, parlé avec C".) and exposed in a manner which conforms to the diary of the eighteenth century.[32]

The pattern of opening and closing the entry on different documented days almost always remains unchanged. To be more precise, the opening is characterized by listing a number of activities related to the personal sphere, which are repetitive and performed, basically, in the same order of priority; the closing usually relates to the family and is primarily dedicated to the family's state of health as well as the location of the King's presence. In this regard, the focus on institutional aspects and details about the movements of the King during the day seem increasingly significant from year to year. The things that change and sometimes increase are data regarding hearings and Councils.

The Journal notes which refer to the year 1781 relate to the entire month of November and the month of December until day 27. However, as evidenced by the Queen's annotation, the transcription of the diary is suspended on the 23rd due to health reasons and resumes on the 27th with the closing of the year. The extension of the text goes from a minimum of 5 lines to a maximum of 12, barring a few exceptions. For example, on 4 November, the Queen, in addition to being worried about her children's health, was also worried about the physical condition of her sister Marie Antoinette, who was to give birth to the heir to the throne of France.[33] The text, therefore, is the longest of the year (15 lines). On the contrary, on 27 December, the Queen lists briefly, in just three lines, the commitments of that day.[34] The language is simple, almost bare-bones but at times unclear and obviously encrypted. For example:

On November. 17

I got up at 7 o' clock – I took care of my little Joseph – Mimi – washed – then I spoke with No. 2. – then 8 – afterwards Mass – spoke to Gravina about his journey.[35]

On November 28

I got up at half past 7 – saw little Joseph – Mimi – the governess – my two firstborn – listened to two Masses – toilette – saw the King while painted – and so I spent the whole morning – I dined with the King – then stayed with little ones – then I read – I spoke with N °. 1 – N °. 3 – then my children – at 6 o'clock, the Council of Carlo de Marco until 8 o'clock – later I prepared myself for confession – I went to confession – I said my prayers I went to bed.[36]

On December 4

I got up at 8 in the morning – I saw little Joseph – Mimi – spoke to the King – ⊙ – then the governess – toilette – Mass afterwards having seen Theresa scolded – at half past 11 the King had lunch – I kept him company – I stayed with him – later spoke to the confessor – then had lunch with Lamberg – my children later played with the small read +++ afterwards wrote – then saw Duchess Sirignano who wants her husband – son of fiscal [lawyer] Caraveda judge and the wife and the daughter of Secondo who want their husband to be counsellors – later saw N °. 1 – then wrote the diary – the post until half past 8 – was present while the King – had milk with coffee –.[37]

The expression "read +++" is seen throughout the diary. The only variation is represented by the number of crosses that were most likely used to connote the subject of the letter or the content. They may have also been used as a value judgement or to identity the author of the text.

One may also notice the different functions of the dual use of the number 8. When it is used to indicate the hour, the number is followed by the clarification *heures*; otherwise, it is mentioned only as an amount. However, even reading it within the text one can understand to what or to whom it refers. Unlike in other years, in the 1781 entries the Queen replaces names with numbers which she uses to conceal their identities in order to protect their privacy, since the noble title, as well as the institutional and/or political role, is mentioned only a few times and usually in reference to the same characters. One might assume that the Queen has an earnest interaction with them (in terms of frequency) and that she therefore participates in the most significant decision-making moments.

The contents of the diary in the year 1782 include the period from 10 September to 31 December. The language continues to be mostly simple with an "essential" vocabulary and in some parts is encrypted and difficult to understand. In this regard, one can no longer identify certain symbols in the pages referring to the previous year, while other symbols and some letters appear (often the initials of names). The Queen apparently sees fit to conceal the names of several people to either avoid unpleasant consequences arising from the disclosure of their identity or simply to shorten the time of writing:

On Wednesday October 9, I got up at 8 o'clock – saw the children – had breakfast – dressed – combed my hair – heard the holy Mass – and then wrote – worked on my affairs – saw Gatti – with my children – talked and kept company to the King – then saw Lady San Marco who the trees on her feud to be cut – then saw S.B.-afterwards went out in a carriage with Mimi up to the channel – back – talked throughout with the King ∗ ⊙ – then the Council afterwards prayed – wrote – saw Lamberg and went to bed.[38]

> The King in the morning went out and afterwards-lunch to San Leucio – the children were fine.

On Sunday the 27th, I got up at 7 o'clock – toilette – dressed – had breakfast – combed my hair – then Holy Mass – saw all my children – then at eleven – went with the lady Gravina and Vasto in town where I met people – SB spoke to me – then A. – Then I read my letters – I had lunch – then I went to pick my winter clothes – and then selected the music papers – read – wrote – at 4 o'clock King arrived – I still continued my affairs – at half past 5 there was the farewell ceremony – in the canopy – in public – of the Ambassador of Morocco with the whole court – afterwards I changed my clothes – I said my prayers and went to Florentines theatre – where I bored myself a lot – at half past ten at home – saw X – I undressed and went to bed.[39]

> The King went out hunting to the net in Carditello – there he had lunch and arrived in town at 4 o'clock – children healthy – Louise better without fever.

On Thursday the 26th, I got up at 7 o'clock – had breakfast – combed my hair – dressed – heard Masses – spoke to a – to SB – to Cim – then had lunch with my children – afterwards spoke again to a – then saw Rocafiorita – the Christmas bishop – Princess Butera – then the two Councils – later to bed.[40]

> The children healthy – in the morning the King went to Carditello – hunting wild boar – and returned in the evening.

Although the structural setting for each day remains almost unchanged, as is the case with the hierarchical arrangement of the arguments as well as the length, the text contains, in the right-hand margin, personal memos concerning the health of Ferdinand IV and the children. Except for a few days in October, November and December (the contents of which take up about three lines), the rest of the daily records extend an average which often exceeds ten lines. But the Queen elaborates in detail on 28 September when she describes with anxiety and trepidation the rescue of young Mimi, her favourite daughter[41]:

On Saturday the 28 I woke up at 7 o'clock – I was informed that dear Mimi had a slight fever – I got up immediately to see her – she was still sleeping – I combed my hair and dressed to go – as I had decided – to college of midshipmen – given that at half past eight she was still asleep – it seemed to me too much – I opened the windows and I realized immediately that it was not sleep but slumber – [therefore] the doctor gave her two emetics of ipecacuanha of two […] at a time – she vomited a lot but still with a terrible sleepiness – she did not complain about anything – and not being able even keep her head straight for a moment – she had enemas for hours – and round the clock she urinated 3 times – although she was always very thirsty – to the touch she was always cool – as the sleepiness still grew – put their feet in gutted pigeons – but after one hour and a half they were cold again – three warm baths at the feet were made – but in vain – she sweated a lot – she was almost black in the face – and the skin and the sweat were cold – when she bled from the foot – the blood came out cold and with difficulty – it were applied two plasters to her legs – cantharide – and she was given camphor by mouth with maidenhair syrup – she was insensitive to everything and the sleepiness increased – in the end energetic and constant rubbing of flannel was applied to the whole body – which combined with other remedies – started to make the frozen blood circulate – as steady – the little girl began to speak – I did not move for anything from the room [during] this whole day and I spent the whole night.

> The other children healthy – the King in the morning went to trawl – in the afternoon on the craggy mountain and in evening to my [prayer] to throw [the javelin].[42]

Regarding the second category, the main topics are represented by the physical condition of the children, the King's commitments, the daily hearings and hunting trips. In the first case, the Queen is confirmed to be a careful and concerned mother. The King's activities are simply mentioned, with no reflection or commentary, like a mere recording. On the contrary, details of walks, excursions and so on are mentioned:

On Saturday October 12th, I got up at 7 o clock – combed my hair – dressed – had breakfast – holy Mass – then read – wrote – went to Louise's room – with all my other children – then had lunch – then arranged my library – afterwards saw Sangro who prays for her affairs – then d.u. – afterwards I went out – with the little Marchioness Hamilton and Lamberg – saw damage of the gulf – and from there I returned on foot through the wood – saw my children – went to Louise's room – then came back down – prayed – then saw my two little children sleeping – afterwards wrote and devoted myself – still go to Louise and I went to sleep.[43]

> The children were quite well – Louise had a quiet night – the new fever took her at nine o'clock – it was slight but the eyes and head dejected. The King went in the morning to the royal tennis – during the day for a short time.

On Tuesday the 29th, I got up at 7 o'clock – combed my hair – had breakfast – dressed – saw my children – heard holy Mass – wrote – read in the library – then the King came – I talked with him – ⊙ – then had lunch – afterwards read – played the harpsichord – saw my children – read – wrote – kept myself busy – went to bed.[44]

> In the morning the King went out to hunting – then at home – it rained – I had the bad thing. The children healthy.

On Monday the 18th, I got up at 6 o'clock – had breakfast – dressed – heard holy Mass at 7 o'clock – afterwards I went hunting to Zingaro with the King – young Altavilla and Gravina – in a carriage – I saw wild boars running – then I fired seven shots and hit five – then dined at 4 o'clock and returned at half past 7 – I changed clothes – saw my children and presided over the Council and to bed.[45]

In 1783, the entries cover all the months of the year, without interruption. The use of coded symbols is greater than in the previous year. Perhaps the Queen participates very actively in politics? Maybe she has intensified her interaction with members of her family of origin or interpersonal relationships with people mentioned for various reasons, within her sphere of interest? There are no citations of any specific topic or foreign policy or domestic policy. Moreover, there are few references to new friends and/or significant new knowledge: the symbols used in previous years remain. In addition, we identified others which were absent before and therefore will be left out hereafter. Furthermore, within the text there is an increase of the initials of some proper and common names:

> On Thursday January the 2nd, I got up at 7 o'clock – had breakfast – combed my hair – dressed – heard holy Masses ♥ – had lunch with my children whom I kept with me until three o'clock, ♥ – afterwards 000 ◣◢ then I prayed and waited for the King who came back at seven o'clock very happy because of the big game hunting – he stayed with me – ☉ – then we had the Cimitile's Council followed by Acton's – afterwards undressed and went to bed. In the morning the King went out – with all the inhabitants of Caserte – to Zingaro where the Duke of Chartres came – there was a great wild boars hunting trip and 147 boars died and everything succeeded wonderfully. I wore my hair with a little bonnet over my hair and [with] a brown polka [jacket]. My children – thanks to God – were healthy – I suffered less than other days from my pregnancy.[46]

> On Saturday January 4, I got up at 7 o'clock – had breakfast – combed my hair – dressed – heard holy Mass – wrote – read – had lunch with my children – spoke to me. – then wrote 000 – afterwards saw Lady Wedel and kept her with me for a conversation – afterwards I dressed s and prayed – then the King returned + – afterwards we went to the theatre – I in the carriage – the King on foot – at the theatre I had the Duke of Chartres – Fitz James – Genlis – Gravina and Migliano in my loge – they played the little music of le Veuvage d'un – then I came back home.[47]

> I went out and returned with the King – my children healthy enough. We killed 125 wild boars. Little Joseph – after a [restless] night – seemed to have a slight fever.

> On Friday January the 10th, I got up at 7 am – had breakfast – dressed – listened to Mass – wrote to Caserta – 000 – saw the ladies – then had lunch with the King with whom I had a long conversation + – then walked out on the terrace three or four times – later my affairs ♥ – then had dinner – later gave hearings – Princess Acquaviva for a domestic affair – Anna Maria Patrizio for her son as a provincial auditor – Saverio Cresconio for his brother judge in Naples – Maria Angiola for her husband [to] settle there – then □ later the King returned, I conversed with him ☉ – afterwards there were two Councils of Finance and War – afterwards which I undressed – I prayed and went to bed.[48]

On Monday January the 13th, I got up at 7 o'clock – had breakfast – combed my hair – heard holy Mass ♥ then r.a.d.a.d'.a.l.d'a.t.t.b.a.t.l.d. – afterwards I talked with Torella for the case of [gulline] of the city – I saw Lamberg – afterwards [I listened to] all my ladies and went to have lunch – and then came Migliano – Cimitile – Sambuca – all informed me of the Council that had been♥ e.c.f.l.p.f.q.j.s.l.v.p.l.s.b.d.m.d.e.c.e.d.h. – then I saw Madame Sambuca complaining – afterwards Faggiano begged me to not to have his brother in law married – the King came back – there was the Council of Sambuca – and then we went to see a comedy of Canito where where I initiately liked the woman who acted – she softened me a lot – from there I went to dress up and to go to the theatre of the ball – I went down a bit with Gravina and Marsico and had Chartres who took leave from my loge – at one o'clock we returned home and I ☉ undressed and went to bed. The King went at 7 o'clock to a fishing pond with Chartres in Castellamare and returned in the evening, the children were well, I was dressed in gray and black polka [jacket] – had started the evening with domino.[49]

On Thursday January the 16th, I got up at 7 o'clock – had breakfast – dressed – combed my hair – heard holy Mass □ then Migliano came to talk with me – I began to write ♥ afterwards had lunch with my children – they stayed with me ♥ ☉ ▲ then wrote – took care – the King came back – he presided over the two Councils and I prayed and went to bed. The King went to Calvi to hunt ducks from morning to night. The children were well – except Amélie and Januarius. I was all *negligee* – the wound reopened – but without pain.[50]

Throughout the year, the use of symbols shrinks but the use of encrypted language still persists:

On Wednesday August the 20th, I got up the morning – heard holy Mass – worked on my affairs – had lunch with my children – stayed with them – spoke to Sambuca – then wrote – read – worked on my affairs – saw old Corigliano – San Marco – read * again – saw my children and went to bed.[51]

On Tuesday August the 26th, I got up at 7 o'clock – at 8 o'clock I walked with Sambuca – then I combed my hair – dressed and started to write my letters – then heard Mass – saw Count Lamberg – Prince Belmonte and his second son – Count Giusepe – all those had lunch with us – later drew – read – wrote – kept myself busy until evening – I kept the King company – ☉ – then read +++ – wrote – prayed – in the evening went out to play a match and had dinner out. The children healthy – in the morning the King went to kill bonitos but in the afternoon he did not go out anymore.[52]

On Sunday the 31st, I got up at nine o'clock in the morning after having had fever all night – I had breakfast – dressed – worked on my affairs – heard holy Mass – then drew – had lunch – drew again – read – wrote these were my occupations +++ – then went out – had dinner and went to sleep – in the morning the King went fishing at the pier – afternoon he went out again to the pier. He wrote to me from Naples that Mimi was getting better – the others healthy.[53]

A graphological examination seems to imply that the Queen, in certain circumstances, for health reasons, entrusted the writing of the daily news to third parties. This was from 18 to 27 July 1783,[54] while Marie Caroline was between life and death in the two days following the birth of a son who died. She therefore had to give up, for a long time, all her commitments and political affairs:

On Friday July the 18th, I got up at half past 7 – had breakfast – dressed – combed my hair – heard holy Mass – wrote the post – saw Sambuca – at midday received the King on his return from Castellamare – had lunch with him – drew – kept him company – saw my children – dressed – combed my hair and went to the two Councils of finance and War – from there feeling not well – I undressed and confessed my sins – after that I began to bleed and have the miscarriage that ended at three thirty in the morning.[55]

On Saturday the 19th, I saw my children in the morning and all day stayed in darkness, lying without talking, the children well. The King did not go out all day.[56]

The contents of the diary in the year 1783 also reveal a significant increase in the commitments of the sovereign. There is an increase in the number of institutional meetings with ministers of the Kingdom and with some notable political figures who were prominent in the diplomatic arena, not only Neapolitans:

On Sunday april the 6th, I got up at 7 o'clock – had breakfast – dressed – combed my hair – heard holy Mass – then the sermon was about the conduct of parents towards their children and subordinates – and then went to have lunch with the King and all the gentlemen in the castle – afterwards played reversis with Gravina – Cassano – at half past 3 went home – read the – then saw Lady Wedel with the 3 sons that I like very much – then Gallo who is leaving for Turin.[57]

On Saturday May the 24th, I got up at half past 7 – had breakfast – dressed – combed my hair – heard holy Mass – read – wrote – devoted myself – had lunch with the King – drew – read – worked on my affairs – to say the rosary – saw my children – in the evening saw Hamilton who talked about the misfortunes of Calabria – and then to bed. The children healthy. The King went a little afternoon for a walk in the grove.[58]

On Sunday June the 8th, I got up at half past 7 – had breakfast – dressed – combed my hair – heard two holy Masses – was present at Mimi's lesson – then saw my children – then had a big lunch for 24 people with the Elector of Bavaria – his two knights.[59]

On Tuesday June 17, I got up at 8 o'clock – had breakfast – dressed – heard holy Mass – went to Mimi's room – saw Acton – then returned to Mimi's room – saw my children – had lunch with the King – drew – wrote my post – went to Mimi – took leave of Count Micheli who will be ambassador to Paris – then prepared for confession and confessed – from there to Mimi's room – had dinner and to bed.[60]

On Tuesday September the 2nd, I got up – had breakfast – dressed – combed my hair – heard holy Mass – read – wrote – kept myself busy – had lunch – later drew – read – wrote – kept myself busy – talked with Sambuca – afterwards kept company with foreigners – went out with Lamberg and Rasoumouski – and Lady Altavilla – afterwards came back home.[61]

Comparing the information regarding the Queen's meetings and her notes about the movements of her husband, it should be noted that the King was often absent, engaged in hunting or visiting various sites in the Kingdom:

On Monday the 3rd, I got up at 7 o'clock – had breakfast – dressed – combed my hair – heard holy Mass – wrote – read – saw my children – went to have lunch with them – afternoon with them – and then wrote – devoted myself – read until the King returned – there was Council and I went to bed The children healthy – the King was in Carditello all day [hunting] pigeons – me – I was always very distressed and sad.[62]

On Friday the 21st, I got up at 7 o'clock – had breakfast – dressed – combed my hair – heard the Mass – went to listen the sermon – had lunch with the King and my brother – and then stayed with my brother until 4 o'clock – afterwards did my things – read – wrote there were the two Councils – then my Theresa played the harpsichord – there were my brother – Hardek – Lamberg – Sambuca – Acton – Gravina and Hamilton in my room until 9 o'clock when I went to sleep and my brother to the pool. The King in the afternoon went to Carbone. The children healthy.[63]

The Queen met daily with her ministers before the Council, which, however, took place only in the presence of the King and often in the evening, since Ferdinand IV was not present at Court during the day. However, there are rarely annotations in the diary concerning the meetings between the King and the ministers of the Kingdom. By correlating these data with each other, one could argue that the Queen took part in the discussions and, therefore, knew the political and institutional decisions concerning the Kingdom. Therefore, Maria Carolina's active role should be spoken of rather than her mere interference. However, there is no mention, except in a few cases, of the topics covered by the Council and at the informal meetings with the ministers. The information entrusted to the text is most frequently that which is relevant regarding the daily meetings with the nobility and their children:

On Tuesday the 29th, I got up around 11 o'clock – had lunch with my two eldest daughters – saw Count Lamberg – Sambuca – Lord Belmonte – Acton – then spent the afternoon with my girls – about 5 o'clock I returned to bed and saw the lady guard and went to sleep, the children healthy – the King went to Caserta – there was a downpour and he returned at half past 11 in the evening.[64]

The range of topics covered by the daily news expands in 1783, the year in which the Queen is visited by her brothers Giuseppe and Maximilian along with her sister, Amelia. But it is also the year of the devastating earthquake in Calabria and Messina, and of a dramatic personal event: the Queen loses young Joseph and gives birth to a dead child. Very deep are the thoughts with which she expresses her emotions and feelings:

On Saturday February the 1st, I got up at 7 o'clock – had breakfast – combed my hair – dressed – wrote – took care of the poor little sick Joseph – had lunch with the children – talked with Migliano – wrote – read – devoted myself – went to Januarius – the King came back – I returned to Joseph's room – Januarius and Joseph – wrote – prayed and went to bed. The King went to the pheasant farm. My children healthy – Januarius with a continual violent cough and fever – little Joseph with a high fever – in the evening he had a new one but more lightly. I was all negligee.

On Wednesday the 19th, I got up at 7 o'clock – the news concerning Joseph was not better – I got up – dressed – I listened to Mass – I took leave of Mimi and went with Teresa – Luisa and Marchioness Altavilla to Caserta – where I arrived at half past eleven – very anxious to have news of my little Joseph – the coldness of which depressed me – I ran up the stairs – I flew into the room of my little one – I found him on his bed he recognized me – he looked at me – shook my finger that handed him [and] a moment later came the hiccups did not let him go until his hands were cold – then the doctor said he no longer had a pulse – I was away from the room I lay down on a sofa – I saw my two eldest daughters – at midday the King returned we cried and talked of this loss – an hour and a half we sat at the table – afterwards I remained with the King – at 4 o'clock the other children were brought to me – it was a new stab to my broken heart – at half past 5 with the permission of the King I went to see my little lifeless one – cold and dead – I kissed his hands – I embraced him – kissed his feet – this caused me in a terrible and painful sweetness – had a face [which was] nice calm [and] relaxed I was touched and I cried so that he would pray for his afflicted mother – I went home, and at 7 o'clock the beloved child was taken to Naples – I lay down – I took care of myself and tried I went to sleep.[65]

On Thursday February 20th, I got up in the morning and I cried a lot – later dressed – listened to Mass ♥ – read – worked on my affairs – lunch with my two eldest daughters – prayed – took care – saw my children – and presided over the two Councils – in my room – later to bed. The King went to the Masseria delle Bufale at ten o'clock and returned at 5 o'clock – my children enjoyed it – we embalmed my little one and we did not find any deficiency – which I knew because he was nice and in a small way perfectly well breeded and of a precocious intelligence and ability – in the evening he was brought to St. Clara, where he remained exposed throughout the night – I was still very sad.[66]

Given the painful events that are recorded in her diary, the Queen continues to predominantly exhibit concerns over the health problems of her children, limiting to just a few references the disaster caused by the earthquake:

On Friday the 14th, I got up later – dressed – heard holy Mass – then breakfast – Sambuca came to give me the bad news that the frigate Saint Dorothy had arrived and brought the news of the destruction of Messina by an earthquake – I had lunch with my children – later came Acton – Carlo de Marco – all with the same news – I spoke to Vincenzo Pignatelli who escaped from there bringing the same details –.[67]

On Saturday the 15th, I got up around 9 am – when we had the bad news that a large part of Calabria ultra had suffered the same misfortune as Messina – I got up – dressed – the King after having summoned the four secretaries to make the resolutions on this unfortunate event – it was decided to send marshal Pignatelli on the spot – to rescue the unfortunate – and reserving at the moment the right to take action depending on the circumstances –.[68]

On Sunday (March) the 16th, [...] the King came back to tell me the details of Calabria – prayed – played the harpsichord – saw my sick children and to bed.[69]

On Friday March the 28th, I got up at 7 o'clock – had breakfast – combed my hair – dressed – saw Sambuca – then went to listen the sermon – had lunch with my brother and the King – then the King was with us – there was the Liparoti exercise – from there he went with my brother across the bridge of Maddalena and then came back – we went to say the rosary and from there to the two Councils – after I had a conversation with my brother – Hardek – Lamberg – the lady – Acton – when around 10 o'clock Don Giovanni came to Naples with a terrible noise informing me that there had been an earthquake in Naples – my fear for this news – for the effects – for everything that interests me was terrible – they spoke about that until late when I went to bed. My children were well, in the morning the King went with my brother to Cacciabella and returned at 11 o'clock, afternoon [he took] exercise and went to the bridge.[70]

On Sunday (April)the 27th, I got up – curled my hair – dressed – heard holy Mass – afterwards there was a long speech by Acton with the King and me regarding the disorders + – and – $\odot$ – then at three o'clock we lunched – afterwards read – later saw Princess Caramanico – stayed with her – changed my dress – went with the King by dray to the blessing of the Augustinians – and home – kept the King company – Rocella informed me about the misfortunes of Calabria – later saw a map – finally went to the lady who was with a lot of people – I played with Altavilla – Belmonte, and then came back home at eleven o'clock at night – very weary – tired and went to bed. The children healthy – the King came out a little after lunch to the revisit and the Liparoti's exercises.[71]

A further detail found in the diary is the Queen's reflections concluding the year and her wishes for the future of her family:

On Wednesday December the 31st, I got up at 7 o'clock – combed my hair – dressed – His Majesty the Emperor came to breakfast with me and kept me company – then I saw my children – went to church and then my brother and my sister came with me to the aqueduct – from there to home to make the toilet – the departure of my sister was scheduled for Sunday, we had lunch at a table of 16 seats – Belmonte Sambuca Gravina Marsico and Migliano everything else was my sister or of His Majesty the Emperor – afterwards Teresa played the harpsichord – then his Majesty gave me the grace stay with me – afterwards we went to the theatre Fiorentino that had been made to come to this small theatre and at home, – the children well – the King went in the afternoon to St. Leucio with my sister to kill wild boar, and so ended the year 1783. A year in which I had infinite pains with public sorrows of Calabria and Messina all the details of this dreadful were terrible catastrophe losses measures filled almost the whole year – I also lost a son whom I warmly loved and whom it cost me to raise him and his precocious spirit was my consolation, I had a bad birth that reduced me to death having received all the Saint sacraments – I had the misfortune of giving birth to a dead child – Briefly that is the result of much deep anguish which has caused me great pain. The consolations were the arrival of my brother Maximilian that of my sister from Parma and especially that of His Majesty the Emperor with whom I had the happiness to start the new year, I dare to hope that under these auspices it will be happier in my pain and sorrow not to do that thanks to the divine Providence that has supported me – and invoke it so that [I] use the life which he has left me, well.[72]

NOTES

1. "from this diary … who knows well the facts and people of the time, will make a contribution to history". B. Croce, *La Biblioteca Tedesca di Maria Carolina d'Austria Regina di Napoli*, in "La Critica", 32 (1934), fasc.1, (Bari: Laterza, 1934), 72.

2. M.Traversier, "Chronique d'un royal ennui. Le Journal de la reine Marie Caroline de Naples (1781–1785)" in *Acte de colloques Écritures de famille, écriture de soi*, M. Cassan (ed), (Limoge: Pulim, 2010), 127–150; U. Tamussino, *Des Teufels Großmutter: eine Biographie der Königin M. von Neapel-Sizilien*, (Wien : Deuticke, 1991); E. Caesar Corti, *Ich, eine Maria Theresias Tochter: ein Lebensbild der Königin Marie Karoline von Neapel*, (Munchen : Bruckmann, 1950) ; B. Croce, "La Biblioteca Tedesca di Maria Carolina d'Austria Regina di Napoli", in *La Critica* ; L. Tresoldi, *La biblioteca privata di Maria Carolina d'Austria regina di Napoli*, (Roma: Bulzoni, 1972).

3. See, S. Rosa, "Un supplemento dal nome poco cospicuo. Linguaggio, genere e studi storici", in *Storica*, n. 20–21, 2001, 65; as well as N. Z.

Davis, *A History of Women: Renaissance and Enlightenment Paradoxes*, (Cambridge: Natalie Zemon Davis and Arlette Farge, 1993).

4. M.L Betri, – D.Maldini Chiarito *Scritture di desiderio e di ricordo: autobiografie, diari, memorie, tra Settecento e Novecento*, (Milano:Franco Angeli, 2002).

5. Amy Culley in her recent study of British women's life, analysing a wide range of print and unpublished sources, as memoirs and journals of courtesans and British travellers' accounts of the French Revolution, provides a new way in which women wrote the stories of their lives and the lives of others. See, A. Culley, *British Women' s Life, 1760-1840: Friendship, Community and collaboration*, (London: Palgrave Macmillan, 2014).

6. See, R. Langford, – W.Russel. (eds), *Marginal Voices, Marginal Forms: Diaries in European Literature and History*, (Amsterdam: Rodopi, 1999).

7. M. Culley, *A day at a time: The Diary Literature of American Women from 1764 to the Present*, (New York: Feminist Press, 1985), 10.

8. According to the French studies tradition on *journal intime*, we mention here some relevant studies published: R. Bizzocchi, "Sentimenti e documenti", *in* "Studi Storici", april–june 1999, 477, *Another Life, Une autre vie*, textes réunis par Mélanie Joseph-Vilain et Judith Mishrahi-Barak, (Montpellier:Presses universitaires de la Méditerranée, 2013); *Archives familiales, modes d'emploi : récits de genèse*, sous la direction de Véronique Montémont et Catherine Viollet, Louvain-la-Neuve (Belgique), 2013; *Les Archives personnelles: enjeux, acquisition, valorisation*I, édition Françoise Hiraux, Françoise Mirguet, Editions Academia, Louvain-la-Neuve 2013; *L'Autobiographie entre autres. Ecrire la vie aujourd'hui*, Fabrice Arribert-Narce, Alain Ausoni (éds.), Berne, Peter Lang, 2013; *L'Autoportrait dans la littérature française du Moyen Âge au XVIIe siècle*, Elisabeth Gaucher-Rémond et Jean Garapon (dir.), Presses Universitaires de Rennes, Rennes, coll. "Interférences", 2013; *L'Écriture de soi*, dossier du Magazine littéraire, avril 2013.

9. For the first time, thanks to the school of autobiographical studies at the University of Hawaii, all the contributions of Philippe Lejeune about the diary have been collected in the work of recovery and translated in English, *On Diary*, Jeremy D. Popkin & Julie Rak (eds), (Honululu: Hawaii University Press, 2009), 2.

10. P. Lejeune, "Relire son journal", in *Pour l'autobiographie*, (Paris : Éditions du Seuil, 1998), 226–228.

11. B. Ackermann, "Paratextes et journal non intime: le journal de Denis de Rougemont" in *Litterature*, vol.18, n.98, 1995, 24 – 44.

12. A. Girard, *Le journal intime*, (Paris :Presses Universitaires de France, 1963), 3 – 4.

13. See, P. Lejeune, "Le journal: genese d'un pratique", in *Genesis*, 32–2011, 30.

14. *The Diaries of* George *Washington*, 5 vol., (Charlottesville: University Press of Virginia, 1976), 211.

15. The *hypomnemata* constituted a material memory of things read, heard or thought, to be offered as an accumulated treasure for rereading and later meditation. See, M. Foucalt, *History of sexuality: the care of self*, trad. Robert Hurley, (New York:Pantheon books, 1986) K. Mesiter, "Autobiographische Literatur und Hypomnémata", in Studia Hellenistica, 30 (1990); J. Engels, "Die Hypomnemata-Schriften und die Anfänge der politischen Biographie und Autobiographie in der griechischen Literatur", ZPE, 96 (1993), 19–36.

16. P. Summerfield, "Conflict Power and Gender in Women's Memoirs of Second World War: A Mass Observation Study", in *Miranda, revue disciplinaire du monde Anglophone*, 2-2010, 1–10; G. Braybon – P. Summerfield, *Out of Cage: Women's experience in Two World Wars*, (London: Routledge, 1987).

17. See, A. Gibelli, *La grande guerra degli italiani: 1915-1918*, (Bologna: Biblioteca Universitaria Rizzoli, 2007); F. Caffarena, *Lettere della Grande Guerra: scritture del quotidiano, monumenti della memoria,fonti per la storia*, (Milano: Edizioni Unicopli, 2005); G. Procacci, *Soldati e prigionieri italiani nella Grande Guerra: con una raccolta di lettere inedite*, (Torino: Bollati Boringhieri, 2000).

18. F. Martini, *Diario 1914-1918*, G. De Rosa (ed), (Milano: Mondadori, 1966).

19. M. Culley, *A day at a time: The Diary Literature of American Women from 1764 to the Present*, (New York: Femminist Press, 1985), 3.

20. Ibid., 4.

21. "Those historian who have known about the diary have not quite to do with it". L.T. Ulrich, *A Midwife's Tale. The Life of Martha Ballard, based on her diary, 1785-1812*, (New York: Vintage Books, 1991), 8–9.

22. Ibid., 33.

23. See in this regard, the study of J. Hinton, *Nine wartime lives, Mass – Observation and Making of the Modern Self*, (Oxford: Oxford University Press, 2010).

24. L.T. Ulrich, *A Midwife's Tale. The Life of Martha Ballard, based on her diary, 1785-1812*, 39.

25. L. Tresoldi, *La biblioteca privata di Maria Carolina d'Austria regina di Napoli*, 15.

26. According to some stylistic peculiarities and theme of Maria Carolina'diary (such as the characteristics of materials and graphics, the structure, the doctors mentioned, the outputs hunting and theatre) see the recent and remarkable essay of M.Traversier, *Chronique d'un royal ennui. Le Journal de la reine Marie Caroline de Naples (1781–1785)*, 135–150.

27. On aspects concerning the methodology of the research in this context, are the reference: M.B. Miles, A.M. Huberman *Qualitative data analysis: an*

expanded sourcebook, (Thousand Oaks: Sage Publications, 1984); R. Trinchero, *I metodi della ricerca educativa*, (Roma-Bari: Laterza, 2004).

28. P. Lejeune "Le journal: genèse d'une pratique" in *Genesis*, R. Barhtes, *Variazioni sulla scrittura seguite da Il piacere del testo*, (Torino: Biblioteca Einaudi, 1999); F. D'Intino, *L'autobiografia moderna. Storia forme e problemi*, (Roma: Bulzoni, 1998), pp. 125–126.

29. Archive of State of Naples, *Archivio Borbone*, 96, *Journal*, f. 1r. It is our translation from French of the diary's entries, which we have reproduced here and in the subsequent pages of this volume.

30. Ibid., f.179v.

31. See E. Caesar Corti, *Ich, eine Maria Theresias Tochter: ein Lebensbild der Konigh Marie Karoline von Neapel*, 114–115.

32. In this regard, see the considerations of P. Lejeune, "Le journal: genèse d'une pratique" in *Genesis*, 28–29; G. Antonelli, "La grammatica epistolare nell'Ottocento" in *La cultura epistolare nell'Ottocento. Sondaggi sulle lettere del Ceod*, G. Antonelli, C. Giummo, M. Palermo (eds), (Roma: Bulzoni editore, 2004), 27–50.

33. ASN, Archivio Borbone, f.96, *Journal*, f.1 v.

34. Ibid., f.15v.

35. Ibid., f. 5 v.

36. Ibid., f. 8 v.

37. Ibid., f. 10 r.

38. Ibid., f. 25 r.

39. Ibid., f. 29 v.

40. Ibid., f. 42 r.

41. Ivi, ff.20v–21v

42. ASN, Archivio Borbone, 96, *Journal*, f.20v.

43. Ibid., f.25v

44. Ibid., f.30v

45. Ibid., f.34r.

46. Ibid., ff.44r–v.

47. Ibid., f. 45 r.

48. Ibid., f.47v.

49. Ibid., f.48.

50. Ibid., f.49 v.

51. Ibid., f.106r.

52. Ibid., f.107 r.

53. Ibid., f. 108v.

54. Ibid., ff.100–101.

55. Ibid., f. 100v.

56. Ibid., f.100r.

57. Ibid., f. 72r.

58. Ibid., f. 87r.
59. Ibid., c. 90v.
60. Ibid., c. 93r.
61. Ibid., c. 109r.
62. Ibid., c. 62v.
63. Ibid., c. 66v.
64. Ibid., c. 102r.
65. Ibid., cc.59r–59v.
66. Ibid., c. 60r.
67. Ibid., cc. 57v–58r.
68. Ibid., c. 58r.
69. Ibid., c. 65v.
70. Ibid., c.68v.
71. Ibid., c. 78v.
72. Ibid., cc.139v–140r.

CHAPTER 3

Complex Interdependence Between Public and Private Moments: Queenly Audiences, Meetings and Precouncil

The drafting of the diary in the year 1784 proposes a chronological arrangement of topics, simplicity of vocabulary, repetition of semantic implications and limited use of punctuation, which is incorrect. It should be noted that there is a change in handwriting that runs from 13 to 17 December. In those days, the Queen had given birth to Antoinette, the youngest daughter, whom she named after her dear sister, the Queen of France. The formal change is represented by a coded language, which has been revised and reduced. The text lacks many symbols, however, in the pages of previous years. On the other hand, it seems to have perfected her codes for "read", "wrote" and "spoke":

> On Friday January the 30th, I got up at six o'clock – combed my hair – dressed – heard holy Mass – then at half past six I left [with] – Gravina – Marsico – and the lady – at midday arrived Naples – I found my children healthy thanks to God – I saw Sambuca – de Marco – I lunched – afterwards I unpacked – arranged my things – saw Acton – read + – kept myself busy.[1]
>
> On Monday February the 2nd, I got up the morning – combed my hair – dressed – had breakfast with Francis – took part with affection in the communion of Teresa – then Mass – read – wrote – kept myself busy – talked with St. Nicola – with Belmonte – had lunch with my girls – saw Sambuca – Acton – gave numerous hearings – two brides [came] to introduce themselves, a certain Simone to put his niece in a convent – Ferrante for his brother – then the Council – afterwards the opera where the Count of Haga came to visit us – then I went to sleep.[2]

© The Author(s) 2017
C. Recca, *The Diary of Queen Maria Carolina of Naples, 1781–1785*,
Queenship and Power, DOI 10.1007/978-3-319-31987-2_3

On Friday February the 6th, I got up – dressed – had breakfast – combed my hair – heard holy Mass – read[+] – wrote – talked with San Marco – then Sambuca – lunched – saw a nice drawing table – then read + – wrote – saw Acton – then had a number of audiences.[3]

On April the 11th Easter Sunday, I got up at half past 6 – went at seven o'clock with the King to the public chapel – there received communion and made my Easter – then returned – I had breakfast with the King and my children – heard Mass with my children – then talked a long time with Pignatelli who returned from Rome – then combed my hair – dressed – went to the hand-kissing – then public table – then changed dress and had lunch – afterwards kept the King company – then saw San Marco – then read….[4] – afterwards saw Duchess la Vella and my children – went with the last to the blessing of the parish – afterwards talked Gravina about my son – undressed – arranged my papers – had dinner and to bed

On Tuesday May the 4th, I got up – dressed – had breakfast – combed my hair – heard holy Mass – wrote my post – preached Theresa – saw de Marco – Sambuca – then had lunch – saw Ventapane – then wrote – saw Acton – a sharp pain took me that was forced to lay – then read ++ – wrote – kept myself busy – went to [say] the rosary – finished my post +++ –.[5]

On Sunday June the 27th, I got up – dressed – lunch – combed my hair – heard holy Mass – kept myself busy – read – wrote – lunched with the King – read ++++ – kept myself busy – read my letters +++.[6]

Given that the Queen, as is seen in the pages from previous years, used to meet political figures and, in any case, belonged to the noble class (not only Neapolitan), it would appear that Maria Carolina strengthened her position as Sovereign and exercised responsibilities even in the absence of her husband. In order to ensure the confidentiality of the information and the identity of the interlocutors, she also perfected her "coded message" in reference to the sessions of the Council of State:

On Wednesday June the 16th, I got up at 7 o'clock – had breakfast – dressed – combed my hair – brought Holy Viaticum to a poor sick – then talked with de Marco – the Countess Althan – afterwards went to the chapel – talked with Belmonte – Gravina – San Nicola – Marsico – lunched with the children – took care of them – read + – wrote – kept myself busy – saw Acton – Monsignor Saluzi – kept myself busy – then spoke to Gravina – saw the King – presided over the Council +.[7]

There remains a lack of references to political issues, both domestic and foreign as well as administrative, while news events are noted.

Perhaps Maria Carolina considers them more important or wants to show the potential readers of her diary an accurate self-image: the Queen consort who does not deal with political affairs, but only with the care of her family and "public relations" with polite society. Yet in the diary, even in the absence of the King, she meets daily with ministers, advisers and ambassadors and also participated in festivals, dances and so on.

On April the 12th Easter Monday I got up at half past 6 – dressed – combed my hair – had breakfast – still arranged my affairs – heard two Masses – then at 9 o'clock went with the King to listen to the sermon – then the commander of miquelets brought us the news that the two famous bandits Angiolello del Duca and Rosso were arrested half dead-.[8]

On Thursday May the 27th, I got up – dressed – combed my hair – had breakfast – heard holy Mass – had breakfast with my three daughters and heard Mass in St. Pasqual – then Caravita – at home I met Breme who spoke to me – then arranged my affairs – went to Naples with my three daughters – on arrival – settled – arranged – talked with Acton – saw my children – talked with Lamberg – with San Marco – gave audiences and went to bed –.[9]

On Friday August the 13th, I woke up at 7 o'clock – got up – dressed – had breakfast with my children – made my toilette – heard holy Mass – saw those who had come to wished me [happy birthday] – lunched with the world – and then read +++ kept myself busy – kept the King company – ⊙ – afterwards saw a little dance performed by my children – Princess Caramanico came to thank for her husband who was appointed ambassador to France –.[10]

On Wednesday August the 25th, I got up in the morning – celebrated the birthday of Louise – had breakfast with my children – then made my toilette – heard Mass – wrote – kept myself busy – talked with the viceroy Caracciolo – lunched – kept the King company to – ⊙ – then undressed – read +++ – kept myself busy – afterwards dressed again – went with my two eldest girls and the King by one horse carriage – to the nun – received the blessing – then to the convent – preached Theresa – dinner and to bed.[11]

Often, as we can see, next to the expression "m'ocuper" (kept myself busy) there also appears "faire mes affaires" (worked on my affairs) without any explanation or annotation. What is the meaning of the one and of the other? It would be interesting to be able to decode the language of drafting, correlating it to correspondences with her brothers and other political figures and institutions with whom Maria Carolina entertained an epistolary exchange, and to try to "decipher it" in light of the historical events of the time:

The use of the letter "A", which the Queen used to indicate, at some point in the diary, a character whose identity she wished to conceal, is intriguing. The cross-matching of information contained in the second half of the year (which mentions epistolary exchanges with Spain and transcribes some reflections) is interesting as well as those present almost daily during the previous months. In this period, meetings with Minister Acton without the presence of third parties are mentioned. Therefore, one might infer that assumptions about an alleged romantic relationship between the two have some basis. Moreover, the arrival of news from Spain provoked the wrath of Charles III and had crippled the already precarious relationship between Maria Carolina and the Iberian Crown. However, in the "Summary" reflections that conclude the diary, the Queen refers explicitly to her state of mind regarding the need to maintain relations with Spain:

> On Tuesday June the 22nd, […] sent letters of Spain and to bed – the children well – the King remained all day at Castellamare.[12]

> On Thursday August the 5th, I got up – dressed – had breakfast – went to walk for a while – saw my children – heard holy Mass – read – wrote – kept myself busy – had lunch with the King – read the letters – busy with my children – my affairs until evening – walked with the children – Ardore, Popoli – whose informed me that their wives have given birth to a son [Caivane] – Cimitile – Cimitile who was appointed to the charge of State director – came to thank me in the evening – on returning – Spanish courrier came to ruin [my day] – it brought me the news that a boat was blown with our two brave young men and also brought many other inconveniences – spent a bad night – had not dinner and went to bed –.[13]

> On Thursday September the 2nd, I got up at 7 o'clock – dressed – had breakfast – combed my hair – heard holy Mass – spoke to Dom Cicio Pignatelli – San Nicola – Cattolica – San Marco – went to church with my children – lunched with them – saw Sambuca with letters from Spain – then Acton –.[14]

> On Thursday November the 25th, I got up – dressed – had breakfast – combed my hair – heard holy Mass – read – wrote – kept myself busy – talked with...... [15] – then had lunch with my children – took care of them – read – wrote – kept myself busy – went to my son's room – kept myself busy in my room and [went] to bed.[16]

On Thursday December the 9th, I got up at half past 7 – had break-fasted – dressed – combed my hair – heard holy Mass – kept the King company – ⊗ – then went to arrange the library – afterwards heard another Mass – had lunch with the King – saw Lamberg – kept myself busy – read – talked with ... [17] – then kept myself busy and went to bed.

On Monday December the 13th, I got up at 1 o'clock – dressed – combed my hair, heard two Masses – spoke to Vasto to ... [18] – went to lunch with the children, kept myself busy read and wrote, On Monday December the 13th, I got up at 1 o'clock – dressed – combed my hair, heard two Masses – spoke to Vasto to ... [19] – went to lunch with the children, kept myself busy read and wrote.[20]

On Friday December the 31 st[...] – And so ended 1784 – I began it with the Emperor – [and] my sister – they left the same month – the King of Sweden came to visit, and there were months of quiet – I happily had Mimi inoculated – I was pregnant – later I had sudden and intense sorrows from Spain – a deadly disease for my eldest son and then a happy birth. God will grant me a happier year.[21]

The pages written in 1785, the last year covered by the surviving section of the diary, are mostly filled with short notes. The exceptions are the month of January, where there is a range of a minimum of 4 lines to a maximum of 12, and December, which include thoughts arising from the proximity to religious holidays. Here are two examples:

On April 20, Wednesday I stayed in bed all day as a precaution but had no fever – I saw K – S. Marco Belmonte – did the Council – the children well – the King walked to the sea.[22]

On Wednesday November the 9th, I got up – dressed – had breakfast – combed my hair – heard holy Mass – was busy – had lunch with the King – wrote – worked – saw Lady Belmonte – presided over the Council and [went] to bed.[23]

Although the language appears simple at first, in reality this is often not the case. Like the pages compiled in previous years, those related to 1785 are characterized by the presence of a cryptic language designed to prevent some information from reaching "troublesome people". So, the clarity of the content is significantly compromised by a scant use of punctuation, and sometimes it is not very appropriate to the text. If one considers, in addition to the semantic core, the presence of different symbols which the Queen uses as well as the frequent mention of personal names (without any reference to the surname or institutional position held or at least to the social role of the characters mentioned), the understanding of the text is sometimes problematic:

> On Friday March the 18th, I got up – dressed – had breakfast – combed my hair – heard holy Mass – worked on my affairs – then had lunch with the King – worked – kept myself busy – talked with Virieux – Genzano – Belmonte – saw the King – kept him company – ⊗ – then went to the sermon ++++ – from there to the Council – then [went] to bed – the children well – in the morning the King went to hunt curlews-to Torre – after lunch in town and returned by the promenade on bridge.[24]

> On Monday March the 28th, I got up at 6 o'clock – dressed – went to my son's room – had breakfast – dressed – combed my hair – heard holy Mass – everybody with him – and then [went to listen] the sermon – afterwards walked with him and my daughters – on returning I made the big affairs to pass him the hands of men – Ayo – Duke of Gravina – preceptor – the eldest Hauss – young Hauss – and Poli the preceptor – four valets of rooms – finally the child behaved very well in everything – I was there until 4 o'clock when he left – I returned at six o'clock – he came back for the blessing – then presided over the Council – kept myself busy and [went] to bed – the children fine – the King went to lunch at castles – afterwards to kill little egrets at the wood several times.[25]

> On Sunday April the 10th, I got up – dressed – had breakfast – heard holy Mass – kept myself busy – went with the King and my three daughters to castles – had lunch at the table that goes up and down – and then I came back and at half past three went with the King to the city – where I took care of my children – saw Lady San Marco Belmonte – hearings to some ladies – and the Florentine theatre to see *le Roi Teodore* which bored me a lot – and where I still recognized the nation by the crowd that there was – we returned – ⊗ – and I went to sleep – the children well – the King was with me all day.[26]

The Queen's mornings seemed to be characterized by the same personal rituals: domestic chores, institutional commitments, hearings, walks. The evenings were occupied primarily by visits to the theatre and dances. Therefore, domestic activities and all other formal commitments alternately marked a typical day for the Queen.

The sequence laid out in chronological order regarding other institutional and informal commitments seems to follow an almost script-like pattern. The Queen, in fact, does not stop to explain her reflections or critical comments and concerns or even personal interpretations about conversations or meetings. On the contrary, the language clearly expresses her opinions regarding both characters who, with various noble titles, asked for a hearing but did not play any decisive role in State affairs, and situations which could be termed "free time" and which were considered typical for the role of a Queen (e.g. trips, parties, theatre meetings, lunches, Reversino [a game where the rules are reversed, meaning the player with the least number of points wins], etc.):

> On Wednesday February the 2nd, I got up at 7 o'clock – dressed – had breakfast – combed my hair – heard holy Mass – saw my children – presided over the Council – had lunch with the King – kept him company – played piquet with him – ☉ – then read – wrote – kept myself busy – saw my children – talked with Lady Belmonte – took leave of Lamberg – gave hearings to the ladies – afterwards went with my two eldest daughters to the comedy of cadets – then returned – domino dressed and went to ball where there were 1,200 masks – I did a tour with uncovered domino – afterwards went to my children that were there and at one o'clock home – there was a figurative minuet and contra dance – just six children – of Lady de Amicis – very pretty and interesting – there being with children we [have been lively] my children well – the King because of bad weather could not go out during the day – in the evening went to the Florentine.[27]

> On February the 8th Fat Tuesday, I got up at 8 o'clock – dressed – had breakfast – combed my hair – heard holy Mass – read – wrote – kept myself busy – tried a mask with my children – saw my son Francis – Amelia – then had lunch with the children – read – wrote – kept myself busy – saw Lady San Marco – participated at the wedding of Giovanina with Vantitelli – which I wish them a lot of happiness – but I am very sad – because I loved her very much and was well served – after having violently grieved and saddened – I made my toilette – dressed as Venus – the girls as Graces – Mimi dressed cupid and – and so dressed – I prepared a framework and presented sonnets to the King – then I kept him company – ⊗ afterwards I kept myself busy – then domino dressed [went] to the ball at the theatre – at half past one from there home – the children well – the King went to the masks parade only after lunch for a short time.[28]

No event of a purely political nature is mentioned. For example:

> On Monday February the 14th, I got up at 6 o'clock – worked on a few domestic arrangements with my papers and affairs – then had breakfast with my children – dressed – heard holy Mass – gave them my blessing – and at

quarter past 8 went by carriage with the King to Venafro – I left the bridge and arrived at half past twelve – whence I lunched – arranged my affairs – kept Lady Hoyos company – then took part in the decree made by the King during the Council – later wrote to my children – I kept myself busy – took part in the Council and went to sleep – I left all my dear children – thanks to God – healthy – the King had a short wild boar hunt.[29]

Why did the Queen decide not to leave traces of her Kingdom's "political plot" at that time? Was it due to cunning, prudence or pure disinterest? Proceeding with an intersection of data on information gathered from daily news and the frequency of meetings with some institutional figures belonging not only to the Kingdom of Naples, the results favour cunning and prudence and not lack of interest. In fact, Maria Carolina almost constantly met with ministers of her Kingdom, court nobles, diplomats and ecclesiastical representatives.

Although Ferdinand IV's Kingdom was not vast and certainly not extravagant compared to the big European courts, life was magnificent and lively. Ladies, courtiers, judges, ministers, ambassadors and scientists gravitated around the Sovereign, who after marriage joined high-ranking people arriving from Vienna, following Maria Carolina.[30] This large group followed the Bourbons when they moved to Caserta, Capodimonte and other royal residences.[31]

Although less frivolous than her sister Marie Antoinette, Maria Carolina was, however, taken by an ambitious lust for power and an equally intense desire to demonstrate it. She was therefore surrounded by obsequious people who were ready to pander to her will. In the wake of the splendours of Versailles, the Queen, supported by the King, wanted to impress. Following his visit to Naples in 1769, Emperor Joseph II wrote: "the Court looks Grand and magnificent, but is full of low-ranking people".[32] The Court of Naples was made up of, with a few exceptions, idle and ignorant representatives, as well as strenuous supporters of feudal legacy.[33]

In 1782, Gaetano Filangieri had described her to an unknown person:

Io mi confermo sempre più nelle mie idee. Nella corte gli uomini nascondono i loro vizi e le loro e le loro virtù. Il perfido e l'eroe sono coperti dalla stessa maschera, perché il primo è ugualmente interessato a nascondere i suoi vizi, come il secondo ad occultare le sue virtù. Per conoscersi bisogna allontanare dalla reggia incantata, dove il bastone del tiranno, simile alla verga del mago, metamorfizza gli oggetti che si presentano e dà allo schiavo l'aspetto dell'eroe ed all'eroe quello dello schiavo.[34]

Insensitive to the rumours that were circulating at Court about the alleged extramarital romantic relationships, including the one with Lady Hamilton, the Queen did not change her behaviour although her brothers[35] and trusted advisers, such as Caracciolo and her nephew, the Marquis de Gallo, suggested using more discretion and developing diplomatic strategies useful for the good of the Kingdom. Those who were unresponsive to her displays of vanity, or tried to politically accomplish something which was not within her plan of gaining power, fell into disgrace. This is what happened, for example, to Prime Minister Tanucci.[36] The direction of Tanucci's internal policy had encountered the resistance of the Sicilian barons and the viceroy. So the Queen skilfully took advantage of the unrest to achieve her objective: to achieve a modern state in which all power was centralized in the hands of the Sovereign.

The heart of life at the court of Naples was represented, therefore, by the Queen with whom no one dared argue, at least until the tragedy of the Neapolitan revolution in 1799. It seems that until that time Maria Carolina made the Court her favourite place in which to exercise her function as absolute ruler, choosing for others a supporting role or appearance depending on the "compatibility" of their characteristics with her political aims.[37]

The way Maria Carolina wove her friendly relationships played a strategic role in the politics of the Kingdom. A careful analysis of the short time span covered by the Journal (1781–1785) shows that in her diary notes, the Sovereign revealed nothing about her friendships and the alleged extramarital ties. The diary, as we have already stated, consists of a series of short annotations. But those are just simple reminders of meetings that bear witness to Maria Carolina's diplomatic and political friendships. Within her private realm, there are at times glimpses where different protagonists of the political and cultural life of the time stand out.

During the Sovereign's daily hearings, in fact, there was always present a welcome group of aristocrats who held positions at Court as well as representatives of the political world, economists, diplomats, the military, clergy, judges, doctors, artists, Italian and European painters. Evidence of the public role and political action carried out by the wife of Ferdinand IV was her practical participation in the administration of power, as well as her ability to manoeuvre between political skirmishes. The meetings, which are often referred to in the pages of the diary, confirm that in the Queen's apartments, important decisions were made.[38]

By reconstructing the biographical profiles of the people welcomed in the Queen's parlours, we can differentiate between the types of hearings.

The salon of Maria Carolina was frequented by not only the great nobles and courtiers, but also by all the most learned intellectual and cultivated people to be found at Naples. Hearings concerning internal politics can be traced to the meetings with President Cimitile and the three Secretaries of State (Sambuca, Acton and De Marco), with the Austrian ambassador Lamberg and the English ambassador Hamilton, with Migliano, Galiani, Filangieri, Caracciolo, Francesco Pignatelli of Strongoli, Vincenzo Pignatelli, Vincenzo Moncada, Prince of Calvaruso and many others. Meetings with Sambuca, Acton and De Marco occurred almost daily. It is remarkable that the Sovereign, on the days when councils were held, faced the three Secretaries of State first thing in the morning (either called together or individually). These "unofficial" morning meetings were followed by "official" evening meetings. For example, Maria Carolina wrote on 28 October 1782:

> On Monday the 28th, I got up at 7 o'clock – dressed – had breakfast – combed my hair – heard two holy Masses – and talked with Lord Belmonte – then Acton – Sambuca and de Marco – afterwards at eleven o'clock I went to Caserta – I arrived at half past twelve – I met the King and all my dear healthy children – we had lunch – then I wrote – I devoted myself – saw my children – then I saw old bishop Onorati who returned to his diocese – afterwards saw my children – read – prayed – the Council and to bed.

Regarding the hearings related to foreign policy issues, the diary records the names of heads of State and diplomats, among whom stand out the Frenchmen Tayllerand and Breme, the Pole Scavronsky, the Swede Gustav III, King of Sweden and his first chamberlain Count Armfelt, the Moroccan Muhammad ibn Uthman Al-Miknasi and the Russians Rasoumovski, Dashkova, Vorontsova and Morkov. Regarding relations with Russia, between 1782 and 1783, they had entered into an agreement, falling within the terms of the League of Armed Neutrality promoted by Catherine II.[39]

With the Russian presence in the Mediterranean, the Kingdom of the Two Sicilies became a crossroads between strong internal and external tensions. People came to realize how the international political order was upset by the risky contrast between two opposing directives: the Russian opening to the east and the Franco-Spanish closure to the west. The Russians had an urgent need for footholds, and especially port bases in the Mediterranean basin. This was the area, which Peter the Great had long tried to gain and that only now became accessible for the Russian Empire. A further complication in the international framework contributed to the conflict of interests, predominantly commercial in nature, which motivated the political decisions of France and Spain. While the French wanted to safeguard commercial relations with the East, the Spaniards did not intend to endanger their projects in the Mediterranean area.[40]

Among the people mentioned by the Queen in her diary, representatives of the clergy are also included. In any case, they are very prominent people (e.g. Ignazio Gaetani Boncompagni, Domenico Orsini d'Aragona, François-Joachim de Pierre, Cardinal of Bernis, Rudolf Edling, Archbishop of Gorizia and Filippo Lopez y Royo). A careful reading of the text shows that the Queen entertained some of them only during religious festivals. Maria Carolina met with her children's tutors (Giuseppe Rossi and Fernando Strina) in their apartments, presumably to discuss the children's education. Finally, she granted certain hearings for reasons not specified in the Journal.

Proposing a unitary framework of the period covered by the diary, we have tried to place the dynamics of the relationship between the Kingdom of Naples and the Holy See within a given historical context. Representatives of different religious orders were invited to speak with the Queen or, on their own initiative, had asked to meet her.

As is well known, even after the fall of Tanucci in Naples the rulers had continued to pursue a policy aimed at the abolition of the centuries-old feudal privileges of the Church. Starting in 1779, a series of rules were written with the intention of reducing the Pope's intrusiveness. It considered, for example, the downsizing of the jurisdiction of the bishops, the reduction of the fees payable to the Roman Curia, the control of papal bulls concerning the Neapolitan church, the suppression of various religious orders and forfeiture of their assets in favour of the Royal domain, the abolition of the right of asylum in churches and monasteries and the abolition of the Tribunal of the Inquisition.[41] This position is also confirmed by several events regarding the initiatives taken by Maria Carolina against the Holy See. For example, the reinstatement, for only a year, of the reception of the homage of Chinea for the Pope at the behest of Maria Carolina who, in this way, intended to show the change using Roman consent to silence the pro-Tanucci party. Therefore, the tribute to Chinea took place in 1777, which did not mean that the Queen wanted to abandon the anticlerical policy previously undertaken by the former Minister, but it was only an act of force to prove that decisions were now made only by the Sovereigns.[42] Moreover, after the expulsion of Tanucci, Maria Carolina launched an even more centralized policy, fashioned after the Habsburg model and enlisting the support of Freemasons who acted as intelligence agents. However, the diary does not reveal any reference to governmental actions or diplomatic strategies inherent in the "new course" of the policy implemented by the Bourbons towards the Church.

The Queen was surrounded by politicians, literary and scientific men and with enthusiastic interest she entered into discussions and enthusiastic plans for regenerating human race. Among the latter were Domenico Cirillo, the celebrated botanist and physician; Giuseppe Maria Galanti, a well-known author of jurisprudence; Conforti, a professor of history at the University of Naples.

She also used to meet economists such as the famous Domenico Grimaldi and Ferdinando Galiani. In November 1781, Grimaldi paid tribute to the Queen by offering his most recent work, "Plan to usefully employ convicts, and by their labor ensure increased grain collections in Puglia and in the other provinces of the Kingdom": "Le 2. novembre [...] ensuite Grimaldi m'a présenté son livre".[43] The following year the Calabrian economist joined the Supreme Council of Finance together with the famous Ferdinando Galiani, who had acquired a reputation with his *Dialogues on the grain trade* (1770). At times, the diary also includes the name Bernardo Filingieri, Royal Councillor of Commerce, who in 1785 became Minister of the praetorian council in Palermo.

The variety of professional responsibilities that these people as well as others fulfilled shows that Maria Carolina was the engine behind some key decisions and assertive changes that transformed the fate of the Kingdom. The Queen also had important contacts in the judicial environment. Within the ranks of the men of law who were received at Court, several stood out: Giuseppe Maria Secondo, adviser to the Court of Justice in Naples; Giuseppe Caravita, Member and *caporuota* of the Royal Council and President of the Royal Chamber in Sommaria; and Ferdinando Corradini who in October 1782 became part of the Supreme Council of Finance; Gaetano Filangieri, author of *La Scienza della Legislazione*. When Filangieri was only 21, he had been distinguished by the Queen after gaining a legal success. In 1777, Maria Carolina made Filangieri gentleman of King's bedchamber and officer of the volunteers in the Navy. But it was with his work on legislation that Filangieri gained a lucrative charge in the Royal Council of Finance.[44]

The Naples of that time attracted tourists, travellers, writers, artists and scientists from all over Europe. In order to attract Italian and foreign visitors, in 1748 Charles of Bourbon started an impressive archaeological recovery operation in Pompeii, a symbolic city which had preserved the majestic vestiges of Roman civilization. In Naples, delegates of the most advanced medical research passed through. In the diary, the names of prominent men of science appear: the aforementioned Angelo Maria Gatti, called to Court for his innovative experimental research on the smallpox vaccination; Samuel Auguste Tissot, also a staunch supporter of inoculation; the Court doctors Michael Troja, Ferdinand IV's head surgeon, Domenico Cotugno, an anatomist and expert in botany, and François Guillaume Le Vacher, a renowned professor of surgery at the University of Parma and, for a brief period, Maria Carolina's personal obstetrician.

Maria Carolina inherited from the Viennese Court, which was the cradle of reform for European opera, a passion for music and the theatre.[45] It is significant that she mentions composers, musicians, singers and playwrights. Among others, there were Ranieri de Calzabigi, a poet and member of the Academy of Arcadia and a librettist of great success, who was a guest for some years at the Viennese court and since 1775 had been a fervent promoter of cultural life in Naples; Gaetano Pugnani from Turin, who was often present in Naples; Maria Bertaldi from Liguria, alias "Balducci", an acclaimed singer of the Teatro San Carlo; Vincent Cammarano, known as Giancola, a star of the Neapolitan dialectal theatre; and Gaetano Latilla from Puglia, a famous composer at that time, a close friend of Goldoni and a prolific playwright.

The Queen also pushed for the cult of figurative arts, defending and calling to Court, as can be deduced from the diary, established painters of the period. Those coming from the Germanic region include Jacob Philip Hackert, appointed by the Bourbons as first court painter and Heinrich Fuger, who was commissioned to decorate the third room of the library of the Royal Palace in Caserta. Another who gravitated towards the Bourbon court was a Swiss painter, Angelika Kauffmann, the author of many fine portraits, two of which were devoted, respectively, to Ferdinand IV and the entire royal family. In addition to playing a decisive political role, Maria Carolina undertook to confer cultural prestige and artistic excellence on her Court, aiming to raise it to the level of the great European courts.[46]

The massive presence in the pages of the diary members affiliated to Freemasonry and other lodges (about 60 are mentioned) must be interpreted in light of the changes that swept the Freemasons during Maria

Carolina's reign. At the height of the 1780s, within Italian Freemasonry rationalist thought was taking hold, not only because of the spread of English lodges, but also due to a particular structuring of the Templar lodges itself belonging to the system of Rectified Regime, which was still commonly called by the name of Strict Observance. The phenomenon was found, for example, in Cremona where, since 1776, a lodge had been opened by the Austrian officers of the garrison.

In 1780, the Enlightenment revolution also involved Naples, where the Duke of San Demetrio was the venerable of a lodge called The Equality, registered in that year with the number 525 by the Grand Lodge of London. The following year another English lodge in Naples, called "La Verità",[47] was registered with the number 440. These English lodges, although less respectful of internal discipline, primarily included members of the bourgeoisie and especially intellectuals. Suffice it to say that in one lodge there was Mario Pagano as Venerable and Gaetano Filangieri as Deputy Grand Master.

The constant expansion of Freemasonry in Naples dated back to the 1770s and coincided with the arrival of Queen Maria Carolina in Naples. In the lodges, there was in fact a gathering of the local nobility hostile to Minister Bernardo Tanucci. In the lodges, more than anywhere else, the spirit of the changing times, which did not separate itself from mundane frivolity, and which was so dear to the Queen, and thus opposed by the Spanish Court was felt.

Francisco d'Aquino, Prince of Caramanico, was a Venerable in the Neapolitan lodge. This fame gave him the privilege of being the Queen's lover. After convening a meeting with the most important Neapolitan "brothers" in the second half of 1773, the Prince of Caramanico declared the dependence of "the free Neapolitan nation" on a foreign centre to be improper. Therefore, he implemented a coup with the consent of the majority of the "brothers", which separated the "Zelo", lodge from the Grand Lodge of London, of which he was a member, transforming it into a National Grand Lodge in which the executive positions were divided as follows: National Grand Master: Francesco D'Aquino (Prince of Caramanico); Deputy Grand Master: Giovanni Gironda (Prince of Cannito); First Grand Warden: Diego Naselli (of the princes of Aragon); Second Grand Warden: Eugenio of Sora; Secretary: the lawyer Felice Lioy.

The lodge of the "Zelo" became the national Grand Lodge and its dignitaries were appointed inside the major offices. Two of these dignitaries, Caramanico and Naselli, were personally related to the Queen.

This suggests that the initiative to create a national Neapolitan lodge was launched by Maria Carolina to have lodges as an independent political force that supported her pro-Austrian and anti-Spanish policy.

In June 1776, the Duchess of Chartres arrived in Naples. She was the wife of Louis Philippe d'Orléans—the future Égalité—Grand Master of French Freemasonry and she herself was the Grand Master of the female lodges, the so-called lodges of adoption in France. The Duchess, received with the highest honours at the court of Capodimonte, pleaded the cause of the "brothers" so much so that shortly after her arrival, the prisoners were released from isolation. There was then a plebiscite of sympathy and solidarity with the detainees by the Neapolitan Masonic world. Among the visitors, there were the Prince of Ottajano, the Duke of San Demetrius, many officers, numerous cadets from Nunziatella and others.

Above all, in French lodges there was great rejoicing. A chorus of praise exalted the work of Maria Carolina. In Paris, there came a point where a new lodge called "Caroline Louise, reine de Naples", was established. The Grand Orient decided that in ritual banquets the typical toast would be, "Caroline, reine de Naples, protrectrice des Maçons persécutés."

In 1779, Diego Naselli changed course and adhered precisely to the Reformation of Lyon. With this new appearance, the Neapolitan Grand National Lodge initially had a rapid growth. In 1782, Naselli sent a list of all the lodges that were dependent on him to Vienna.[48] Meanwhile, the case against Pallante followed its course with ups and downs and long pauses until in 1782 when the same Tanucci, who had been left with the task of monitoring the cause of the Freemasons, informed the president of the State that the King had decided to abolish "Sovereignly all those crimes, inquisitions, penalties, cases and decrees which included all the varied causes that had proliferated. Therefore there is no harassment or inconvenience for some individuals." In this way, even Gennaro Pallante was freed of all charges and placed in retirement.

In the English lodges, one could find the Duke of San Demetrio and Prince Filangieri. The "knights" of the rectified regime there included a lawyer called Felice Lioy as well as a professor of Greek, Pasquale Baffi.

In 1784, the Lutheran theologian Friedrich Münter arrived in Italy. He had received from Copenhagen a twofold task, informational and organizational. His first assignment, given by the Duke of Brunswick and Prince Charles of Asia, was to see how much he could save of the old Templar building, restructuring it according to the criteria set at Wilhelmsbad.

The second assignment was given by the authority of the Order of the Illuminati and concerned the Order's propaganda and rationalist Masonry in Vienna. On 1 September 1785, Munster arrived in Naples, where he found a swarm of regular and irregular Masonic and para-Masonic lodges. They considered themselves regular subordinates of Naselli and San Demetrio. Among the irregular lodges were a lodge directed by the Prince of San Severo Paolo Di Sangro, one of Francesco Pignatelli, and those of Zappatori and Adamiti.[49]

In that same year, Münter made a trip to Sicily where he found the Masonic situation not very prosperous. During his trip, the Danish theologian met two brothers, Agamemnon Spanò and Giuseppe Zurlo. The latter provided Münter which the chance to get in touch with a group of brothers in Naples who would give him the opportunity to create a new sectarian organization. Returning to Naples, after a visit with Abbot Caracciolo, he also met Pasquale Baffi and Tommaso Donati. The latter put the Dane in contact with brothers from the English lodge: Domenico Cirillo, Mario Pagano, Gaetano Filangeri, Giuseppe Albanese, Emmanuele Mastellone and Nicola Pacifico. He had two important talks with Don Diego Naselli. After this series of meetings, Münter travelled to Rome where he established a lodge, but in spite of everything his interest was always focused on Naples where he met with friends who wanted to erect an Illuminati lodge. While he was in Rome, Münter met with Marquis Costanzo who decided to give life to Enlightenment in Italy.

Afterwards Münter received from Donato Tommasi Giuseppe Zurlo their response regarding the questionnaire with the order of Illuminati gave to candidates. Both had released from their original lodges and they already sent to the Danish theologian their formal commitment.

The six founding members of the first and probably only Illuminati lodge in Italy were the priest Gaetano Carrascal, the jurist Emanuele Mastellone, Mario Pagano, Donato Tommasi, Giuseppe Zurlo and the botanist Nicola Pacifico. All six members were leaders or martyrs of Neapolitan Jacobinism, like almost all the Neapolitan friends of Münter, from Pasquale Baffi to Domenico Grillo. After some correspondence with the enlightened German superiors and with Costanzo, the Danish envoy departed again for Naples. His third and final stay in this city lasted for nearly two months, and during this time he was in contact almost exclusively with the members of the Illuminati lodge, with Tommasi, Zurlo and Nicola Pacifico. But he also often saw Mario Pagano, Filangieri and Cirillo.

The Illuminati "brothers" surrendered the cahiers, containing the rites and the plans of the Order, and officially put the lodge under the control of Constanzo.[50] At first, Don Diego Naselli welcomed Münter with open arms, but when he returned to Naples the welcome reserved for him by the Grand Master was no longer the same. Perhaps this was because the arrival of Münter in Naples had highlighted the latent crisis of Neapolitan Freemasonry, as with the chivalric and aristocratic, now overtaken by the different requests of a new generation, and of the English, moving the best men away from its lodges to put in the Order of the Illuminati.

The goal, albeit distant and gradual, to create the State based on a new rational foundation through the secret work of the "brothers", gave a concrete purpose, a political purpose, to the activity of Freemasonry, which had to recruit men of high intellectual and moral standards like those who had given life to the Illuminati lodge in Naples. And if these new purposes might seem subversive to Prince Naselli, a man like Mario Pagano had to give the impression of having finally found in Freemasonry a purpose, a programme that exceeds chivalric antics and the philanthropy of the English lodges. It is clear that this decline of aristocratic Freemasonry and spiritualism would displease Naselli who attributed part of the blame to Münter.[51]

This proliferation of lodges and Masonic unrest, in a rationalist sense, that took intellectual reformers from Cremona and Naples, began to feel its effects not only with the flourishing of English lodges but also by manifesting itself within the same spiritualist Freemasonry of the rectified system. Hence, the decline of Templar lodges and the strengthening of the more modest but more concrete English lodges where, albeit sometimes between excessive libations, there were some essential principles of equality and brotherhood which corresponded better to the spirit of the times. Young people who knocked on the doors of the lodges, now mostly belonging to the Third Estate or the younger nobility, hoped to find in the organization and in the Masonic brotherhood an instrument designed to bring forward new ideas and overcome obstacles that hindered achievement.[52]

Here we quickly reviewed just a few of the numerous people (more than 600) mentioned by the Queen in her diary. For many others, we outlined the bio-bibliographical profile in the footnotes accompanying the text of the journals which we transcribed.

Notes

1. Ibid., c. 147r.
2. Ibid., c.148r.
3. Ibid., cc148v–149r.
4. Like this in the text.
5. Ibid., c. 170v.
6. Ibid., c.184r.
7. Ibid., cc.181r–181v
8. Ibid., cc. 165r–165v.
9. Ibid., c. 176r.
10. Ibid., cc.195v–196r.
11. Ibid., c.198r.
12. Ibid., cc.182v–183r.
13. Ibid., c. 194r.
14. Ibid., c. 200r.
15. Like this in the text.
16. Ibid., c. 218v.
17. Like this in the text.
18. Like this in the text.
19. Like this in the text.
20. Ibid., 223r.
21. Ibid., 226r.
22. Ibid., 249v.
23. Ibid., c. 254v.
24. Ibid., c. 243v.
25. Ibid., c. 245v.
26. Ibid., c. 248r.
27. Ibid., c. 235r.
28. Ibid., c. 236v.
29. Ibid., 238r.
30. E. Caesar Corti, *Ich, eine Maria Theresias Tochter: ein Lebensbild der Königin Marie Karoline von Neapel*, 45.
31. In the daily notes of the Queen are also mentioned royal residences such as Belvedere, San Leucio but also the Academy.
32. Giuseppe II d'Asburgo, *Corte Lazzara. Relazione a Maria Teresa sui Reali di Napoli,* ed. E.Garms – Cornides, (Napoli: Di Mauro, 1992), 97–98.
33. On the visit of Emperor Joseph II, see Giuseppe II d'Asburgo, *Corte Lazzara. Relazione a Maria Teresa sui Reali di Napoli*; E. Caesar Corti, *Ich, eine Maria Theresias Tochter: ein Lebensbild der Königin Marie Karoline von Neapel*, 73–76.

34. "I am more and more convinced of my ideas. In court the men hide their faults and their virtues. The traitor and the hero wear the same mask because the former is concerned with concealing his vices while the second is equally concerned with concealing his virtues. To meet others, one must distance oneself from the enchanted realm, where the tyrant's staff, similar to the magician's rod, transforms objects and gives the slave the appearance of the hero and the hero the appearance of the slave" Extracted by R. Ajello "I filosofi e la regina. Il governo delle due Sicilie da Tanucci a Caracciolo (177–1786)", 685.

35. See on this regard the epistolary exchange of the two brothers: A. Ritter von Arneth, *Joseph II und Leopold von Toscana. Ihr Briefwechsel von 1781 bis1790*, II vol., (Wien: Wilhelm Braumüller, 1872).

36. The institutional and political debate in the early years of the Reign of Ferdinand IV was developed around the constant dualism between the mainland (Naples) and the island besides the lighthouse (Sicily). The effort of Tanucci was to pursue an equal term of conditions between Naples and Sicily just as King Charles III wished.

37. M.C. Charlton Bearne, *A sister of Marie Antoinette the life-story, Queen of Naples*, (London: T.F.Unwin, 1907), 78.

38. The ambassador Simon de Las Casas writes so "en el dispacho, y se determinen los negocios". See R. Ajello, "I filosofi e la regina. Il governo delle due Sicilie da Tanucci a Caracciolo (177–1786)", 450–451.

39. M. L. Cavalcanti, *Le relazioni commerciali tra il Regno di Napoli e la Russia. 1777–1815. Fatti e teorie alle origini del Risorgime*nto, (Gèneve: Droz, 1979), 126–128.

40. See G. Galasso, Il *Regno di Napoli. Il Mezzogiorno borbonico e napoleonico (1734–1815)*, 562–569; M. Mafrici, *Un austriaca alla corte napoletana* in M. Mafrici, (ed), *All'Ombra della Corte. Donne e potere nella Napoli borbonica (1734–1860)*, 60–61.

41. See R. Ajello, "I filosofi e la regina. Il governo delle due Sicilie da Tanucci a Caracciolo (177–1786)", 429; G. Oliva, *Un Regno che è stato grande, la storia negata dei Borbone di Napoli e di Sicilia*, 100.

42. See footnote 28, 7.

43. ASN, Archivio Borbone, f.1r.

44. On Gaetano Filangieri see the detailed work of G. Ruggiero, *Gaetano Filangieri: un uomo, una famiglia, un amore nella Napoli del Settecento*, (Napoli: Guida editore, 1999).

45. In this regard, it should be remembered the Italians Apostolo Zeno and Metastasio Pietro Ranieri de' Calzabigi were called to assume the position of "caesarean poets" at the Habsburg court, who had arrived in Vienna, respectively, in 1718, 1730 and 1761; they were engaged to carry forward the reform of the melodramatic genre, an operation that was brought to

completion by Calzabigi in collaboration with Christophe Willibald Gluck. See, L. Tufano, *I viaggi di Orfeo. Musiche e musicisti intorno a Ranieri Calzabigi*, (Roma: Edicampus, 2012); Id., "Il poeta «cadente» e il re «filosofo» versi ignorati di Ranieri di Calzabigi e altri appunti sul suo secondo soggiorno napoletano" in *Napoli Nobilissima*, serie 5, II gennaio-agosto, 2001, 101–126; as well as the study edited by F. Marri e F.P. Russo, *Ranieri Calzabigi fra Vienna e Napoli*, (Lucca: Lim, 1997).

46. M.C. Charlton Bearne, *A sister of Marie Antoinette the life-story, Queen of Naples*, 78–81.

47. F. Münter, *Aus den Tagebüchern Friedrich Münters. Wanderund Lehrjahre eines dänischen Gelehrten*, (Kopenhagen und Leipzig: Ø. Andreasen ed., 1937), 3 voll.

48. See A. Zucco, *1799: la repubblica napoletana e la massoneria*, (Cosenza: Brenner, 1999), 148–153.; V. Ferrone, *I profeti dell'Illuminismo: la metamorfosi della ragione nel Settecento italiano*, (Roma-Bari: Laterza, 2000), 249–250.

49. A. M. Rao, "La massoneria nel Regno di Napoli", 526–532

50. C.Francovich, *Storia della massoneria in Italia. Dalle origini alla Rivoluzione francese*, (Firenze: La Nuova Italia, 1974), 419.

51. *Ibidem.*

52. P. Maruzzi, "Notizie e documenti sui liberi muratori a Torino nel secolo XVIII", in *Bollettino storico-bibliografico subalpino*, XXX (1928).

CHAPTER 4

The Reformist Impulse of John Acton: an Essential Expert in the Service of the Court

In the spring of 1778, Maria Carolina had begun to take an active part in government affairs and assisted in subjugating the entire State Council. The new government programme by Maria Carolina alternated between innovative causes and motions for a clear reactionary spirit. The new policy had been influenced by suggestions from Ferdinando Galiani, Francesco D'Aquino, Prince of Caramanico, and the Tuscan doctor, Angelo Maria Gatti.[1]

In a letter dated 28 April 1778, which was addressed to her brother Leopold, the Queen wrote of the need for vessels and militia, and following a policy opposing Spanish protection, sought among the Austrians a general of the army and elsewhere an admiral who was not Spanish or French.[2] For the admiral, she demanded the commander John Acton, who at that time was in the employ of Tuscany and was famous for his recent achievement in Algiers:

> Dear brother and friend… I am entrusted with a task by my dear husband. I undertake it fearing to bother you but please answer me with your confidence. Our situation needs a good navy since we are surrounded by the sea, close to the pirates and for our business and not to be insulted [the navy] is necessary for us. My dear husband spends a lot and is badly served, [scams] are excessive and our navy is shameful, not glorious. We have acquired and [will acquire] new funds which will be useful to give us a navy but we lack an honest man, as you know, who is capable of details, incapable of stealing,

© The Author(s) 2017
C. Recca, *The Diary of Queen Maria Carolina of Naples, 1781–1785*,
Queenship and Power, DOI 10.1007/978-3-319-31987-2_4

and knows how to direct. My dear husband, who knows of the reputation of Acton, would have wanted someone a few months ago but seeing in him little support for this idea I was afraid to appear to bother you but now we are even more in need... My dear husband would like to give the secretary of the navy to Acton where the first command of the sea could be more useful, being able to make plans to build and sustain our navy with less expense and do the reviews of "equipment and weapons". As an honest man this could last a few years and if you had the goodness to lend Acton he would be secretary of the Navy ... We have no one in our State. A Spaniard or a Frenchman would be a danger without knowing them ... they too need the British, but our need is such as to make me bother with pain to write on this subject but the necessity has forced me.... a reign of 48 years of Tanucci has caused this plague for which we are understaffed ... fraud is permitted or tolerated, never punished, justice sold, these are the cruel effects that we mourn and weep for a lifetime because it will be necessary for your business and indefatigable application to remedy the situation and that's what we're missing.[3]

For the Grand Duke, it was not so easy to agree to the request. However, he wanted to help his sister; so on 10 May 1778, he responded that he wanted to leave Acton for a certain period only if the latter had agreed:

My dear sister, I received your long letter of 28 last month I saw that in your letter you mentioned your ideas for the navy and your assignment to write asking Acton for his service. Let me tell you honestly and I hope that you do not make use of my letter against anyone. Acton is a man who understands the navy, he studied it in depth .... but I do not know if he would be able to sustain the effort it would take to put in good order the affairs of your navy ... he does everything with a lot of energy, vibrancy and insistence which I've always loved and respected ... If the King wishes his service and believes that it may be useful, for my part there is not the slightest difficulty in sending him, provided that he desires it and he is happy.[4]

In a letter dated 9 June 1778, the Grand Duke Peter Leopold announced Acton's acceptance:

My dear sister, [...] I accomplished with respect to the other Acton committee of which I have instructed and I spoke to him, he is [convinced] of the goodness of the King, but he did not want absolutely to leave my service last year after refusing to move to advantageously service of France as he was offered, he still believes for this reason that he could not accept the offers of the King, however he declared to me, that in the case where the King wants to use him to consult him or let him draw up a plan for the reorganization of his Navy, but not be responsible for the implementation, it would be ready to go to Naples for a few months to work there but the execution of your orders while remaining here where the service would return as soon as the commission would be over, I told him to put in writing his opinion what he has done here in the memory unit about which await what you will tell me if the King wants, when and for how long; Gatti also between him two days to Naples, where he expects to arrive around the middle of next week, here thank God we're all fine.[5]

At the conclusion of the same letter, the Grand Duke of Tuscany informed his sister that he had attached a Mémoire where Acton had declared himself ready to carry out the task entrusted to him, but under certain conditions.

Mémoire

Les nouvelles marques de clemence que S.A.I. a bien voulu donner au soussigné lui imposant le devoir de mettre a ses pieds sa très respectueuse reconnoissance, il vient d'apprendre par ses ordres les vues flatteuses que S.M. le Roy des deux Siciles a daigne concevoir a son egar, et eprouve toute la sensibuilité possible dans la grace que S.A.R. veut bien lui faire de le laisser en pleine liberté d'opter entre l'honneur de continuer a la servir, et celui de presenter ses services a la Cour de Naples.

Le soussigné desireroit vivement pouvoir temoigner en cette occasion combien il seroit empressé de repondre aux idées avantageuses que S.M. lui fait l'honneur de se former de ses foibles lumieres en daignant jetter les jeux sur lui pour l'etablissement de sa marine sur un autre pied, et la direction des plans et operations relatives a cet objet, mais penetré des sentimens ineffacables que lui inspirent le devoir, la plus vive reconnoissance, et son respectueux attachement pour l'auguste persone de son souverain, il ne peut penser a quitter son service et tout choix à cet égard lui est interdit des qu'il lui est permis de consulter sa propre volonté, il zsupplie en consequence S.A.I. de vouloir bien acceuillir avec sa clemence ordinaire la reponse qu lui dicte son cœur, et lui permettre d'implorer l'oracle de ses volontés, pour se conformer uniquement a ce qu'il lui plaira de determiner.

Si le soussigné povoit cependant se flatter qu'il lui fut permis de presenter à S.A.R. un moyen qui lui sembleroit propre a concilier la demande et les intentions de la Cour de Naples avec ce qui concerne egalement les devoirs du soussigné et le desir qu'il auroit de répondre en quelque façon à l'honneur qu'on y a daigné lui faire, il oseroit proposer que sous le bon plaisir de S.A.I., et sans quitter son service la Cour de Naples voulut agrer qu'il s'y portat à reçevoir ses ordres et qu'il y travailla le tems convenable et necessaire à former les opérations qu'on daigneroit lui prescrire relativement a la marine, le soussigné fondé a faire cette proposition sur les exemples connus d'autres officiers pretes dans de pareils cas au service d'autres cours, et pour de semblables effets, seroit très empressé d'employer avec ardeur ses foibles connoissances et tous ses efforts pour temoigner a S.M. le Roy de Naples combien il est reconnoissant et sensible a l'honneur qu'elle a daigné lui faire.

Cette idée qu'il n'ose presenter que dans le cas ou le service de S.A.I. permit l'absence du soussigné le combleroit de satisfaction, si on daigne l'approuver, par le bonheur qu'elle lui procureroit de pouvoir remplir ainsi tous ses dévoirs.

C'est avec la plus parfaite soumission et le plus profond respect qu'il à l'honneur de se mettre aux pieds de S.A.R.

Florence ce 6 juin 1778

Signé – Acton.[6]

After a week, Maria Carolina sent her response:

Mon tres cher et amy j'ai recue votre chere et obligeante lettre et ne saurois assez vous en remercier je l'ai comunique a mon cher mary lequel penetré de vos bontes me charge de vous dire qu'il attend avec beaucoup d'empressement la venue d'Acton nos schiabeck yront vers la fin de ce mois a faire une tournée vers Livourne s'il en veut profiter pour venir yci mon cher mary leur donnera l'ordre d'aller a Livourne s'il veut venir par terre cella dependra de son gout, le bienfait de voir meilleure notre marine nous le devrons a vos bontes et notre reconoissance ne fera qu'augmenter et seulement nous desirons de pouvoir vous assurer a vive voix de nos sentimens.[7]

John Acton, the son of a doctor, was born in Besançon in 1736 to an English family. He had been brought up by an uncle, an experienced officer with the same name who, after working under Lord Bristol, had been hired by De Sartine in Paris. For a period of time he had served in the French navy. Not feeling sufficiently appreciated, he was then transferred to Tuscany.[8]

In Naples, with Tanucci's departure, the Queen launched plans for the end of Spanish protection and the consequent attraction of the Kingdom in the Austrian domain. Maria Carolina wanted a wide-ranging foreign policy, characterized by respect for neutrality, sanctioned by the end of the war of Austrian succession and the reinforcement of military facilities in the Kingdom. There are many examples of the new line followed by the Sovereign regarding international political dynamics: in 1776, diplomatic relations with Russia were initiated, strengthened in 1778 by the exchange of Minister Plenipotentiaries; in 1777, a specially established Committee examined a draft treaty presented by France which proclaimed the Kingdom's neutrality with the edict of 19 September 1778, in the war that saw the major powers engaged in support of the English colonies in America and against England. The promotion of trade relations with Russia and, above all, the expansion projects regarding Sicily's transit trade made the work of rebuilding the Neapolitan commercial fleet necessary, starting with Acton who was called to Naples by the Queen in 1778 as a capable restorer of the Navy.[9]

Acton has been described as a man of pleasant appearance, a rough and tough character who harboured a deep resentment towards France. "Acton […] est un homme qui a tout plein d'autres connoissances, plein de talents d'esprit et de bonnes facons, aimable, plein d'activité, capacité et fermeté, et avec cela tres honnete et desinteressé, excellent pour les details, mais il est extremement vif et rude vis-à-vis de ses subalternes, soupçonneux facile a s'agiter, inquieter, il n'aime pas a etre contredit, et a une tres grande ambition, et aucunement le talent de se faire aimer a cause de son air, ni de ses superieurs, egaux, ni inferieurs, et aimant un peu les nouveautés."

Balanced against the English commander is the opinion expressed by Anna Maria Rao. In Neapolitan history, Acton is described as one who, through the work of reconstructing the Kingdom's merchant ships, promoted trade relations with Russia based on the exchange of iron, lumber and agricultural products. He also favoured the expansion projects regarding the transit trade of the Sicilies.[10]

In the essays of Raffaele Ajello, Acton is presented as a military "despot". Ajello outlines the way in which the admiral had distinguished himself while commanding two Tuscan frigates which had participated in the expedition against Algiers in July 1775. Commissioned by Charles III, the operation ended in disaster. By chance, Acton was compelled to save the Spanish troops who had landed on the Algerian coast (an unsuitable place due to bad weather) and were driven back by the Arabs into the sea. The fact that Tuscan vessels were lighter and did not facilitate fishing turned out to be very fortunate. This was the first step in a long series of successes, driven by his good qualities which included physical prowess, intelligence, willpower and character.[11] Acton, defined by Ajello as "an expert", was therefore a trustworthy man whom the Queen turned to in order to carry out her personal intervention in the management of public financial assets. In addition to this end was the establishment, by Acton and the Queen, of the Supreme Council of Finance.[12]

Therefore, it was in this historical context that Acton arrived in Naples, as highlighted by Vincenzo Cuoco, as a "designer'" and as such he was received.[13] Gatti, after obtaining consent from the Sovereigns, was sent to Florence and asked the Grand Duke Leopold of Tuscany for permission to have the new admiral in Naples.[14] On 11 August 1778, John Acton was transferred to Naples on temporary loan. He immediately adopted a plan for the reorganization of the Navy, increasing the fleet, arming the forts and ensuring all maritime defence work in a country which, surrounded on three sides by the sea, required for this purpose numerous buildings and heavy expenses.[15]

At the time of King Charles of Bourbon's departure to Spain in 1759, the Neapolitan navy, prior to Acton's reorganization, consisted of six xebecs, three frigates—including the San Carlo la Partenope—one vessel, the San Filippo la Reale, and four galleys. In the following two decades, the Sovereign's naval policy changed. It proceeded to repair only some vessels which had been worn by time, and there was no increase in the fleet.[16] Between Acton and the Queen there existed, from the first moment, a relationship of deep and complete understanding. Maria Carolina wrote to her brother on 10 August 1778: "plus que je vis cet home plus il me paroit estimable retiré sachant son metier a fond et en parlant non en fanfaron mais en home qui le possede les connaisances nécessaires."[17]

Ambition was the common characteristic which the Queen and the admiral shared. In addition, Acton, with an independent spirit but amendable when necessary, was in agreement with the Sovereign on the project to remove the Two Sicilies from Spanish interference and to submit them to Austrian subjugation. Maria Carolina and the General shared an antipathy towards France, who took on the rights of guardianship over the Bourbons of Naples and reverence towards England, obviously for Acton since it was his homeland. However, the Queen, who feared the great seafaring power, planned with opportunistic calculation and judged wisely that she needed an alliance with this stronger country[18]: "Among the King's ministers he was the only foreigner and understood before the others that in Naples the Queen was everything and the King was nothing."[19]

Acton formed a Navy Council for the management of arms. He later replaced the Spanish rules, issuing new ones, and eventually pledged the establishment and reorganization of nautical schools.[20] To fight the pirates in North Africa, he made use of the methods used by Tanucci. The Minister's idea, launched in 1770, had been to ensure maritime security and antipiracy by forming a French–Spanish–Neapolitan fleet, based in Naples, well-trained and equipped. The project needed many thousands of ducats since it involved the construction of seven ships with 74 cannons, four frigates with 32 guns, four galleys with 18 benches and four xebecs with 20 cannons. The King was pleased by the reconstruction project and for this reason he personally contributed 500,000 ducats. To get an idea of how costly the project was, the subsidy offered by the Sovereign was added to the proceeds of the Military Fund, or about 100,000 ducats a year. The Seal, issued by Pius VI in 1777, called for indulgences from subjects who in turn paid the cashier money which was then used for maritime defence.[21]

This policy was quite different from the one that the court physician, Giovanni Vivenzio, had launched. In fact, he was entrusted with the Navy during the years of Ferdinand IV's early adulthood. Vivenzio confirmed that "a small coastal flotilla" was sufficient for trade protection, believing Acton's naval project to be detrimental. The navy, as Acton had imagined, "was a giant with feet of clay. It was too small to do good, too big to do evil: it excited rivalry between the great powers without exhibiting necessary force, not to win but at least to resist".[22]

The construction of many ships, frigates and other vessels, commissioned by the Queen thanks to her great ambition and seconded by Acton's arrogance,[23] worsened trade and impoverished state revenue, given the need to maintain many sailors and workers serving these ships. In addition, it caused hostility abroad.[24] Cook highlighted Acton's "diplomatic errors": the army did not grow in proportion to commerce and trade, thus becoming "useless and expensive" and causing a reduction in commercial trade.

Furthermore, port infrastructure was created for this great Navy, and worse, the idea of making the ports of Brindisi and Baia functional was never considered. For this reason and by their nature, it involved a small fee.[25] The ports of Naples and Baia could accommodate no more than four or five big line vessels; rebuilt in 1776, the port of Brindisi was able to accommodate only frigates. The lack of adequate naval port infrastructure designed by Acton meant conducting commercial activities on French, English and Dutch ships. This increased fees and decreased risk, therefore it was possible to be captured by the infidels as well as encounter probable slavery in the seas of the barbarian regencies of the Ottoman capital.

The Actonian Navy was ill-suited to the defence of the Kingdom. The relationship between the risk to which commercial traffic was exposed from one location to another in the Tyrrhenian Sea and the Ionian Sea, as well as the cost of insurance and general expenses, was significant. This would have sidelined the Bourbon navy. Ultimately, Acton pursued a precise politico-strategic goal: the abandonment of the pro-Spanish and pro-French politics for the benefit of a privileged axis with Vienna and with its eternal ally, England. It is understandable that this purpose was perfectly in tune with the thinking of the Queen, as it aims to give prestige to Austria in the Tyrrhenian Sea.[26] Maria Carolina, following a pro-Austrian stance, definitively broke ties with the Bourbons of Spain. Her main objective was to put the Kingdom in a prominent place in the international scene. This required not only of the reorganization of the Navy but the reorganization of the army as well.[27] Acton's thirst was satisfied. To him was entrusted the task of reorganizing and rearranging the army. He became Minister of War in 1779 and combined the two Secretaries of War and Navy.[28] With the Queen's support, Acton began his ascent inside the Court. A special bond quickly developed between the two.

The design to reform the army included the replacement of a static army with a modern and meritocratic military body. It also provided organized educational trips abroad for officers and strengthened the public works department.[29] Acton, when reordering the army, followed the same strategy he used to reform the navy. During the years of his leadership, Carlo III had established in Naples about 30,000 men for the army, but since the Kingdom was able to enjoy a long period of peace, actual ground troops were reduced to no more than 15,000. Even the artillery was organized in such a way that they had no reason to envy foreign counterparts. In reality, Acton ostensibly increased the number of troops, lending itself to cover theft and waste of the Court. This conduct assured the minister an extensive and prolonged protection.[30]

The "expert" in whom the two monarchs had total confidence was Acton. He was valued as a trained naval officer, which his contemporaries acknowledged, but nothing more. His personality was characterized by a strict and haughty attitude, which was in contrast to the mediocrity of the King. Queen Maria Carolina, attracted by the English admiral's haughtiness, understood immediately that he knew quite a lot about the militia and navy but was certainly not an expert in the management of government and State commitments.[31]

Conscious of his own limitations and accused of being a foreign despot, to appease the public hatred that poured against him, Acton surrounded himself with the best men in the Kingdom. He tended to put in prominent positions those who were endowed with a certain cultural background and descended from aristocracy, like Giovan Battista Albertini, Prince of Cimitile and Francesco Pignatelli, Prince of Strongoli. But important positions were also given to leading intellectual supporters of an enlightened policy: Gaetano Filangieri, Giuseppe Palmieri and Domenico Grimaldi.[32]

The royal couple deeply appreciated Acton's dynamism. He shared the King's passion for natural sciences and Anglo-Saxon technology and with the Queen he undertook a comprehensive reform programme. A design destined to converge with a Genoese culture, it had as supporters Ferdinando Galiani, the Grimaldi brothers and Giuseppe Palmieri. This project favoured a technical–practical quality rather than theoretical reflections on sociopolitical order.[33] Genovesi, in fact, hinged his work on issues regarding the need to implement an innovative economic policy in the Kingdom, focused on the promotion of manufacturing, commerce and agricultural production.[34] The southern economy was set back. To raise it again, it was essential to disseminate methods used in more advanced countries, such as England.[35] The willingness to make Neapolitan trade independent of foreign control was at the centre of Genovesi, Intieri and Galiani's neomercantilism concept. It was the latter who guided Acton's policy in the 1780s.

Acton's political action stirred tears and exacerbated the conflict with the Spanish government. This was also due to the excesses that invalidated the moves made at the international level by Acton and Maria Carolina (first of all, the resumption of relations with the Russian Empire). Disorder would result in the court of Naples, with a serious moral and institutional crisis. But in the meantime, on the judicial side, in 1781 the reforms resulted in a new regulation, written by Michele De Jorio, concerning the right of navigation and maritime trade law.[36]

In 1783, the Court of Admiralty and Consulate was born from the merger of the Court of the Grand Admiral and the Consulate of the Sea.[37] Within the vast project to reorganize weapons, a place was found for the creation of a Royal Military Academy in the famous home of the *Nunziatella* at Pizzafalcone, for the vocational training of senior officers trained in applying modern technologies.[38] This situation increased the needs of the nation as well as the needs of the court.[39]

It was urgent for the Queen and Acton to restructure the Supreme Council of the Company, partly as a result of Maria Carolina's discontent with the work of Secretary Juan de Ausencio Goyzueta. The problem soon had a natural solution. In fact, due to an illness and the death of Goyzueta, which took place between 26 March and 16 September 1782,[40] Acton obtained the company ad interim, showing what benefits could be drawn from that place. Obviously this act, which was performed outside of established rules, brought him negative repercussions in terms of public opinion and consent.[41] But he received from the Sovereigns a reputation of praiseworthy efficiency. So Acton, henceforth and forever, had the delicate task of raising capital for various unofficial purposes, even after the birth of the Finance Council.[42]

In reality, historiography expresses an uncertainty towards the creation of the Council of Finance. If, on the one hand, it enhances an innovative aspect, on the other, it condemns it for its failure and describes it as a tool desired by the Queen to cover their incompetence and embezzlement.[43] Not by chance, Anna Maria Rao in *Il regno di Napoli nel Settecento* describes the Council of Finance as an essential instrument of the new reformist policy and its practical demonstration was the task of "reforming the old and pernicious abuses of the confusing system and effectively restoring the nation's dejected energy by promoting the safe channels of the wealth of its subjects and the state". Rao also stated that the establishment of the Council expressed concretely the need for modernization and effectiveness of State power.[44] The opposite opinion is that of Raffaele Ajello who explains how the new image of the Council of Finance was part of a political strategy that aimed to provide superior expertise through the creation of a collegial body that boasted famous names and therefore covered fiscal and financial operations unwelcome to the public. Ajello admits that "in fact he created a financial ministry to immediately overstep and continue to confuse public administration and the Queen's private assets. Not to mention the enormous confusion caused by fragmentation, juxtaposition and a clash of ill-defined responsibilities among multiple authorities, the new and the old: Sommaria, Soprintendenza d'Azienda, Segreteria degli Affari esteri e di Casa Reale, Marina (Summary, Superintendent of the Company, Secretary of Foreign Affairs and of the Royal House, Navy)".[45]

The Council staff had already been established with the dispatches of 18 and 19 October 1782 and was made up of a President (who was Giovan Battista Albertini, Prince of Cimitile, with the title of Councillor of State); ex officio members, that is, the three Secretaries of State (Giuseppe Beccadelli, Marquis of Sambuca, John Acton, Carlo De Marco); and three Councillors (Ferdinand Corradini, Mazzocchi and Filippo Antonio Loffredo, Prince of Migliano).[46]

Acton conceded the title of President to the elderly Cimitile because his mind had been seriously compromised as a result of clashes between Church and State, which had arisen from the controversy over the recovery of Chinea in 1776 and during which he was Ambassador of the Sicilies at the Court in Rome. In fact, he set aside the burden of telling the King about the Council deliberations. This resulted in the ability to decide everything, as usual, with the Queen.

Nearly a month later, on 20 November 1782, Acton published, in 22 points, the Instructions for the establishment of the Supreme Council of Finance, which he wrote on 19 October in Caserta. He also decided on the appointment of three commissioners who would be members of the Council only in the case in which they had responsibilities.[47] The consultants appointed were Nicola Ajello, President of tax lawyers accounts, for which he was assigned to advise on *arrendamenti* (indirect use taxes) and customs; Ferdinando Galiani, a trade consultant; and Domenico Grimaldi, a consultant for manufacturing and agriculture.

> On Wednesday the 20th I got up at 7 o'clock – combed my hair – dressed – had breakfast – holy Masses – read – talked with SB – wrote – devoted myself – then I had lunch with my children and Tissot kept me company – I spoke to him about the health of my children – then I saw Hakert with his portfolio and drawing – afterwards I spoke to A. – then some hearings – all to seek the vacant abbey – afterwards the Council of Carlo de Marco – then General Acton referred the finance papers to Cimitile in the presence of the King and demonstrated – how full of modesty – we had benefits – after that I went to sleep.[48]

The children healthy – except Joseph – had a bad night and showed [having] a fever.

Beyond the different historiographical opinions, the Council became the central coordinator of intellectuals and reformers of the Enlightenment who tried to offer a united economic direction with some innovative proposals: studies on physical reality, demographics, classes of the Kingdom; a debate on the themes of the feudal system, mortmain and domains, the development of agriculture and trade, technical progress; the abolition of many customs, which was part of the tariff reform, considered by the Council to be one of the main goals. However the government was forced to resort to loopholes in order not to diminish royal pensions and also due to the lack of expected development in commerce and industry.[49]

The situation worsened the following year. 1783 brought with it a series of unpleasant events: on 5 February, a violent earthquake hit many cities in Calabria and Sicily, killing 32,000 people.[50] The quake lasted 100 seconds destroying 109 towns and villages that were located in the part of Calabria called Piana. Money, clothing and provisions were sent; doctors, architects and archaeologists were headed by field marshal Francesco Pignatelli who, with a council of judges, controlled the administration. The provinces of the Kingdom that were not affected by the earthquake were imposed an extraordinary tax in order to help the two devastated regions:

In the early days of the following year, Emperor Joseph II arrived in the Kingdom to visit his sister. His trip lasted two weeks. He had arrived in Naples on 30 December 1783, as the Queen had noted:

> On Thursday December the 30th, I got up – When I woke up I was informed by the courier who brought the news that His Majesty the Emperor had slept in Gaeta and hoped to leave again at 7 o'clock – had breakfast – dressed – I heard holy Mass – I made my post at ten thirty went with my sister – Gravina and Virieux – we met outside S. Maria Capua His Majesty the Emperor – was with the King – I went down and hugged him then went in a carriage home I showed my children the house – then had lunch – ke kept me company – later wrote my post and from there his Majesty the Emperor returned for a moment – went to the pool hall – then attended a big concert where all the best singers of the theatre sung – from there had dinner and to bed – children well the King in the morning went to Carditello to meet the Emperor and afternoon for a while in the wood, my sister was always with me.

He wanted to visit Calabria, but could not due to the impracticality of the roads and the weather.[51] The following year, on 30 April 1785, even the Neapolitan sovereigns decided to take a trip, visiting Tuscany, Liguria and Piedmont:

> I leave saturday the 30th, wiithout finishing to write my journal.
> The diary of my journey will be written separately and it will be inserted here – I start again from the day of my arrival on September 7th.[52]

On this trip they spent a million ducats, in so much that the King was given the title "King of gold". Much less was granted to restore the areas affected by the earthquake of 1783, for which the King gave little thought and did not bother to visit.[53] Upon returning from a long trip, on 7 September 1785, Maria Carolina and Minister Acton were implicated.

La Spagna esercitava sul Regno di Napoli una tal quale specie di dominio, il che recava molto pregiudizio a questo stato, togliere La Monarchia di Napoli alla tutela che vi esercitava quella di Spagna, stringere dè vincoli più utili con l'Austria, tali furono le vedute di questo Ministro di cui la sagacità venne pienamente comprovata dal loro più felice compimento. Egli nulla paventò le minacce della Corte di Spagna, che posero la sua vita in pericolo, e per meglio assicurare i vantaggi del Regno, egli fece entrare nel Consiglio di Stato la Regina, che aveva ereditato il genio di Maria Teresa. Il corso della carriera Ministeriale che gli rimaneva a precorrere deveniva di giorno in giorno più difficile, e più spinoso.[54]

So the close political collaboration between Acton and the Queen created a stir at the Neapolitan court. Acton was not well accepted in the local current pro-Spanish so much so that between the end of 1784 and 1785 several attempts were made to discredit him and Maria Carolina, always guilty in the eyes of King Charles to support the European powers which were not welcomed by Spain and to pressure Ferdinand IV to insubordination.

NOTES

1. R. Ajello, "I filosofi e la regina. Il governo delle due Sicilie da Tanucci a Caracciolo (177–1786)", 431–432
2. P. Colletta, *Storia del Reame di Napoli*, 118.
3. Osterreichisches Staatsarchiv, Sammelbände des Hausarchivs, 10, *Lettere della Regina di Napoli e risposte del 1778 relative per la maggior parte alli affari e alla destinazione del General Acton a quel servizio*, ff. 5r-6v. We translated into English the following excerpts contained in manuscripts of the Viennese Archive.
4. Ibid., ff.7r-8r.
5. Ibid., ff. 15v.
6. Ibid., ff.16r-17v.
7. "My dear brother and friend, I received your dear and kind letter and I do not know how to thank you, I communicated to my dear husband who pervaded from your goodness he asked me to tell you that he is going to wait the coming of Acton our xebecs will go toward the end of the month in Livorno if you want to take this opportunity to come here my dear husband will give them the order to go to Leghorn if you want to come by

land it will depend on your inclination, the benefit of seeing our navy improved is due to your kindness and our gratitude will only increase and we only want to be able to assure our feelings." Ibid., ff. 21r-21v.

8. R. Ajello, "I filosofi e la regina. Il governo delle due Sicilie da Tanucci a Caracciolo (177-1786)", 447.

9. A. M. Rao, *Il regno di Napoli nel Settecento*, 111; Id, "Corte e Paese: Il Regno di Napoli dal 1734 al 1806", in M. Mafrici (ed.), *All'Ombra della Corte. Donne e potere nella Napoli borbonica (1734-1860)*, 24.

10. A. M. Rao, *Il regno di Napoli nel settecento*, (Napoli: Guida Editori, 1983).

11. R. Ajello, "I filosofi e la regina. Il governo delle due Sicilie da Tanucci a Caracciolo (177-1786)", 447–448.

12. Ibid., 600.

13. V. Cuoco, *Saggio storico sulla rivoluzione di Napoli*, 99.

14. P.Colletta, *Storia del Reame di Napoli.*, 118.

15. G. Nuzzo, *La monarchia delle Due Sicilie tra ancien régime e rivoluzione*, (Napoli: Berisio, 1972), 31–50; Id., "L'ascesa di Giovanni Acton al governo dello Stato", in *Archivio Storico per le Province Napoletane*, 3, 19 (1980),. 438–545.

16. M. Mafrici, "Il Mezzogiorno d'Italia e il mare: problemi difensivi nel Settecento", in R. Cancila (a cura di), *Mediterraneo in armi (secc. XV-XVIII)*, in «Mediterranea. Ricerche storiche», 4, 2007, t. II, 647–648.

17. Osterreichisches Staatsarchiv, Sammelbände des Hausarchivs, 10, *Lettere della Regina di Napoli e risposte del 1778 relative per la maggior parte alli affari e alla destinazione del General Acton a quel servizio*, f. 36r. "Acton, the more I see the more I think questo'uomo reputable reserved which masters his job and he speaks not as a braggart but as a man who has the required knowledge."

18. A. Bordiga Amedei, *Maria Carolina d'Austria e il Regno delle due Sicilie*, 41–42.

19. V. Cuoco, *Saggio storico sulla rivoluzione di Napoli*,. 72.

20. M. Mafrici, "Il Mezzogiorno d'Italia e il mare: problemi difensivi nel Settecento", 648 .

21. Ibid., 649–650 .

22. V. Cuoco, *Saggio storico sulla rivoluzione di Napoli*, 101.

23. Ibid., 650.

24. P. Colletta, *Storia del Reame di Napoli*, 120–121.

25. V. Cuoco, *Saggio storico sulla rivoluzione di Napoli*, 100.

26. The same objective was adopted by Acton in Tuscany, during the time spent at the court of Lorraine, when it brought success in Algiers in 1775 with a small team consisting of frigates and light. See M. Mafrici, "Il Mezzogiorno d'Italia e il mare: problemi difensivi nel Settecento", 654–656.

27. G. Astuto, "Dalle riforme alle rivoluzioni. Maria Carolina d'Asburgo: una regina «austriaca» nel Regno di Napoli e di Sicilia", 41.
28. P. Colletta, *Storia del Reame di Napoli*, 119.
29. G. Astuto, "Dalle riforme alle rivoluzioni. Maria Carolina d'Asburgo: una regina «austriaca» nel Regno di Napoli e di Sicilia", 41–42.
30. V. Cuoco, *Saggio storico sulla rivoluzione di Napoli*, p. 101.
31. R. Ajello, "I filosofi e la regina. Il governo delle due Sicilie da Tanucci a Caracciolo (177-1786)", 440.
32. Ibid., 440–441.
33. G. Astuto, "Dalle riforme alle rivoluzioni. Maria Carolina d'Asburgo: una regina «austriaca» nel Regno di Napoli e di Sicilia", 42.
34. R. Ajello, *Dalla magia al patto sociale. Profilo storico dell'esperienza istituzionale e giuridica*, (Napoli: Arte Tipografica editrice,2013), 240–251.
35. A. M. Rao, *Il regno di Napoli nel Settecento*,99.
36. R. Ajello, "I filosofi e la regina. Il governo delle due Sicilie da Tanucci a Caracciolo (177-1786)", 401.
37. A. M. Rao, *Il regno di Napoli nel settecento*, 115.
38. G. Astuto, "Dalle riforme alle rivoluzioni. Maria Carolina d'Asburgo: una regina «austriaca» nel Regno di Napoli e di Sicilia, 42–43.
39. V. Cuoco, *Saggio storico sulla rivoluzione di Napoli*, 108.
40. On 16 September 1782 the Queen wrote in her diary: "I saw the King learned of the sudden death of Goysueta did the Council and went to sleep."
41. R. Ajello, "I filosofi e la regina. Il governo delle due Sicilie da Tanucci a Caracciolo (177-1786)", p. 662.
42. Ibid., 448–449.
43. G. Astuto, "Dalle riforme alle rivoluzioni. Maria Carolina d'Asburgo: una regina «austriaca» nel Regno di Napoli e di Sicilia", 35.
44. A. M. Rao, *Il regno di Napoli nel settecento*, 112–113.
45. R. Ajello, "I filosofi e la regina. Il governo delle due Sicilie da Tanucci a Caracciolo (177-1786)", 450.
46. G. Galasso, Il *Regno di Napoli. Il Mezzogiorno borbonico e napoleonico (1734-1815)*, 538.
47. R. Ajello, "I filosofi e la regina. Il governo delle due Sicilie da Tanucci a Caracciolo (177-1786)", 669–671.
48. ASN, Archivio Borbone, *Journal*, f. 34v.
49. G. Astuto, "Dalle riforme alle rivoluzioni. Maria Carolina d'Asburgo: una regina «austriaca» nel Regno di Napoli e di Sicilia", 35.
50. On the earthquake see the valuable contribution Sul terremoto sia di riferimento il pregevole contributo A. Placanica, *Il filosofo e la catastrofe. Un terremoto del Settecento*, (Torino: Einaudi, 1985).
51. P. Colletta, *Storia del Reame di Napoli*,. 122, 129.

52. On 30 April 1785, the Queen and the King left for a long trip in Northern Italy, which ended five months later, on 7 September of the same year.
53. E. Caesar Corti, *Ich, eine Maria Theresias Tochter: ein Lebensbild der Königin Marie Karoline von Neapel*, 127–128.
54. This excerpt is taken from an unpublished biography of John Edward Acton preserved in the State Archives of Naples, f.110, c. 119v–124v. "Spain exercised over the Kingdom of Naples a kind of domain which bore much prejudice toward this state, removing from the monarchy in Naples the protection that was exercised by Spain, tightening the more useful restrictions with Austria. Such were the views of this Minister whose sagacity was fully proven by his most successful accomplishments. He was not scared by the threats coming from the Spanish Court, which put his life in danger. To ensure the benefits of the Kingdom, he allowed the Queen, who had inherited Maria Teresa's intelligence, to be part of the State Council. The remainder of the course of his Ministerial career which he pursued became more difficult and thornier day by day."

CHAPTER 5

1785: Conspiracies and Attempts to Overthrow the Queen

The close political collaboration between Acton and the Queen created a stir at the Neapolitan court. Acton was not well-accepted in the local current pro-Spanish so much so that between the end of 1784 and 1785 several attempts were made to discredit him and Maria Carolina, always guilty in the eyes of King Charles to support the European powers which were not welcomed by Spain and to pressure Ferdinand IV to insubordination.

The first plot was hatched by Minister Sambuca. The Marquis of Sambuca, Giuseppe Beccadelli, succeeding Bernardo Tanucci in 1777 (remaining in office until 1786), accepted Acton as the restorer of the Navy. Because of his loyalty to the Iberian monarchy, Sambuca had raised the hopes of the party in favour of the Spaniards. However, the first Secretary of State fell into disgrace for having favoured the influence of Acton in the Kingdom.[1] Sambuca was then swallowed up by the whirlwind of court scandals in those years, being accused of a theft which took place in the house of the Russian Ambassador, Andrei Kirillovc Razoumovskij, who was the alleged lover of the Queen and the recipient of her letters. The Queen had asked in vain for Razoumovskij to return the incriminating letters.

Maria Carolina ordered Sambuca to retrieve those letters. It was the minister who later confessed to having carried out the robbery, aided by the Russian diplomat's manservant. But the Queen did not trust Sambuca, whom she disliked very much, and was convinced that the latter had not

© The Author(s) 2017
C. Recca, *The Diary of Queen Maria Carolina of Naples, 1781–1785,*
Queenship and Power, DOI 10.1007/978-3-319-31987-2_5

handed over all the letters and had kept some for himself in order to be able to blackmail her.[2]

In 1785, Sambuca, being bypassed by Acton and hoping to gain the support of the King of Spain against the English general, allied himself with the Spanish Minister, Simon de Las Casas. Ferdinand received a secret letter written by his father, who warned him of the relationship between Maria Carolina and Acton, and the King Charles invited his son to get rid of the uncomfortable minister[3]; Ferdinand's reaction was violent. He rushed into his wife's room and threw the letter in her face but the Queen, knowing well her husband's character, knew how to deal with the storm. Playing the part of the outraged wife, she accused Ferdinand of not being able to defend his reputation and, in tears, told him about the expectation of another child, after which she fainted. When she came to, she found herself shut in a room with her husband for 24 hours. When they emerged, now reconciled, the King was convinced that his wife had been wrongly accused and that Acton's presence was indispensable to the Kingdom of the Two Sicilies. Obviously, the sovereign's revenge was immediate. Ambassador Herreria[4] was sent to Madrid while his replacement, Count Simon de Las Casas, was not received by the Royal couple. He was not even allowed to present his credentials to the Court.[5] All this happened, not by chance, from the return of the royal couple from a journey in Northern Italy, which seemed to confirm the will of Ferdinand, of course instigated by his wife, to develop a new policy on the peninsula that fell within the guidelines of Vienna. It is no coincidence that in response to a shift that was performed to question the precarious balance in the Mediterranean, it was said that Madrid were contemplating extreme measures, such as the repudiation of Maria Carolina by King Ferdinand or even the removal of the royal couple, although the full allegiance of the King and Queen with respect to the lack of an infant of acceptable age narrowed much room for manoeuvre in both directions.[6]

The Queen's private writings, the journals and letters, sometimes alluded to the controversies and the intrigues that stirred that troubled historical situation. Another attempt to torpedo Acton and put Maria Carolina in a bad light was implemented by the new French minister, Baron de Tailleyrand, who wanted to resume relations with France. But even before allying with Las Casas to carry out his plan, Tailleyrand was publicly accused, unjustly, by the Queen of stealing secret documents from Acton's study. In reality, they were not secret documents but, once again, the Sovereign's compromising letters which had not been stolen by the

Baron, but by Sambuca. Indeed, the latter would then be dispatched to Madrid to attempt a hypothetical betrayal by Acton and Maria Carolina. This would have triggered a chain reaction of fear and blackmail.

The accusation spread panic among the various embassies. Everyone burned papers and dispatches in fear of a search warrant. It was clear that, while Acton began his reforms and was consolidating his position, the Spanish ambassador reported to Charles III harsh criticism of the policy of the Kingdom of Naples and the behaviour of the Court. The Spanish party, having acquired the documentation of two diplomats, the viscount de la Herreria and Simón de las Casas, who had collected the testimonies hostile towards Acton and the Queen, pondered extreme remedies: the repudiation of Maria Carolina by King Ferdinand or the removal of the Royal couple. But the first measure was unenforceable because Ferdinand, deeply in love, was manipulated by Queen; the second solution was impractical due to the lack of an infant of an acceptable age. The Queen was furious against the Spaniards and publicly threatened to get back her letters. Meanwhile, marital passion was reignited in Ferdinand so much so that it alleviated his suspicions about his wife. It was no wonder, then, that the King denied a meeting with Las Casas and refused to see the letters. "I am not interested in fake documents", Ferdinand IV wrote under his wife's dictation to the Spanish Ambassador who had scolded him harshly for his participation in the nefarious plot.

Despite having avoided the scandal, rumours about the Queen were spreading in the European courts. Having returned from a long journey and embittered, she wrote in the Journal on 24 September 1785:

> The numerous affairs at the time of my return – the violent troubles I have had from the minister of Spain Mister de las Casas – I was dazed to the point that I have lost the faculty of doing anything and I did not know and could not do absorbed by my pains here my cruel position that continues on October the 10th we went to Caserta and whence that I write about my situation and always painful.

After a few weeks, the Sovereign, concerned about a situation she could not deal with, resorted to the protection of the brothers. Here we report long passages of a long letter of 12 October, in which Maria Carolina gave their version of events and she sincerely confided her mood, showing all her weaknesses and calling for help. She wrote to her brother Peter Leopold on 12 October 1785:

Depuis mon arrivee je n'ai eue que des chagrins, tout le tems du voyage on nous a laisse en paix craignant, que peut-etre quelque lettre, montre ou quelque conseil donné pouroit nous illuminer, mais depuis alors cella est bien diferent ; le ministre d'Espagne le celebre Las Casas a eté a Rome tout le tems de notre voyage, a notre arrivée il n'est pas venus au scandale du public qu'apres neuf jours et plus, mais de cecy je n'aurois pas pris garde meprisant les petitesses. A peine arrivée, il a cherche de parler au roi! il lui a dit devoir lui parler des affaires d'Alger, lui a donées copie d'un office de Florida Blanca, ou s'exprimant sur cette affaire, [...], que si l'on ne chasse Acton, jamais il n'y aura ni paix ni bien, lui etant la racine de tout le mall et inimitie, sur cella il a dit au roi, que lui Las Casas avoient recuelli des preuves evidentes qui lui prouveroient, que Acton etoit un traitre un malhonete home si indigne de la confiance, le roi y acceda et ils resterent de se parler quelque part secretement et surtout/: car c'etoit le pacte principal:/a l'insue de moi, et dans un endroit ou je ne puisse venir les voire ni surprendre, le soir Las Casas me parla de chasser Acton, battit la campagne en disant, que nous le comblions d'honneur pourvu que nous l'eloignions, puisque un ou deux ans, le vieux roi pourroit vivre, et qu'alors il revient glorieux et triomphant, enfin il me comenca a m'attaquer tres insolenment, que c'étoit par tendresse de cœur, que je le soutenois, que mon gout etoit bien mauvais et chose pareille, enfin impertinemes, mais cachant toujours avec soin qu'il avoit demandé une entrevue secrette, que j'ygnorois alors, lui demandant mais quelles etoit les delits et crimes pour lesquels nous devoins sacrifier un honnete home, qui nous sert bien, il dit : aucun, que l'obstination du roi d'Espagne, qui s'occupant peu de la politique, c'est mis cella en tete; je lui ai demandé quelles idees quelles preuves lui memes avoient de cet home? il m'a repondue etre trop peu de tems yci pour en juger, mais que personellement il l'auroit estimé et recherché, si sa cour ne le lui defendoit, nous restames ainsi. le jour d'apres je sue la trahison secrette per la bouche de mon mary, les bruits public me parvinient de tous cotùés que cet home dit, que non seulement il fera chasser Acton, mais ruinera pour toujours a moi.[...]Pour mon cher mary il a mall fait de tremper dans la promesse de l'entrevue secrette, il a ensuite remedié par le billet, il n'ose faire un coup d'eclat, come chasser Sambuca, exiler l'infame Facy qui tient des propos et les a toujours tenus a faire horreur, et defendre d'approcher a la cour a Las Casas jusqu'au reponses d'Espagne ce seroit un parti, l'autre seroit ceder, rester pupille, jusqu'à la mort du vieux roi, et doner une honorable demission a Acton, pour aquerir sa tranquilité, mais cella quoique le seroit mon parti favori, il n'est pas a persuader. Je le voudrois a cause de moi, pour finir ses discours, pour conserver la vie a cet honete home, et un peu par mechancete, pour faire sentir au public le manque qu'il feroit, en Marine, Justice, verité, et soutien du gouvernement, car c'est l'unique, Actuellement mon cher mary se montre tres pique et faché contre Las Casas, de ce qu'il a ose blesser son honneur, et lui vouloit montrer des preuves diaboliquement forgées, ce secret, cet eloignement de moi, que prouve t'els qu'un ordre qu'on lui vouloit faire souscrire, pour faire des violences et me deshonorer, car que ce ne sont point des preuves, de service d'Acton, cella est constaté par tout ce qu'il a dit au roi, a moi, a l'ambassadeur de France qui est venue a l'infame compensation de chasser Acton avec honneur meme, et les preuves seront detruites, mais je n'ai pas peur et on ne m'epouventera point, des preuves forgées par des falsaires :/et tels ils doivent etre:/se peuvent renouveller a chaque instant, et contre tout autre je proteste, et le nie, et abjure pour la vie. Nous verrons ce que Pignatelli obtiendra je n'espere rien de bon, le vieux roi obstinne come un roce, per puntiglio n'en demordera point, au moins sauront nous si c'est lui, qui veut deshonorer une bille fille apres dixsept années, j'ose dire d'un prudent mariage, qui n'a rendue que de bons services a son fils, l'a fait paroitre, faire figurer, rendue home, jamais pensé a elle-même, car je n'ai ni un sous d'argent, ni jamais fait de dettes, pas un arpens de terrein, ni creatures, ni parti, ni intrigues, qui a mis douze enfans dans cette maison, qui n'a jamais fait d'eclat, et souferte beaucoup de peines privées, qui pour n'etre pas violentes n'en sont point moins sensible etant continuelles nous verrons si le vieux père pour me recompenser, permette cette infamie, qu'aucun home honete se permetroit. Voilla ce qui au moins sera eclairci et pourra nous servir de regle, au reste je n'en attend nul bien, mon cher mary est foible, le père obstiné, si Pignatelli n'obtiendra rien, il parle toujours de partir sur l'heure, moi grosse alors de 7. a 8. mois que dois-je faire ? partir paroit repugner le bon sens, rester je jure que dans mes presentes circonstances je ne reste point, on feroit soulever le pays, et on m'en feroit un crime d'Etat, car on veut m'aneantir, si mon mary va seul en Espagne, j'ai fini d'exister pour lui, on l'impoisonera contre moi de facon a ne pouvoir y revivre, et si j'y vais aussy, et puis obtenir un delai jusqu'apres mes couches, je serois exposé a tout ce que l'atrocité dans un pays propre peut faire entreprendre, a en juger ce qu'on a fait chez nous. Voilla ma situation triste et malheureuse, c'est a vous cher frere que j'ose recourir, pour vous demander vos conseils […] Je vous prie jettez un regard et pensée a une sœur et amie malheureuse, et a laquelle on trame d'oter plus que la vie, en lui otant la confiance de son mary, l'honeur et en deshonorant ainsi la mere et sept enfans vivans moi enceinte, je ne sais come j'y survis, enfin mon sentiment est tel, que j'espere de vous conseils, secours, et amical avertissement, mon mary est tout pour moi, il me rend justice, et fortifiée contre toutes les impostures se conduit tres bien, mais on peut le surprendre quoiqu'il est tres prevenue que tout est imposture, conseillez moi, daignez vous conduire en frere, amy, pere, et protecteur, je ne puis voire dans cette crainte de noirceurs qu'on me trame, mon ame sera toujours en suspens, et je devrois toujours craindre trahison".[7]

Also Ferdinand, in a letter to the brother-in-law the same day, affirmed that only the help of the Habsburgs would allow him to keep pace with the wishes of his father and confirmed, in turn, all his fragility. A copy of the letter from the King of Naples to his Royal Highness on 12 October is as follows:

> Dearest brother-in-law, the only consolation I have left, considering my continuing afflictions and the experiences of renewed persecutions against us now more than ever, is the thought that other people we have seen and known may judge our honesty and onoratezza. Now also this give our malevolent remove, cling, and publicly slander the honesty of my wife, your sister. After arriving at such a perfidy of this gesture I do not trust to appear anymore, and I do not know if I am in this world or the next. I do not trust anymore, I only recommend//a miserable and desolate family.[8]

So Peter Leopold used the occasion to intervene, writing separately to both spouses and at the same time he cared to inform his brother Emperor Joseph. To Ferdinand was given a government lesson, asking him, in the name of honour of his sister, to hold in front of the father and proceed to the expulsion of those who were plotting against the royal couple.

> Carissimo cognato, ho ricevuto la vostra lettera, che subito io non intesi, fino a che non ebbi letta quella di vostra moglie, confesso che allora, attaccato sinceramente come io vi sono, non seppi in che modo io mi **fussi** tra la rabbia, l'indignazione, di una cosi infame ed insolente calunnia, non credevo mai che la malignità ardirebbe avanzarsi a tanto, né che l'insolente Las Casas avrebbe coraggio di parlarvi costi, tremo per la salute di mia sorella gravida, viva, e sensibile come io la conosco, la vostra tenerezza può solo consolarla, e la fermezza che dimostrerete in questa occasione contro tutti nel sostenere la riputazione e decoro do vostra moglie nel gastigare chi ardisse essere insolente, ò parlare contro di lei, e nel sostenere i vostri buoni servitori contro la cabala dei loro e vostri nimici può solo acquistarvi e mantenervi quella stima del pubblico e di tutta l'Europa, che per//il vostro carattere meritate, che nei vostri viaggi vi siete meritamente acquistata e che perdereste affatto col cedere e mostar paura in quest'occasione cosi solenne pubblica ed importante della vostra vita, simile alla quale forse mai più veruna si presenterà, perdonate alla mia sincera amicizia e attaccamento se vi parlo così e al desiderio mio di vedervi contenti e tranquilli se non mostrate in un occasione

come questa di saper essere Rè e tener a dovere gl'insolenti e gastigare con allontanare da voi i capi che da tanto tempo vi fomentano tante inquietudini non goderete mai una vera pace e quiete che io di tutto il mio cuore vi desidererei, mia moglie sensibilissima a quest'affare ne scriverà forte in Spagna giacchè per questo corriere non ha potuto il medesimo avendo fatto una diligenza incredibile per procedere[9]//Pignatelli come li è riuscito avendo anticipato di più ore la sua venuta qua. Desidero sapere presto migliori nuove di voi e di vostra moglie; la mia vi fa i suoi complimenti ed io vi prego di esser persuaso della tenera amicizia e attaccamento col quale sono.[10]

On 22 October 1785, Peter Leopold suggested to his sister not to lose her temper, not to repeat too many mistakes already made and to take control of the situation, guiding her husband in the choice of a strong resistance to the claims of the old father:

Très cher sœur et amie [...] L'etat violent dans lequelle je vous voyois me fait tant craindre pour votre santé pour votre tete, pour l'amour de dieu et de toute votre famille [...] si vous voulés vivre si vous ne voulés pas devenir folle oui folle parceque c'est ainsi qu'on la devient quand on se laisse aller et que la raison ne dirige plus les combinaisons, vous venés de faire un eclat sur quoi, car je ne vois ni ne conais encore la vraie donnée que Las Casas a voulu parler au roi seul [et bien] quelle droit avés vous d'y etre les propos repandues dans le publique sur votre honeté et vos liasons avec Acton sure comme vous l'éte de votre fait vous devriez mepriser ces propos et par la vous leurs [daniés] une bien plus grande improbabilité qu'en s'en emportant comme vous avez faite; ces maudites ecritures multipliés, les lettres que vous ecrivés a tort a travers a tant de personne les expressions fortes dont vous vous servés l'envie demeurée que vous avez d'acquerir par la des sufrages d'obliger les confiances qu'indistinctement vous faite a tant de personnes meme etrangeres tout cella si vous ne les reformes exactement doivent vous jetter dans les embarras et inconveniens continuelles. Si le roi eut parle a Las Casas vous auriés eus en main des preuves de perfidie au lieux qu'ainsi vous n'aves rien. Il serait ridicule que le roi aille en Espagne pour engager son père à lui promettre d'avoire Acton pour ministre et de chasser Sambuca pendant qu'il en est le maitre. Si ce voyage a lieux vous ne pouvez en etre [grasse] et dans cette saison et apres vos couches je me flatte toujours qu'a la fin le roi voudra etre ce qu'il peut pour cella faire j'ai couché ces reflexions que je vous envoys et que vous lui liréz avec attention elles contienent je crois tant ce qu'on peut dire pourvu que votre chere mari fasse toutes ces histoires seronts finies pour la vie. Pardones ma chere amie la franchise avec laquelle je vous ecrit mais je suyis trop interessé a votre bonheur et conservation pour ne pas etre energicque quand elles sont comme dans des pareilles cas en jeux adieu j'attents d'ulterieures nouvelles avec bien de l'impatience et c'est en vous embrassant tendrement que je serai pour la vie votre.

Voici une lettre que je vous prie de remettre au roi.[11]

In addition, the Grand Duke of Tuscany, in a series of letters sent to the Emperor from 15 October to 1 December 1785, informed him of the cabal hatched against his sister:

> sachant que la Reine vous en fait tous les details. Vous verrez les infamies qu'on a osé répondre et la conduite insolente, le langage et le ton de Las Casas, qui m'etonne point [...] je me suis pris la liberté de vous avertir de propos qu'on avait osé tenir sur la Reine et sur Acton [...] et quoique je connaisse la vivacité, la sensibilité de la Reine et que je sache son imprudence à écrire, dans cette affaire elle a toutes les raisons posibles et je suis persuadé que vous ne souffriez pas qu'elle soit diffamée et traitée de cette façon. Le Roi s'aflige de tout cela, mais ne se fâche point, ne montre point les dents et ne renvoie pas Las Casas ni ne chasse Sambuca, qui sont pourtant les premières choses qu' il aurait dû faire, et de cette façon ces Messieurs deviennent toujours plus insolentes [...] La cabale ourdie contre Acton et contre l Reine a le marquis Sambuca et presque tous les seigneurs de la Cour à la tête et tous les Siciliens, et ce qui s'appelle à Naples les parti espagnol, qui y est fort nombreux.[12]

On 22 October 1785, Emperor Joseph responded to his brother Peter Leopold showing his disappointment for the inability of his sister who in so delicate circumstances seemed to have lost her mind. And so with her rash she was threatening to ruin the political line conquered in a few years:

> Voila une nouvelle absurde affaire, et la Reine et tout le monde a pris l'alarme bien mal a propos. Il fallait parler a Las Casas, il fallait voir et prendre les papiers qu'il dit avoir, pour avoir un fait, un document de méchanceté en main; mais ainsi on a rien, et l'on envoie Pignatelli en Espagne pour demander la permission d'être Roi de Naples. On lamente, on s'afflige et on ne chasse pas ceux qui en sont cause. [...] La Reine peut se fairegrand mal avec ses violentes afflictions et coleres. [...] Dieu sait si ce que Las Casas a voulu donner au Roi la regardait. Enfin si ces bonnes gens ne changeant de conduite et ne prennent le parti que je leur insinnue, il faut qu'il renoncent à être Roi et a à être hereux de leur vie. Veuillez bien, mon cher ami, leur parler dans la même ton et calmer les premiers mouvemens de la Reine et animer le courage du Roi pour faire seul les affaires de son Etat.[13]

Indignant, he urged Ferdinand IV to take effective and concrete action against those who had woven the vile, slanderous plot and to dictate, in the first person, the line at the court of Naples:

> Carissimo amico don Fernando con somma pena hò letto per il corriere, che mi mandò Richecourt, il dettaglio delle pene, nelle quali dei malvaggi vi hanno messi, e quanto hanno osato calumniare mia sorella; felice lei ed io, che tanto teneramente l'amo, che queste calumnie atroci non hanno fatto nessun effetto sopra voi caro amico! Che siete giusto, savio e onesto, e che non vi lasciate soprafare di bugie cosi nere, conoscendo il merito e la virtù della vostra compagna, e il cuore fido e onesto della madre dei vostri figli. Credetemi se non agirete da Rè, da padrone indipendente come siete, non avrete mai riposo. Ne mando alcune riflessioni su di ciò in confidenza alla regina, pochi esempi di fermezza basteranno a rimettere tutti in ordine, ma quelli ci vuole e ci va dell'onor e della riputazione vostra; quell paragon delle due regine Caroline infame vi compromette gravemente, mettendovi voi, che avete datto in tutte le città d'Italia saggi di vostro spirito, della vostra penetrazione, in parallelo con quel Rè scemo e incapace di Danemarca; ne son così arrabiato, che se ne conoscessi l'autore, glielo farei pagar caro. Addio! Vi ringrazio caro amico! Ancor una volta di tutte le finezze che dimostrate a mia sorella, e recomendandola di tutto cuore v'abbraccio e saro sempre.[14]

The letter written by Joseph II was prepared on 22 October 1785. On the very same day, Ferdinand IV wrote to his brother-in-law:

> Cognato carissimo corrispondendo alla vostra affettuosissima risposta alla mia fattavi pervenire per mezzo di Pignatelli, vi ringrazio infinitissimamente per la giusta parte che avete voluto prendere in un affare che tanto è interessa, e delle amorosissime espressioni che mi fate riguardo a tal assunto. Fin'ora mi avete conosciuto bastantemente, per poter essere sicuro della mia fermezza in sostenere un punto così giusto, e se fin'ora mi son contenuto a non far novità alcuna, è stato per il solo rispetto, che ò per mio padre, e non per debolezza, ma ora che non ne posso più non attendo altro che le nuove che mi darà Pignatelli per regolarmi. Grazie a Dio quest'ottim'aria e le amene campagne che vi sono d'intorno mi anno alquanto sollevato, ma mia moglie non stà come io desidererei. Il Signore intanto conservi voi e la vostra amabile famiglia per consolazione di chi vi ama e stima infinitamente.[15]

In the meantime, the Queen had decided to send Prince Francesco Pignatelli to Spain to plead her cause with her father-in-law, King Charles, since the Prince was opposed to the lies that were spread about her. But the monarch proved inflexible and the mission failed. In fact, Pignatelli misunderstood Charles's underlying attitude, making a mistake in the Neapolitan Court. The Spanish King had decided to dismiss Acton in order to remove the minister from his ministerial responsibilities. Pignatelli had hinted to the Neapolitan court that Charles III would not be opposed to the permanence of the English commander and would have avoided future interference in matters pertaining to the Kingdom of the Two Sicilies. Involved in this ruthless political mechanism that swept her private life, Maria Carolina asked her Emperor brother for support in saving the throne as well as Acton's place. The Sovereign interpreted this as permission to dismiss Sambuca, as reported by Pignatelli, who was considered the main culprit of the conspiracy. At this point, it was possible to wipe out the pro-Spanish faction.[16]

In the fall of 1785, Acton, tired of conjecture, speculation and rumours that he had been persecuted, wanted to retire to private life. At the end of November, as seen in a letter written by Maria Carolina to Peter Leopold, the general reiterated his intention to resign. But his request was not accepted, especially since he possessed documents potentially harmful to the Queen. It was feared that the content of those documents could be made known throughout the European courts.[17]

Sambuca's successor was Domenico Caracciolo, Ambassador to France and an expert in economic matters. He was tasked to improve the public finances.[18] With the substitution of Sambuca, the Sovereign had achieved her goal: to remove the influence of the Spanish Kingdom from the Two Sicilies. In fact, Caracciolo, now elderly and tired, would not have exercised great influence at Court and would be needed, without knowing or at least not caring, to shine the light on Acton, whom the Queen wished to exalt instead. The fragility of the situation, however, did not allow her to fulfil this aspiration. Maria Carolina then waited for the right moment to arrive when she could redeem Acton's reputation. With Caracciolo's death in 1789, she was able to carry out her plans: Acton was placed at the top of State affairs and De Marco was given less relevant assignments, such as organizing tasks within the court.[19] The Neapolitan government was noted for its successful adherence to the ideals espoused by the Enlightenment. But at the same time it was at the centre of very damaging scandals, losing credibility which resulted in significant changes in the tone and character of public life.[20]

The early 1780s that represented a time of major reorganization of government,[21] marked by the exponential growth of the political personality of Maria Carolina. In the few pages of the diary of the Queen saved from the flames emerge clearly that particular political situation. On the political front, changes of the diplomatic balances were decisive to the relocation of the two southern kingdoms in the international context, while on government action, they saw a strong reform momentum in Naples as in Sicily, which in the overall ministerial reorganization was a very significant test. Just the creation of the Supreme Council of Finance in 1782 symbolized the change of government in those years, where the public government had requested the assistance of the best reformist minds such as Domenico Grimaldi, Gaetano Filangieri and Giuseppe Palmieri. It was a choice that accompanied Acton's triumph of the government, more and more needful for the royal couple. And not surprisingly, these are the years where a picture of a sly and libertine queen took shape.[22] It seems clear that these testimonies of diplomats and travellers reflected the pro-Spanish intentions. It aimed to damage the Queen, hinted at her intimate relations with the ministers who in turn would guide the affairs of government. Such as Prince Caramanico (soon dismissed by the will of King Ferdinand and sent to guide the embassies of London and Paris). There were also some whispers regarding the relationship with the Marquis of Sambuca that soon was replaced in his role in 1786 by Domenico Caracciolo. And especially with Acton, whose liaison with the Queen was considered evident and indisputable. As all those allegations were, however, primarily an instrument of political struggle, it is showed by the last backlash of what was left of the Tanucci's group on the occasion of cabal of 1785. As we saw in that occasion, Spanish diplomats, denouncing Maria Carolina and Acton as lovers, convinced Charles III to issue an ultimatum to his son with the clear intention to move away from the Kingdom the Minister and to return the Queen to her mere functions of consort.[23] For the occasion, however, once Peter Leopold and Joseph themselves actively supported his sister and allowed her to come out winner from the deaf power struggle within the Court.

In the light of the correspondence examined, it appears clear why the attempt to overthrow Acton by the party's pro-Spanish ended with nothing coming out of it: the Habsburg power had intervened directly on the foreign policy of the southern kingdoms, entering into the conflict between father and son in order to guide him to their side and to also compensate for clamorous weaknesses for the circumstance that Maria Carolina showed. In fact, the victory on the elderly King Charles III was the certification that another protection was substituted for that of Madrid, but in this smooth handover, the Queen had been everything except a decisive figure. Thus in Naples and Sicily another political season was started, where the new balances of government seemed to get stronger, but in reality they were connected in an even more subordinate manner to the new Austrians centre of power, that through the streets of Tuscany, went back to Vienna. And Maria Carolina rather than victory would have left only the stain, no more erasable, of an unfaithful and lustful wife.

NOTES

1. V. Cuoco, *Saggio storico sulla rivoluzione di Napoli,* Milano, p. 73 (Vedi nota n. 17).
2. R. Ajello, "I filosofi e la regina. Il governo delle due Sicilie da Tanucci a Caracciolo (177–1786)", 710–711.
3. Osterreichisches Staatsarchiv, Sammelbände des Hausarchivs, 10: *Lettres de S. Mte. La Reine de Naples et Reponses 1784,* ff.123r-124r. Maria Carolina in a letter wrote to her brother Peter Leopold on 21 August 1784 reported an excerpt of a letter of King Charles to his son Ferdinand in which he denounced Acton as troublesome intruder.
4. Viscount de Herreria was the one who had delivered the letter of King Charles to Ferdinand.
5. E. Caesar Corti, *Ich, eine Maria Theresias Tochter: ein Lebensbild der Königin Marie Karoline von Neapel,* 127–130
6. Ibid., 88–89.
7. Osterreichisches Staatsarchiv, Sammelbände des Hausarchivs, 10: Korrespondenz Großherzog Leopold von Toskana mit Kaiserin Maria Theresia und Maria Karoline von Neapel: Lettere e copie relative alli affari ultimi di Napoli seguiti dal mese di ottobre a tutto il dicembre 1785 relativi alli affari con la Spagna, Las Casas e la dimissione di Acton. From the letter of 12 October 1785 Maria Carolina to Peter Leopold, ff. 11v-16r. "Since my arrival, I have had nothing that sorrow, during the whole trip we were worried, that perhaps some letters, shows or any advice given could enlighten us, but since then everything is different; the Spanish minister, the famous Las Casas, was in Rome the whole time of our trip, when we arrived it become a public scandal only after nine days and more but of this I should not have taken guard contemptuous pettiness. Just arrived, he tries to talk to the king! he said him he needed to talk about Algiers affairs, gave him a Florida Blanca's offices copy, expressing on this matter, [...], that if he does not dispel Acton, he will never find neither peace nor good, as he was the reason of all bad things and enmity, this is what he told the

king, that he himself Las Casas had collected obvious evidence that demonstrate it, that Acton was a traitor, a dishonest man, such unworthy of
trust, the king entered and they stayed somewhere to talk secretly and
above all/: as it was the main pact:/unbeknown to me, and in a place
where I could not see or surprise them, that evening Las Casas talked to
me about Acton's dispel, beating the campaign while talking, that we
should fill him with honours providing that we take him away, since one or
two years, the old king could live, and then he comes back glorious and
triumphant, finally he start attacking me very saucily, that it was by tenderness of heart, that I have to sustain him, that my taste was very bad and
other similar things, even impertinences, but still concealing carefully he
had asked for a secret appointment, a fact that I ignored at that time, asking what the offenses and crimes were, for which we have to sacrify an
honest man, that serves us well, he said: none, except King of Spain's
obstinacy, who is few interested in politics, this has to be put in mind; I
asked him what ideas, what evidence he had of that man? he answered me
that time was too little to judge it, but he would have personally estimated
and searched for, if his court forbade him, so we agreed like that. the day
after I knew the secret treason from my husband's mouth, the public
rumors come to me from all over, that this man says that not only he will
dispel Acton, but he will also ruin me forever. […]
According to my dear husband he did not do a good thing by promising a
secret appointment, he then remedied by a note, he did not dare to make
an exploit, such as dispelling Sambuca, exiling the infamous Facy that
always talks just to do horror, and ban to approach Las Casas to the court
until Spain responses, it would be a party, the other would be to assign, to
become ward, until the old king's death and to give Acton an honourable
resignation, in order to gain his tranquility, but whatever my favourite
party would be, he has no to persuade me. I would like it for myself, to
finish his matters, to preserve this honest man's life, and a little because of
my wickedness, to make the public feel the lack he will do in the Navy, the
Justice, truth, and the support to the government, because it is the only
thing. Now my dear husband shows himself sting and very upset with Las
Casas, because he dared to hurt his honor, and he wished to show him
evidence wickedly forged, this secret, this remoteness of me, that proves
nothing else that an order they wished to ascribe to him, to violence and
dishonour me, because, that there are not any evidence, of Acton's service,
this is a fact recognized from all that he said to the king, to me, to the
ambassador of France who came to the infamous compensation to dispel
Acton and even his honour, and the evidence will be destroyed, but I'm
not afraid and they will not scare me, evidence made up by forgers:/and
they should be:/they can be renew every moment, and I protest against

any other thing, and deny and swear on my life. We'll see what Pignatelli will obtain, I don't hope anything good, the old king is stubborn like a rock, he will not give up absolutely for obstinacy, at least we will know if he wants a beautiful girl to be dishonoured after seventeen years, I venture to say, of a prudent marriage, who has rendered only good services to his son, has made him come into view, rendered him a man, never thought to herself, because I do not have neither money, nor debts, not acres of ground, nor creatures nor parties nor intrigues, who took twelve children in this house, who has never been ostentatious, and has suffered many private pains, which even though not violent there are not at all less sensitive because continuous, we'll see if the old father, to reward me, will allow this infamy, that no honest man would take the liberty. At least, this will be clarified and could serve as a rule, for the rest I do not expect any good, my dear husband is weak, the father is stubborn, Pignatelli will get nothing, he still talks about leaving, then I'll be to 7 from 8 months pregnant, what should I do? Leaving seems to repulse the common sense, remaining, I swear that in my current circumstances I do not remain at all, they will rouse the people, and accuse me of a State crime, because they want to annihilate me, if my husband goes alone in Spain, I have finished to exist for him, they will poison him against me so that we could not live together anymore, and if I go too, and then can obtain a period until my childbirth, I will be exposed at whatever the atrocity in their own country can undertake, by judging what they did here. That is my sad and unhappy situation, it is to you dear brother that I dare to speak, to ask your advice [...] Please take a look and think at an unhappy sister and friend, against whom they conspire to rub out more than her life, to take her out her husband's trust, her honour and thus dishonouring this way a mother and seven children since I am pregnant, I do not know how I will survive, my feeling is such that I hope in your advice, help, and friendly warning, my husband is everything for me, it makes me justice, and fortify me against all the impostures he behaves well, but he could be surprised though he is very warned that everything is fake, please advise me, act as a brother, friend, father and protector, I cannot even see in this fear of vileness that are conspired against me, my soul will be always pending, and I'll have always to fear betrayal."

8. From the letter of October 12, 1785 by Ferdinand IV to Emperor Joseph. Ibid., ff. 52rv.

9. Wrote in the line spacing.

10. Peter Leopold to the King of Naples, on 15 October 1785. Ivi, ff. 54rv. "Dearest brother-in-law, I received your letter which I immediately did not understand until the moment I read the one of your wife, I confess that in that moment, I felt sincerely connected to you like as I am, I can't tell in

which state of mind I have been, between rage and indignation, for such an infamous and insolent slander, I never thought that malignancy dare to advance like so, nor the insolent Las Casas would dare to speak that way to you, I tremble for the health of my pregnant sister, full of life, and sensitive as I know her, only your tenderness can console her, and the firmness that you will show on this occasion against everyone in supporting the reputation and dignity of your wife and chastise those who dare to be insolent, or to talk against her, and support your good servants against the plots of their as well as your enemies which only you can buy and keep for yourself the esteem of the public and of the whole of Europe, which you deserve for your character, that in your travels you have deservedly obtained and that you would lose absolutely by giving up and show fear on this occasion such a solemn public and important part of your life, similar to what perhaps will never again be present, forgive my sincere friendship and my attachment if I talk to you in that way and my desire to see you happy and peaceful if you do not show in an opportunity like this to know how to be King and to detain properly the insolent and chastise, pushing away from you the leaders who for so long stir so much unrest no one ever will enjoy real peace and quiet that I above all wish with all my heart, my wife is very sensitive to this business, she will write with intensity to Spain since this same courier cannot do an incredible diligence to proceed//Pignatelli managed to have, anticipating having more hours in advance of his coming here. Let me know soon the best news about you and your wife; my wife sends you her compliments and I beg you to be persuaded of the tender friendship and attachment which I have."

11. Passages from the letter of 22 October 1785 written by Peter Leopold to Maria Carolina. Ibid., f.54bisv. "Dear sister and friend [...]. The violent state I've seen you makes me so worried about your health, about your head, for God's sake, and about your family's sake [...]. If you want to live, if you don't want to get crazy, because it's so that you became when you give yourself up and the reason doesn't manage the combinations anymore, you are going to do a grand gesture, because I do not see nor I know yet the real fact that Las Casas wanted to speak to the King alone [and well] what right have you to have a public answer to your intentions, about your honesty and your relationship with Acton, sure as you are about it, you should despise these intentions and that way you'll give them a much greater improbability that you have loosed your temper as you did; those numerous wretch writings, the letters you have wrongly written, to many people, the strong expressions that you have used within, the extreme desire to acquire support through them, to oblige to the confidence that you indistinctly made to many people, even irrelevant to all of that, if you do not reformulate it more exactly, should throw you in continual embar-

rassment and inconveniences. If the king had talked to Las Casas you would have in your hand evidence of perfidy instead of having nothing this way. It would be ridiculous for the King to go to Spain to require his father to promise him Acton as minister, and to dispel Sambuca while he is the master of him. If this trip take place, you cannot participate to, [fat] and in this season and after your childbirth I still flatter myself that at the end the king will intend to do all what he can to make it work. I have inscribed these thoughts that I send you and that you will read to him carefully as they contain, I believe, all that it can be said as long as your dear husband do so that all these stories will finish for ever. Forgive, my dear friend, my frankness in writing you this way but I care too much your happiness and conservation that I cannot put all my energies as they are in any case in running. Goodbye, I wait for further news with great impatience and kissing you tenderly I am for your life.

Here there is a letter that I ask you to give to the King."

12. Reproduced in A. Ritter von Arneth, *Joseph II und Leopold von Toscana. Ihr Briefwechsel von 1781 bis1790*, I vol., (Wien: Wilhelm Braumüller, 1872), 303–304. "Knowing that the Queen gives you all the details about it. You will see the infamy that he dared to answer and the insolent behavior, Las Casas's language and tone, who doesn't amaze me at all […] I took the liberty to warn you about the intention that it was dared to have on the Queen and on Acton […] and although I know Queen's liveliness, the sensitivity, and I know her imprudence in writing, in this case she has all the possible reasons and I am sure that you will not tolerate she to be defamed and treated that way. The King is worried about all this, but he is not angry at all, he doesn't show much the teeth and does not return Las Casas nor dispel Sambuca, that are the first things that he should have done, and this way these gentlemen become ever more insolent […] the cabal formed against Acton and against the Queen has Marquis Sambuca and almost all the lords of the Court to the head, and all the Sicilians, and what in Naples is called the Spanish party, which is there very numerous."

13. Ibid., 307. "Here there is a new absurd affair, and the Queen and everyone took the alarm very badly. It is necessary to speak to Las Casas, the papers he said he possess have to be seen and taken, to have a proof, a document of wickedness in hand; but so we have nothing, and Pignatelli was sent to Spain to ask for the permission to be King of Naples. We lament, we grieve and we do not dispel those who are the reason of this […] The Queen can harm much herself with her violent afflictions and angers. […] God knows if what Las Casas wanted to give to the King concerns her. Finally, if these good people don't change their behavior and take the party I suggest them, he must resign from being the King and being happy of his live. Please, my dear friend, talk to him in the same tone and calm the Queen's

first movements and animate King's courage to do only the affairs of his State."

14. Osterreichisches Staatsarchiv, Sammelbände des Hausarchivs, 10: *Lettere e copie relative alli affari ultimi di Napoli*, "Copia della lettera di Sua Maestà l'Imperadore a Sua Maestà il Re di Napoli in data dei 22 ottobre 1785", f. 82r. "Dearest friend don Ferdinando I read with great sorrow through the courier, who sent me Richecourt, the detail of the prison where wicked men have put you, and how they dared to slander my sister. Happy she and I are that I love so dearly, that these atrocious slanders do not have any effect on you dear friend! You are right, wise and honest, and do not let the black lies overwhelm you, knowing the merit and virtue of your partner, and the trust and honest heart of the mother of your children. Believe me if you do not act as King, the independent master as you are, you will never have rest. I send in confidence some thoughts on this to the Queen, a few examples of firmness will be enough to put everything in order, but they are necessary and there goes your honor and reputation. The paragon of the two infamous queens Caroline will seriously compromise, putting you, who have given in all the cities of Italy trials of your spirit, your penetration, in parallel with that stupid and incapable King of Denmark. I am so angry that if I knew the author, I would make him pay dearly. Goodbye! Thank you dear friend! Once again, all the kindness that showed my sister, and recommending it wholeheartedly I embrace you and I will always be."

15. Ibid., f.63r. "Dearest brother-in-law I'm replying to your affectionate response to mine which Pignatelli delivered. I thank you many times over for the proper role that you decided to have in a business that is so interesting, and for the very loving expressions that you addressed to me about this hire. Until now you have known me well enough to be sure about my firmness in supporting a point so correct, and if until now I am content with myself to not to do any change, it had just been out of respect for my father, and not due to weakness, but now that I can't stand to wait anymore for the news that Pignatelli is going to give me so I can control myself. Thank God for this fresh air and the beautiful country that have been around for a year and helped me somewhat, but my wife doesn't desire what I do. May the Lord protect you and your lovely family for the consolation of the person who loves and respects you infinitely."

16. V. Cuoco, *Saggio storico sulla rivoluzione di Napoli*, 73.

17. Osterreichisches Staatsarchiv, *Sammelbände des Hausarchivs*, 10: Korrespondenz Großherzog Leopold von Toskana mit Kaiserin Maria Theresia und Maria Karoline von Neapel: Lettere e copie relative alli affari ultimi di Napoli seguiti dal mese di ottobre a tutto il dicembre 1785 relativi alli affari con la Spagna, Las Casas e la dimissione di Acton. From the letter of 12 October 1785 Maria Carolina to Peter Leopold: "Meanwhile

Acton has resisted every attack of the British, Austrians and all slander charges, death threats, which continuously received, to all the pains, hardships, pains, obstacles that were made, withstood it all, knowing they can remove, that the examination would prove his conduct and sacrificing his life for his lord, Acton could not resist these vile attacks in which I compromised and gave the 6th month resignation, the king wanted them to accept This man who is honest and dying in pain, because I'm attacked due to his kills him."

18. P. Colletta, *Storia del reame di Napoli*, 163; G. Oliva, Un Regno che è stato grande, la storia negata dei Borbone di Napoli e di Sicilia, 107.
19. Ibid., 73–74.
20. R. Ajello, "I filosofi e la regina. Il governo delle due Sicilie da Tanucci a Caracciolo (177–1786)", 399.
21. G. Galasso, *Il Regno di Napoli. Il Mezzogiorno borbonico e napoleonico*, 527–531; G. Astuto, "Dalle riforme alle rivoluzioni". Maria Carolina d'Asburgo: una regina "austriaca" nel Regno di Napoli e di Sicilia, 27–51.
22. See this issue highlighted by M. Mafrici, "Un'austriaca alla corte napoletana", in M. Mafrici (ed), *All'Ombra della Corte. Donne e potere nella Napoli borbonica (1734–1860)*, 57–58.
23. G. Galasso, *Il Regno di Napoli. Il Mezzogiorno borbonico e napoleonico*, 546–547.

CHAPTER 6

Between Praise and Condemnation: A Look at the Historical Debate

As was previously mentioned, Maria Carolina has been denigrated by many historians who have painted her as a monster, unscrupulous both with men and women. Ten years later at the storming of the Bastille, the Kingdom of Naples was overwhelmed by a revolution which led to the establishment of the Republic (23 January 1799).[1] It was during the Neapolitan revolutionary period that the first slanders began against the Royal Bourbons, especially towards Maria Carolina. This defamation was spread by the Republican press and circulated within European public opinion.

The official newspaper of the Neapolitan Republic was *Il Monitore napoletano* followed by *Veditore napoletano*, *Vero repubblicano*, *Giornale Estemporaneo*, and *Corriere di Napoli e Sicilia*.[2] Analysing all of these publications, we were able to note that the allegations against the Queen of Naples renewed, when not reproduced faithfully, some of the clichés observed in the French pamphlets against Marie Antoinette. Even across the Alps, there were charges present in Neapolitan newspapers, which corresponded to three categories respectively: character (Amazon, Messalina of the north), psychological (tribade, scoundrel, insane, and delusional) and, above all, political (the creator of a corrupt government, tyrant, usurper of the Royal treasury, despot, and deceiver of information).[3] After the revolutionary period, polemical attacks focused on the links between

© The Author(s) 2017
C. Recca, *The Diary of Queen Maria Carolina of Naples, 1781–1785*,
Queenship and Power, DOI 10.1007/978-3-319-31987-2_6

the sovereign's private life and her political life, where she was seen as a foreign tyrant, vile, wicked and corrupt.

The most interesting aspect of this political literature concerns the channels which allowed the circulation of these stereotypes from Paris to Naples. In this regard, it seems the main link between the birth of Republican France and the Neapolitan Republic of 1799 is represented by Giuseppe Gorani's *Mémoires secret set critiques des cours, des gouvernements et des mœurs des principaux états de l'Italie* which was published in Paris in 1793. The portrait which Gorani paints of the Queen outlines two distinct points: on the one hand, he emphasizes Maria Carolina's intention to establish Austrian hegemony in Naples,[4] while, on the other, the story he proposes regarding the personality of the sovereign is used to demonstrate that Gorani simply took the same charges traditionally addressed to Marie Antoinette, *sic et simpliciter*, and applied them to Maria Carolina.

The Milanese intellectual described the wife of Ferdinand IV like so "silly and pedantic, only able to repeat the thoughts of others like a parrot, master of intrigues and plots, cruel toward her husband, stepmother to the children, tyrant to the people, a woman who combines all the lubricity of a Messalina and the unorthodox tastes of a Sappho".[5]

Gorani's attacks on Maria Carolina were, first and foremost, on her origin as well as her ethical and personal character, and later, on the way she governed. The writer explicitly expressed his distaste for the Sovereign. He also sought to persuade readers to negatively judge the political and administrative decisions made by Maria Carolina. According to Gorani, they had caused a state of absolute degradation which affected every part of the Kingdom: from the Royal House, to the nobles and the common people.

Republican witnesses of the time such as Carlo Botta and Pietro Colletta, having biased ideological attitudes, were not magnanimous with Maria Carolina. They described her as a "being" equipped with exceptional ingenuity and strength of character but fell prey to unmentionable vices, like a relentless fury thirsting for blood and revenge for the death of her beloved sister, Marie Antoinette.[6] In truth, in several letters written at the time to her brothers, there emerges a deep resentment, revenge, an unyielding desire to confirm and strengthen the image of the Queen regnant, making it fearsome and stronger.[7] But the Queen knew also to pay attention to the needs of her subjects. In fact, in 16 letters sent to Antonio della Rosa, Director of the General Neapolitan Police in 1799, she recommended justice, moderation, forgiveness and order.[8]

And it amazes that the tragedy of 1799—which sees Maria Carolina always in the dock along with the Spanish—too many myths of a Naples launched to the path of progress were created. So that only the blindness of the ruling house would have impeded the success of the society's renewal.[9] But we have not to impress that the Queen, right in front of so many violent attacks, had also zealous defenders.[10] This is the case of the Prince of Canosa, who in 1831 responded to the words of Luigi Angeloni, who portraited Maria Carolina as "a dreadful woman, unjust, cruel and bloodthirsty".[11]

But among these defences of Bourbon one part especially deserves to be remembered; in the course of our research, we found a rare praise written by Carmine Lancellotti in 1829. The man, belonging to a family of recent nobility and who had certainly attended the court circles, harked to all allegations against Maria Carolina to refute them, though indirectly, one after the other, and offered a portrait of the Queen replicating with a tenacity worthy of attention all the ideological traits that held the image of the monarchy in the ancient regime.[12]

From Lancellotti's paper emerges a portrait of the Queen, which is very different from that handed down by historians over time.[13] In particular, Lancellotti describes her as a wonderful mother who cared about her children: she often went to visit them in their rooms to see if they needed anything. If any of them were ill, she stayed awake with them all night:

> Una madre premurosa, amorevole, interessata all'educazione dei propri figli, come ogni altra madre andava a visitarli durante il giorno, voleva essere informata dei loro bisogni e dei loro malanni. Scelse per i suoi figli i migliori educatori e direttori di spirito ai quali aveva ordinato di negare tutto ciò che i pargoli chiedevano sotto forma di comando e con ostinazione; [...] Inoltre si impegnava a educarli alla beneficenza e ad essere generosi, punendoli invece, quando mostravano questi difetti.[14]

The wife of Ferdinand IV was also an excellent educator. In order to better instruct her children, she had extensively researched many authors who had dealt with the issue of education. She did this not to ignore the multitude of theoretical constructions but to seize the best educational system in order to build one of her own: "entendre la répétition de Thérèse et Louise de géographie histoire je fus parfaitement contente de la premure".[15] The Queen entrusted her children to great spiritual advisers, placing religion at the foundation of their education.

Maria Carolina, despite her commitments to govern, never lost sight of her children and demanded a daily log of their conduct from their tutors, who were selected with a "Habsburg" rigour.[16] In addition, in order to accustom the princes and princesses to behaving appropriately during court ceremonies, plays were presented in the private theatre of the Royal apartments which other members of that milieu also attended.[17] In addition to being a good mother and a good educator, Maria Carolina, according to the testimony of Lancellotti, was also a generous woman who tried to teach her children to be magnanimous, punishing them severely if they were selfish[18]: "she could not breathe or live without helping others, her generosity grew in relation to the modesty of others and the needs which she saw in those who presented themselves before her".[19] There are many examples of such generosity: for the marriage of Princess Maria Cristina in Palermo, about 10,000 ducats were distributed in one day to poor girls so that they could marry. Many retreats and monasteries were maintained at her own expense. Those who benefited from her generosity included the poor, orphans, widows, officers and soldiers in need, as well as French emigrants.[20]

So far we are in the reassuring circle of a sovereign's image of the ancient regime, whose Christian virtue would be attested by the exemplary life conduct. However, the insistence with which Lancellotti suggests the role of mother, of sovereign, seems closely related to the great fertility of Maria Carolina, who between 1772 and 1793 had even 18 pregnancy, of which 16 completed. This trait certainly impressed the court circles, not only because fertility was a model of virtue, but also because it was not clear how, precisely for that reason, Maria Carolina was no longer only the wife of the King, but a regal figure in some ways even more important than Ferdinand. So, to Maria Carolina applied punctually the words of Adriana Cavarero, when she finds a way to remember that during the gestation of delivery, we can say that, to the letter, include in its body the continuity of his royal role. It is clear that the incorporation of the body politic in the natural body of the King is even more radicalized when it goes to coincide, in absolutely perfect shape, with motherhood, with a royal body that is fraught of an heir.[21]

Following this indication, it appears that Maria Carolina, almost always pregnant, had acquired in the eyes of the society court an exceptional dimension, which of course should lead to assume also functions of government. In the imagination of the time, in short, we could say that Maria Carolina was the constant representation of Queenship in her most complete expression. While on a parallel—and subordinate—side, the Queen's fecundity confirmed incontrovertibly her virtue. If we keep this in mind, the reasons of her rapid rise on the ground of the government practice find deeper reasons than those that lead to the carelessness and indolence of Ferdinand.

But the Queen was not frequently appreciated. While often maintaining a misogynistic position, historians have consistently recognized Maria Carolina's remarkable skills when it came to strategy and policy. In some cases, the slanderous criticisms were the result of a post-revolutionary vision still strongly influenced by Jacobin ideas and from the great trauma of 1799. There were other cases of prejudiced attitudes against the female gender. The wife of Ferdinand IV was pilloried by memoirists, historians and biographers, both in her time[22] and in the centuries to follow.[23]

Due to this common disparaging approach by French–Italian historiography,[24] those who mainly drew from Austrian sources painted a different, more positive picture of the Queen. Among them two stand out: Baron Joseph Alexander von Helfert[25] and Count Egon Caesar Corti, authors of two exemplary biographies which appeared, respectively, in 1878 and in 1950. In fact, starting with the clear intention of rehabilitating the image of the Queen, they have contributed greatly to Neapolitan history and have provided copious amounts of important evidence about the events of the late eighteenth century. Differing greatly from Baron Helfert's opinion were the interpretations expressed by Schipa, Simioni, Bouvier and Laffargue. But despite the accusations made by several parties, "whatever she may have been, she was better than how she was depicted"—as Bozzo claimed in 1879.[26]

The English historian and archivist John Cordy Jeaffreson published a peculiar biography about Maria Carolina and Lord Nelson, on which he denied the French thesis turning over the French assertions, reconstitutionalizing, through documents coming from the English archives, the Queen of Naples's political activity and the relations with the Anglo-Saxon world. In 1907, following Jeaffreson, Mary Charlton Bearne published in London another biography about Maria Carolina, for whom she used a part of Austrian unpublished documents kept in private archives, and whom she had the aim to highlight to the English-speaking audience who knew very little about a Queen so widely celebrated, so flattered and worshipped by many, and so cruelly slandered by others. Bearne's intent was in fact writing a biography totally different from the previous works rich of accusations written by those who for political reason were the bitterest enemies of the Queen.[27] So the English historiographic operation changed the general meaning of the Neapolitan Queen's commitment, with an interpenetration totally opposed to the French–Italian tradition.

While in Italy, few years later, Benedetto Croce still wrote about her, "How anyone could justify a woman who, over the misconduct and turpitude of private life, has been caught in a series of flagrant lies and violations of solemn commitments of honor and faith, I can not to understand. Then about the admiration for her energy and for her ingenuity, I confess that I find it quite obscure, at least as long as the energy and ingenuity, do not become one with the restlessness and gossip. A turbid spirit, she had neither loftiness of mind nor was she expedient and prudent; and she damaged herself as well as the others."[28]

According to the Neapolitan historian and journalist Amalia Bordiga Amadei, who had written a biography about Maria Carolina, she performed her sovereign duty to a very high degree which never wavered. But when managing power she committed many mistakes, especially regarding the means by which she used her power. Bordiga Amadei considers, however, that in an age of such strong philosophical and political upheavals it was not easy to make the right decision. In addition, the Sovereign governed alone. Nobody, apart from Acton, possessed the necessary qualities to moderate the dangerous impulses and to merit esteem.[29]

After a long time, an attentive historian such as Raffaele Ajello, who established the portrait of the Queen based primarily on diplomatic sources in Spain and Turin, reprised Croce's severe opinion which defended Maria Carolina as "a very ambitious woman, unprincipled, spoiled, arrogant, and like all the daughters of Maria Theresa, prone to corruption. She had every expression of self-righteousness and traditionalism and immediately breached the mix of libertinism and enlightenment that young people had practiced in those years."[30] In the words of Ajello, it was the return of many of the stereotypes of the eighteenth-century ancestry that the dramatic results of Republican events in Naples would help to exaggerate. This is a confirmation of how the reading of the patriotic part has informed not only the historiography of united Italy, but also that of more recent date, which ascribes to the season of the Enlightenment in Naples the advantage of a great cultural renewal destroyed by the will of a dynasty, backward and reactionary, whose Queen Maria Carolina's mediocrity would have the main responsibility.

A review of the unpublished manuscripts housed at the State Archives of Vienna, to which we have already referred, can further enrich the broad repertoire of sources used by historians up to now. From the exchange of letters between Maria Carolina and her siblings, one can, in fact, infer the peculiar opinions which have so far been almost completely neglected and to allow for an overturning of established accusations.[31]

The jagged segment of time referred to by the precious legacy of testimonies (Journal and letters) which we examined delivered an unexpected image of Maria Carolina. Finding herself holding the fate of the Kingdom of the Two Sicilies, the Sovereign implemented a decidedly pro-Habsburg policy and therefore not pleased of the Spanish monarchy, which had tried repeatedly to limit and contain the growing power of the wife of Ferdinand. But these efforts fell on deaf ears. Skilful in the art of flattery if circumstances required it, the Queen, however, was able to keep the severity, energy, tenacity and ruthlessness necessary to face the trials of history.

NOTES

1. On the Neapolitan revolutionary and Republican period cite the following work: A. De Francesco, *1799. Una storia d'Italia*, (Milano: Guerini e associati, 2004); A. Rao, *La Repubblica Napoletana del 1799*, (Roma: Tascabili Economici Newton, 1997), E. Chiosi, "Il regno di 1734-1799", in *Storia del Mezzogiorno*, vol. IV, (Roma:Edizione del Sole, 1986).

2. *Il monitore napoletano,* directed by Eleonora de Fonseca Pimentel was the most popular Republican newspaper, publishing 35 issues and three supplements from 2 February to 8 June; Il *Veditore Repubblicano* was edited by Gregorio Mattei that brought to the press four issues, from 21 March to 19 April 1799; Il *Vero Repubblicano* characterized by the publication of only two issues, 19 April to 10 May 1799 *Giornale Estemporaneo*, weekly, 9 issues spanning 31 March to 21 May 1799, il *Corriere di Napoli e Sicilia*, ten issues published, from 17 February to 27 April 1799, marked by the publication in two versions, French and Italian. In this regard, see, M. Battaglini, *Napoli 1799. I giornali giacobini*, (Roma: Libreria Alfredo Borzì, 1988).

3. According to the allegations mentioned, see the following numbers of newspapers: *Il monitore napoletano,* diretto da Eleonora de Fonseca Pimentel, N. 4, 12-02-1799; *Il monitore napoletano,* diretto da Eleonora de Fonseca Pimentel, N. 7, 26–021799, Corriere estemporaneo, 3-03-1799; *Vero Repubblicano*, N.1, "Repubblica Francese dal Quartier Generale di Napoli 25 Germile. Il Commissario del Governo Francese al Popolo Napoletano"; *Giornale   Estemporaneo*,   N.2,   6-04-1799;   *Giornale*

Estemporaneo, N.5, 27-04-1799; *Corriere di Napoli e Sicilia*, N.3, 24.02.1799; *Corriere di Napoli e Sicilia*, N.4, 3-03-1799.

4. G. Gorani, *Mémoires secret set critiques des cours, des gouvernements et des mœurs des principaux états de l'Italie*, (Paris : Buisson 1793), I, 253–254.

5. Ivi, pp. 255–256.

6. C. Botta, *Storia d'Italia dal 1789 al 1814*, Tomo I, Italia, 1824, 31, 308; P. Colletta, Storia del reame di Napoli, (Capolago: Tipografia elvetica, 1834), in A. Bravo (ed.), *Storia del reame di Napoli*, (Torino: UTET, 1975), 143.

7. Ivi, p. 159.

8. S.V. Bozzo, *Maria Carolina e le pubblicazioni di documenti a lei relative*, in «Archivio Storico Siciliano», nuova serie, anno IV, fasc. I-II, (Palermo: Stabilimento Tipografico Virzì, 1879), 3.

9. A. De Francesco, *1799. Una storia d'Italia*, 65–120.

10. J. A. von Helfert, *Konigin Carolina von Neapel und Sicilien im Kampfe gegen die franzosische Weltherrschaft (1790–1814)*, (Wien: Braumuller 1878); Egon Caesar Corti, Ich, eine Maria Theresias Tochter, 10.

11. A. Capece Minutolo, *In confutazione degli errori storici e politici, esposti da Luigi Angeloni contro Sua Maestà la defunta Maria Carolina di Napoli*, Marsiglia, 1830, 5.

12. See C. Lancellotti, *Elogio di Maria Carolina arciduchessa d'Austria, Regina del Regno delle Due Sicilie*, (Napoli: Tipografia Flautina, 1829), 34–35.

13. C. Lancellotti, *Elogio di Maria Carolina arciduchessa d'Austria, Regina del Regno delle Due Sicilie*, 34–35. "A caring mother, loving, concerned with the education of her children, who like every other mother visited them during the day, she wanted to be informed of their needs and their illnesses. She chose the best educators for her children and a spiritual advisor who had been ordered to deny everything that the kids were asking for if stubbornly demanded; [...] She also taught them to be beneficent and generous, punishing them instead when they exhibited defects such as selfishness and greed."

14. Ibid., 7–8, 10–11. This behavioural trait of Maria Carolina is well documented in the *diary*. See, for example, the entry of 9 December 1781.

15. See on this regards, the *diary* (may 1784).

16. The preceptors of the princes were personally chosen by the Queen. See in this regard in the *Journal*, the biographical notes on Charlotte Frendel, and the brothers Hauss.

17. In the daily annotations are numerous examples of the diligence with which the Queen personally took care of even the entertainment of their children. Here is an example: "Je dus entendre jouer le clavesin avec mes deux filles aînées", in *Journal, Le 25* (novembre 1781).

18. C. Lancellotti, *Elogio di Maria Carolina arciduchessa d'Austria, Regina del Regno delle Due Sicilie*, 11–12.
19. Lancellotti in his praise claims to be an eyewitness. Ibid., 15.
20. Ibid., 16.
21. A. Cavarero, *Corpo in figure. Filosofia politica della corporeità*, Milano: Feltrinelli, 1995, 165. On this issue see also M. Axton, *The Queen's two bodies: Drama and the Elizabethan Succession*, London: Royal Historical Society, 1977 and the still more recent K. Robertson, "The Body Natural of a Queen", in *Renaissance and Reformation/Renaissance et Réforme*, 26, n. 1, 1990, 25–36.
22. We remember, among others, Giuseppe Gorani, Francesco Lo Monaco, Vincenzo Cuoco, Carlo Botta, Pietro Colletta.
23. R. Palumbo, *Carteggio di Maria Carolina con Lady Hamilton. Documenti inediti*, (Napoli: Yovene, 1877); A. Gagniere, *La reine Marie Caroline de Naples, d'apres des documents nouveaux*, Paris : Ollendorf, 1886; M. D'Ayala, "I liberi Muratori di Napoli nel secolo XVIII" in *Archivio Storico per le Provincie Napoletane*, 22–23, 1897–1898; A. Bonnefons, *Une ennemie de la Révolution et de Napoleon. Marie Caroline reine des Deux-Sicilies (1768–1814)*,(Paris: Perrin, 1905).
24. According to the French biographies see by A. Gagnière, *La Reine Marie Caroline de Naples, d'après de documents nouveaux*, A. Bonnefons, *Une ennemie de la* Révolution *et de Napoléon. Marie Caroline reine de deux Siciles (1768–1814)*, Perrin, Paris 1905 ; M. Lacour-Gayet, *Marie Caroline, reine de Naples : 1752–1814. Une adversaire de Napoléon*, (Paris:Tallandier, 1990).
25. J. A. von Helfert, *Konigin Carolina von Neapel und Sicilien im Kampfe gegen die franzosische Weltherrschaft (1790–1814)*.
26. S.V. Bozzo, "Maria Carolina e le pubblicazioni di documenti a lei relative", in *Archivio Storico Siciliano*, a. V, fasc. I-II, 1879, 10.
27. M.C. Charlton Bearne. *A sister of Marie Antoinette the life-story, Queen of Naples*, VI.
28. B. Croce, *La Rivoluzione napoletana del 1799. Biografie, racconti, ricerche*, (Bari: Laterza, 1926), XIX.
29. A. Bordiga Amadei, *Maria Carolina d'Austria e il Regno delle due Sicilie*, 215.
30. R. Ajello, "I filosofi e la regina. Il governo delle due Sicilie da Tanucci a Caracciolo", 450–452.
31. Excerpts of this correspondence are contained in the volume biography of Maria Carolina published by Count Corti. See E. Caesar Corti, *Ich, eine Maria Theresias Tochter: ein Lebensbild der Königin Marie Karoline von Neapel.*

CONCLUSION

In rebuilding the image of a woman once so widely celebrated, so flattered and worshipped by many, so cruelly slandered by others, I have tried with this research to throw fresh light upon what is already known and recorded concerning her: her diary. In fact, what I have perceived about Maria Carolina is that amongst general readers, students and historians what little is known about her is generally bad. Some people had no idea who she was at all, many depicted her in a hazy manner as an upstart interloper who usurped the Bourbon throne, which was a travesty of the real Maria Carolina.

Maria Carolina was the fortunate daughter of the Empress-Queen Maria Theresa; in fact, most of her children were overshadowed by a fatality which doomed them either to an early death, a disappointed life, or else to sorrows, dangers and calamities, which, as well as the grandeur of their birth, separated her from ordinary women. A woman of whom the magnificent prosperity of the earlier part of her life and the perils and misfortunes which clouded her later years. Those only exceeded by the still more lofty position and more terrible fate of the favourite sister Marie Antoinette for whom she strained all her energy to save, and whose murder changed and embittered the rest of her days.

I have attempted to portray Maria Carolina in such a way to disprove the accusation brought by those who for political and nationalist reasons were her bitterest enemies. So I have tried to "cross-analyse" the various writers from her age until ours and the documents preserved in the Archives of Naples and Vienna—her personal diary and letters—with references and descriptions of that time, besides explanations and information as to the character, motives and credibility shown by past historiography. The material contained in the unpublished sources proves not only the improbability but the strong unreliability of many charges brought against the Queen. I have examined the surviving pages of the diary which I hope may interest those who are acquainted with the fuller histories of Maria Carolina's life and that of her still more illustrious mother given by the distinguished authors I have quoted in the previous pages.

The diary, as has been said, is made up of a series of short annotations. The sequence arranged in chronological order of institutional and informal commitments, seems to respect a pattern almost like a script. The mornings of the Queen appear to have been characterized by the same personal rites: family duties, institutional commitments, hearings, walks, while the evenings were divided between government commitments and moments of worldliness. However, Maria Carolina never reveals her thoughts, criticisms, doubts or personal interpretations about the talks or hearings, and she seems to insist with greater clarity of language on convivial situations. The Queen therefore opted to leave no trace on the canvas of her political commitment for sovereign prudence; it was as if the repeated absence of the King (the few times that King Ferdinand took part in the Council meeting were regularly recorded) made her assume, if possible, an even more reserved attitude in writing.

It is precisely these simple reminders of meetings of the Queen of Naples that testify to the years of her brilliant and eventful career. Her handwritten notes give us glimpses of the way various protagonists of the political and cultural life of the time stand out. In the daily hearings of the Sovereign, in fact, there was constantly present a welcome group of aristocrats who held positions at Court, as well as members of the political establishment, economists, diplomats, clergy, military, judges, doctors and artists. By reconstructing the biographical profiles of the characters who met in the salons of the Queen, we can differentiate the types of hearings. And it is this intersection between private and court life, including marital duties and obligations of government which is one of the most interesting aspects of the diary that follows here, from which we can derive—that is the hope—an interest in both the social and political history of the Kingdom of Naples in the difficult balance between reformist impulses and resistances of the ancien régime.

Consequently, the proof of the public role and political action carried out by the wife of Ferdinand IV was her effective participation in the administration of power, but also the ability to manoeuvre in the midst of political skirmishes. The meetings which are often cited in the pages of the diary confirm that it in the apartments of the Queen important decisions were made.

The correspondence with her two brothers, the Emperor Joseph II and Leopold, of which I have introduced here a few excerpts and which is the subject of my next monograph, confirms her strong position of power enriched by her personal thoughts and the certain presence of far-sighted and older brothers to whom she refers in moments of indecision and crisis, both familial and political. It is clear that the interest that Maria Carolina's brothers showed in the Neapolitan court and in the Queen herself, was the manifestation of their intent to retain the orbit of their family sphere in the Kingdom without feeling its weight. In fact, the exchange of letters between Maria Carolina and her family continued to maintain caring familial relationships and sought both confirmation of her belonging to the House of Habsburg, as well as alliances to continue the policy of marriage strategies undertaken by her mother, whose ultimate goal was to "allocate" the Habsburgs in the major European courts and protect the interests of the house of Austria on the European scene.

Only after the death of Maria Carolina were the people, who had played a major role in her life, vindicated. The Queen in fact could not live to witness the solemn day on which her spouse ascended the throne of Naples again, for which she had given her soul; she could not attend the royal weddings of her daughters, for which she had prepared the way; and she could not see her bitter enemy Bonaparte exiled on a faraway island.

If the French Revolution had not brought unrest and discord to the Kingdom, Maria Carolina would have remained in her enlightened intentions of advanced freedom of her early reign and would happily have guided her husband. And perhaps the result would have been a long series of happy years, instead of the pain and struggles that embittered the last 20 years of the Queen's life.

EDITORIAL CRITERIA

In the translation of the original diary of Maria Carolina preserved in the folder 96 of the Bourbon Archive at the State Archives of Naples we followed an extremely preservative criterion. The intent was to produce, in the truest possible way, the image of the manuscript. Thus we avoided standardized interventions, which would inevitably alter the linguistic and cultural features of the text. All this has led to the revival of the humble French known by the Queen, and of all the many spelling uncertainties present in the text. So we have been as faithful possible to the original version bearing in mind that Maria Carolina's French was by no means perfect and that the meaning is not always clear. Moreover sometimes we added some words to make the reading clearer.

The criteria has maintained the articulation of paragraphs in the manuscript. It was decided, however, to intervene in the text by changing the elements that would have affected the reading to a contemporary reader following the instructions provided in this regard by A. Grésillon, *Elements de critique génétique*, Gunter Narr, 2000, W. Speed Hill, E. M. Burns, *Text: an interdiscièplinary annual text of studies*, vol.11, The University of Michigan Press, 1998, so we have adopted the following editorial criteria:

The original manuscript contained, in the right-hand margin, personal memos concerning the health of Ferdinand IV and the children in the year 1872, which have been set here as boxed text.

© The Author(s) 2017

C. Recca, *The Diary of Queen Maria Carolina of Naples, 1781–1785*,
Queenship and Power, DOI 10.1007/978-3-319-31987-2

- Owing the insufficient punctuation of the daily notes we decided to insert a dash –.
  - Regarding the date reported each day in the diary we standardised the way in which the date is written.
  - When we were uncertain about the transcription of some word or even uncomprehensible words we used (...);
  - We used [...] to add words to the text;
  - As it regards the names of trhe persons received in audience by the Queen such as *lui Belmonte* or *elle San Marco* we translated in the following way: Lord Belmonte or Lady San Marco.
  - We maintained abbreviations (Act: per Acton e SB: per Sambuca) and we reproduced symbols which often Maria Carolina used in her notes. In the case of words or groups of letters Unable to read, we inserted square brackets [...] and we also chose to highlight the parts of text written in the margin, representing them in their original location

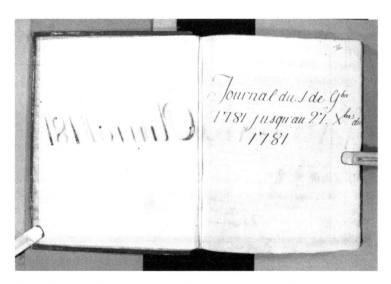

Archive of State of Naples, Archivio Borbone, 96, cc IIv-IIIr by gracious permission of "Ministero per i Beni e le Attività Culturali e del Turismo", authorization number 3/2016

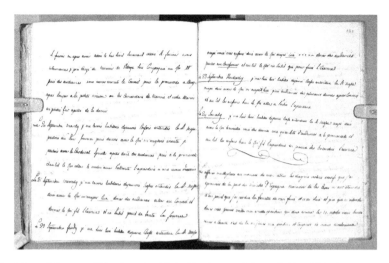

Archive of State of Naples, Archivio Borbone, 96, cc 252v-253r by gracious permission of "Ministero per i Beni e le Attività Culturali e del Turismo", authorization number 3/2016

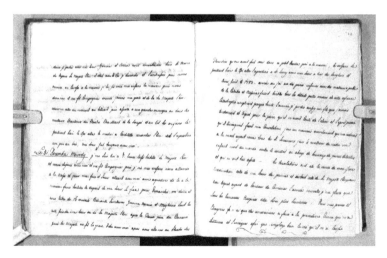

Archive of State of Naples, Archivio Borbone, 96, cc139v-140r by gracious permission of "Ministero per i Beni e le Attività Culturali e del Turismo", authorization number 3/2016

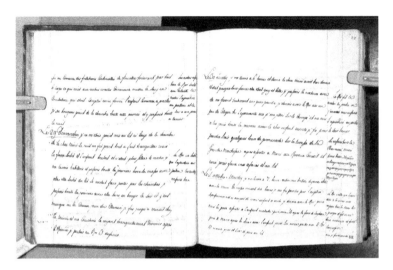

Archive of State of Naples, Archivio Borbone, 96, cc 21v 22r by gracious permission of "Ministero per i Beni e le Attività Culturali e del Turismo", authorization number 3/2016

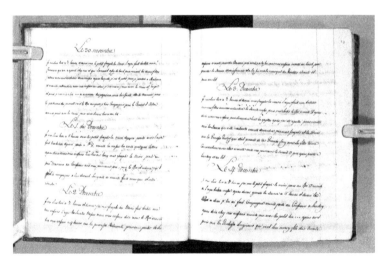

Archive of State of Naples, Archivio Borbone, 96, cc 9v-10r by gracious permission of "Ministero per i Beni e le Attività Culturali e del Turismo", authorization number 3/2016

We finally put in italics all the words written in Italian by the Queen as well as the titles of theatre works. In the apparatus was finally provided, where possible, a detailed indication of the numerous characters mentioned in the autograph, indicating briefly the role that covered at the court as other useful information and insights on the subject.

JOURNAL FROM 1 NOVEMBER OF 1781 UNTIL 27 DECEMBER OF 1781

This November 1, 1781
I got up at about 8 – saw my little ones – made my toilette – dressed – then talked with Ci. and M. – listened to two Masses – afterwards +++ read – afterwards saw my children – read the letters received in the mail – saw the King, who was returning from the pheasant farm where he had killed 24 pheasants – later dined with the King – then read – took care of little baby – of the toilette of Mimi,[1] – afterwards read – later conversed with the King – afterwards prayed the rosary – vespers of the dead – said my prayers – afterwards the Council of Finance – so wrote my diary and saw Count Lamberg [2] and went to bed – my health was the health of a pregnant woman – I was beginning to feel a toothache – in particular the last molar that was broken and I went to bed at ten o'clock.

On November 2
I spent a slightly restless night – as usual – I woke up at half past 7 – got up – saw my little boy – then combed my hair – dressed – listened to two Masses – saw my daughters – took care of the little boy – then read +++, and later – I saw people – had lunch with my children – down from there – took little Joseph[3] – Mimi – started to arrange my papers – afterwards I spoke with S. – then Princess Caramanico[4] came to speak to me – then Grimaldi[5] showed me his book – there I saw the children – afterwards said the office of the dead – then the King came back – there was the Council – later said the rosary – my prayers – for a moment Lamberg – at ten o clock to bed.

On November 3
I woke up at half past 7 – was with the King – had breakfast with my two eldest daughters – then combed my hair – put curlers – played with Joseph and Mimi – then talked with N. 2 – afterwards the Mass had lunch with my children – afterwards talked with Gatti[6] about my children – I showed him Joseph and little Marie[7] – then put in order my paper – saw the daughter of Marsico[8] – Butera's mother and the old Marsico – her daughter – who is going to become a nun in Regina Coeli – then I finished arranging papers – I wrote the post – and then played with Mimi – went

up with her and remained there until half past 8 – went down – said the rosary – my prayers – Lamberg for a while and went to sleep.

On November 4

I woke at 7 in the morning and I was informed both by the coachman and Gravina[9] – that the French courier had passed by Capua – it distressed me a lot – I finally learnt – around 10 o'clock – that thank God the Queen should give birth to a Dauphin which made me extremely happy – my child has been very agitated and I was forced to let him take different medicines – my toilette – the one of my daughters – it took a long time – at a quarter past eleven we went to the public hand-kissing – then the table – then I undressed and had lunch at my convenience – afterwards I was with the King + until half past three then I saw a while No. 1 – later the ambassador[10] returned and gave me details of the happy childbirth of my dear Queen[11] – Princess Ferolito[12] introduced to me the Roman Princess Santa Croce[13] – then I saw the French courier – a wet nurse – afterwards Donna Teresina Sangro[14] – then I got changed my dress – saw my children and went with my two daughters to the eternal opera San Carlo[15] that ended at half past eleven – where I spoke again to the King for half an hour, and then to bed – where a shiver run through me that I thought I had fever – but fortunately it dissipated during night so I slept from exaustion and discouragement.

On November 5

I got up at 8 o'clock – saw my son – attended to my little daughter playing with the wet nurse and and her child – then I combed my hair – scolded Theresa[16] and went to Mass – afterwards I read the letters of the day before – then I saw the ambassador – my children and a few men – I made a standing conversation – then – since all the kitchens were closed and the King brought his meal I had lunch at 2 o' clock – the King came back and wanted to eat – it was necessary to prepare [a meal] – afterwards at three o'clock he went out again, and I began to read +++ then I was with Mimi – Joseph – afterwards I did my payment accounts – Francis[17] and Mimi came to play in my room – my confessor came with great lamentation about a lost prebend in Vienna – there was a long conversation – then the Council of Sambuca[18] where it was decided to send Gravina to Paris to convey our congratulations and also to see there to choose someone for my son – afterwards – then the Council – I wrote my notes and went to sleep.

On November 6

I got up at 7 o'clock in the morning and went to my poor little one where he was given two enemas – then I got dressed and combed my hair and returned him – I took care of him – serving in his room until eleven o'clock when I listened to the Mass – then had lunch – went up and down the stairs to see 8 wet nurses – brought milk to the child and I did nothing but write and be with the child until 8 o'clock when I said my prayers – isomething and children up to 8 hours when I started to say the Rosary and went to sleep.

On November 7
I got up at 7 o'clock took care of Joseph who was a little better – then combed my hair – dressed washed entirely – was *gala dress* for the birth of the Dauphin[19] – then read +++ then took care of my children – heard Mass – had lunch with the King who came at half past twelve – then I conversed with the King – ☉[20] – then at [3] o'clock went out – I continued to take care of my little one thanks to God who was better then j.. p.... a d.. s h....:.... [21] a long time – then I took care of the little boy – for my three daughters – read a little – then the Council where Agostino[22] was made Country Comissioner – . In the evening afterwards the Council I said my prayers and then I talked with Lamberg about a library that I want to get someone to do it.

On November 8
I got up at seven o'clock and went to my little child – then curled my hair – had breakfast – saw my daughters – heard Mass, Migliano[23] talked to me a long time about the affair of her sister – then I spoke to No. 1 – then ambassador – knights – afterwards I had lunch with my children in Francis's room – afterwards lunch also Mimi came and I stayed some time with Francois and she – afterwards I went down in my room – I took care of little Joseph – then I saw Lady Melissano[24] who begged me to appoint her husband chamberlain – then I spoke to Lady Belmonte,[25] and Count Michele Pignatelli[26] to allocate aid for his embassy – then a poor Sicilian named Peroni[27] – then Princess – then with my children until the return of the King where I presided over the Council and after that wrote my diaries – my prayers and to bed.

On November 9
I got up at 8 o'clock – having had some collic I took an enema which had a positive effect – I spent a long time with my little Joseph – then Mimi – afterwards the two eldest girls – later the Mass – then I started to write – read some papers – afterwards I had lunch with the King and – ☉ – afterwards I played with Mimi – little Joseph – I spoke to N. 1. – then came Francis – three daughters and I passed the evening with them – afterwards there was the Council and the King granted to Fagiano[28] and Sacco[29] a pension of each of 300 ducats and to the first a promotion to the rank of captain – wrote again – later my diaries – prayers and went to sleep.

On November 10
I got up at 7 o'clock – I took care of Joseph – Mimi – my two eldest daughters – the governess came to report – and toilette – then I spoke to No. 2. – later with Gravina – then the Mass – then Migliano spoke to me – afterwards the French ambassador[30] of the odious Marseilles affair – then I had lunch with the children – there returning I played gith my little children – read some papers – wrote the post – at 6 o'clock Francis and Mimi came to my room – then Prince Hessenstein[31] who remained in company of my children to the music – where he came for it – and it lasted until half past 9 – where I undressed and went to bed.

On November 11
I got up at half past 7 – I saw Joseph – little Mimi – I had breakfast with Theresa – Louise,[32] then toilette – two Masses – afterwards I read +++ – then I exlusively took care of a little child after another – also having Francis in the arms – then I spoke to Duchess of Palme about her ugly affair – afterwards the ambassador brought me news of my sister who thank God was fine – and then I went to have dinner with my children – on my return I [sat] with small children and started to write – at 6 o'clock the King came back – I saw him a moment + – afterwards said the rosary – and I wrote – afterwards there was music and singing of the *Roi et du fermier* – and then I went to sleep.

On November 12
I got up at half past 7 – then I combed my hair my hair – I dressed *half gala* and I saw my children – then the Mass – from there I started to play the harpsichord – 8 – and at eleven I saw Prince Hesenstein with Altavilla,[33] [and] – I waited for the King who came back at 13 o'clock – I conversed with him – ☉ – I had lunch with him – then I took care of my children – I read +++ – I spoke to N 1. – Lord Belmonte[34] – Princess Santa Croce – to whom I introduced my children – then French courier – afterwards I read again – then the Council afterwards which I still took some notes – I saw Lamberg and went to bed

November 13
Afterwards a very restless and bad night – I got up at 8 o'clock and I went to my little boy – where I had a violent pain in one shoulder – one arm and one side – so violent and spasmodic that I stayed in bed – I took an enema and it almost lasted an hour – afterwards I made my toilette – my poor little Joseph had such pain and cried so much that I constantly was by him – at eleven o'clock I heard Mass – and then with the child until one o'clock – I had lunch with my children – then again with little

Joseph until half past 3 – I started writing – then I saw Maria Acejo in connection with a problem with her brother – then Princess of Jacy for her brother Calvaruso[35] governor in Messina – afterwards Don Nicolas Spluga[36] – returned from Portugal with the vessel showed me a painting of that country then my children – wrote – prayed – and French musical – *Roi et fermier* – and then to bed.

On November 14
I got up to 7 o'clock – toilette – took care of the little boy – played with Mimi – wrote – read – then Mass – waited for the King and had lunch with him – afterwards played with my children – read – put my documents in order – saw Vanvitelli Palmena[37] who begged me to help his son navy guard – Sossi for her husband the auditor[38] – then Gagliani[39] along time – afterwards a widow of a Spanish oficier – then Scalatta[40] – with my future child – afterwards wife and children of the judge Secondo[41] crying misery – afterwards I went to my children – the King returned + – I prayed – then a Council of two hours and a quarter where del Giudice[42] has had a post worth 8 ducats at the Secretary of justice – afterwards to bed.

On November 15
Woke up at 7 o'clock – the little child – then Mimi – an entire toilette – then heard Mass – heard the King playing the lyre – then I conversed with him – ⊙ – then was present to his lunch – afterwards saw Miglianowho reminded me of his sister – and Gravina – then Ambassador – afternoonwith my children and then wrote – saw my little children – then No. 1 – afterwards Duchess Giordano[43]who wants Vespoli[44] superintendent – talked a long and very well about Rome with the benedectin father Cordua[45] – then with my children – the King came back – afterwards his milk – the Council – and wrote – prayed – saw Lamberg for a moment and went to bed.

On November 16
I woke up at 7 0'clock – got up – went to see little Joseph who thank God had a good night – I combed my hair my hair – saw the governess – little Mimi – heard Mass – I did some account – I had lunch with the King – then I was with my children – afterwards-dinner I read ++, and then Tarsia spoke[46] to me – afterwards Gaetano Ventimiglia[47] for having given a commendam to dom Inocenzio Pignatelli[48] – then I did my accounts – played with my little children – was present with the King who took his milk to taste – then Acton[49] 's Council – afterwards wrote – prayed and afterwards went to bed.

On November 17
I got up at 7 o' clock – I took care of my little Joseph – Mimi – washed –
then I spoke with No. 2. – then 8 – afterwards Mass – spoke to Gravina
about his jouney – then had lunch with my children – afterwards I was
present to the painting of a portrait of Mimi that was already started –
then I wrote – then I had the hearings – the Bishop of Aversa[50] for justice – Turito[51] for having his son nominated judge – […] to ask leave – and
father Mariano[52] for giving me the report of his [journey] – Then I saw
my little children – afterwards wrote my post – saw the King on his return
+ who took the milk – then continued to write my post – saw my eldest
daughters – afterwards listened to the music of the deserter in my apartments – then bed at ten o'clock.

November 18
I got up at half past seven – took care of my little children – combed my
hair – dressed – spoke with governess[53] – heard two Masses – arranged
some papers – had lunch with King + – and read – [rewrote] letters of two
ordinaries – played with my children – spoke to the eldest daughter – saw
[and] swaddled the little one – gave hearing to Salandra[54] and Pignatelli –
then the King returned – took his snack – wrote – arranged my diaries –
marked my letters – prayed – saw my children – Lamberg and to bed.

On the 19th
I got up at half past 7 – saw little Joseph – played with Mimi – spoke to the
governess – saw my eldest daughters – I washed – went to Mass – afterwards in my cabinets where the King painted – there I wrote until midday
when I returned + – and had lunch with the King – ⊙ – afterwards read –
took care of my two little children – wrote and kept the King company,
who did not got out – at five o' clock I went with him to listen the *la
musique du déserteur* – at 6. o'clock I returned – saw Francis – my daughters and let them dance – I presided over the Council – and – feeling for
some days swolen breast and oppression – I bled for Santolillo[55] with four
ounces of blood – I remained still slightly to calm down and then to bed –
I took my soup and performed the unction of pregnancy water.

The November 20
I got up at half past 7 afterwards a fairly quiet night – and then went to
see little Joseph – played with Mimi – a baby tooth, incisor bottom was
removed from Theresa – who had a root more much longer than the
tooth – then I had breakfast with her – made my toilette – heard Mass –
wrote in the cabinet where the King painted – took care of Francis – my
two daughters – had lunch with the King – read – stayed with Mimi –

wrote my post – diary – saw little Joseph who cried – and then prayed and afterwards made *la musique du déserteur* – afterwards to bed.

On the 21st

I got up at half past 7 – saw my little one cry aloud because of a tooth irritation – I washed going in and out from his room – afterwards came the little Mimi – the two eldest daughters – the governess – I went to Mass – afterwards I always took care of my littleone who shouted jumped and I was worried – then I drove Mimi to the pool hall – I went with her and the King upstairs in the little child's room to see Januarius[56] who makes compassion ruined by a veneral disease – and I decided with sorrow that he should be given syrup of smilax aspera – finally we went down – I had lunch with the King – ⊙ – then I took care of little Joseph who was better – then I amused myself with Mimi to scold Theresa – afterwards wrote diary – tales – prayed – there was the Council where we discussed the possibility that the abbey of Acquaviva might give the pension to one of our children – afterwards the Council – my children were still with me – I read, and then went to sleep

On the 22nd

I got up at 8 o'clock – went to see little Joseph – then Mimi – the governess – my eldest daughters – afterwards Mass – arranged some papers and took care of the children – and so I spent the morning – I had lunch with the King – and then I read the letters – I began to do accounts – Tarsia told me – then No. 1. – then Princess Jacy introduced to me Duchess Montalba[57] – afterwards came donna Teresina told me about her issues – then King returned – who took milk – I played with Mimi – Joseph – then the Finance Council – afterwards I was with my children – where there was also Francis until 9 o'clock – I prayed and to bed.

On the 23rd

I got up at half past 7 – I tock care of little Joseph – had breakfast – played with Mimi – spoke with governess – combed my hair – washed – saw the two eldest daughters – read +++ – scolded Louise – heard Mass – put some papers in order – had lunch with the King – and read – later then attended to see Mimi painted – playing with Joseph – Mimi – then wrote – read – in the evening the King came and took his snack – then the Council of Acton – afterwards saw Prince Hessenstein – with my children – half past 8 saw Lamberg and went to bed.

On the 24th

Woke up at 8 o'clock in the morining – saw Joseph – little Mimi – made great toileitte for the birthday of J: D: – then Mass – read – afterwards went out for a moment to see the world of Caserta – then at eleven o'clock had lunch with King – read and went out and I saw my three eldest children – spoke to Gravina about his journey and future commission – afterwards 8 – and then played with little Joseph – Mimi – saw some goods – afterwards Lamberg – wrote the post – and then saw Prince Hessenstein – Gravina and Migliano – afterwards the King came and drank his milk – ☉ – then continued to write – afterwards great music where Hesenstein participated.

On the 25th

I got up at half past 7 – had breakfast with my two eldest daughters – that during my toilette – they wanted to speak to me about their spiritual reading – saw little Joseph who was healthy – though he had not slept all the night – then governess – finally my toilette – afterwards heard two Masses – 8 – and saw the people who were going hunting with the King – afterwards read +++ – then came Francis from his walk and I went and returned from the little one – when all of a sudden I was informed that he had a paroxsym which lasted about ten minutes – was certain it was over – that Mimi fell down and she had a terible blow on the front – very worried I went to have lunch with my two eldest daughters and I always stayed with Joseph – at three o'clock with my two eldest daughters I heard harpsichord being played – afterwards I saw Lady Belmonte who came to tell me her troubles – afterwards I heard singing Palmina Vantitelli – then by my littleone – my girls went in their rooms – then the King came – I attended him during his milk, he detailed me his hunting plans for the Russians – afterwards to the poor little one's room, who fell asleep at half past 7 – afterwards wrote my diary – read – wrote my letters of the post.

On the 26th

We had a big storm – during the night at half past one I went to see my little Joseph and I found him asleep – then I woke up at 7 o'clock – the littleone – Mimi – had breakfast – the governess – my daughters – the toilette – then Mass – afterwards theKing could not go out because of the bad weather – just read – saw Francis – my two eldest daughters kept me company while I had lunch with the King – and then read + – then due to my tiredness I slept one hour – I stayed the rest of the time with little Joseph and Mimi – I scolded my two eldest daughters – afterwards read +++ – then it Sambuca[58] – the King who remained nCounty an hour – the little child – the Council – then my little girl – my diaries – a moment with Lamberg – then I went to sleep.

27. November

I got up at half past 7 – I saw little Joseph – Mimi – the governess my two daughters – toilette – I heard Mass – in the morning having had a cruel headache I did not write – and I went in and out where while the King painted – played with my small children – saw Francis – then had lunch with the King – then read – afterwards attending where the King painted – ⊙ – at a half past five I started to write until half past 8 when children danced – I attended it and gave an enema to Mimi – later when the children left – the King sung and we sung the music of the French deserter – afterwards I went to sleep.

On November 28

I got up at half past 7 – saw little Joseph – Mimi – the governess – my two firstborn – listened to two Masses – toilette – saw the King while painted – and so I spent the whole morning – I dined with the King – then stayed with little ones – then I read – I spoke with N °. 1 – N °. 3 – then my children – at 6 o'clock, the Council of Carlo de Marco[59] until 8 o'clock – later I prepared myself for confession – I went to confession – I said my prayers I went to bed.

The always fatal and unhappy 29.[60]

I got up at 6 in the morning – I dressed – reconciled and went to the Holy Table to offer my unworthy prayers for the most excellent and adorable of mothers – then I had breakfast – saw Joseph – Mimi – the governess – heard three Masses – went to see Januarius – and then had lunch with my two eldest daughters with whom I can talk and I did so until 4 o'clock – then read – wrote – wrote my diaries – saw the little ones – afterwards the Council – prayed – at quarter past 8 I said the office of the dead with all my people – Theresa and all the priests of the chapel – in order to understand the cruel time when the best mother died – afterwards this cruel and painful duty I went to bed.

On the 30th November

I got up to 7 o'clock – for little Joseph – Mimi – the governess – made toilette – saw Genarino[61] who was brought to my room and he enjoyed enough of everything – then the two girls came – I went with them to hear two Masses afterwards that I saw the little boy – then I spoke to Migliano afterwards I went to have lunch with my children – on return I played with Mimi and Joseph, and then I read + ++ – put my papers in order – saw Lord Spiriti[62] – Lady Mancini[63] – later the little child – wrote diaries – then came the King whom I kept company – and the Council of Acton – then prayed with Mimi – played and good time to bed.

On 1 December
I got up at 8in the morning – saw little Joseph – Mimi – had breakfast with the governess – made my toilette – had breakfast – spoke to No. 2 – then Mass – read – wrote some letters – then had lunch with my children – read a long time – saw Joseph – Mimi – spoke to Father Mariano – to the confessor – wrote my diaries – prayed, and the King came back – I kept him company during his lunch – later played music and then went to bed.
On December 2
I got up at 7 o'clock – I saw Joseph – Mimi – made toilette – saw my children – the governess – Holy Masses – saw my children again – had lunch with the King – then – read – my children – at 4 o'clock saw Princess Belmonte to tell me about her [problems] – then played harpsichord – prayed – at the end wrote – for my children – went up to scold Theresa and see Januarius and – at the end – saw *la musique du déserteur* – sung and then to bed.
On December 3
I got up at half past 7 – saw Joseph – Mary – the governess – made my toilette – saw my eldest daughters – heard Mass – then saw the King going out – then 8 – afterwards had lunch with my children – and went downstairs – read the gazette – afterwards I was called to go upstairs to see Theresa who was nasty – then went down – played with Joseph and Mimi – saw Princess Daskof[64] who she was introduced to me by Princess Jacy with her daughter – I conversed with them – then wrote my diaries – the Council – ⊙ – prayed – afterwards talked with Lamberg and to bed.
On December 4
I got up at 8 in the morning – I saw little Joseph – Mimi – spoke to the King – ⊙ – then the governess – toilette – Mass afterwards having seen Theresa scolded – at half past 11 the King had lunch – I kept him company – I stayed with him – later spoke to the confessor – then had lunch with Lamberg – my children later played with the small read +++ afterwards wrote – then saw Duchess Sirignano[65] who wants her husband – son of fiscal [lawyer] Caraveda[66] judge and the wife and the daughter of Secondo who want their husband to be counsellors – later saw N °. 1 – then wrote the diary – the post until half past 8 – was present while the King – had milk with coffee – afterwards attended the deserter Music that I could not sing because of goiter – at half past two to bed.
On December 5
I got up at 8 in the morning – saw Joseph – Mimi – spoke to the governess – toilette – Mass – afterwards 8 – then brought little Joseph in

all the rooms – afterwards Lady Cassano[67] and Altavilla – spoke to Lord Belmonte – had lunch with my children – on return saw my little children – read +++ – then saw Freda[68] – then the wife and daughter of Secondo – afterwards the wife of colonel Leon[69] with their daughter – afterwards my young and old children – then the Council – prayed – saw Lamberg and to bed.

On December 6

I got up at 8 o'clock – went to little Joseph's room – Mimi – then came to my room – had breakfast – made toilette – involved to see and to show the kit linen and lace for a value of 17 thousand ducats – then saw Masses – saw Mimi while she was painted – attended to her lunch with Francis – Louise – Gatti – afterwards lunch with the King – read – unrolled a scroll – afterwards I went because I was called from Theresa's room who was nasty – I stayed there nCounty two hours when I went down – then I saw the mother of the resident of Venice and I introduce Louise – Francis – Mimi and little Joseph to her – afterwards – I saw Princess Villa[70] – the wife of Patrizio[71] – afterwards the King returned – there was Council – I wrote my diaries – made payements and [saw] Lamberg and to bed

On December 7,

I got up at half past 7 – saw little Joseph – Mimi – the governess – had breakfast – saw my two daughters – heard Holy Mass – 8 – afterwards went out with Altavilla[72] – Corleto[73] – Priore[74] – Diomede[75] – Mimi with her lady – I went to the channel by one horse carriage wrhere I found the King – then came Louise – I saw fishing – then the King returned – had lunch with the King – saw little Joseph – 8 – then the ambassador of France – one hour and a half – then Centola,[76] Celano,[77] a widow with her daughter who wants to be a lady in waiting, a widow Lafatta – the [project] for the plan where to place the archive – afterwards the King came back–then the Council – wrote my diaries – afterwards prayed – Lamberg and to bed.

On December 8

I got up at 7 o'clock – I saw little Joseph – Mimi – the governess – my two eldest daughters – No. 2 – heard two Masses – then saw some knights – afterwards had lunch with my three girls and the boys – then went down – 8 – afterwards wrote – then talked with Gravina about his journey and commission – afterwards with Father Mariano – then came the King and – afterwards I wrote my post – my diaries – saw my children meanwhile attended the music that the King and the others sung the [deserter] afterwards that to bed.

December 9th

In the night I got up half an hour to go to see my little one who was awake – then I got up at 7 o'clock – saw little Joseph – Mimi – made toilette – saw my eldest daughters – the governess – heard two Masses – 8 – afterwards saw the kights of Cascile – then had lunch with Theresa and Francis – afterwards went to scold Louise who had been very nasty – then 8 – then took care of little Joseph – stayed a long time with the young Salandra[78] who came to take leave of me – afterwards the King returned – I wrote my diary about my business – spoke with the King – ⊙ – then I made the children come – and I stayed with them until half past eight – where I went to hear the rehearsal song of the French music and afterwards to bed.

December 10

I got up at 7 o'clock and went to little Joseph – to Mimi – the governess came – made toilette – saw my eldest daughters – read +++ – heard Mass – arranged some papers – had lunch with all my children – that is the four oldest children – and then I let them play – jump – until four o'clock – afterwards they went to do their homework – I saw Princess Caramanico who prayed for the Mataloni[79] – and N ° 1 – then wrote my diaries-worked on my affairs – afterwards saw my children – the King returned happy from his hunting – he presided over the Council of Sambuca and then we went to sleep.

December 11th

I got up at half past 7 – saw little Joseph – Mimi – the governess – made toilette – saw my eldest daughters – started to write letters – heard Mass – had lunch with the King – afterwards talked with him – ⊙ – then saw my children – wrote – afterwards I had hearings – the wife of judge Secondo and her daughter – then the wife and daughter of a cavalry captain – a widow of a lieutenant colonel – then I saw Princess Potoski[80] with Marchioness Sambuca – to whom I showed my children – and Count Lamberg – Marquis Sambuca – Prince Stigliano[81] – Count Cereto[82] – Finally the King returned – I kept him company – then continued to write letters – afterwards made Francis and Mimi dance – then attended a rehearsal of *la musique du déserteur* – then went to sleep.

On December 12th

I got up at 7 o'clock – saw little Joseph – Mimi – the governess – dressed – then 8 – afterwards scolded Theresa – then Mass – arranged some papers – saw Valignari[83] to ask for the place in the Farnese State – and Cantelli[84] for a pension – then I saw gentlemen who serve in Caserta – I went to have lunch with Teresa – Louise and Francis – then I went down to see Joseph – played with Mimi – spoked to Lusciano[85] – saw the jewels of my children, then talked with Ayiello[86] – to the widow of counsellor Caraciolo,[87] Monsignor Spinelli[88] – to a French person – then No. 3 – and the King returned – we presided over the Council of de Marco – afterwards that I wrote my diary – prayed – saw Lamberg and to bed.

On December 13th

I got up an hour afterwards midnight and stayed up until half past 4 because of the illness of unhappy little Joseph who did not cry – but shouted – this lasted until half past 4, then came back I went to sleep – at 8 o'clock I woke up – saw little Joseph – the governess – my eldest daughters – Mass – wrote – put some papers in order – talked with No. 3 – No. 1 then – then had lunch alone – and then played with Mimi – Joseph – read +++ – saw an engraved book, then talked with confessor – afterwards with Dentici[89] – with Pignatelli the [director] – then the King returned – I wrote suggestions – wrote my diaries and saw Lamberg for a moment and went to bed.

On December 14th

I got up at half past 7 – saw little Joseph – Mimi – and then – the governess – my eldest two daughters – then 8 – afterwards Holy Mass – and then saw Prince Hessenstein with Lady Altavilla[90] – Corleto and Migliano – at one o'clock I went to have lunch with my children – then went down – read several papers – then read +++ – afterwards wrote my diaries – saw my children – afterwards received Hessenstein – Vasto[91] – Marsico and Corleto – I sent Marsico and Vasto to Naples to see their wives and sister – then the King came back – I was with him + afterwards King played to read it and I saw Hessenstein again – Gravina – Lamberg until I went to bed.

On December 15th

I got up at 7 o'clock – saw little Joseph and went upstairs to Theresa's room – a lower tooth was removed from her – and I had breakfast with her – Louise and Mimi – and then I was to see Francis – Januarius – I went down – made my toilette – heard Mass with Francis – then I started to write a little – I had lunch with the children – then 8 – afterwards Lord Belmonte wanted to speak to me – then Tarsia – afterwards King came back – I gave two hearings to Residents of Venice – then the King came + – afterwards I made up – continued to write the diaries until 6 o'clock I went to the theatre – saw the comedy at the Florentiness Theatre[92] which bored me to death – this lasted until 9 o'clock – there was Gravina –

Migliano – Montalto[93] – Hoyos[94] and Marchioness Altavilla with me – in the evening I went to bed.

On December 16th

I got up at 7 o'clock – saw little Joseph – Mimi – then made toilette – 8. – afterwards saw the child again – had a long and unpleasant conversation with the governess – then two Masses – then read my post – afterwards had lunch with my three daughters and son – then down – read +++ – afterwards the children – saw Mr. Wedel[95] who came to thank for having had his wife baptized – then saw Tripalda,[96] my little children – afterwards King returned – I talked with Bean who announced the successful childbirth of poor Princess Marsico – when the King returned I heard that afterwards a quarter hour she had suddenly died this made me very sad – then King came to me + – afterwards ⊙ – then I wrote – saw my children – an engraved book – very sad – to bed.

The always painful 17th.[97]

I got up in the morning at half past 7 – saw little Joseph – made toilette – saw with with a sensitive tenderness my beloved Mimi – living portrait – of the ever dear and loved and for me lost – Charles – then spoke to the governess – saw my eldest girls – put my papers in order – heard Mass – played with Joseph when a pain in the kidneys and in thighs got me that forced me to go to bed and I was rubbed with hot sheets – then had lunch with the King in the presence of daughters – then read +++ – then arranged papers – at half past three I talked with No. 1 – with Princess Daskof with her daughter to whom I introduced my children – then the King came back his milk – then the Council was over – then wrote my diaries – saw my daughters and at nine o'clock to bed.

On December 18,

I got up at half past – saw little Joseph – beloved Mimi – the governess made toilette – heard Holy Mass – saw my two eldest – then 8. – afterwards I saw painter Füger[98] and Lamberg for some painting – had lunch with three daughters and son – and then down – started to see Joseph – I conversed with my confessor – then went and read ++ + – afterwards wrote eleven letters – the notes – in the mean time the King returned from hunting – feeling the need of eating – I took milk with coffeee – continued to write until nine o'clock – interrupted by Mimi and the other daughters – at nine o'clock from my writing desk to my toilette – undressed and went to bed.

December 19th

I got up at half past 7 – then saw Joseph – made toilette – and 8 – afterwards saw Mimi – the governess – afterwards arranged business –

Mass – then spoke to Gravina – Count Micheli Pignatelli – had lunch with my two eldest daughters and Francis – then down – saw beloved Mimi – Joseph – read +++ – then arranged some memoirs – afterwards unpacked papers to form an archive – then saw the secretary of the Sicilian Junta[99] – then Princess Belmonte – afterwards Marchioness de Sambuca – then the King came back – then the Council – saw Lamberg for a moment and to bed.

December 20,
I got up at half past 7 – saw little Joseph – Mimi at breakfast – made toilette – spoke to the governess – saw my two eldest daughters – scolded Theresa – heardthe Holy Mass – saw Father Mariano – worked on my future archive – to decipher the papers – had lunch with Louise and Francis – and 8 – then donna Teresina Sangro who came to talk with me for her brothers – afterwards San Marco[100] – then the King came back – presided over the Council – then played with Mimi – made my accounts – went upstairs with Mimi – I saw her having dinner and sleeping – afterwards down – wrote my diary – accounts – a moment Lamberg time and to bed.

On December 21
I got up at half past 7 – saw little Joseph – Mimi – the governess – my two eldest daughters – made toilette – 8 – and Mass – then had lunch with my two daughters and son – afterwards lunch played with Mimi and Joseph – read +++ – then spoke to Sambuca – afterwards Roccella[101] for Colege – to Malaspina[102] for the ministry – to the wife and beautiful daughter of Marquis D'Anna[103] – to Vespoli to thank – then played with the children – presided over the Council and played until nine o'clock in the evening with Mimi and Francis – went upstairs to see Mimi sleeping and then stayed with the other until the evening.

On December 22,
I got up at half past 7 – saw the governess – little Joseph – Mimi – and then made toilette – heard Holy Mass – saw my two eldest daughters – saw the wise woman – No. 2 – then Lamberg with the painter to see saw the paintings of the rooms – had lunch with my children – 8 – then saw the confessor – spoke with him – afterwards saw Calvaruso – a woman known as French – afterwards wrote my post – and then waited for the King – spoke with him – Acton – then saw Lamberg for a moment and to bed.

On December 23
I got up in the morning at 8 o'clock – saw little Joseph – Mimi – the governess – 8 – heard my two Masses – then spoke to Acton – – – +

A strong inflammation in the right eye impeded me to write and record the days 23-24-25-26-until [27].

December 27th
I got up at 8 o'clock – saw little Joseph – Marie – saw the governess – heard Masses – saw Carlo de Marco – Sambuca – had lunch with my children – afterwards playing with the little ones – saw Diego Naselli,[104] Acton, a poor woman – and the children – wrote.

JOURNAL FROM 10 SEPTEMBER 1782 UNTIL THE END OF DECEMBER 1782

On September 1782
On Tuesday the 10th I left Naples in a carriage with all my dear children to go to Portici – fortunately we happily arrived at half past six – the King returned immediately after us – afterwards having a little arranged the children – we went to the blessing – the rest of the evening was spent in arranging my business papers – in calming down the children – saw Count Lamberg for a moment and at ten o'clock to bed.

The King went to Volla for quails [hunting].

On Wednesday the 11th morning I got up at 7 o'clock – toilette – had breakfast – visited all children – arranged my affairs – read – wrote – Holy Mass – so the morning passed – I had lunch with my children and spent afternoon with them – at three o'clock I started reading and devoted myself[105] – at five o'clock SB[106] came – spoke about his affairs – and Duchess of Tursis[107] talked with me about her affairs for a permission to marry the second daughter outside of Milan – from there I went for a walk with my daughters to the wood above Caravita[108] and from there home – then I went to receive a blessing and afterwards to the Council of Carlo Marco,then saw for a moment Lamberg and at ten o'clock undressed – had dinner and put to bed.

Thanks to God all in good health – The King was S. Leonardo – he went there at midday and returned at 7 o'clock from the quails hunting.

On the 12th Thursday I got up at 6 o'clock – saw my children – played with them – had breakfast – powdered my face – curled my hair – dressed,

Holy Mass – and then talked to the King – ☉ – then dressed – after dinner – unpacked a box of new German books – which kept me busy until four o'clock – read all my post letters – recorded them – afterwards Cicio Pignatelli[109] spoke to me for a moment – then A. [110] – afterwards I took care of my children until the time of the rosary and of the blessing – then the Finance Council – changed dress to be warmer [when I went] to the woods with the King – Theresa to see hunting sparrows – we took those 1400 – and then we came back home – we undressed – dinner and bedtime.

> All healthy thanks to God. The King went hunting quail in Volla at one o'clock and returned at six.

On the 13th Friday I got up at 6 o'clock – saw my little children – had breakfast – combed my hair – dressed – then Holy Mass – afterwards wrote my post – talked to confessor; at eleven o'clock Kaufmann[111] came to paint me for an hour – then I had lunch with the King – in the afternoon during his light sleep I started to read and afterwards to write – then I spoke to SB – then I went out to walkin low wood – I was in one horse carriage with Theresa – Mimi and theirs ladies and made a tour around Granatelle[112] as far as the house of Ricia[113] – then I came back home – I went to say the rosary and afterwards to the Council – then I saw Count Lamberg – I undressed – had dinner and went to bed

> The King spent the morning trawling at the sea – Thanks to God all in good health, at three o'clock the King went out to hunt in the mountains and came back at half past 6.

On the 14th Saturday I got up at 8 o'clock – afterwards having had bad hips during the night – toilette – had breakfast – my children – this almost took the morning – the arrival of the good Bohminin[114] – went to see Louise – heard Holy Mass and took little Joseph to be painted – then lunch – then Mimi fell down – I remained a bit 'to console her – and afterwards I started to read – then to write – afterwards hearing an A. Mess. – then Louise's room who is not well – afterwards this the rosary and then with my children until the time to go to bed.

The King purged as a precaution – because he wanted to start his tea – he came out afternoonnnn to exercise the volunteers of the navy. Louise had a little fluxional fever – the rest of the family are fine.

On the 15th Sunday I got up at 7 o'clock – made toilette – saw my children – heard two Masses – then attended to the lunch of the King and to his departure for hunting – read my post letters – afterwards saw a moment Tarsia – then had lunch with my children – then played with Mimi on the porcelain factory and Theresa with her books – afterwards arranged my papers – talked with Gravina – SB – with Cicio Pignatelli – saw my children – dressed and went to the blessing of St.Antony – accompanied by lady Corleto Montalto Spinnelli and my Theresa – returning I found the King at home – took the second blessing – I remained and conversed with him – ⊙ and afterwards I made my business – saw my children sleep and at ten o'clock I went to bed.

All healthy – the King went at 12 o'clock to hunt quails and came back at 7 o'clock.

On Monday the 16th I got up at 7 o'clock – toilette – Mass – saw my children – wrote a little – Kaufmann came – I saw her painting Louise – then I had lunch with my children – having previously been through the Palace with the Grand Master[115] and Macedonio[116] to decide the apartment for my children among the men – then I spent the after lunch with my children, read – wrote – and then talked with Cicio Pignatelli on forages – clothing soldiers – afterwards saw San Marco a while – I ride for a walk in the woods at the top – from there I returned – went to say the rosary – saw the King after the unexpected death of Goysueta[117] – presided over the Council and went to sleep.

Thanks to God all in good health – the King went at 8 o'clock to Volla and then to St. Leonardo and did not return until the evening.

On Tuesday the 17th I got up at 7 o'clock – toilette – Mass – saw my children – wrote – and then the King came with Acton to talk about an hour – then I conversed with him – ⊙ – afterwards lunch – then read – wrote – then played with my beloved Mimi – finished writing the post, afterwards saw Princess of Jacy to pray for me Pietra Persia – then SB – afterwards Sangro to beg me for the affair of Noya – then to say the rosary – then took care of my children – and read and wrote until the dinner time and to bed.

All fine. The King for fatigue of the previous day and a slight headache went out just a little to the craggy mountain afternoon

On Tuesday (sic) the 18th I got up at 7 o'clock – dressed – combed my hair – played with the children – heard Holy Mass – then started to write afterwards I saw a painting and enjoyed myself with my children until 1 o'clock – when I had lunch with my Theresa – then played with Mimi – afterwards attended to the King's table – after that read – wrote – stayed my children – then I went to the top of woods to the craggy mountain to pick the King up – and we went together in town – by dray – I gave hearing to Surchiarola for her husband – to Felingeri[118] for a largest commendation – and to Avellino[119] for his wedding – afterwards there was the Council of Justice – when finished – I undressed – had dinner and to bed.

All healthy – at midday the King went to trawl – until 2 o'clock at the sea – afternoon with me in town.

On Thursday the 19th I got up at 7 o'clock – had breakfast – full dress – Holy Mass – then at ten o'clock in the main chapel – at the podium – where only the Duke of andria[120] took part in the procession – afterwards my hand was kissed by all order of the knights – then undressed – changed my dress – read the letters of the post – had lunch afterwards the Finance Council – then ⊙ – afterwards read – kept myself busy – changed my dress – at half past 4 we went in a carriage to the cathedral to kiss the blood of Saint Januarius – then to St. Ferdinando – I got on a dray with the King and went to Portici – where my dear children waited for me with the greatest eagerness – played with them until the time of the rosary – when I undressed – received a blessing – arranged a few affairs – and then played music – where I sung – at half past ten had dinner and went to sleep.

Thanks to God all healthy – the King went out only with me.

On Friday the 20th I got up at 7 o'clock – combed my hair – dressed – had breakfast – saw my children – heard Holy Mass – at ten o'clock – spoke to A. – then had lunch with the children – then talked with Gatti who attended to the games of children – and then spoke to Dentici – then with SB – afterwards read – wrote – worked on my affairs – saw my children – the King came back – I attended to his toilette – then to the blessing of the Council – and afterwards undressed – had dinner and to bed.

All healthy – except Januarius – a slight cold – the King went in the morning to the [fair] of Salerno and did not return until evening.

On the 21st Saturday I got up at 8 hours – dressed – combed my hair – Mass – saw my children – at half past two I kept the King company – who was painted by the Kaufmann – at midday we had lunch – then in the children's room – wrote – then received the Bishop of Nola[121] in audience who requested the grand priory of the constantinian order – then went for a walk in the woods from above – afterwards went to the children – saw the little ones and Louise – until the return of the King – the blessing – then make my business – took care of my children and go to bed at ten.

Januarius is still cold Janvier – also Francis but he had fever – the other well. The King went at 1½ to Volla and returned at 6½.

On Sunday the 22nd I got up at 8 o'clock – saw my children – toilette – Mass – afterwards visited my other sick children – read the letters of the post – waited for the King until one o'clock – when I had lunch with him – then read – wrote until half past 5 – when Lord Hamilton[122] came – together with Lamberg – I really suffered from this meeting it reminded me the loss of so worthy of [excellent] Miledy[123] – irreparable loss for humanity and for her friends – afterwards this sad talk – I went to the blessing by the Augustinian – afterwards to bed.[124]

The King went trawling – afterwards dinner to the craggy mountain and to the blessing with me; l the children healthy – Louise wanted to go to bed because her feet were slightly sore.

** Here the text is interrupted; on the next page it starts from September 27

On Friday the 27 I got up at 7 o'clock – the children – combed my hair – had breakfast – dressed – heard Holy Mass – saw and kept the King company while he was painted – had lunch with the King – took care of Mimi – took care for my books – while the King was seated in his office – wrote – read – worked on my affairs – then received in audience the wife of the official Ramet[125] who would like to stay in Naples – the daughters of Ristori who would like to serve – Strongoli who would wish to receive the cordon[126] – Ayello to discuss about the customs disorders – the brother of Cattolica[127] to go to Sicily – afterwards which I went to the high woods to find Louise with Mimi and Theresa – to half I had to make the King go back to see the children – presided over the Council – wrote and spent the evening doing my affairs – at ten o'clock slept.

> My children all better – dear Mimi with a strong sickness but no fever – the King went out only one hour and a half up the craggy mountain.

On Saturday the 28 I woke up at 7 o'clock – I was informed that dear Mimi had a slight fever – I got up immediately to see her – she was still sleeping – I combed my hair and dressed to go – as I had decided – to college of midshipmen – given that at half past eight she was still asleep – it seemed to me too much – I opened the windows and I realized immediately that it was not sleep but slumber – [therefore] the doctor gave her two emetics of ipecacuanha of two […] at a time – she vomited a lot but still with a terrible sleepiness – she did not complain about anything – and not being able even keep her head straight for a moment – she had enemas for hours – and round the clock she urinated 3 times – although she was always very thirsty – to the touch she was always cool – as the sleepiness still grew – put their feet in gutted pigeons – but after one hour and a half they were cold again – three warm baths at the feet were made – but in vain – she sweated a lot – she was almost black in the face – and the skin and the sweat were cold – when she bled from the foot – the blood came out cold and with difficulty – it were applied two plasters to her legs – cantharide – and she was given camphor by mouth with maidenhair syrup – she was insensitive to everything and the sleepiness increased – in the end energetic and constant rubbing of flannel was applied to the whole body – which combined with other remedies – started to make the frozen blood circulate – as steady – the little girl began to speak – I did not move for anything from the room [during] this whole day and I spent the whole night.

> The other children healthy – the King in the morning went to trawl – in the afternoon on the craggy mountain and in evening to my [prayer] to throw [the javelin].

On Sunday the 29th I did not go to bed – nor I did move from the room of dear Mimi – the night was not peaceful at all – so the fever came and and the little girl was hot and was no longer frozen – in the morning I washed – I dressed and spent the whole day – except Mass – with her – with her [who] got up – she wished to be carried from one room to another – I spent the whole day with her – without moving – in the evening there was musical where Theresa played the harpsichord – I was until midnight in Mimi's room and I went to bed afterwards saw her sleeping peacefully – afterwards the rosary – spoke to the King – ⊙ of [Affairs].

> The King went out only after dinner to the craggy mountain – other children healthy.

On Sunday the <u>30th</u> Sunday I got up at half past 6 – in Mimi's room – she had slept well and was almost without fever – she was cheerful and beautiful – I spent the morning with her – I was painted only for a short time – I had lunch with the King – I had a little colic as a result for fright – I plopped myself down on the sofa – and began to read – then the whole day with the dear child – afterwards I took air walking on the terrace of the Great Maîtresse[128] – afterwards took care of Mimi – the rosary – Council and wrote – prayed – did my business and to bed

> The King in the morning went fishing there I sent the children – after dinner to the craggy mountain – in the evening to throw. The children – except the beloved Mimi – all well. [It Followed by code words].

On Tuesday October the 1st, I got up at 7 o'clock – between my toilette – having breakfast – being with Mimi – Mass – it was ten o'clock – I was painted by Angelica Kaufmann and took care of my child – at midday I half lunch with the King – and then wrote the post – took care of the sick child – then saw SB – the wife of Feydau[129] – thenSan Marco – afterwards the evening with the child – then read – wrote – talked with the King – ☉ – then prayed and read, and afterwards to bed.

> The King went only after lunch to the [net] – my children healthy – Mimi purged and was still very sick – I felt pity for her – I was unwell.

On Wednesday October the 2nd, I got up at 7 o'clock in the morning – dressed – combed my hair – Holy Mass – afterwards took care of the children – at ten o'clock Acton came and spoke to the King and to me, and then I wrote – saw SB – saw the papers – I burned it – then dinner with my eldest daughters – afterwards with them I packed my books – then organized a money lottery for the maids of Mimi – afterwards I saw a sicilian lady Tornabene who wanted a pension[130] – Casabono[131] for assistance and pension – and don Antonio Spinelli[132] as lawyer of his brother – later Lady Tarsia[133] and Tripalda to tell me that to tell me the marriage paper to sign – then I saw Mrs. Sangro – afterwards Butera, then I made the lottery and I gave a bonus to the servants for the consolation of dear Mimi who s escaped from this disease – which by killing her would have desolated and deprived me of all consolation and satisfaction in this world, then stayed with Mimi until time of blessing – afterwards that – I went to the Council and then I went to sleep.

> All my dear children healthy – Mimi Mimi purged wihout effect – this dear little girl is getting better but slowly – in the morning the King did not go out – at midday he went to Mortella – where he hunted hares and returned at 6 o'clock.

On Thursday October the 3rd, I got up at half past 6 – worked on my affairs – wrote – arranged – then I saw my dear Mimi – had breakfast with two eldest – and combed my hair – dressed – the Mass – at two o'clock I went to the college of midshipmen with the young Altavilla – Gravina and Corleto – there they well trained – they presented themselves wonderfully – I appreciate for the maintenance of their decency and cleanliness throughout – then I returned home – still my affairs – afterwards I went to have dinner in Count Lamberg's house – in one horse carriage the King – Sambuca – Migliano – Gravina – Altavilla and me – in another there was the Priore and Onorato[134] – there we found Hamilton and Rasowmouvski[135] – we had dinner – played in the small pretty house of Count – afterwards we went home – where we took care of children until 6 o'clock – we went in town where – just arrived – we did the two Councils and then straight to bed.

Mimi is recovering – the others well – the King went out at 6 o'clock to hunt in the mountains – the rest always stayed with me.

On Friday October the 4, I got up at 8 o'clock – combed my hair – unpacked – arranged – dressed – lost the time – at half past eleven I went to the public hand-kissing – from there to the public table – undressed – kept the King company – ☉ then saw lava and stones of Sicily – read wrote post in advance for tomorrow – talked a long time with the Great Maîtresse – changed my dress – the hand-kissing of ladies – wrote to my children – dressed – undressed – went to the theatre – where I stayed until the second ballet – afterwards home – undressed – prayed and to bed.

All the children healthy – the King – in the afternoon – went for a while to the porcelain factory.

On Saturday October the 5th, I got up at 6 o'clock – prayed [prepared] – confessed – received communion – then Princess Jacy told me that I could not have her daughter here – then had breakfast – combed my hair – at 9 o'clock went to the Florentines church to hear Holy Mass and receive the blessing – and then I picked up the King from the [factory] porcelain and went to Portici – where we met our children again – Mimi all weak and pale – Januarius sad – again all out – we saw the house for the boy when he becomes a man – afterwards we had lunch – then Marsico spoke to me and I recomended him – then I wrote – went with my children – I combed my hair – then the King returned – afterwards a while with our children – we left for the city – when arrived I saw the daughter of Tarsia who on Monday will become a nun at Regina Coeli or Jesus delle Monache – I forgot it – and a Roman lady took leave, I dressed and prayed – and then we went to the new performance of comic opera at the Florentines [theatre] – the theatre was full – it bored me so much – after the 2nd act we returned home – I still spoke with the King – ☉ – then had dinner – undressed and to bed.

My children – Mimi weak and sad. Januarius again agitated – Joseph the dedication – the others well – King went to [ride] and porcelain – afterwards with me Portici – at 7 o'clock to Volla and at 5 hours he returned and spent the rest of the day with me.

On Sunday October 6th, I got up at 8 o'clock – then had breakfast – combed my hair – dressed – at ten o'clock I went to the main chapel – to the sung Mass – at eleven I went with the King – to the riding stables to see a British man and a woman who rode on horseback very skillfully and fast – then back had dinner – afterwards wrote – read my post – kept company the King company who went out at 3 o'clock – so I sat down to write – at 4 o'clock I saw SB – then A. – then lady Cariati in a audience for a bigger pension – to widow of Artale[136] for her son to become master rational – to the mother of Palma[137] so that we will not take place the trial for the escape of her daughter – afterwards I saw Sangro[138] – Belmonte and Cenzano[139] – then Lamberg brought me a nice paiting – King returned and also saw it with pleasure – then to the theatre – afterwards the second act the King left – I undressed and went to bed.

My children were all a bit better. The King at 3 ½ to Portici and came back at half past 6.

On Monday October 7th, I got up at half past five – dressed – combed my hair – Holy Mass – worked on my affairs – all arranged – at 7 o'clock I went with Marchioness Altavilla and Rocella to Portici – we went down to the Strada Nuova[140] – because we saw the Blessed Sacrament there – at 9 o'clock we left Portici – me in the last carriage with Mimi – then we arrived all well and quietly – at midday I put the children in order and then I had lunch with the King and gentlemen – afterwards I was in Mimi's room until a terible storm – which did not worry her – it vanished – then I began to arrange all my little affairs – papers – books – writing – this lasted until 6 o'clock – when I was with Mimi and wrote again half an hour – at half past 6 I presided over the Council of Sambuca – then my affairs – then I went to make a General visit to all the children – then I began to write and at ten o'clock to bed.

We made the jouney – fortunately the children behaved well – Joseph just a little sick – in the evening Theresa – for her badness – fell down broke a tooth and hurt a lip. The King at 7 o'clock left Naples – went to Carditello – when I arrived in Caserta he was already there and he could not go out anymore for the rest of the day.

On Tuesday October 8th, I got up at half past 6 and went to my little childrens' room – to see them dressed – had their breakfast – this took me time – then I had breakfast – I combed my hair – dressed – at 9 o'clock I went to Holy Mass – at half past nine I began to write and to finish my post – at midday I went to have lunch at Teresa's room – Louise and Francis – I went down with the two girls – who they kept me company – they both played the harpsichord – paraded with me – then I began to write my papers and work – then I spoke No. – afterwards I went outside with my three girls in a carriage – to the wood and the channel – I returned and began to write and stay with Theresa – then the King came – I still read – wrote – saw my children – prayed – paraded until the time of undressing and going to bed.

My children were quite well – little Joseph much better and I wish him well. – At 8 o' clock the King went to San Leucio and came back at 6:00 afterwards – dinner.

On Wednesday October 9th, I got up at 8 o'clock – saw the children – had breakfast – dressed – combed my hair – heard the Holy Mass – and then wrote – worked on my affairs – saw Gatti – with my children – talked and kept company to the King – then saw Lady San Marco who the trees on her feud to be cut – then saw S.B.-afterwards went out in a carriage with Mimi up to the channel – back – talked throughout with the King * ⊙ – then the Council afterwards prayed – wrote – saw Lamberg and went to bed.

The King in the morning went out and afterwards-lunch to San Leucio – the children were fine.

On Thursday October 10th, I got up at 7 o'clock – dressed – had breakfast – saw my children – heard Holy Mass and spoke to C.D.M[141] – then arranged my papers – afterwards had lunch with Louise and Francis – kept them company – then wrote – afterwards talked with Ayello – then Acton – then wrote – worked on my affairs – saw the children – the King returned – there was the Council – afterwards I prayed and went to bed.

I had a terrible cold all day – my children healthy – the King went out in the morning to hunt wild boar and returned in the evening –

On Friday October 11th, I got up at 7 o'clock – had breakfast – toilette – Mass – my children – went to Louise's room who I was informed had a paroxsym – and then down with Teresa – worked on my affairs for a while – at ten King came back – I kept him company – started to write – worked – then went to Louise's room – saw the soldiers with new uniforms that Acton presented to the King – had lunch – kept the King company – ⊙ – then read – wrote – my children – took care of them – prayed, and presided the Council – then still in Louise's room – afterwards saw Lamberg and [went] I went to sleep.

Louise was sick apparently fluxional fever – she had a long parosym – but [worth] and was better in the evening. The King went in the morning to the roral tennis – in the afternoon to the wood.

On Saturday October 12th, I got up at 7 o clock – combed my hair – dressed – had breakfast – Holy Mass – then read – wrote – went to Louise's room – with all my other children – then had lunch – then arranged my library – afterwards saw Sangro who prays for her affairs – then d.u. – afterwards I went out – with the little Marchioness Hamilton and Lamberg – saw damage of the gulf – and from there I returned on foot through the wood – saw my children – went to Louise's room – then came back down – prayed – then saw my two little children sleeping – afterwards wrote and devoted myself – still go to Louise and I went to sleep.

The children were quite well – Louise had a quiet night – the new fever took her at nine o'clock – it was slight but the eyes and head dejected. The King went in the morning to the royal tennis – during the dayfor a short time.

On Sunday October 13th, I got up at 6 o'clock and went to Louise's room – where – between her and my other children – the Time passed until 8 o'clock when I combed my hair – dressed – heard two Holy Masses – in Louise's room until the return of the King – when I returned with him to Louise's room – then talked with King – ⊙ – then had lunch – afterwards read – wrote – saw the young and pretty wife of Troya[142] – then Duchess Gravina[143] – afterwards I went out with Gravina – Migliano – to Canalone in the carriage – on return walking – then I went to Louise's room – King returned – he joined me there – he went down with me and we talked about our children and their future education – afterwards what I saw my children sleeping – prayed – wrote and saw a moment Lamberg – so spent the rest of the evening and then to bed.

> Louise better – the others fine – in the morning the King went to Carditello and in the afternoon to Carbone.

On Monday October 14, I got up at half past 7 – combed my hair – dressed – saw my children – heard Holy Mass – at ten o'clock I went to Carditello by one horse carriage where the King hunted boars – with us there was Lamberg – Hamilton – Rasoumovski – Breme[144] – Gravina – Migliano – Corleto Priore Altavilla – Cusano – Don Onorato Domenico Spinelli[145] – Caldanisetta[146] – de Marco – Diomede and – with me – the little marchioness – Lamberg – Gravina – Hamilton and Migliano – we saw the hunting – we did two hunting trips in a one horse carriage – at three o'clock we went to have dinner – and then we started to return on foot – and we finished in dray – I returned with the King – I undressed – went to Louise's room – saw all my children – presided over the Council – prayed – and then undressed and to bed.

> Louise had a fever – but slight – all others fine – at 8 o'clock the King went to Carditello – at 10 o'clock I joined him and returned with him.

On Tuesday October 15, I got up – dressed – combed my hair – had breakfast with Theresa – then I heard two Masses – because of the sad birthday of the most adorable of mothers – then wrote – saw SB – had lunch alone withTeresa – then listened to her playing the harpsichord – finished my post – then I went to Louise's room – I saw Princess GonzHaga[147] – who saw all my children and we conversed – and then I went out with the young Altavilla and Gravina and I went to the channel – where I met Theresa and with with her I returned on foot – I wrote – prayed – then saw Lamberg and went to sleep.

> Louise had fever – but slight – the others well. In the morning the King went out – remained to to have lunch to San Leucio – went to the pheasant farm and did not return until evening.

On Wednesday October 16, I got up at 7 o'clock – combed my hair – dressed – had breakfast – heard Holy Mass – saw my children – and then I went to Carditello – found the King with Hamilton – Lamberg – Gravina – Marsico and the lady – we saw two hunting trips – then had lunch at home and from there by dray – with the King I went to Naples – I spoke with the King – ⊙ – then received Aflito[148] who is in a convent – by the will of her husband – it appears to me a little unfair – then Lady Butera[149] – afterwards undressed – then at nine o'clock to the new theatre – to the new opera composition of Corleto that seemed detestable – afterwards to bed.

> Louise had fever – but slight – Francis – who should have been served at 18 o'clock – he served himself with the help of his wet nurse and he behaved well – In the morning the King to Carditello and spent all the day with me.

On Thursday October 17, I got up at 6 o'clock – curled my hair – dressed – had breakfast and Mass – then I saw Acton – then the widow of Gosueto[150] – afterwards I returned with Gravina and Vasto in a carriage and the lady in Caserta – thanks to God i found all my children healthy – and Januarius weaned – fortunately without much annoyance – Louise still sick – Mimi weak and convalescent – Joseph [in] bad [conditions] – Theresa – Francis and Amélie[151] well – afterwards having embraced them – the King came – I had lunch with him – unpacked my books – saw some paintings – ⊗ – then I undressed and I began to write and work – then I went to Louise's room – saw my other children who live upstairs – afterwards the King returned – I prayed – there was a long Council – and then slept.

> Louise had fever once again – but more lightly – Januarius happily con-tinued his weaning – the King went in the morning to the net to hunting larks – in the afternoon to San Leucio.

On Friday October 18, I got up at half past 6 – dressed – had breakfast – went to Holy Mass – spoke to Carlo de Marco – then I did a long
walk – with my three chambermaids – to the channel and the path – then
return – I combed my hair – dressed – then went to see Louise and the
other children – had lunch with the King – afterwards read – wrote –
worked on my affairs – talked with A. – afterwards the wife and beautiful
daughter of Paterno[152] in audience – then S.B. – then saw my children –
worked on my affairs – later the Council – talk a little and to bed.

> The King went to the net and afterwardswards-lunch to the mountain to
> [hunt] patridges. The children healthy – Louise had still – but slight – fever.

On Saturday the 19th, I got up at 6 o'clock – had breakfast – dressed –
combed my hair – the Mass – then spoke with A. – then saw Louise – my
children – then went to Carditello[153] by one horse carriage – with those of
the other day – on arrival we saw the hunting with net – then the one of
deers – where we did two hunting trips – afterwards there was lunch – at
5 o'clock – and I returned by dray with the King – then – afterwards having talked to him – saw my children – we talked with Acton along about
a paper on finance [154] – and then prayed and undressed – bed – ⊙ – then
I went to sleep.

> In the morning the King went to the net – the day he was still with us.
> Children healthy – Louise stood up for the first time – but she had still fever.

On Sunday the 20th, I got up at 7 o'clock – saw my children – had breakfast – I dressed – combed my hair – heard Mass – wrote – then went
by carriage with Altavilla – Gravina and Migliano up Aversa – I found
the King, who came with us – then to Giuliano – to the feud of Prince
Stigliano – where we found his wife – beautiful daughter – and Duchess
Termoli[155] – all don Felice's son and other oficiers – we saw the house –
we had dinner – the King led Altavilla – Cassano[156] – Onorato Priore –
Hamilton and Breme – we saw the house – and then we had dinner – I had
close to me the two ladies of the house – then we saw a buffalo hunt that
was spoiled by the bad weather and the rain – then the journey back and
we returned home due to the rain and bad weather – I worked on myaffairs – saw my children – prayed and then to bed.

In the morning the King went to the net – then he picked me up in Aversa and he was with me all day. The children were well – Louise was almost all day up and much better.

On Monday the 21st, I got up at 7 o'clock – combed my hair – dressed – had breakfast – heard the Holy Mass – then saw my children – started to write my post – at half past eleven I went to Mimi's room – where there was Gatti – at midday we had lunch – then I went with the King to Louise's room – then wrote – worked on my affairs – Tarsia – Cicio Pignatelli wanted to talk with me – Princess Butera – my children – wrote – presided over the Council and went to sleep.

The King went out to Carditello at 3 o'clock and returned at 7 o'clock. The children healthy – Louise got up at theer o'clock – Joseph had a slight fever.

On Tuesday the 22nd, the I got up at 7 o'clock – then dressed – combed my hair – had breakfast – saw my children – wrote – heard two Holy Masses – prayed to God about the change of wet nurse for little Joseph will be fine – saw Louise – played with my children – had lunch – then I was always on the move for the change of wet nurse from Januarius to Joseph – so that gods bless us – afterwards wrote – arranged books, then received the daughter of Molina[157] in audience – who shouted and cried for injustice – afterwards in my childrens'room – and then I went up to the top to visit donna Gesualda – who is very ill with dysentery – then to Louise's room – afterwards went down – wrote – prayed – marched and thus the evening ended.

Louise got up twice and had a modest fever and was very weak, at 3 o'clock afternoonnn I changed to the trembling Joseph 's wet nurse, in the morning King went out to the net and he was all day at home.

On Wednesday the 23rd, I got up half past 5 – saw my little Joseph – who had spent a restless night and I began to write – dressed – combed my hair – Holy Mass – then wrote for my son – then (saw) Lady Migliano – (Fama) and the old (......) – who came to thank for Migliano – then

Belmonte spoke to me few minutes and showed me sketches-then I had lunch with my children – then I stayed in Louise's room – then I brought Theresa with me – with her – Mimi and Joseph – so I spent the afternoon – then MarchionessSan Marco came to beg me to cut some tress of the wood – afterwards S.B. – then a lady fromTurin was presented me by Duchess del Gesso[158] – then spoke to Fagiano – then thanked Conradino[159] – afterwards I wrote – prayed – read – saw my children – the Council of de Marco and to bed.

> In the morning the King went out to hunt – afternoonnn he went to Carditello – he did the race and did not return all day until 7 o'clock of theevening. Little Joseph had an anxious night – a quiet day – Louise had a very slight fever and was better – the others well.

On Thursday the 24th, I got up at 7 o'clock – afterwards I felt all night a bit upset – combed my hair – dressed – had breakfast – I started to talk with de Marco – then Holy Mass – afterwards we heard the news ….. [160] – then my children – S.B. – waited for the King – had lunch – talked with him – ⊙ – afterwards read my letters – wanted to write – then talk with A. – then don Ferrante[161] – afterwards Lady Belmonte – for her problem with his brother – read – wrote – the Council – prayed and went to sleep.

On Friday the 25th, I got up at 7 o'clock – combed my hair – dressed – had breakfast – heard Holy Mass – spoke to A. – then had lunch in childrens's room – with Francis and Theresa – stayed with children – wrote a little – at half past 3 Princess Jacy came to tell me not let her daughter come – then SB – afterwards I saw the brother of Wintersee[162] – engineer lieutenant colonel at the service of the Emperor – then my children – the Council – worked on my affairs and went to bed.

> [code words] In the morning the King was in to the net – had lunch at Carditello and did the […] buffalo of afternoon. The children were well – Louise nearly without fever.

On Saturday the 26th, I got up at 7 o'clock – dressed – combed my hair – had breakfast – read – wrote – hear two Holy Masses – saw my children – then had lunch – afterwards talked with the King – ⊙ – later read – wrote – saw the children, played the harpsichord – showed the library to the King – the small illuminated theatre – then still talked – afterwards prayed – then there was music in the King's apartment – a famous violinist called Bügano[163] – at the service of Turin – there he played excellently, then we went to sleep.

The King went out to the Net – afternoonnn he stayed at home – The children healthy – Louise without fever.

On Sunday the 27th, I got up at 7 o'clock – toilette – dressed – had breakfast – combed my hair – then Holy Mass – saw all my children – then at eleven – went with the lady Gravina and Vasto in town where I met people – SB spoke to me – then A. – Then I read my letters – I had lunch – then I went to pick my winter clothes – and then selected the music papers – read – wrote – at 4 o'clock King arrived – I still continued my affairs – at half past 5 there was the farewell ceremony – in the canopy – in public – of the Ambassador of Morocco[164] with the whole court – afterwards I changed my clothes – I said my prayers and went to Florentines theatre – where I bored myself a lot – at half past ten at home – saw X – I undressed and went to bed.

In the morning The King went out hunting to the net in Carditello – there he had lunch and arrived in town at 4 o'clock – children healthy – Louise better without fever.

On Monday the 28th, I got up at 7 o'clock – dressed – had breakfast – combed my hair – heard two Holy Masses – and talked with Lord Belmonte – then Acton – Sambuca and de Marco – afterwards at eleven o'clock I went to Caserta – I arrived at half past twelve – I met the King and all my dear healthy children – we had lunch – then I wrote – I devoted myself – saw my children – then I saw old bishop Onorati[165] who returned to his diocese – afterwards saw my children – read – prayed – the Council and to bed.

The King went hunting – then he had lunch at home – later at three o'clock he went to San Leucio and retuned at 6 o'clock – the children healthy.

On Tuesday the 29th, I got up at 7 o'clock – combed my hair – had breakfast – dressed – saw my children – heard Holy Mass – wrote – read in the library – then the King came – I talked with him – ⊙ – then had lunch – afterwards read – played the harpsichord – saw my children – read – wrote – kept myself busy – went to bed.

> In the morning the King went out to hunting – then at home – it rained – I had the bad thing. The children healthy.

On Wednesday the 30th, I got up at 7 o'clock – had breakfast – dressed – combed my hair – wrote – at eleven o'clock Monsignor said Mass – then confirmed the daughter of Belmudy – who is getting married – I gave her brilliant pins and a precious cloth [enough] – I was with my children – then I had lunch – then I kept the King company – and then wrote – read – devoted myself – then at 5 o'clock I participated at the wedding of the daughter of Belmudy with a certain Vito St. Mary of Capua – the marriage grieved me because she seemed a victim of her father's greed and I doubt that she will be happy – afterwards I remained with the children – I prayed and went to the Council – I played the harpsichord – worked on my affairs and went to bed

> The King did not go out due to the bad weather – in the afternoon he went to San Leucio. The children healthy.

On Thursday the 31, I got up at 7 o'clock – had breakfast – combed my hair – heard two Holy Masses – Carlo de Marco – read – wrote – talked with Acton – saw the wife of Stefano Patrizio – then wrote – saw Dentici who wants to be financial adviser – and then the King came – the Council and to bed.

> In the morning the King went hunting in the afternoonnnn to San Leucio. The children healthy.

On Friday november 1, I got up at 7 o'clock – I dressed – had break-fast – combed my hair – heard two Holy Masses – spoke to Acton – and then I went to Carditello to the hunting – with the marchioness we did a nice chase – in spite of the bad weather and returned at 7 o'clock – the was Council and at nine o'clock to bed.

> The King went hunting – hunted with me and he reurned with me.The children healthy.

On Saturday november 2, I got up at 5 o'clock – I dressed – confessed – afterwards received communion – I heard two Masses – then I had breakfast – heard two Masses – had lunch with my children – spent the afternoon with them – then I wrote – at half past 3. I spoke a long time with Gravina – then once again with my children – in the evening there was a great concer of Bugani who played the violin – afterwards we went to sleep.

> The King went out in the morning and returned in the evening – Joseph spent a bad night and a bit of fever – the others well.

On Sunday the 3rd I got up at 7 o'clock – I dressed – combed my hair – heard Holy Mass – I had breakfast – and then I went with Theresa – the little marchioness – and Gravina in Naples where I saw S.B. – afterwards I had lunch – then I worked – and read with Theresa – then came A. – which I spoke – afterwards King arrived – who I talked with him ⊗ – then I prayed – saw pregnant ladies and I received their compliments – afterwards we went to the concert opera where Balduci[166] was sick – so they rehearsed only the ballets – then at home I went to sleep.

> The King went hunting – then had lunch there and at 4 o'clock in Naples – all the children healthy.

On Monday the 4th I got up at 7 o'clock – had breakfast with Theresa – then combed my hair – heard two Holy Masses – worn court dress – afterwards the hand-kissing – public table – then undressed – had lunch – saw the lugger that Acton with the young Thurn[167] brought to the King – afterwards talked with the King – ⊙ – then worked on my affairs – took care of Theresa – heard the harpsichord being played – [Serrao] – then changed my dress – the hand-kissing of the ladies – then undressed and

went to the theatre – where Balduci – lead singer – was sick – they perdormed the Florentines opera – with two big ballet of *Cleopatra and love
between weapons* that are pretty good – afterwards undressed – theatre and
to bed.

> The King did not go out all day – in the morning he only went a moment
> to the porcelain factory and in the afternoon to the parade of Liparoti. The
> children healthy – thanks to God.

On Tuesday the 5th I got up at 6 o'clock to write my post letters – I
dressed – combed my hair – had breakfast – listened to the Mass – I spoke
to A. – then at half past 10 I went to Strone by one horse carriage with the
lady in waiting – Princess Migliano[168] and gentlemen – there was a boar
hunt where between stalking wild boar and killing them with the shot-
gun – we killed 76 – we had dinner there and we returned – I changed my
dress – spoke to the King and then to the Florentines theatre – to a dull
tragedy entitled *Cambise*[169] where there was nobady – at nine o'clock at
home and had dinner on bed.

> The King left for Strone an hour before me – the rest of the day [with
> me]. The children – according to my news and letters received – thanks
> God – healthy.

On the Wednesday 6th I got up at half past 6 – did my accounts – my
affairs – dressed – combed my hair – had breakfast with Theresa – heard
the two Masses – talked to A. – then saw doctor Tissot[170] who I esteemed
him – afterwards at 10 o'clock I returned to Caserta where I saw my
healthy children – and then had lunch with the King – read – wrote –
worked on my affairs – afterwards the Council – then I went to sleep.

> In the morning at nine o'clock the King left. The children were well.

On Thursday the 7th, I got up at 7 o'clock – had breakfast – combed my
hair – dressed – Holy Mass – saw my children – read – devoted myself –
then had lunch with the King – ⊙ – afterwards read – played the harpsichord – wrote – kept myself busy – saw my children – in the evening the
Council and to bed.

The King went out. The children were healty.

On Friday the 8th, I got up at 7 o'clock – combed my hair – dressed – had breakfast – heard two Holy Masses – afterwards wrote – Mars. [171] – Mig. [172] both spoke to me about their children and affairs, – then I saw Louise who came down for the first time with me – then I went to have lunch with Theresa and Francis – I went down with Teresa and went to the library – then wrote letters – devoted myself – played harpsichord with the teacher – talked with A. – then read – wrote the Council and to bed.

The children healthy

On Saturday the 9th, I got up at 7 o'clock – I dressed – combed my hair – had breakfast – then Holy Masses – afterwards wrote – read – devoted myself – had lunch – afternoon played harpsichord – appliedmyself – read – wrote – my children and like so until the hour to go I went to sleep.

The children healthy – In the morning the King went to San Vito and retuned in the evening.

On Sunday the 10th, I got up at 7 o'clock – dressed – combed my hair – had breakfast – heard Holy Mass – saw Cimitile[173] who arrived today and talked with him – and then at half past 10 I went by one horse carriage to the pheasant farm – it was a heavy journey and it was the first time I passed by San Leucio – that sad and fatal house – we went down to the pheasant farm where we ate – afternoon we made three hunting trips – I saw more than 4,000 pheasants – a prodigious amount – the King with 102 shots killed 100 pheasants – we returned – afterwards the hunting – I undressed – changed my dress and listened music which the violinist Bugnano played – then I went to sleep.

The King went out at 9 o'clock to prepare everything – the rest of the day he was with us. The children healthy.

<u>On</u> Monday <u>the 11th</u> I got up at 7 o'clock – dressed – combed my hair – had breakfast – heard Mass – then I sent down Theresa and Louise – the first played the harpsichord in the presence of Bugnano – and I went to Belvedere by dray with the lady and we had lunch there – – in the afternoon we did hunting trip – [in] Mount Brianza – of wild boar – I did ten shots and I hit 5 – we returned to the house where we had a load courier that spoke about a disease of the Emperor[174] – then I spoke to the King – ⊙ – afterwards the Council and to bed.

In the morning the King went to San Leucio to prepare everything – returned with me. The children healthy.

<u>On Tuesday</u>the 12th, I got up at 7 o'clock – had breakfast – combed my hair – I dressed half gala – then wrote the entire post – heard Holy Mass – attended to the lunch of the King – and then finished writing – afterwards went to have lunch in the childrens'room – l.6.q.m.d.[175] – then I worked on my affairs – packed – finished writing – afterwards at half past 3 I went to town with the Lady Marsico and Migliano – shortly after my arrival the King came – I said my prayers and then we went to San Carlo opera house – where we saw two acts and two ballets – then to bed.

The King went to Carbone at halp past twelve and from there home – the children well, me – I had a slight cold.

On Wednesday the 13th, I got up at 7 o'clock – dressed – combed my hair – had breakfast – heard Holy Mass – at nine o'clock spoke to A. – at eleven to the famous doctor Tissot that I appreciate very much – then S.B. – then received people which were in the waiting room – then in the afternoon I played the harpsichord for a while – saw Carlo for Marco – afterwards LadySan Marco then Sangro – Wedel later Lady Tripalda[176] – Artale – the King returned – I spoke to him – X – then prayed and to the theatre – where we remained two acts and a ballet and then I went to sleep.

The chidren healthy – my cold is better but it did not finish yet. In the morning the King went to Varcaturo and returned in the evening.

On Thursday the 14th, I got up at 7 o'clock – combed my hair – dressed – heard Holy Mass – talked to A. – then read my letters – chose some cloths – talked – returned to Caserta with the lady in waiting – arriving I saw my children – had lunch with the King – talked read – wrote – played the harpsichord – and the Council of Carlo de Marco – then a long speech with the King and Acton – where a fatal matter was solved by Sambuca and the money allocated for my daughters – then I went to sleep.

At 8 o'clock the King left Naples – returned to Caserta – had lunch and after-lumch went to San Leucio. The children healthy.

On Friday the 15th, I got up at 7 o'clock – had breakfast – combed my hair – dressed – heard Holy Mass – talked to A. – had lunch with my children – worked on some little affairs – payments – read – wrote – talked to S.B. – the Council and then to bed.

In the morning the King went to Carditello to brand foals and he spent all day there.

On Saturday the 16th, I got up at 7 o'clock – had breakfast – heard Holy Mass – wrote – at half past ten I went to the hunt by one horse carriage – saw wild boars running – the hunting was very great – we had lunch – there was whole Stigliano[177] family – men and women – we hunted – we had lunch at four o'clock – returned at six o'clock – I undressed and started to write – doctor Tissot came – I showed him all my children and so I spent the evening.

The King went to Catditello at 7 o'clock in the morning – he spent the rest of the day with me – the children healthy.

On Sunday the 17th, I got up in the morning at 7 o'clock – dressed – combed my hair – had breakfast – heard two Holy Masses – had lunch with my children – where there was Tissot – I stayed a little with him – then wrote – played harpsichord – read – wrote – then saw my children – prayed and thus passed the day ⊙.

The children healthy. The King went out in the morning and did not return until evening.

On Monday the 18th, I got up at 6 o'clock – had breakfast – dressed – heard Holy Mass at 7 o'clock – afterwards I went hunting to Zingaro with the King – young Altavilla and Gravina – in a carriage – I saw wild boars running – then I fired seven shots and hit five – then dined at 4 o'clock and returned at half past 7 – I changed clothes – saw my children and presided overt the Council and to bed.

I went out and returned with the King – my children healthy enough. We killed 125 wild boars. Little Joseph – after a [restless] night – seemed to have a slight fever.

On Tuesday the 19th I got up at 7 o'clock – lunch – combed my hair – dressed – wrote the post – Holy Mass – at midday I had lunch with the King – afterwards my girls kept me company – then I played the harpsichord – saw Tissot – talked with him – finished my post and had some hearings – prayed and then the King returned – ⊙ – afterwards I went to bed.

In the morning the King went to the pheasant farm where he killed over 50 pheasants – then he had lunch in San Leucio and hunted.

On Wednesday the 20th I got up at 7 o'clock – combed my hair – dressed – had breakfast – Holy Masses – read – talked with SB – wrote – devoted myself – then I had lunch with my children and Tissot kept me company – I spoke to him about the health of my children – then I saw Hakert[178] with his portfolio and drawing – afterwards I spoke to A. – then some hearings – all to seek the vacant abbey – afterwards the Council of Carlo de Marco – then General Acton referred the finance papers to Cimitile in the presence of the King and demonstrated – how full of modesty – we had benefits – after that I went to sleep.

The children healthy – except Joseph – had a bad night and showed [having] a fever.

On Thursday the 21st I got up at 7 o'clock – combed my hair – dressed – had breakfast – heard Holy Masses – wrote about business – read the post – took care – then had lunch with my children – kept them with me afternoon – afterwards played the harpsichord – talked with Tissot – the King came and spoke with me – ⊙ – then first Council presided by Cimitile – afterwards I went to sleep.

> Le Roi alla à 9 heure à Calabricitra et retourna le soir. Little Joseph spent a good night – but around noon fever strongly arose with constant crying which made me feel sorry sorry for him.

On Friday the 22nd I got up at 7 o'clock – had breakfast – dressed – combed my hair – heard Holy Mass – spoke to Tissot – to see me for my health – afterwards had lunch with the children – then went down with them and my two eldest daughter that kept me company – afterwards I saw Lady Molinas who came for an appeal – then I saw A. – later the King came back and spoke with Acton to inform about the Finance Council – how it went since it was his first – afterwards saw my children – then the Council and I went to sleep.

> The King was in Carditello all day for the woodcock. Joseph had the fever again – spent a sleepless night – we stated to purge him with the chicory syrup – he became very ill – other children healthy.

On Saturday the 23rd, I got up at 7 o'clock – had breakfast – combed my hair – dressed – heard Mass – then spoke to Tissot about the health of my children – then with A. – afterwards had lunch with my children – then stayed with them – and wrote my post and papers – all day I was agitated and upset – saw and changed little Joseph's wet nurse and thus spent this bad day.

> The King out all day at the buffalo farm and at Carditello – little Joseph was very ill – new fever and pain – I changed his wet nurse.

On Sunday the 24th I got up at 7 o'clock – combed my hair – dressed – had breakfast – heard Masses – wrote – read – took care of my poor sick child – I had lunch with children and stayed with them after lunch – read my letters – the gazettes felt so sorry for the little patient – saw two wet nurses – chose one – let her change – prayed read – wrote – spent bad day – the King on his return told me – ⊙ and was a while with me – then I went to sleep.

The King went to Lady Spinosa – then to San Leucio – came back in the evening. The children healthy – little Joseph very bad – lots of cold – fever – I had to change his wet nurse.

On Monday the 25th, I woke up at 7 o'clock – had breakfast – combed my hair – heard the. Masses – then wrote – read – devoted myself – afterwards had lunch with Francis and Januarius – afternoonread – wrote and spoke to Ayiello – took care of my children – especially the little patient – then prayed – later the Council after that I went to sleep

The King was all day at the pheasant farm – little Joseph is still very ill – my others well.

On Tuesday 26th, I got up at 7 o'clock – dressed – had breakfast – combed my hair – heard Masses – wrote – afterwards had lunch with the children – then I wrote my post and began to play the harpsichord – then I saw S.B., afterwards my children – the King returned from hunting and I spent my day between writing – praying and my children.

The King went to Carbone all day – the children healthy – beloved little Joseph better – but his voice still very (weak).

On Wednesday the 27th, I got up at 7 o'clock – had breakfast – combed my hair – dressed – heard Masses – went upstairs to see my children – and then wrote – devoted myself – played with my children – had lunch with the King – read – devoted myself – played the harpsichord – talked to Tarsia and S.B. – then prayed – went to the Council – worked on my affairs and I went to sleep.

The King went out only at three o'clock to [San Leucio] – little Joseph is better – Louise a little cold – the others well.

On the 28th Thursday I got up at 7 o'clock – combed my hair – dressed – had breakfast – heard Holy Masses – saw my children – played the harpsichord – wrote – had lunch with the children and talked with Tissot – then with A. – afterwards I saw MadamTeresina Blanca – afterwards the Council – then I confessed – afterwards to bed.

The King went to San Leucio all day – the beloved children better.

On the 29th Friday I got up at half past 6 – prayed – recapitulated and then went to church to receive communion – heard two Masses – saw my children – read – wrote – heard two Masses – had lunch with the children – then to the library arranged books with Theresa – afterwards read – wrote and prayed – saw the children – at 8 o'clock I said the cruel office of the dead for the most beloved and adored of mothers.

The King went to Carbon – at noon to Paloma – returned in the evening, Louise was a little upset – other children healthy – I missed my period than I expected in this day.

On the 30th Saturday I woke at seven – had breakfast – combed my hair – dressed – heard Holy Mass – did spiritual readings with Theresa – saw Louise – the other children – had lunch with them – held Francis and Theresa with Mimi until four o'clock – then had some hearings – Princess Caramanico – afterwards wrote – read – prayed – the King returned – held a long conversation with him – afterwards read – wrote and so thus spent the evening.

The children thanks to God well – King went hunting for all the day.

<u>On December the 1,</u> I got up at 7 o'clock – had breakfast with Theresa – combed my hair – dressed – heard Mass – went to see my children – afterwards I went to Naples with the ladies Migliano and Corleto – since I left at half past eleven – I arrived at half past one – I had lunch – then I began to write – arranged – read – at 3 o'clock I saw A. – afterwards I had some hearings – the King returned and – after a while – I saw Count Richecourt[179] who was introduced to me – as also the young Salandra[180] – then we went to the opera – after that I spoke to the King – ☉ – then had supper – undressed and to bed.

> In the evening the King came from San Leucio in Naples – the children healthy.

<u>On Monday December the 2nd,</u> I got up in the morning – had breakfast – combed my hair – dressed – heard Mass – wrote my letters to my family in Caserta – then went to church – heard Mass and received the blessing – as there was the exibition of the octave of the Holy Virgin – then I returned – saw Sangro who wanted to talk with me – then I had lunch – afterwards S.B. came to talk with me – then A. – both told me about the speech delivered by the King during the Finance Council – then the King came – then there was the Council of Sambuca – afterwards to the San Carlo opera house and later to bed.

> The King went to Strone at midday. The children healthy

<u>On Tuesday December the 3</u> I got up at 6 o'clock – I started to write – then dressed – combed my hair – afterwards talked with ::: – then dressed – went to church – talked with de Marco e and Cimitile – then had lunch – afterwards had a hearing – then talk with Lady Gengano – then A. – afterwards the King came back – finished my post – prayed – talked with the King – ☉ – then Florentines opera – which bored me to death – I was introduced to a Florentines lady.

> In the morning the King went to (Cicola) to kill wild boars – The children healthy (it followed by code words).

On Wednesday December the 4, I got up at 7 o'clock – dressed – combed my hair – had breakfast – heard Mass – arranged my affairs – presided over the Council of Carlo de Marco – then left Naples with the King – Marsico – Migliano – I accompanied nCounty Caivano – where they went hunting – I saw my children – had lunch with them – then unpacked books – writing – reading – devoting myself [made up] my day and evening.

> The King left Naples with me – afterwards in the half-way hunted 4 (…). The children healthy.

On Thursday December the 5, I got upat 7 o'clock in the morning – I had breakfast – combed my hair – dressed – listened to the Mass – I started to read the letters from the post – had lunch with my children – and then talked to A. – then the children – the two Councils – Finance and war – wrote – devoted myself – prayed – thus ended the day.

> The King spent all day his at his manor farm – the children thanks to God well.

On Friday December 6, I got up at 7 o'clock in the morning – had breakfast – combed my hair – dressed – heard Mass – took care of my children – spent the day with them – had lunch with the King – and then read the letters – those I did not finish those for the courier – then saw Marchioness San Marco – afterwards Ventimiglia and fra Nicola Luigi Pignatelli[181] for commendam of Malta – then came the King – I kept him company – ⊙ – afterwards read – prayed – took care – until the hour to go I went to sleep.

> The King made [exercise] in the morning – afternoonnnn he went to San Leucio. The children healthy – little Amelia was (…) the first time. The other children healthy.

On Saturday December the 7, I got up at 7 o'clock – had breakfast – combed my hair – dressed – heard Holy Masses – wrote – saw my children – had lunch with them – then my two eldest stayed with me – spoke with

Mig. – with Princess Butera – an audience – afterwards the King came back – talked with him – then wrote post – read – prayed – applied me.

> The King went up a mountain to hunt partridges – the children healthy.

On Sunday December the 8, I got up – combed my hair – had with Theresa – dressed – heard Holy Masses – saw my children and went to Naples with the King – I left the King in Caivano and went to Naples at half past one – I had lunch – saw Sambuca – Acton – then read – wrote – unpacked my papers – King came – I said my prayers and then to the – on return I had some complaints – two hours afterwards […] from the King – ⊙ – then I went to sleep.

> The children healthy – the King went hunting at Caivano – I led hin there and he returned in the evening.

On Monday December the 9, I got up at/7 o'clock in the morning – had breakfast – combed my hair – dressed – and then talked with a * – then Holy Mass – wrote to [those who were staying in] Caserta and about my affairs – afterwards saw Rocella who spoke to me about affairs – then saw all the ladies – had lunch – saw S.M.[182] – then S.B. – then A. – afterwards hearings – the sister of Marchioness Altavilla – wife [Aeto] – was introduce to me – and the Council of Sambuca – prayed and went to San Carlo's theatre – evening talking with the King – ⊙ – afterwards I went to sleep.

> The children healthy – the King left at 8 o'clock in the morning to hunt in Fusaro and returned to five hours.

On Tuesday December the10th, I got up at 7 o'clock – had breakfast – dressed – heard Mass and then wrote and did a few affairs – afterwards at half past 10 I left Naples with the King – he stopped at half way in Caivano and I went to Caserta – where I found my dear children – thanks God all healthy – I had lunch with them and took care of the in the afternoon – and read – wrote – played the harpsichord, feeling very tired and ill – I went to bed at 8 o'clock in the evening.

The King went to Caivano with me – then he came back in the evening – the children thanks to God well.

On Wednesday December the 11th, I got up at 10 o'clock – had breakfast – dressed – combed my hair – heard Masses – wrote – read – took care – saw my children – had lunch with the King – kept him company all day while he was working – then played the harpsichord – saw my children – prayed – in the evening the Council and then to bed.

The children healthy – the King did not go out all day.

On Thursday December the 12th, I got up at 7 o'clock – had breakfast – dressed – combed my hair – heard Mass – saw the children – read – wrote – ocuper me – saw my children – had lunch with the King – afterwards read – or A. – then Cim. [183] – then the Council – prayed – saw S.B. – afterwards to bed.

The children healthy – the King went to an hunting trip San Leucio (it followed by code words).

On Friday December 13, I got up at 7 o'clock – dressed – combed my hair – had breakfast – Holy Masses – read all the letters that I could not read yesterday – had lunch with my children and stayed with them until about four o'clock – then Lord Paterno spoke to me – then the brother of Wintersee who is leaving and he is a very polite man – afterwards my children – the King returned – I began to write and work until bedtime.

In the morning the King went out to the wood where he took exercise – then had lunch at San Leucio – The children healthy – excluding poor Joseph – a violent cough. I suffered so much from the disorders of pregnancy.

On Saturday December the 14, I got up at 7 0'clock – had breakfast – dressed – combed my hair – heard Holy Masses – wrote – worked on my affairs – had lunch with the children – stayed with them – played the harpsichord – saw Migliano who spoke about the Finance Council – and MarchionessSan Marco – then read – wrote – devoted myself the King returned and talked for two hours with me – ⊙ – then being very exausted went to sleep.

The King took the exercise and then at eleven o'clock went to dine – afterwards he went to hunt pigeon in Carditello – the children healthy.

<u>On Sunday December 15</u>, I got up at 7 o'clock – had breakfast – combed my hair – dressed – heard Masses – read – wrote – worked on my affairs – had lunch with my children – the girls stayed with me, then read – wrote – played the harpsichord – saw the wife of don Giovanino Carafa[184] – to intercede for his brother in law – then the father of the Carmelites General Francis – afterwards Ms. Wedel[185] – then the King and back – ⊙ – then prayed – saw my children – afterwards wrote and to bed

The King went out at ten o'clock in St. Arcangelo – hunting wild boars. Children healthy – Januarius appears to me every day [quick] – Joseph with a [convulsive] cough which caused him so much trouble.

On Monday December 16, I got up at 7 o'clock – had breakfast – combed my hair – dressed – heard Masses – read – wrote – had lunch with the King – read – then played music with the King until the evening – when I had audience with Lady Ottajano[186] – for her brother – with a provincial lady for oppression – then the Council – prayed and to bed.

The children healthy – King did not go out all day.

On Tuesday December 17, I got up at 7 o'clock not having slept all night – having always infront of my eyes the fatal and painful disaster of the loss of my dear son Charles who – even though it happened four years ago – is always present and torments my heart – I got up – dressed – heard Mass and wrote all morning – then had lunch with my two eldest daughters – afterwards had the unsurpassed weakness of not being able to see my children in this fateful day – then wrote again – talked with S.B. – then Roccella – afterwards prayed – played music against my will – the King – who had ordered me – came to hear him sing it – then finished my affairs and to bed.

The children healthy – King stayed from morning to night in San Leucio – saw the wood being cutting.

On Wednesday December 18, I got up at 7 o'clock – dressed – had break-fast – saw the children – heard Holy Masses – wrote – read – had lunch with my girls – then afterwards lunch they stayed with me – then talked to S: B: afterwards had some hearings – afterwards the Council – worked and to bed.

The children healthy – the King went hunting on Monte Calvo.

On Tuesday December 19, I got up in the morning – had breakfast – combed my hair – dressed – heard Holy Masses – read – devoted myself – had lunch with the King – then talk to $\underline{a}$[187] – saw the children – talked with the King – ☉ – afterwards the two Councils Finance and war – then prayed and to bed.

The children healthy – in the morning the King went to San Leucio – after-noonnn to the grove.

On Friday December 20, I got up at 7 o'clock – had breakfast – combed my hair – dressed – heard Masses – wrote – then around midday I went out with my three daughters – Marsico and the lady – to the wood – in Canalone – afterwards a very short path – I met Gatti – I returned and had lunch with all the children – then I took care of them – afterwards read – wrote – and then the King came back – he took his milk with coffeee – I kept him company – continued to do my affairs – until time to go to bed.

The children healthy – the King went to the [swamp] at Acerra.

On Saturday December 21, I got up at 7 o'clock – had breakfast – combed my hair – dressed – Holy Masses – saw my children – and at eleven – I left Caserta with Theresa – the lady and Marsico and arrived at quarter past one – where I had lunch with Theresa – afterwards saw Sam: then Sangro – then Act: – then Lady Tripalda – Marquise Sam – then the King came – afterwards saw the little [Loperol] – Theresa – prayed – did my little affairs and paraded and went to sleep.

> The King went to St. Vito – then to the pheasant farm and he came back in the evening

On Sunday December 22nd, I got up at 7 o'clock – had breakfast with Theresa – combed my hair – dressed – heard Holy Mass – then worked on my affairs – afterwards half past eleven I went with the lady and Gallo[188] to Posillipo – I met the King – with Migliano – Cassano – Altavilla – Corleto – Acton – Rasoumowski and third commander and commander Russian – Dinna is – afterwards lunch – I left and came back home – I kept myself busy with a – then I spoke of my business – afterwards I saw the King and spoke to him ⊗ – to the French lady – Madame de Chalais[189] – then the Great Maîtresse – prayed – listened to the music and to bed.

> The King went to the Russian vessel – then had lunch in Posillipo where he did the (…) – the children healthy.

On Monday the 23rd, I got up at 7 o'clock – had breakfast – combed my hair – dressed – listened to Theresa – during her homework – afterwards a – then talked withSan Marco – afterwards went to the chapel – to the Mass and blessing – then saw people – afterwards talked with Lady Belmonte – then Gengano – afterwards had lunch with Teresa – later spoke to Sangro – SB – to a – then the King came back – I spoke with the King ⊗ – then I had some hearings to the poor S.Lorenzo[190] and San Felice[191] – then the Council – afterwards worked on my affairs and to bed.

> The King went to Fusaro at half past 8 in the morning and returned at half past 4. The children healthy.

<u>On Tuesday December the 24th,</u> I got up at 7 o'clock – had breakfast – dressed – combed my hair – heard the children – had lunch with them – and afterwards I saw them playing – then I started to write and to do my affairs – prayed – at nine o'clock I went with my two eldest daughters in the King's bedroom – where there was a large cantata sung by the best teachers and it lasted until midnight – where we went to hear the three Masses in the main chapel and afterwards a dinner for 40 guests.

> In the morning the King went to Carditello and returned in the evening – children healthy – dear Mimi a little cold.

On December 25, Christmas Day I got up at 8 o'clock – had breakfast withTheresa – afterwards dressed – combed my hair – hear Holy Masses – then the hand-kissing – where – a moment before going ou the King – had the terrible fear that the Duke St. Elizabeth[192] fell dead as a doornail at his feet – there was hand-kissing – the public table – the King bled himself and I – afterwards the table – I undressed – had lunch – saw MadameSan Marco – then <u>a</u> – then I prayed and spoke to the King on his return – ☉ – afterwards we went to the theatre where there was the opera ballet – to which I took my two eldest daughters – after the theatre we went home.

> The King afternoonnn went to San Leucio – the children – thanks to God – well.

<u>On Thursday the 26th,</u> I got up at 7 o'clock – had breakfast – combed my hair – dressed – heard Masses – spoke to <u>a</u> – to <u>SB</u> – to <u>Cim</u> – then had lunch with my children – afterwards spoke again to <u>a</u> – then saw Rocafiorita – the Christmas bishop – Princess Butera – then the two Councils – later to bed.

> The children healthy – in the morning the King went to Carditello – hunting wild boar – and returned in the evening.

On Friday the 27th, I got up at 7 o'clock – had breakfast – dressed – combed my hair – heard Holy Masses – wrote – read – had lunch with the children – they stayed with me – and saw Princess Belmonte who announced of the marriage of her son – then again with the children – a long conversation with the King – prayed – wrote and looked afterwards all evening.

> Les enfans bien – le Roi alla à St. Arcangelo à une chasse de sungliers.

On Saturday December 28, I got up at 7 o'clock – had breakfast – combed my hair – dressed – heard Holy Masses – worked on my affairs – had lunch with the children – take them with me – then saw Migliano – then read – wrote – prayed – kept myself busy – at 8 o'clock I went to bed with a slight fever.

> Les enfans bien – le Roi alla à St. Leucy à dîner et à la fesanerie.

On Sunday December 29, I got up at 7 o'clock – had breakfast – combed my hair – dressed – heard Holy Masses – spoke to the children – arranged my affairs – then saw the Duke of Chartres[193] – whom Sambuca introduced to me with Mr. Genlis[194] and Fitzjames[195] – I I found them quite well and not as bad as I had imagined – they all dined with us at table 20 guest – afterwards they saw our children – and afterwards a conversation – they went to see the wood – afterwards I undressed – worked on my affairs and having fever went to bed early.

> In the King did exercise with Liparoti – in evening he went to a little wood. The children healthy.

On Monday December 30 I got up at 7 o'clock – dressed – combed my hair – had breakfast – heard Holy Masses – worked on my affairs – had lunch with my children – saw Lord Salandra that arrived – wrote – saw Lady Tripalda – Rocafiorita – Patrizio – then the Council – prayed – worked on my affairs and to bed.

> Little Joseph had a strong cold – the others well – the King in the morning went to San Leucio and then to Carbone.

EDITORIAL CRITERIA 165

On 31 Tuesday I got up at 7 o'clock – had breakfast – combed my hair – dressed – heard Holy Mass – wrote my post – had lunch with the children – Rocella spoke to me of Trabia[196] that nominated his relative for the Sicilian Junta – then saw my children playing and writing – spoke to Cicio Pignatelli for [the *asiento*] and for clothing of the trope – afterwards the young Salandra – the King returned – kept me company – then wrote – prayed – I confessed myself – and went to sleep – and thus for me ended the year 1782. My children are – in good health and Theresa is improving well in her education – Louise sickly – feeble in body and mind – but learns and follows her education – Francis high spirit – healthy – strong spirit of judgment but impolite, Mimi cheerful healthy very nice does not know anything but without caracter flaw – Januarius of poor health – weak – retarded – does not stand even up – Joseph – weak – pale – unhealthy – full of spiriy witty – Amelia healthy – strong – well being – the King well and I two months pregnant – God bless us – save all. Amen.

Little Joseph continues with his cough – the others healthy. The King went to Casertavecchia – for a partridges hunting.

JOURNAL 1783

1. The January 1783
On Wednesday January the 1st, I went in the morning to church where I received communion – then I had breakfast with Theresa – received the compliments from my children – for everything that there was at Caserta – combed my hair – dressed – prayed – and then heard two Masses – had lunch with my children – worked on my affairs – wrote – read – saw ◣◢ Lady Cariati Seminarone[197] for her affairs – she begged me to not to be at the mercy of of her miserly husband without money – and Countess Gaetani[198] for her issue – then the King came – I spoke to him – ⊗ – afterwards there was the Council of Justice and from there I undressed and went to bed. The King went to the grove in the morning to shoot duck – then with the Prior went to Zingaro to prepare everything for hunting in Zingaro. My children were well – poor little Joseph has a dangerous and nasty cold in his small body. I wore a dress of white satin embroidered with green and gold and combed my hair and jewelry – I suffered because of pregnancy as usual.

On Thursday January the 2nd, I got up at 7 o'clock – had breakfast – combed my hair – dressed – heard Holy Masses ♥ – had lunch with my children whom I kept with me until three o'clock, ♥ – afterwards 000 ◣ ◢ then I prayed and waited for the King who came back at seven o'clock very happy because of the big game hunting – he stayed with me – ☉ – then we had the Cimitile's Council followed by Acton's – afterwards undressed and went to bed. In the morning the King went out – with all the innhabitants of Caserte – to Zingaro where the Duke of Chartres came – there was a great wild boars hunting trip and 147 boars died and everything succeeded wonderfully. I wore my hair with a little bonnet[199] over my hair and [with] a brown polka [jacket].[200] My children – thanks to God – were healthy – I suffered less than other days from my pregnancy.

On Friday January the 3rd, I got up at 7 o'clock – had breakfast – dressed and heard Mass – then wrote 000[201] – read my letters that I had not read – saw my children – had lunch with the King – and I wrote until eight o'clock in the evening – finished all my particular accounts books and other writings of the old year and start the new year – I was only interupted by the hearing of Princess Ottajano – who spoke to me about her issue and begged me to give more time to the two judges Porcinari[202] and Patrizio for her famous lawsuit, then Ferrante – who asked me a letter of recomendation for her son who will travel to Italy to marry a Milanese lady. In the morning the King went to the pheasant farm to prepare everything for the hunting trip – he had lunch at home and went out again at two o'clock to go to San Leucio for the same reason. My children – thanks to God – were well – a cough bothered little Joseph. I wore a big bonnet over my hair and yellow house jacket – very sad and sickly – in the evening I prayed – I saw my children and I went to bed.

On Saturday January the 4th, I got up at 7 o'clock – had breakfast – combed my hair – dressed – heard Holy Mass – wrote – read – had lunch with my children – spoke to m. – then wrote 000 – afterwards saw Lady Wedel and kept her with me for a conversation – afterwards I dressed s and prayed – then the King returned + – afterwards we went to the theatre – I in the carriage – the King on foot – at the theatre I had the Duke of Chartres – Fitz James – Genlis – Gravina and Migliano in my loge – they played the little music of *le Veuvage d'un* – then I came back home – at nine o'clock we were at home – I prayed – I undressed – had dinner and went to bed. My children were – thanks to God – healthy, in the morning the King went out with Chartres to the pheasant farm where they killed 180 pheasants – then they had lunch in San Leucio and after dinnerthere was a wild boar hunting trip where they shot 30. I wore a little bonnet over my hair, [and] wore with a green british dress.

On Sunday January the 5th, I got up at 7 o'clock – had breakfast – combed my hair – dressed – saw my children – heard Holy Mass – read – wrote – had lunch with the children – they stayed with me afterwards lunch – wrote – saw Paterno, Father Gagliani – the King returned – he conversed with me – ⊙ – then I prayed – saw my children and the eldest daughters played the harpsichord in the presence of Migliano – Gravina and Lamberg – then bedtime. The King went to his guardianship – all day with Migliano. The children – thanks to God – well. I wore polka green jacket and a bonnet over my hair.

On Monday January the 6th, I got up at 7 o'clock – had breakfast – combed my hair – dressed – saw my children – had breakfast with Theresa – heard Holy Masses – then took care of my children – afterwards had lunch with them – write 000 – and then stayed with the children who played around me – afterwards came Princess Caramanico – then ◣◢ – afterwards Altavilla introduced me to the Russian lady Waraskon[203] – and then the King came – kept me company – ⊙ – then I prayed – saw my children – presided over the Council of Sambuca – and went to sleep. The children healthy, I wore a little bonnet over my hair and a lilac and white dress. The King went to have lunch at the castle in the woods and then to Carbone – to hunt.

On Tuesday January the 7th, the I got up at 7 o'clock – combed my hair – dressed – had breakfast – heard Holy Mass – wrote the post – dinner with my children – talked with LadySan Marco – for cutting her wood, saw the wife of Luigi Galeota[204] – then Laurino[205] for an for an injustice done to his sister in law – who by force was put in a convent against the wishes of the parents who did not want her there at all, and Palmira for being lady during the hand-kissing ceremony afterwards ◣◢ – then Francis – afterwards prayed – gave a small ball to my children – to my three daughters – to the two of Altavilla of [Caitone] – the daughter of Madame Roche Wintersee – they danced – the spectators were Gravina and Vasto – then I gave them dinner – I undressed – wrote to the King – and then worked on my affairs and to bed. In the morning at six o'clock the King went to Monteragone with Chartres and Fitzjames and all ministers and gentlemen. The children were well – afterwards-dinner Francis complained of headache and went to bed – the doctor found he had a fever, I was dressed with night hat with muslin blazers all *undressed*.[206]

On Wednesday January the 8th, I got up at 7 o'clock – had break-fast – combed my hair – heard Holy Mass – 000 – talked a long time with Gravina for arrangements for my son, had lunch with Louise – saw the gallantry of Madiot – unpacked new books from France, then played with the little one and Mimi – spoke to Montalto about his problems to ◣◢ – wrote – prayed – saw my children at 8. O'clock. The King returned from Monteragone – presided over the Council of Carlo de Marco and went to bed. My children – thanks to God – were well – Francis was healthy and was up all day and I suffered a lot – all day ills of pregnancy. I wore a large hat and a muslin jacket, all *undressed*. The King came back from Mondragone since yesterday morning – the first day killed 20 boars on the second day 1200 ducks but he was not satisfied with this hunt.

On Thursday January 9, I got up at 7 o'clock – had breakfast – combed my hair – dressed – heard Mass – saw my children – arranged my little affairs – at eleven o'clock I left Naples with Gravina – Marsico and the lady in Toledo [Detio] fell from her horse – but – thanks to God – not hurt – then I arrived – saw the first assault of people and then I had lunch – read my letters – the gazettes of the post – arranged my papers and began to read ♥ then I saw the young Salandra who would like a home for her hus-band in Caserta – Then the King returned – I prayed – we went to the Fondo theatre where the new comic opera – entitled l'*astrologo*[207] – was a composition of all the imaginable horrors – little unpleasant pot-pourri and long – on return I undressed – put […] and went to the San Carlo theatre with Lady Gravina and Marsico – I could not go down – not feel-ing well – Chartres came twice to my loge and also Fitzjames – we stayed until half past one and from there [went] at home. The children – thanks to God – healthy – I suffered most of the day from the pregnancy, and from the effort to vomit. The King went hunting at lunchtime in San Leucio – and at the pheasant farm he killed a wolf four ducks and 58 pheasants – he returned about six o'clock +. I wore a little bonnet over my hair with a yellow polka jacket.

On Friday January 10, I got up at 7 am – had breakfast – dressed – listened to Mass – wrote to Caserta – 000 – saw the ladies – then had lunch with the King with whom I had a long conversation + – then walked out on the terrace three or four times – later my affairs ♥ – then had dinner – later gave hearings – Princess Acquaviva[208] for a domes-tic affair – Anna Maria Patrizio[209] for her son as a provincial auditor – Saverio Cresconio[210] for his brother judge in Naples – Maria Angiola[211] for her husband [to] settle there – then ≤ later the King returned, I conversed with him □ – afterwards there were two Councils of Finance and War – afterwards which I undressed – I prayed and went to bed. The King in the morning went to the dock – to see the lugger – in the afternoon at half past one went to Portici to hunt skylarks. I knew from Caserta that my children were well thank God. I wore a little bonnet over my hair and a green polka [jacket].

On Saturday January 11, I got up at 7 hours – had breakfast – combed my hair – heard Holy Mass – wrote to Caserta – wrote the post – had lunch with the King – and held a comversation with afterwards ♥ – then I had a world of intoductions – Aciajoli[212] – Tuscany court lady, – (Sanhagar) a milanese introduced by Civitella, Feroleto introduced me to another whose name I have forgotten – then prayed and went to San Carlo theatre. In the the morning the King went to the porcelain [factory] – afterwards lunch at half past one he went to Capo di Monte to shoot larks and returned in the evening – thanks to God I had the good new about my children. I wore polka [piece] with a bonnet over my hair.

On Sunday the 12th, I got up at 7 o'clock – had breakfast – dressed – combed my hair – heard and received the first compliments for the day – and then I received a present of 2000 ounces from the King with a card which I wanted to answer – then went out for Mass – I wore court dress and went out to the hand-kissing and public table – where the Duke of Chartres – as to one as to another – appeared as a simple stranger and was very polite – afterwards I undressed – had lunch – kept company with the King – who came out for an half hour for the royal tennis and then returned home – where * afterwards ⊗ – then I wore again court dress – I gave hand-kissing to the ladies – after that I changed my white polka [jacket] – prayed and went to the well lit theatre with a great illumination – then we went to sleep before the second ballet. The King went out for a while to the royal tennis, my dear children were well – while I wore a blue satin court dress with laces, and in the evening a white polka [jacket] with all the jewelry I have.

On Monday January 13, I got up at 7 o'clock – had breakfast – combed my hair – heard Holy Mass ♥ then r.a.d.a.d'.a.l.d'a.t.t.b.a.t.l.d.[213] – afterwards I talked with Torella[214] for the case of [gulline] of the city – I saw Lamberg – afterwards [I listened to] all my ladies and went to have lunch – and then came Migliano – Cimitile – Sambuca – all informed me of the Council that had been ♥ e.c.f.l.p.f.q.j.s.l.v.p.l.s.b.d.m.d.e.c.e.d.h.[215] – then I saw Madame Sambuca complaining – afterwards Faggiano begged me to not to have his brother in law married – the King came back – there was the Council of Sambuca – and then we went to see a comedy of Canito where where I initiately liked the woman who acted – she softened me a lot – from there I went to dress up and to go to the theatre of the ball – I went down a bit with Gravina and Marsico and had Chartres who took leave from my loge – at one o'clock we returned home and I ⊙ undressed and went to bed. The King went at 7 o'clock to a fishing pond with Chartres in Castellamare and returned in the evening, the children were well, I was dressed in gray and black polka [jacket] – had started the evening with domino.

On Tuesday the 14th, I got up early and started to write letters – dressed – combed my hair – heard Holy Mass ♥ – and then wrote – talked with Rocella – Princess Butera – then went to Caserta where I went with the young marchioness and Gravina – I found my children who welcomed me with their innocent joy – I had lunch alone with Louise – Theresa has been very nasty – the then morning did not have this honour – the littleones had already dined – I remained with them, and then began to write – then the King came back and I finished my post – began to pray and then to bed The children were well – thanks to God. The King went at 5 o'clock to Carditello where there was an hunting run from where Monsieur de Chartres – Genlis Fitzjames left for Rome. I wore a great bonnet with a gray and black jacket.

On Wednesday the 15th, I got up at 7 o'clock – had breakfast – combed my hair – dressed – heard Holy Mass – read – wrote – worked on my affairs – had lunch with the King – read – kept company saw engravings, then he ent out ◣◢ – afterwards wrote – read – saw my children – talked with the King – ⊙ – and the Council – prayed and bled myself. My children were well, the King came out in the afternoon to the little grove. I was dressed in a jacket and big bonnet.

On Thursday January 16, I got up at 7 o'clock – had breakfast – dressed – combed my hair – heard Holy Mass ≤ then Migliano came to talk with me – I began to write ♥ afterwards had lunch with my children – they stayed with me ♥ ⊙ ▲ then wrote – took care – the King came back – he presided over the two Councils and I prayed and went to bed. The King went to Calvi to hunt ducks from morning to night. The children were well – except Amélie and Januarius. I was all *negligee*[216] – the wound reopened – but without pain.

On Friday January 17, I got up in the morning – went to congralulate Mimi who – thanks to God – turned four years – I had breakast with her and Louise – heard Mass – 000 – did some accounts – gave presents – received wishes for this dear little girl – had lunch with them – saw clothes that had arrived from Paris – gave them to my children – to the whole house – after lunch Sangro and Salandra came – and Serra Capriola[217] to take leave – Roccafiorita for some affairs – then the King returned – we saw Cardinal Bandini[218] – then I spoke to him ⊗ – then there was a childrens' ball – to please the children and after dinner – at eight o'clock it was all over – I undressed – prayed and went to bed. The King went to Carbone to hunt ducks. I was dressed in white and sable pleated satin with a bonnet and jewelry.

On Saturday January 18, I got up at 7 o'clock – had breakfast – dressed – heard Holy Mass – went to see the library – wrote – saw my children – then had lunch with Francis and Mimi – the two eldest were punished – afterwards lunch – I kept them with me – afterwards came MarchionessSan Marco – then I spoke to Migliano – afterwards some hearings – the wife of Anguissola[219] to entrust herself – and a poor woman from Bitonto for justice – then I finished my post – prayed – saw my children – prayed – at 8 o'clock the King returned – I received him – and then went to sleep. The children – thanks to God – well – except Januarius who continued having a cold, the King went at 6 o'clock to Monteragone – hunting ducks – and came back in the night. I wore a big bonnet over my hair and jacket – all *negligee*.

On Sunday January 19, I got up at 7 o'clock – had breakfast – combed my hair – dressed – heard Holy Mass – wrote – read the letters – saw Duchess Gravina – then had lunch with my children – kept them with me – then wrote – afterwards saw Countess Vigolino[220] for the affairs – Lady Bischi[221] for her sons – then Lady Wedel – the King returned – kept me company – I saw my children – sermonised Theresa – then wrote – prayed and went to bed. The King went to the feast of San Leucio at eleven o'clock – dined there and then went to the pheasant farm. The children healthy. I wore a little bonnet over my hair and dressed with a polka color pink and black.

On Monday January 20, I got up at 7 o'clock – had breakfast – dressed – combed my hair – heard Holy Mass – read – wrote – then at half past eleven went out at the hand-kissing with all the children – except Januarius – the eldest were dressed in cherry color [and were] on the embroidered cart – my dear Mimi had a lilac dress and lace – Joseph blue emperor and lace – and Amelia pink and lace – we took the hand-kissing – held Francis and the four girls at the big hand-kissing – then I undressed – had lunch – kept company with the King – saw engravings ⊗ afterwards affairs ♥ Lord Belmonte spoke to me – then I prayed – saw the children and went to the theatre – there was the Florentines opera, where I took my two eldest daughters – on return I undressed and I went to bed. The King did not go out. In the morning I was dressed in a gala silver dress embroidered in green and gold – in the evening with lilac frock-coat.

On January 21, I got up at 7 o'clock – had breakfast – dressed – combed my hair – heard Holy Mass then ♥ then had lunch with the children – in Francis's room – afterwards wrote the post ◣◢ – then the King came back – kept company with him – afterwards continued to write until 8 o'clock – when I prayed and went to bed. The children healthy. In the morning at nine o'clock the King went to Madalona to hunt wild boars and returned at 6 o'clock. I wore a little bonnet over my hair and a pink and black polka [jacket].

On Wednesday the 22nd, I got up at 7 o'clock – had breakfast – combed my hair – dressed – slept most of the morning – eyes closed on a sofa – wrote a little – heard Holy Mass – had lunch with the King – kept him company – laid myself on a sofa – read the papers – affairs – wrote – saw the children – masking books – with the King to the Council of Carlo de Marco and went to bed at eight o'clock.The King did not go out for the bad weather – the children healthy, and I all *undressed* [and] very sick.

On Thursday the 23rd, I got up at 7 o'clock – had breakfast – combed my hair – dressed – heard Holy Mass – then saw and talked with Carlo de Marco ♥ – then had lunch with my children – stayed with them ♥ – afterwards worked on my affairs – the King came back – I prayed – saw my children, and then the two Councils, my children were well, King went to Carditello and returned in the evening. I wore a little bonnet over my hair – gray and black polka [jacket].

On Friday the 24rd, I got up at 7 o'clock – had breakfast – combed my hair – dressed – saw my children – heard Holy Mass – talked with Trej about the porcelain for the Prince of Asturias – then wrote – later had lunch with the King – read – wrote – Salandra spoke about the end of the marriage of her mother – finished after 23 years and that he [father] is so adverse – afterwards a lady from Sorrento for family affairs – then wrote – put my papers in order until half past 8 – then prayed – saw Lamberg and to bed. In the morning the King went to the grove for a walk – the afternoon in San Leucio. All children healthy – I wore a big bonnet over my hair and quite *negligee*.

On Saturday January 25, I got up at 7 o'clock – had breakfast – dressed – combed my hair – heard Holy Mass – started to write and work – had lunch with Teresa – Francis and Mimi – afternoon draw silhouette portraits – I did the one of Francis and Theresa and then I did so in miniature with a pantograph – afterwards I saw Migliano – then Princess Villa who wants the vicar of Naples to continue to defend her – then wrote – the King returned – I saw my children – worked on my affairs and went to bed. In the morning the King went to Carditello with the Prior by dray – did not dine – and then afternoonwent to Carbone – the children healthy. I was completely *negligee*.

On Sunday the 26th, I got up at 7 o'clock – had breakfast – dressed – combed my hair – heard Holy Mass – wrote – arranged papers – saw my children – had lunch with them – afternoon stayed with them – then went for a walk with Teresa and Louise in Canalone – on return I met Gravina who accompanied me – I saw Feydeau e Amignano[222] who both asked me for a nomiation as land agent in Capo di Monte for their husbands, I spoke to Gravina – Count Micheli Pignatelli – then came the King – I conversed with him – ⊙ – then I prayed – undressed and to bed. The King went [hunting] ducks in Piedimonte. The children healthy. I wore a little back bonnet over my hair – white polka black topped. In the morning Füger painted me.

On Monday 27th, I got up at 7 o'clock – had breakfast – dressed – combed my hair – heard Holy Mass – wrote – worked – had lunch with my children – saw MarchionessSan Marco to thank for a cut of the grove that she got – then Vigolino for his affairs – read – wrote – until the return of the King – presided over the Council and went to bed. The King went to the first hunt (…) – which was copious. The children healthy – Genarino is consumed – annhilated but without illness, I was all *negligee* with a big bonnet.

On Thursday January 28, I got up at 7 o'clock – had breakfast – combed my hair – dressed – heard Holy Mass – wrote – worked – saw my children – had lunch with the King – kept him company – read – did some portraits in shadow – ⊙ – then saw Vigoleno who came to thank me for being nomiated land agent of Capo di Monte – then wrote – read – saw my children and went to bed. The King could not go out all day because of bad weather. The children healthy. Me all *negligee* with a big bonnet.

On Wednesday the 29th, I got up at 7 o'clock – dressed – combed my hair – had breakfast – saw the children – spoke to Migliano – then stayed relaxed on a chair – my mind is unable to <u>concentrate</u> – having had a violent convulsive headache night – I was sick all day – I had lunch with my children – afternoonFrancis and Mimi stayed with me – then ◣◢ – afterwards two hearings – one widow of already three husbands and another poor woman – the King returned – there was Council – I prayed and then went to bed. The King went to the pheasant farm to hunt pheasants. My children healthy, me *negligee* with jacket and big bonnet.

On Thursday January the 30th, I got up at 7 o'clock – had breakfast – combed my hair – dressed – heard Holy Mass □♥ – worked on my affairs – had lunch with my children – then kept myself busy – saw Acton – then a – then my children ◇ the King returned – there were two Councils – I saw Lamberg, and then went to bed. My children healthy. The King went hunting to (…), I was half hairdo with a gray and black polka.

On Friday January the 31st, I got up to 7 o'clock – had breakfast – combed my hair – dressed-I was forced to put myselfu on the bed – not feeling well – then heard Holy Mass and went out to walk with Theresa – Mimi and Gatti – then had lunch with children – plopped down on the couch to read, then Sangro came to beg to me for her problems – then Rocella talked me for a long time – then the King came back – kept me company – ⊙ – afterwards saw Joseph – worked on my affairs – prayed and went to bed. The King went hunting to Capajo – the children healthy – except little Joseph in the evening the cough increased and he had a slight fever. I was all *negligee*.

On Saturday february the 1st, I got up at 7 o'clock – had breakfast – combed my hair – dressed – wrote – took care of the poor little sick Joseph – had lunch with the children – talked with Migliano – wrote – read – devoted myself – went to Januarius – the King came back – I returned to Joseph's room – Januarius and Joseph – wrote – prayed and went to bed. The King went to the pheasant farm. My children healthy – Januarius with a continual violent cough and fever – little Joseph with a high fever – in the evening he had a new one but more lightly. I was all *negligee*.

On Sunday february 2, I got up at 7 o'clock – combed my hair – dressed – had breakfast – heard Holy Mass – saw my children – wrote – worked on my affairs – had lunch with my children – they stayed with me after lunch during which I read – then saw my little boys – countess Gaetani – then again my children – the King came back – he had milk with coffeee – I kept company with him – ⊙ – then read – worked on my affairs – prayed and went to bed. The King went at eleven o'clock to the swamp in Acerra to kill ducks. My dear children were quite well – Januarius was a little better during night – but as the violent cough and slight fever continued he did get up from the bed – Joseph was a little better at night but the fever never stopped – it stated again at five o'clock in the evening – the cough was violent and the child did not stop crying – both afflicted me and did not like it at all. I wore a little bonnet over my hair and a polka [jacket] colour pink and black.

On Monday february 3, I got up at 7 o'clock – had breakfast – dressed – combed my hair – heard Holy Mass – saw my children – wrote – went to my childrens' room – had lunch with my girls – then went out to the wood with them to Peschiera[223] – afterwards returned – wrote – read – devoted myself – saw my sick children – the King returned – there was the Council – afterwards I went to bed. The children so-so – Francis started having a little cold – Januarius was a little better – as Joseph – the girls well – King went hunting for Capajo – for me I was all negligee.

On Tuesday February 4, I got up at 7 o'clock – had breakfast – combed my hair – dressed – heard Holy Mass – wrote the post – had lunch with my girls – walked with them to Canalone – and then Migliano spoke to me afterwards ◣◢ – then saw my sick children – the King came back – I did some affairs and went to bed. The King went to the Bufaleria[224] and was there all day – I was all negligee, Januarius is better – Francis has having a nasty cold and fever – Joseph was very uneasy [with] continual cough and terrible sleepiness.

On Wednesday February 5, I got up at 7 o'clock – had breakfast – dressed – combed my hair – heard Holy Mass – wrote – read – worked on my affairs – had lunch with my children – took them with me – then went to see all the sick children – afterwards wrote – devoted myself – saw Duchess of Ostuni – for her issue the wife of the Anguissola – for poverty another ◣◢ – then saw my sick children – the King came back – I kept him company – ☉ – afterwards the Council and to bed. The King went out in the morning and returned afterwards half an hour because of bad weather – he left again afternoon in San Leucio. The little boys were better – Francis had fever and Louise had also a little. I wore a yellow polka jacket without mourning and with a little bonnet in occasion of the name of little Altavilla.

On Thursday February 6, I got up at 7 o'clock – had breakfast – combed my hair – dressed – heard Holy Mass□♥ – then saw my sick children – I devoted myself and dinner with Theresa ♥ then devoted myself – saw my sick children – and had both Councils and from there to bed. In the mornoing the King went to hunt at Capajo – the children better – Francis had fever and was purged – but slight – I was all negligee – but I had a bit cold with fever.

On Saturday Friday the 7th, I got up at 7 – I had my breakfast in bed having a nasty cold and stayed there until nine o'clock – got up – dressed – Holy Mass – worked on my affairs – saw my children – had lunch with Theresa – took some books – put all my papers in order – wrote – worked – had some hearing of ladies – father Mariano for his order and then prayed and went to bed – I had fever and violent cough all day – headache – my children were all better – Mimi started to cough and to have warm hands, the King was at *****[225] and then at the grove – I was all of *negligee* and sickly.

On February 8, I got up to 7 o'clock – had breakfast – dressed – combed my hair – heard Holy Mass – saw my children – took leave and at ten o'clock I went to Naples with my three girls – by carriage where I arrived at half past twelve – I had oil put on my skin and put on the sofa – then I had lunch with my two eldest daughters – then I unpacked – worked on my affairs – and began to read – then I saw Count Weissenwolf[226] – introduced by the minister of communication – afterwards I spoke to my ladies – to de Marco – I began to pray – the King returned from Caserta – we went to the opera in San Carlo where only the first ballett was beautiful – during the second I went to the King's room. Then went to sleep. The King went hunting to Morrone – then saw the children in Caserta – and afterwards returned here. Francis began to have evacuations of bile – Joseph to have more cough – Mimi had more cough – I had a big cold. I was half combed my hair with bonnet and jacket color pink and black.

On Sunday the 9th, I got up at 7 o'clock – had breakfast – combed my hair – dressed – heard Holy Mass – remained a little in bed – and then had lunch with the King and spent the after lunch together – afterwards wrote – read – prayed – Genzano kissed my hands – then to the Florentines theatre where we saw a new and very graceful performance of comic opera – afterwards returned – undressed and dolled myself up and to the ball where there were many masks – most of them domino dressed – I did not go down because of my cold – at 2 o'clock we went to bed. The King went out only to go to Toledo – dressed domino – by carriage – at 3 o'clock and returned at 5 o'clock, my children Mimi's cold was better – from Caserta I was informed that Francis was getting better and that Joseph had a cold again, me – I was very uncomfortable with my cold – to the point that evening I took 2 opium pills. I wore a little bonnet over my hair and dressed a black frock-coat the – to the ball with domino dress in the loge.

On Monday the 10th, I woke up at 8 o'clock and got up at f^{27} o'clock because of my cold – dressed – combed my hair – heard Holy Mass – I attended the Council of Sambuca – then Gatti saw Mimi – afterwards lunch with the King – where there were the children – kept company with the King until half past 3 – ☉ – afterwards I wrote – read – saw my children – arranged books – prayed – saw my children dancing – took care of myself and went to bed – where I coughed. The King – because of bad weather – could not go out all day, my children – those who are here – are well Mimi has still a slight cold. From Caserta I was informed that little Joseph has a cold – Francis better. My cold was better – I did not move at all from home in order to treat myself with pills and I was all *negligee*.

On Tuesday the 11th, I got out of the bed at 9 o'clock – after having remained in bed owing to my cold – got up – heard Mass and began to write – dressed – had lunch with the King – kept him company – afterwards I worked on my affairs and wrote them – saw my children – several ladies – then I continued to write and to see my children and to bed. In the evening the King went to Fondo, after lunch to Portici. I was all *negligee*, from Caserta I was informed that little Joseph was very ill – which it afflicted me.

On Wednesday the 12th, I a little late – had breakfast – dressed – heard Holy Mass – saw my children – lunch with the King – kept him company until he went to Capo di Monte – then wrote my ordinary letters – wrote – saw the children – prayed – presided over the Council of Carlo de Marco and afterwards went to see young Popoli[228] dressed as a woman – with whom the King went to the masked ball – for me – still with my cold – I went to bed and there I dined. Joseph a little better.

On Thursday the 13th, I got up at nine o'clock – dressed – combed my hair – heard Holy Mass had breakfast with the children – the King went hunting at Agnano – I had lunch with the children – then saw Sambuca – then – read – wrote – did my business – saw the children – the King came back – there were the 2 Councils – afterwards we went to bed.Little Joseph was better, my cold still very nasty – the King went to Agnano.

On Friday the 14th, I got up later – dressed – heard Holy Mass – then breakfast – Sambuca came to give me the bad news that the frigate Saint Dorothy had arrived and brought the news of the destruction of Messina by an earthquake – I had lunch with my children – later came Acton – Carlo de Marco – all with the same news – I spoke to Vincenzo Pignatelli[229] who escaped from there bringing the same details – I prayed – read – saw my children and waited for the King who came back at half past 9 – and then he received the bad news – after having talked about it – we slept. The King was in Caserta where he wrote to me – and then told me in person – that little Joseph was better – though very weak – and the others well.

On Saturday the 15th, I got up around 9 am – when we had the bad news that a large part of Calabria ultra had suffered the same misfortune as Messina – I got up – dressed – the King after having summoned the four secretaries to make the resolutions on this unfortunate event – it was decided to send marshal[230] Pignatelli on the spot – – to rescue the unfortunate – and reserving at the moment the right to take action depending on the circumstances – afterwards I had lunch with the King and kept him company – I wrote my post – saw my children – spoke to Pignatelli who had to leave – finished writing – worked on my affairs – prayed and went to bed. The King went out all day. The children better – me with my cold – everybody dismayed.

On Sunday the 16th, I got up in the morning and perdormed my devotions – then had breakfast – dressed – heard another Holy Mass – read – wrote – had dinner with the King – kept him company – did my accounts – afterwards saw my children – before four o'clock I went with the King to the blessing – which was in the chapel and then took care of myself – saw my children and to bed. The children quite well – little Joseph better – me – always with my cold and very sad – the King took exercise after lunch.

On Monday the 17th, I woke up late and got up at 10 o'clock – dressed – combed my hair – heard Holy Mass – had lunch with my children – spoke to Acton – Carlo de Marco – took care of myself – was with my children – the King came back – I went with him to the blessing and kept him company – during that [time] he took tea with milk – ⊙ – afterwards there was the Council – then did some affairs – prayed and to bed. Mimi had again a new cold with fever – she was quite annoyed – little Joseph still in pain – me the same with my cold which makes me suffering – the King at 2 o'clock went hunting at Agnano and returned at 4 o'clock – he also has a slight cold. I was always very dismayed by the bad news that still arrives.

On Tuesday the 18th, after having spent a very bad night – I woke up at 8 o'clock and received bad news regarding the health of Joseph – I thought a bit with the King on what we had to do – then I sat down to write – read – combed my hair – dressed – heard Holy Mass – saw Mimi who was better but still in bed – had lunch with the King – kept him company – read – worked on my affairs – saw my children – go to blessing – write my letters – worked on my affairs – the children – prayed and to bed – the news concerning the children is very bad – Joseph ill – Mimi in bed with her cold – me very sad. The King after lunch went to Portici.

On Wednesday the 19th, I got up at 7 o'clock – the news concerning Joseph was not better – I got up – dressed – I listened to Mass – I took leave of Mimi and went with Teresa – Luisa and Marchioness Altavilla to Caserta – where I arrived at half past eleven – very anxious to have news of my little Joseph – the coldness of which depressed me – I ran up the stairs – I flew into the room of my little one – I found him on his bed he recognized me – he looked at me – shook my finger that handed him [and] a moment later came the hiccups did not let him go until his hands were cold – then the doctor said he no longer had a pulse – I was away from the room I lay down on a sofa – I saw my two eldest daughters – at midday the King returned we cried and talked of this loss – an hour and a half we sat at the table – afterwards I remained with the King – at 4 o'clock the other children were brought to me – it was a new stab to my broken heart – at half past 5 with the permission of the King I went to see my little lifeless one – cold and dead – I kissed his hands – I embraced him – kissed his feet – this caused me in a terrible and painful sweetness – had a face [which was] nice calm [and] relaxed I was touched and I cried so that he would pray for his afflicted mother – I went home, and at 7 o'clock the beloved child was taken to Naples – I lay down – I took care of myself and tried I went to sleep.

On Thursday February 20th, I got up in the morning and I cried a lot – later dressed – listened to Mass ♥ – read – worked on my affairs – lunch with my two eldest daughters – prayed – took care – saw my children – and presided over the two Councils – in my room – later to bed. The King went to the Masseria delle Bufale[231] at ten o'clock and returned at 5 o'clock – my children enjoyed it – we embalmed my little one and we did not find any deficiency – which I knew because he was nice and in a small way perfectly well breeded and of a precocious intelligence and ability – in the evening he was brought to St. Clara, where he remained exposed throughout the night – I was still very sad.

On Friday the 21st, I got up – dressed – went to the Mass – worked on my affairs – wrote – read – had lunch with the King – kept company with me – took care of myself ◣◥ – then wrote – made all the rewards for those who had served my beloved Pepe – I will never forget it – then played – prayed – saw my daughters and went to bed. In the morning the King went to the grove and after lunch to San Leucio where he returned in the evening – the children healthy – my little Joseph was after religious service admitted to eternal rest with his brother Charles and sister Mariane[232] – here are three parts of me [which are] cold and buried under ground.

On Saturday February 22, I got up around 9 o'clock – after having spent the night coughing – I had no need to rest and had my break-fast in bed – dressed – combed my hair – heard Holy Mass – wrote my post – embraced Mimi who arrived from Naples – saw other children – had lunch with the King – kept company with him – saw the people of my late beloved Pepe – then wrote – saw Duchess Gravina – once again the King – languished – dragged myself – stayed with the King during his lunch – worked on my affairs – prayed and to bed – my children healthy – the King did not go out because of bad weather – for me my cold tormented me – I felt ever sadder and dejected.

On Sunday February 23, I had a restless night – I got up at half past 7 and took an ounce of salt of England – afterwards I walked and then dressed – combed my hair – then Holy Mass – read – wrote – had lunch with my two eldest daughters – spent the after lunch with them – read the letters – wrote – ◣◢ then took care of myself – then saw Tarsia – afterwards took care of myself – saw the children – prayed and to bed – in the morning the King went out for breakfast at Carditello – returned at noon – he went out again at two o'clock on horseback to have lunch at 4 o'clock at the Belvedere.[233] The children healthy – my heart – has beeb broken a thousand times – I go to the door of my little one imagining to find him and the cruel certainty that I will never see him again.

On Monday February 24, I got up a little late to take care of my health – I dressed – combed my hair – heard Holy Mass – wrote a few early letters – had lunch with the King – kept him company – then took care of myself – read – wrote – ◣◢ prayed – saw my children – attended the King during his tea with milk – ⊙ – afterwards Council of Sambuca – and then to bed. The King went out in the morning to the grove – the afternoon at Carditello – the children healthy – me – my health better but soul [very] sad.

On Tuesday February 25, I got up late – the King kept me company during mybreakfast – ⊙ – then I wrote – still in bed and I gor up at half past 10 – I dressed – combed my hair – heard Holy Mass – saw my children – had lunch with the King and kept him company – after I began to write – saw Marquise San Marco – ◣◢ – then wrote – took care of myself – prayed and to bed. The King went in the morning to the royal tennis – after lunch at the pheasant farm where he killed 70 pheasants. The children healthy – I am better but sad.

On Wednesday February 26, I got up at 9 o'clock – dressed – combed my hair – heard Holy Mass – wrote – took care of myself – saw my children – had lunch with my two eldest daughters – spent the after lunch with them – saw Princess Caramanica ◣◢ took care of myself – then read – wrote – the King returned took care of myself – presided over the Council of Carlo de Marco again took care of myself, and then to bed. The King was in Piedimonte hunting woodcocks – the children healthy – me all in pain.

On Thursday February 27, I got up at 9 o'clock – had breakfast – dressed – combed my hair – heard Holy Mass – had lunch with my children – wrote – read – devoted myself – the King came back – I was all day in a bad mood – dark – highly strung and very annoyed, my children healthy – the King went to dinner at San Leucio – the weather was very bad.

On Friday the 28th, I got up – dressed – wrote – heard Holy Mass – read – prayed – dinner with the King – see prints – ☉ – saw my children – then Acton – afterwards I began to read – prayed – then the King came back – there were the two Councils afterwards I went to bed. The King went in the morning to Carbone – after lunch at the grove – the children healthy – me better.

On Saturday March 1, I got up in the morning – had breakfast – dressed – combed my hair – heard Holy Mass – wrote my post – worked on my affairs – read – saw my children – had lunch – kept myself busy – read – wrote – saw Serra Capriola who is leaving for Russia as minister – then wrote – saw my children – prayed – kept myself busy until the time of going to bed. The children healthy – the King was in Carbone and did not return until half past five when he had dinner with my company – and then we saw the Cardinal Archbishop of Naples – the weather was quite passable.

On March 2, Sunday I got up as usual at half past 7 – dressed – had breakfast – combed my hair – heard 2 Holy Masses – wrote – worked – worked on my affairs – had lunch with my children – afternoon kept them with me – read – applied and prayed – the King came back – we stayed a while all together to keep ourselves company – ☉ – then I let my children dance – music – the joy filled me with great sadness and so I went to bed. The children healthy – the King went to San Leucio to have lunch.

On Monday the 3rd, I got up at 7 o'clock – had breakfast – dressed – combed my hair – heard Holy Mass – wrote – read – saw my children – went to have lunch with them – afternoon with them – and then wrote – devoted myself – read until the King returned – there was Council and I went to bed. The children healthy – the King was in Carditello all day [hunting] pigeons – me – I was always very distressed and sad.

On Tuesday the 4th, I got up at 7 o'clock – had breakfast – dressed – combed my hair – heard Holy Mass – read – wrote – I devoted myself – had lunch with all my children and the King who wanted to see them – played – afternoon – then wrote – devoted myself – talked with Gatti – with Lord and Lady Sambuca – afterwards my children were all disguised and all the maids danced – had supper – at ten o'clock it was all over – I undressed and to bed – the King went out only in the evening to San Leucio – all with some men to have dinner – played – danced and had the carnival. The children healthy – me – I sadly finished my sad carnival.

On March 5, Ash Wednesday I got up at 7 o'clock – had breakfast – combed my hair – dressed – heard Holy Mass – then went to the Carmelites sermon which I did not please me – had lunch with the King – kept him company – ⊙ – and read – wrote – kept myself busy – ◣◢ – saw my children – the King returned – prayed and the Council – then [went] to bed. The children healthy – in the morning King went with me to listen the sermon – afternoon in San Leucio.

On Thursday March 6, I got up at 7 o'clock – had breakfast – combed my hair and dressed – heard Holy Mass – was painted by Marsilli[234] – had lunch with my children – stayed with them – read – wrote – worked – saw Lady Sangro – King – prayed – kept myself busy – read and went to bed – the King in the morning went to Carditello [to hunt] pigeons, my children were well – me so-so.

On Friday March 7, I got up in the morning at 7 o'clock – had breakfast – combed my hair – dressed – read – wrote – heard Holy Mass – I was painted by Marsilli for the medallion for my sister in Innsbruck – the King came and spoke with me and Acton – then we had lunched together – then I kept the King company – ⊙ – afterwards read – wrote – worked on my affairs – and then prayed – children – the two Councils where we had the unpleasant news that the earthquakes were still continuing to ruin Calabria. The children healthy. The King did not go out in the morning – after-dinner he went to the woods and to San Leucio.

On Saturday March 8, I got up at 7 o'clock – had breakfast – dressed – combed my hair heard Holy Mass – worked on my affairs – read – afterwards at 11 o'clock I went out in a carriage with my two eldest daughters – I met the King – Marsico and Rasoumowski on horseback accompanied me as far as Canalone where I dismounted and returned home on foot – then I had lunch with the King – I kept him company during his tea with milk – and I prayed and kept writing until I went to bed. The children healthy – King came in the morning and returned on horseback with me – afternoon he went to Carditello.

On Sunday March 9, I got up at 7 o'clock – had breakfast – dressed – combed my hair – heard Holy Mass – then afternoon went with the King to listen the sermon – afterwards kept him company – then saw Marchioness San Marco going to the estates – then wrote – read – applied myself – prayed – kept company with the King – saw children – breaking the piñata – afterwards heard a concert and a quartet of a German composer – then I went to sleep – my children were well – King went afternoon to Carbone – I was very nervy.

On Sunday the 10th, I got up in the morning – had breakfast – combed my hair – dressed – heard Holy Mass – read – wrote – I devoted myself – went out with my two eldest daughters – Frendel[235] – Lisette[236] – went to Canalone and returned on foot – had lunch with the King – kept him company – then I started reading – writing – and praying – presided over the Council of Sambuca – afterwards saw the children and to bed. The children healthy – me very so sick with nerves – in the morning the King went on horseback to Carditello – afternoon to the wood and San Leucio.

On Tuesday March 11, I got up in the morning – had breakfast – dressed – combed my hair – heard Holy Mass – wrote my post – worked on my affairs – had lunch with the children – they stayed with me while Theresa played the harpsichord – and then returned with the King at half past 2 and had lunch – I kept him company at dinner and after – $\odot$ – at half past 4 I went out with him by dray tot Belvedere – and got off at the big fountain and returned with him alone on foot to the house where I started reading – writing – played the harpsichord – did my duties – finished writing – afterwards prayed – saw the children and went to bed. The children healthy – in the morning the King went hunting foxes in Carbone and came home on horseback – in the afternoon he went out with me.

On Wednesday March 12, I got up at 7 o'clock – had breakfast – dressed – combed my hair – heard Holy Mass read – wrote – devoted myself – saw my children – had lunch with the King – kept him company – read – wrote – played the harpsichord – presided over the Council and to bed. The children healthy – in the evening put my son Francis to bed – he complained that his legs swollen – the King could not go out all day because of the weather – in the morning we received news that earthquakes were continuing and that atCatanzaro everything had fallen.

On Thursday March 13, I got up – dressed – combed my hair – heard Holy Mass – read – wrote – worked on my affairs – saw my children – had lunch with the King – kept him company – worked until evening making continually accounts for the necessary and difficult economy that I fore-see. The children healthy – the King could not go out in the morning to Carditello – after-dinner he was at home.

On Friday March 14, I got up at 7 o'clock – had breakfast – dressed – hear Holy Mass – the King spoke to Actonin my presence regarding the business discussed during the Council – then the sermon – kept company with the King – ☉ – then had lunch – read – wrote – devoted myself – there were the two Councils – afterwards received and read letters from Vienna – the King summoned Acton tohave Toscano's reply in relation to navy guards and officers – the children healthy – the King did the review and exercise with Liparoti[237] in the woods.

<u>On Saturday the 15th,</u> I got up – dressed – combed my hair – heard Holy Mass – <u>read</u> – wrote – worked on my affairs – saw the children – had lunch with the King – afterwards read – devoted myself – saw Duchess of andria[238] – did the post – in the evening went to the sick children – played the harpsichord and to bed. In the morning the King went to Carditello – afternoon to the pheasant farm.Louise was ill with an inflam-mation – Francis well.

On Sunday the 16th, I got up – sent Theresa with my German ladies to have lunch in the countryside at Carditello – I dressed – had breakfast – combed my hair – Mass – the sermon – kept company with the King – ☉ – then undressed – had lunch – read – wrote – kept myself busy – went to see the house apartments for my eldest daughters that are coming – saw old Salandra[239] for her business – kept myself busy – read – wrote – the King came back to tell me the details of Calabria – prayed – played the harpsichord – saw my sick children and to bed. The King afternoon to the wood – Francis was with arthritis which is swellng both a leg and the arms – to bed – Louise was with an inflammation – in bed – the others.

On Monday the 17th, I got up at 7 am – had breakfast – dressed – combed my hair – heard Holy Mass – read – wrote – saw my children – had lunch with the King – afterwards read – then worked – saw Teresina de Sangro then Caramanico – then kept doing my affairs – prayed – attended the Council and to bed. The King in the afternoon went out to Carditello. Louise was recovering from her fever. Francis was without fever but his arms and hands were enormously swollen.

On Tuesday March 18th, I got up at 7 o'clock – had breakfast – combed my hair – dressed – heard Holy Mass by the ◣◢ – then wrote – devoted myself – had lunch with Teresa – saw engravings – then wrote – devoted myself – gave audiences – went to see my children – prayed – wrote and to bed. The King went in the morning to Carbone – had lunch at Carditello and hunted there. Louise was without fever – Francis kept having a swelling.

On Wednesday the 19th, I got up at 7 o'clock – dressed – combed my hair – had breakfast – heard Holy Mass – afterwards arranged my affairs – papers – saw my children – had lunch with Theresa – and read – devoted myself – saw Sambuca – wrote – read – saw my children – prayed – there was the Council and to bed. The King went to Carditello – the children were quite well – Louise better – Francis stood up until evening when he complained of [pain] in the legs and lay down.

<u>On Thursday the 20th,</u> I got up at 7 o'clock in the morning – and then I wrote to the King ◇ before having received the news that my brother would arriv at lunchtime – I combed – dressed – arranged the home – waited for my brother who arrived at one o'clock – dressed as an abbot fattened in the face but not in the rest of the body – even much better than before – dressed in uniform he had lunch with me face to face – and then saw the house and my children – stayed with me until 4 o'clock – then he went to his room – I began to write – worked on my affairs – the King came back – I kept him company – ⊙ – then my brother came back – I spent the evening with him – Lamberg – Hardek – Hamilton and Gravina and the lady – at 9 o'clock I went to bed. The children healthy – Francis still with this arthritis – the King went in the morning to prepare everything for a great hunt at Carditello – having known that my brother had arrived he went to meet him in St. Agata – accompanied him as fas as Capua where he left him and came here – my brother and the King went hunting.

On Friday the 21st, I got up at 7 o'clock – had breakfast – dressed – combed my hair – heard the Mass – went to listen the sermon – had lunch with the King and my brother – and then stayed with my brother until 4 o'clock – afterwards did my things – read – wrote there were the two Councils – then my Theresa played the harpsichord – there were my brother – Hardek – Lamberg – Sambuca – Acton – Gravina and Hamilton in my room until 9 o'clock when I went to sleep and my brother to the pool. The King in the afternoon went to Carbone. The children healthy.

<u>On Saturday the 22nd,</u> I got up at 7 o'clock – had breakfast – combed my hair – dressed – heard Mass – read – wrote – worked on my affairs – saw my children – my brother – the King returned – at three o'clock had lunch – conversed with the King and my brother – then read – wrote – kept myself busy – in the evening we talked and conversed each other. The King in the morning went to Carditello – after lunch at San Leucio. The children quite well.

<u>On Sunday the 23rd,</u> I got up at 7 o'clock – had breakfast – combed my hair – dressed – heard Holy Mass – worked on my affairs – my luggage – put all my stuff together – and then had lunch with my brother – kept him company – then read – wrote – kept myself busy – saw my children – afterwards the King – then my brother came and there was music with King – then to bed. The King went out with my brother – in the morning had breakfast at Carditello where there was also an hunt on horseback nting – afternoon the King went to the Pantano Cerra. The children quite well.

On Monday the 24th, I got up in the morning – wrote for the courrier – then combed my hair – dressed – heard Holy Mass – and then I went to Naples with the lady and Corleto – arrived in my room I ran to the terrace to meet the King and my brother whom I introduced to my ladies – then we had lunch – afterwards I went throughout the house and apartments of Naples with my brother – and then we came to Portici where we did the same thing – afterwards the rosary – Council of Sambuca and to bed. The King went to Naples in the morning with my brother and afternoon he went to his lugger and from there came with us to Portici. The children healthy – Francis – Januarius Amelia moved to Naples – Theresa – Louise and Mimi in Portici.

<u>On Tuesday March the 25th,</u> I got up at 7 am – breakfasted – dressed – ccombed my hair – heard Holy Mass … [240] then wrote mail – see my daughters – then my brother dined with us we remained together until half past 4 – and – then wrote ◣◢ – devoted myself – went to say the rosary – kept company with the King – afterwards and the rest of the evening with my brother – then I went to sleep. The King took exercise – the children healthy.

On Wednesday March the 26th, I got up at 7 o'clock – had breakfast – combed my hair – dressed – heard Holy Mass – read – wrote – devoted myself – had lunch with my brother – saw my children with him – played – he enjoyed himself – stayed with him until 4 o'clock – later read – wrote – saw a German lady named the Countess Althan[241] – then Gepo[242] – afterwards lady Gravina – I went out with my brother – Gravina and the lady in the garden of Jacy – then at the Casa Galenda[243] – saw the house – on return I read – wrote – afterwards went to say the rosary – then King came back – I kept him company – + ☉ – afterwards I was with my brother – Hardek – Lamberg and the lady the rest of the evening. In the morning the King went out to walkwith my brother – at midday he went to hunt great snip in Carbone – the children healthy.

On Thursday March the 27th, I got up at 7 o'clock – had breakfast – combed my hair – dressed – heard Holy Mass – read – wrote – devoted myself – had lunch in town with my brother and the King – before lunch-time saw the children – Don Giovanni's electric machines – then had lunch – talked – went to the theatre in the dark – porcelain factory – then my brother went to see the studi[244] – walking on Chiaia – the ing went to his lugger and I remained to write and to see my children – at six o'clock we came back to Portici – my brother and me went to say the rosary and there was musical – there Theresa played the harpsichord very well. The King was with us all day. The children were fine – bad weather spoiled the walk that the King wished to go at Castellammare.

On Friday March the 28th, I got up at 7 o'clock – had breakfast – combed my hair – dressed – saw Sambuca – then went to listen the sermon – had lunch with my brother and the King – then the King was with us – there was the Liparoti exercise – from there he went with my brother across the bridge of Maddalena and then came back – we went to say the rosary and from there to the two Councils – after I had a conversation with my brother – Hardek – Lamberg – the lady – Acton – when around 10 o'clock Don Giovanni came to Naples with a terrible noise informing me that there had been an earthquake in Naples – my fear for this news – for the effects – for everything that interests me was terrible – they spoke about that until late when I went to bed. My children were well, in the morning the King went with my brother to Cacciabella and returned at 11 o'clock, afternoon [he took]exercise and went to the bridge.

On Saturday the 29th, after not having slept a wink during the night for fear – I got up – had breakfast – combed my hair – heard Holy Mass – then we went – my brother the King and I – to see the establishment of navy guards – from there to the house where + – and then we went into the large carriage – King – my brother – Hardek – Lamberg – the lady Gravina – Migliano – Marsico – Salandra – Onorato – Altavilla – Priore and I at dinner at the castle in the conspiracy table – we talked afternoon and then we returned home where I kept company with the King – ⊙ – then I began to read – then wrote – the rosary in the evening musical played by Bley.[245] The King went with me to the navy guards at the castle in the evening – only a moment in the quarters. The children were well.

On Sunday March 30, I got up at half past 7 – had breakfast – some coffeee with milk with my brother and the King – and then went to Mass – combed my hair – dressed – then went to listen the sermon – afterwards read my post – talked with my brother – at half past twelve we went in a carriage – the King – my brother – Hardek – Gravina – Marsico – Onorato – the lady – I – Acton to the house of Lamberg in Portici where we in addition found Richecourt and Scotti – we had lunch – the King played music and I held the conversation – at 4 o'clock the King went to do the Liparoti exercises and I came back to do my affairs – read – then at half past 5 I went down in a carriage to take the King and my brother to the quarters and take them with me to town – along the way we found that a fire broken out the granaries – but it was soon extinguished – arrived in town we saw our children – and I kept company with the King – ⊙ – then I washed a little – afterwards at 8 o'clock we went to the Academy to introduce my brother to the nobility – there was musical – then I played reversis[246] with Gravina – Salandra and Marchioness of Sambuca – I stayed there until half past 10 – and then went home. The King came out with me all day – the children healthy.

On Monday March 31st, after having slept in town – I got up at 7 o'clock – had breakfast – dressed – combed my hair – went to the Council of Sambuca – then to the childrens' – there heard Holy Mass – stayed with them – after went down – attended the table of the King who was going out hunting – at midday my brother came back – we danced with him and Francis – I introduced Gatti to him – and we were together until 4 o'clock – afterwards I worked on my affairs – read – wrote – devoted myself with great zeal – afterwards saw my children – at six o'clock I returned with my brother – the lady and Gravina to the house of Portici – we met the King who had just arrived – we went to say the rosary and from there worked on some affairs – saw my children and music and to bed. The King went [hunting] great snip – pigeons at the Acerra – the children were well.

On Tuesday 1 of April, I got up in the morning at 7 o'clock – had breakfast – dressed – combed my hair – heard Holy Mass – wrote my post and saw my brother and the King – left – had lunch with my children – took care of them – read – wrote – worked on my affairs with particular zeal – and finished the whole work – saw the children – the King returned – we went to say the rosary and I spent the evening in the company of my brother. The children healthy – King went around 5 o'clock with my brother and the gentlemen on xebec[247] to Castelamare where he dined – stayed there all day and returned in the evening.

On Wednesday 2 April, I got up at 7 o'clock – and my brother came to keep me company during my breakfast and we stayed together – then I washed – dressed – combed – talked with Acton who came to take leave of my brother – then Mass – worked on my affairs – spoke to my brother – the King returned – we had lunch together and continued to chat until 4 o'clock – so the King went to take exercise – I went to my brother's room – spoke to Hardek and then I saw my brother again until half past 6 when he left – which made me very sorry because I am very fond of him – he deserves it – he has an excellent and reliable character – we went to say the rosary – thence to Carlo de Marco Council and to bed. In the morning the King went to see his tonara[248] in Posillipo – afternoon he took exercise and children are healthy.

On Thursday 3 April, I got up at 7 am – had breakfast – dressed – heard Holy Mass – then worked on my affairs – read the post – arranged my papers – had lunch with the King – kept him copmpany until 5 o'clock – wrote a little and then went out – walked with Theresa to Granatello [where] I met the King who drove in a one horse carriage – went to say the rosary – kept company with the King – ☉ – then kept myself busy reading – writing – with my children and to bed. The children healthy – the King went out a little in the morning and afternoon played bowls in Granatello.

On Friday 4 April, I got up at 7 o'clock – had breakfast – dressed and combed my hair – heard Holy Mass – listened to the sermon which was about predominant sin – then kept company with the King – ☉ – then had lunch with him – read – afternoon wrote and started my post – then saw Brindesi who demanded a further increase – afterwards the wife of an inhabitant of Dubrovnik praying that the seizure be removed – afterwards Count Carinola[249] and his wife who claimed the order that his father had – then read a little – afterwards played the harpsichord, then came Sambuca who informed the King that on the 28th a strong earthquake had done damage – my terror was not small – and then we presided over the 2 Councils and then to bed. The children were well – in the morning the King went out to a walk a little and also afternoon in the high wood.

On Saturday April the 5th, I got up in the morning – had breakfast – dressed – combed my hair – heard Holy Mass – at 2 o'clock went to town with Marchioness Altavilla and Gravina where I met the King who heard the letters of the unfortunate Calabria being read – then I took care of the children – had lunch with them – then Princess Butera spoke to me about her problems – afterwards I wrote – then saw Sambuca, who brought me the papers of what they had decided and spoke to me of the matter – later I chose my entire wardrobe for the half season – then I saw Acton – then my children and from 6 o'clock to Naples – I came – went to say the rosary – and talked with the King – then finished my post and to bed – in the morning the King went by boat – saw the vessel – in the afternoon he returned to have lunch in Portici and spent his day shooting […] in low wood.

On Sunday April the 6th, I got up at 7 o'clock – had breakfast – dressed – combed my hair – heard Holy Mass – then the sermon was about the conduct of parents towards their children and subordinates – and then went to have lunch with the King and all the gentlemen in the castle – afterwards played reversis[250] with Gravina – Cassano – at half past 3 went home – read the – then saw Lady Wedel with the 3 sons that I like very much – then Gallo who is leaving for Turin – later went with the lady and her father to San Agostino's blessing – from there returned – saw officiers of the French frigate for a moment – then with the King – + ☉ – after felt ill – undressed and to bed. The children healthy – in the morning the King went for an hour to Granatello – had lunch with me to the castle – came back with me – went out again at 5 o'clock to shoot some birds – went to the blessing and came back with me.

On Monday the 7th April, I got up at 7 o'clock – had breakfast – combed my hair – dressed – heard Holy Mass – and then at 11 o'clock I went with the small canopy and Gravina to town – there I saw my children – had lunch – in the afternoon I was with Francis – then I saw Sambuca – later Acton – Teresina Sangro claimed for her son – for her problems – afterwards hearings – then the King came back and we presided over the Council – at 9 o'clock to bed. The children healthy – the King had lunch at the castle – took exercise in the afternoon and came back to the cityduring the night.

On April the 8th, I got up – dressed – combed my hair – prayed – heard Holy Mass – read – wrote – kept myself busy – saw my children – the King – had lunch with him – and then plopped myself down on the sofa and read – then write my post – DD – afterwards saw Lady San Marco – Belmonte – then Monteaperto – other persons – returned with Altavilla and Gravina to Portici – rosary – finished my post – saw my children and to bed. The children were well – in the morning the King went fishing in Fusaro which filled him well – he returned at 1 o'clock and left again afternoon for Carbone to hunt great snips.

On Wednesday April the 9th, I got up at 7 o'clock – had breakfast – dressed – combed my hair – heard Holy Mass – started to put my papers in order – had lunch with the King – kept him company – wrote – worked on my affairs – [tonic] – Micheroux[251] kissed my hand is leaving for Turin – Martha Columessa begged me to remove her sister out of convent – Duchess Mota Bagnara[252] anticipated me that she wanted take legal action against her sister – the King returned – we went to spirituals exercises that were about the past times badly spent – the present which runs away and how an uncertain future should be undertaken – from there there was the Council of ecclesiastic and then to bed. The children were well – in the morning the King went out and afternoon a little in the wood hunting little egrets.

On April the10th, Thursday I got up at 7 o'clock – had breakfast – dressed – combed my hair – heard Holy Mass – was painted by Füeger – then had lunch with the King – kept him company – ☉ – then read – wrote – worked on my affairs – Vigolino[253] spoke of workable economies for Capo di Monte – then the old Duchess Bovino Castel Franco and her problems – then Sangro [came] to claim permission for his son to stay another year more – then the spiritual exercises where the preacher spoke about Holy baptism – of obligations that we have incurred – then worked on my affairs – recorded my current affairs – sung a bit and to bed. The children healthy – the King went in the morning by boat to Naples to see his lugger – afternoon he went to the low wood to shoot little egrets.

On Friday April the 11th, I got up at 7 o'clock – had breakfast – dressed – combed my hair – heard Holy Mass – wrote – read – worked on my affairs – was painted by Füeger – had lunch with the King – kept him company – read – wrote, worked on my affairs – saw a Florentines lady named Pazzi introduced by Lanfranchi[254] – then Gengano – then kept the King company – ☉ – afterwards the sermon – then the Finance Council – then a General discussion with all four secretaries regarding the affairs of Calabria – and the Council of War and Navy – it lasted until late – I went to bed. In the morning the King went out to walk a little, and afternoon he [took] exercises with the Liparoti. The children healthy.

On Saturday April 12th, I got up at 7 o'clock – had breakfast – dressed – combed my hair – then wrote my post – at eleven o'clock played – went to town with Marchioness Altavilla and Gravina – on arrival there I met the King and my children – we had lunch with Francis – after having wished Januarius [a happhy birthday] – then saw the ladies – afterwards read – kept myself busy – wrote my post – saw the children – the servants of my children – chose fabrics – returned to Portici – was present to listen the sermon it was about the universal judgment – then worked on my affairs – played the harpsichord for while and to bed The children healthy. The

King went to town by sea to see his lugger – afternoon to the porcelain factory and at halp past 3 he returned to Portici.

On Sunday April the 13th, I got up at half past 7 – I dressed – combed my hair – had breakfast – heard two Holy Masses – did some little affairs – had lunch with the King – then kept him company – read – then read the letters – later played the harpsichord – prayed – prepared myself – went to listen the sermon – then confessed and later to bed. The children healthy. The King did not go out all day because of bad weather

On Monday April the 14th, I got up at 7 o'clock – had breakfast – combed my hair – dressed after having performed my devotions, having finished my toilette – I heard another Mass – then was painted by Füeger – afterwards had lunch with the King – kept him company until 4 o'clock – ☉ – afterwards wrote – worked on my affairs – saw a Sicilian lady – and Sambuca – then was present at the sermon – afterwards the Council and to bed. The children were well, in the morning the King rode out and afternoon a bit to Granatello.

On Tuesday April the 15th, I got up at 7 o'clock – had breakfast – dressed – combed my hair – heard Holy Mass – was painted by Füeger – then had lunch with the King – read – wrote my post – kept myself busy – saw a poor woman with her daughters – then ◣◢ – afterwards I went out with Gravina and the lady to the Jacy's garden of – King came to pick me up – I returned with him – there was the blessing – then worked on my affairs and to bed. In the morning the King went to town by sea – afternoon to Granatello where he came to pick me up to Jacy's garden. The children healthy.

On Wednesday April the 16th, I got up at 7 o'clock – had breakfast – combed my hair – heard Holy Mass – then had myself painted – had lunch with the King – kept him company – ☉ – then drew – afterwards gave some hearings – a girl who complains of her parents and seeks alms – the wife of judge Crispo,[255] afterwards a visit to my good Bohmin who thanks to God is already fine – then Sangro came to talk about her affairs – later saw the children – prayed – kept the King company and went to bed. The children healthy – the King went in the morning and afternoon to Granatello for a bit.

On Holy Thursday April the 17th, I got up at 7 o'clock – had breakfast – dressed – combed my hair – heard Mass with Theresa – then drew – at half past 10 went to the chapel where all the major functions of the day took place – afterwards had lunch with the King – then drew – and then at three o'clock did the washed the feet of twelve poor girls where my daughters were present – afterwards kept company – worshipped Jesus Christ in the Sepulchre – again kept the King company – at 7 o'clock went to hear the sermon of the Passion after that I did some little affairs – then I undressed and returned to worship Jesus Christ in the Holy Sepulcher until the time to go to bed. The children healthy the two eldest daughters went to confession and behaved very well. The King came out a little afternoon to shoot 31 little egrets that had arrived.

On Good Friday April the 18th, I got up at 7 o'clock and went to worship Jesus Christ in Holy Sepulcher until quater past 8 – then combed my hair – dressed – at half past 9 I went to church to the big functions of Holy Week – which finished at midday when the King had lunch – and then I began to draw – then had coffee with milk – afterwards read – wrote – worked on my affairs – then saw Princess Ferolito for her affairs – after prayed – saw my children – wrote – played some music and went to bed. The children healthy – the King afternoon went out for a little walk.

On Holy Saturday April the 19, I got up at 7 o'clock – dressed – combed my hair – had breakfast – then at eleven we went to church – then I kept the King company – ⊙ – then I had lunch with my girls – afterwards drew – then saw Marchioness San Marco – afterwards kept the King company after until 8 o'clock – then curled my hair – and then confessed and I went to bed. The children healthy. The King went out to have lunch at the castle with a many people – there he ran a bit and returned in the evening.

On Saint Saturday April the 20th, Saint Saturday I got up at 5 am – dressed – prayed – reconciled myself – at half past 6 I went with the King at the chapel of the Church to receive the Holy Sacrament of the Eucharist – on returning there was the lunch table with the paschal lamb – then I had breakfast with my girls – made my toilette – heard two Masses – one with Mimi – one on my own – then the public hand-kissing where there were a lot of people – then public table – afterwards I undressed and went with Gravina to Granatello to pick the King up in a dray with which I went to the blessing at San Augustino – from there we returned – King took coffeee with milk – I kept him company – ⊗ – afterwerwards we came back to the lady's house where we met 14 or 15 ladies – many men – I played a reversis's match with Belmonte – Termoli – Gravina – then we returned and I went to bed. The children healthy – the King went several times to walk at Granatello.

On Monday April the 21st, I got up at 7 o'clock – had breakfast – dressed – combed – heard two Masses – then the sermon – afterwards drew – then had lunch with the King – then read while he was sleeping – at

3 o'clock I woke him – wrote – read – kept myself busy – Monsignor Tufo came to apologize – then Francis came from Naples – I went with him – Mimi – Theresa – Louise to the castle to have a snack at the table of conspiracies – and I went on foot with Francis to Granatello so that he could kiss the Kin's hand – from there children returned to Naples and me with the King at home – then the rosary – Council of Sambuca – then worked on my affairs and to bed. The children healthy – King went to have lunch in the morning with many pepole in Granatello where they played the game of war to run – then afternoon to [hunt] little egrets in Granatello.

On Tuesday the 22nd, I got up to 7 o'clock – had breakfast – combed my hair – dressed – at nine o'clock I went with the King and Gravina in a carriage into town to see the children where I heard two Holy Masses – and then saw my children – wrote afterwards I kept the King company – ⊙ – later I had lunch with Francis – then I read – wrote – I saw Princess Migliano who told me her husband could not go to the Ministry – Don Inocenzio Pignatelli for his wedding, the Great Maîtresse for her affairs – Carlo de Marco – Acton – I returned here and went to say the rosary and then drew – wrote and went to bed. The children healthy – the King came to town with me – saw his lugger went to the dock – to the porcelain [factory] and returned to Portici – lunched at the castle and in the morning killed a few little egrets.

On Wednesday the 23rd, I got up in the morning – had breakfast – dressed – combed my hair – heard Holy Mass – then worked on my affairs – was painted by Füeger – then had lunch with the King – afterwards read – drew – wrote – saw my children – talked with Count Micheli Pignatelli about his affairs – then Sambuca – afterwards the King returned – I went to say the rosary – to the Council of Carlo de Marco and to bed, the children healthy, afternoon the King went to hunt great snips and to Granatello.

On Thursday April 24th, I got up at 7 o'clock – had breakfast – dressed – combed my hair – heard Holy Mass – was painted by Füeger – had lunch with my three daughters – then stayed a little with them – drew – read my post – kept myself busy – then talked with Acton – afterwards dressed – the King came back – we went to [say] the rosary – I kept him company – ⊗ – then we went down to Altavilla's house where there were a lot of people – I played reversis with Belmonte – Termoli – Gravina and at half past ten we came back home. The children healthy, the King went in the morning at 4 o'clock to Granatello to hunt quails – then at half past 8 with Breme – Marsico – Onorato – to Caserta to see his lands and returned at 7 o'clock of the evening.

On Friday the 25th, I got up at seven o'clock – had breakfast – dressed – combed my hair – heard Holy Mass – drew – devoted myself – then had lunch with the King – read while he was sleeping – later talked with Tarsia regarding issues of expenses – afterwards drew – <u>read</u> – wrote – worked on my affairs – the King returned – I kept him company – ⊙ – then the rosary – both Councils and to bed. The children healthy – in the morning the King went to Granatello – afternoon at two o'clock hunting quails whence he returned at 6 o'clock.

On Saturday the 26th, I got up at 7 o'clock – had breakfast – combed my hair – then I went with the King and Gravina to town – there I heard Holy Mass – saw my children – dressed – saw the King – spoke to Sambuca – had lunch with Francis – wrote my post – <u>read</u> – wrote – saw the Great Maîtresse – and so spent the day – saw my children – back to Portici with the lady and Gravina – heard the rosary – saw Duchess Frias[256] – worked on my affairs and went to bed. The children healthy – the King went in the morning with me to town – went to see the lugger – then to Posillipo – returned to have at the castle in Portici – afternoon he played bars.

<u>On Sunday the 27th,</u> I got up – curled my hair – dressed – heard Holy Mass – afterwards there was a long speech by Acton with the King and me regarding the disorders + – and – ⊙ – then at three o'clock we lunched – afterwards read – later saw Princess Caramanico – stayed with her – changed my dress – went with the King by dray to the blessing of the Augustinians – and home – kept the King company – Rocella informed me about the misfortunes of Calabria – later saw a map – finally went to the lady who was with a lot of people – I played with Altavilla – Belmonte, and then came back home at eleven o'clock at night – very weary – tired and went to bed. The children healthy – the King came out a little after lunch to the revisit and the Liparoti's exercises.

On Monday April the 28th, I got up at 7 o'clock with a slight fever – had breakfast – dressed – heard Holy Mass – arranged my papers – wrote – kept myself busy – had lunch with the King – drew during his light sleep – then wrote – listened to him – playing the (Roi de la vieille) – then saw Princess Ottajano in connectin with her affairs – Marchioness D'Anna and her daughter regarding their poverty and misery – the Bishop of Mileto[257] about his affairs – Lord San Marco for his brother. ◣◢ – then wrote – went to say the rosary – saw the King – the archbishop – afterwards the Council – worked on my affairs and to bed. The children were well. In the morning the King went for a short walk and the same in the afternoon.

On Tuesday April the 29th, I got up at 7 o'clock – had breakfast – dressed – heard Holy Mass – drew – had lunch with the King – read – wrote – drew – worked on my affairs – saw lady. San Marco – later other hearings – Lady Blancho who was leaving for Lucera where there her husband's military district – then drew – went to say the rosary – in the evening fever was higher – I bled myself and after lay a bit on the sofa – where my daughters kept me company – I went to bed. The children healthy – the King went to Granatello morning and evening.

On Wednesday April the 30th, I got up at half past 7 – combed my hair – dressed – had breakfast – heard Holy Mass – arranged some papers – read – wrote – worked – had lunch with the King – drew – read – afterwards Lady Wedel came to take leave of me and stayed a bit – later to say the rosary – the King returned – we went to the Council but since I felt the fever I was forced to lie down during the Council. The children healthy, King went at two o'clock in the afternoon to Mortella[258] to shoot quails and returned at 7 o'clock.

On Thursday May the 1st, I got up at 7 o'clock – had breakfast – dressed – combed my hair – heard Holy Mass – worked on my affairs – drew – had lunch with my three girls – saw the flowers of Portolano with them – later drew – kept myself busy – read my letters – Acton came to enquire about my health – I had several hearings with widows – then Mr. and Mrs. Wedel came to listen to Theresa play the harpsichord and they took leave of the children – afterwards I dressed and waited for the King with whom I went to the lady's house – there I played my ordinary reversis match with Belmonte – Termoli – Gravina – at half past 10 we were at home – we had supper and to bed. The children were well – I was still in poor health but without fever – the King went out early [to hunt] quails – from there at eleven o'clock he went to Granatello and then to Mortella – he only returned at 8 o'clock.

On Friday May the 2nd, I got up at 7 o'clock – had breakfast – dressed – combed – heard Holy Mass – worked on my affairs – kept the King company – ☉ – then had lunch – afterwards drew – read – wrote – worked on my affairs – gave some hearings – then went out to walk on the high wood – afterwards drew – went to say the rosary – the King returned and we presided over the two Councils. The children healthy. In the morning the King went to Granatello to shoot quails – afternoon at 2 o'clock he went to Mortella for the same reason and came back at half past 7 .

On Saturday May the 3rd, I got up – had breakfast – combed my hair – dressed – heard Holy Mass – read – wrote – worked on my affairs – had lunch with my girls – drew – then saw San Marco Ardore[259] Lord Rocella – Lady Salandra Monteleone [Crapa] – all these people took up the whole of my day – I met the King who came back – we went to say the rosary – talked together – I worked on my affairs and went to bed. The children healthy – in the morning the King came to go to the fair of Aversa – from there to Carditello and came back at half past 7.

On Sunday May the 4th, I got up at 7 am – had breakfast – dressed – combed my hair – heard Holy Mass – at nine o'clock went with the King and Cassano to town by land where I heard Mass – saw my children – wrote – spoke to de Marco – Sambuca – and several ladies – then had lunch with Francis – later saw him at liberty – then read lying on a couch – walked through all the rooms – wrote – read – devoted myself – afterwards talked with Acton – later saw Duchess Monte Mileto who introduced me to her daughter[260] who is going to become a nun – then I retuned – ◣ ◢ – then I undressed – saw my daughters having dinner and went to bed. The children healthy – the King went with me into town – from there to the dock where a boat went to Posillipo to take the big galliots with which he went to the Mortella to hunt quails – then evening in Capri – he slept on board and returned only the day after.

On Monday May 5th, I got up at half past 7 – I had breakfast with my three daughters and spent a good part of the morning with them – I dressed combed my hair – heard Holy Mass – had lunch with my children – made them play in my room – read – wrote – drew – saw Countess Gaetani – told me about a marriage for her daughter – then wife of Paschali the judge[261] with her daughters – then I went out on the terrace with Mimi but the King came back – I spoke to him – we went to say the rosary – (Council) and to bed The children healthy – the King at 10 o'clock left Capri – went into town – returned by boat at 7 o'clock.

On Tuesday May 6th, I got up at 7 o'clock – had breakfast – dressed – combed my hair – heard Holy Mass – read – wrote – kept myself busy – had lunch with the King – drew – then saw Reil[262] who is leaving for Vienna – then Duchess Avagliano – afterwards at five o'clock I went with the King in a carriage [to the celebration of] St. Januarius – we adored the saint and then went into town – there I saw my children and took care of them – then the King came tospeak to Acton for a while in my room – then I finished my post – then I attended the music and later to bed. The King did not go out in the morning – went with me to St. Januarius and came back a little to the dock with his lugger. The children healthy.

On Thursday May the 7th, we slept in town – I woke up in the morning – had breakfast – dressed – combed my hair – at half past nine we had Carlo de Marco's Council where the King announced the promotions in his ministry – gave jubilation to useless people – then I had lunch with the King – then read and kept him company – read a little – wrote – saw my children – Princess Migliano with her beautiful sister – in – law who became a nun – then at half past 6 – I returned by dray – with King we went to say the rosary – then he kept me company until 9 o'clock + – ⊙ – (being) tired – weary – I went to bed. The children healthy – the King went out all day.

On Thursday the 8th, I got up in the morning at 7 o'clock – had breakfast – dressed – combed my hair – heard Holy Mass – read – wrote – devoted myself – at midday had lunch with the King – drew – kept myself busy – changed my dress – saw Acton for a moment – then Termoli – Ardore – Baroness [Din] – and other women and hearings – then to [say] the rosary – after kept myself company – ⊗ – then other ladies with whom I played – there were a lot of people – I played my ordinary game and returned at eleven o'clock, to bed The children healthy – afternoon the King went for a walk at Granatello.

On Friday May 9, I got up at half past 7 – had breakfast – combed my hair – dressed – heard Holy Mass – *read* – wrote – drew – then had lunch with the King – then drew – <u>read</u> – wrote – worked on my affairs – then the rosary – to both Councils and to bed. The children healthy – the King went to town in the morning trying to bear galliots – he could not because of bad weather – afternoon he walked a little in Granatello.

<u>On Saturday the 10th,</u> I got up at half past 7 – had breakfast – combed my hair – dressed – heard Holy Mass – read – wrote – worked on my affairs – had lunch with my children – they stayed with me afternoon – then wrote the post – saw Lady San Marco, who came to thank me for her brother who had become a judge – then kept writitng my post – the King came back – I began to draw – later the rosary – then with my eldest girls – worked on my affairs and [went] to bed. The children healthy – the King went to Naples about half past nine by dray to see the children and worked on his lugger and came back at half past 6.

On Sunday May the 11th, I got up at 7 o'clock – combed my hair – dressed – had breakfast – heard Holy Mass – spoke to the King – to Acton on our affairs – had lunch with the King – drew – dressed – read – wrote – gave some hearings – then went by dray with the King to the blessing at Sant' Agostino – then the blessing – home – kept the King company – and then went down to [see] the lady – after having previously seen Cardinal Buon Compagno[263] in King's antechamber – I went to play my usual reversis match at the lady's house until 10 o'clock and then I went to bed. The children healthy – the King only went out to walk a little afternoon.

On Monday the 12th, I got up around 8 o'clock – had breakfast – dressed – heard Holy Mass – at ten o'clock went to town with the lady and Gravina – I saw my children – and then I went down to Molosiglio to see the launching of the lugger ton which the King had lunch – Belmonte – Gravina – Filingieri – Pignatelli – Galatolo – Gepo – Acton – the lady and me – disembarked from the lugger at five o'clock – until half past five I went home – saw my children – de Marco – Duchess Coscia – <u>read</u> a bit and then I returned – went to the rosary – kept the King company – ⊙ – afterwards the Council and went to bed. The children were well – King got up at half past 4 went by sea to town and stayed there all day and returned at half past five in the evening by sea.

On Tuesday the 13th, I got up at 7 o'clock – had breakfast – combed my hair – dressed – talked with the King – ⊙ – then finished dressing – heard Holy Mass – wrote the post – had lunch with my girls – walked through the rooms with them – drew – saw Caramanico – Sangro in connection with their affairs – finished writing my post – went to say the rosary – worked on my affairs until the time to go to bed. The King went out only afternoon at lugger and there spent the day – the children healthy.

On Wednesday the 14th, I got up at half past 7 – combed my hair – dressed – heard Holy Mass – then worked on my affairs – had lunch with the King – read afternoon – then the King went [hunting] quails – I began to <u>read</u> – wrote – worked on my affairs – drew – later the rosary – the King returned – there was Carlo de Marco's Council – then from the balcony with the King I listened to music played by Rasoumowski – afterwards to bed. The children healthy – in the morning the King went out on foot and afternoon to Mortella [to hunt] quails.

<u>On Thursday May 15th,</u> I got up in the morning – combed my hair – dressed – had breakfast – heard Holy Mass – later worked on my affairs – read – wrote – had lunch with the King – read while he was sleeping – and drew – gave numerous hearings – San Marco took leave to go to the feuds – the wife of San Lorenzo[264] for having dared to stay out of the convent – two for misery – and <u>read</u> – worked on my affairs – then the rosary and the two Councils – from there to bed. The children healthy – in the morning the King went to town to see the lugger – afternoon he went ou on foot.

On May the 16th, I got up at 7 o'clock – had breakfast – combed my hair – dressed – <u>read</u> – wrote – worked on my affairs – hear Holy Mass – then talked with Cari with Rocella – then Gatti – had lunch with my children – took care of them – drew – <u>read</u>+ – wrote – worked on my affairs – the rosary and waited for the King – later to bed. The children healthy – King went to Caserta at 7 am and returned at ten in the evening.

On Saturday May the 17th, I got up at half past 7 – had breakfast – dressed – combed my hair – heard Holy Mass – wrote my post – had lunch with the girls – then stayed with my children – wrote – arranged papers – drew – later dressed – gave hearings to a few ladies such as Malena the widow las Casas – husband died under the ruins of Messina – and then went out with Gravina and Altavilla to the low wood – from there to the blessing in St. Pasquale – afterwards to the pier – home – undressed – worked on my affairs and went to bed. The children healthy – the King got up very early to go fishing in Granatello – then went to see his lugger and returned from Naples at five o'clock – went with me to the blessing in St. Pasquale – he accompanied me home and in the evening went to the pier to play music.

On Sunday May the 18th, I got up in the morning at half past 7 – had breakfast with my girls – dressed – combed my hair – heard Holy Mass – went with the lady and Gravina to Granatello – then went on board a galliot with the King and went into town to see my children – spruced myself up a little – had lunch with the King – later read worked on my affairs – kept the King company – ⊙ – then went to comb and dress – at [6] o'clock went out by dray with the King to the garden of Francavilla²⁶⁵ we saw the house – garden and returned – I saw my children – the young Ferante was introduced to me – I spoke to the Great Maîtresse and we went to the theatre of the Florentines saw an act of an unbearable opera and then to bed. The children healthy – the King was present all day and only went out with me.

On Monday May the 19th, I got up at half past 7 – had breakfast – heard Mass – at half past 8 there was the Council – and I made my toilette – had lunch with King – I read – then wrote – worked on my affairs – walked on the terrace – saw Carlo de Marco – some hearings – the widow of San Lorenzo²⁶⁶ and others – at 7 o'clock I left – returned to Portici – undressed – went to say the rosary – saw my children and began to write until I went to bed. The children healthy – the King spent the morning at home – afternoon he went to the dock and was there almost until nightfall – he returned by sea at 9 o'clock in the evening.

On Tuesday May the 20th, I got up at half past 7 – had breakfast – dressed – combed my hair – heard Holy Mass – wrote my letters – dinner with the King – and then kept him company – ⊙ – drew – read – wrote – devoted myself – saw Donna Teresina in connection with her affairs – then my children – to say the rosary – kept the King company – finished my post and to bed. The children healthy – in the morning the King went out a bit on foot – after-dinner he could not go out because of bad weather.

On Wednesday May the 21st, I got up at half past 7 – had breakfast – combed my hair – dressed – heard Holy Mass – read – wrote – saw Sambuca – worked on my affairs – had lunch with the King – drew – saw Predicatella who is leaving for the feuds – Countess Althan who is a German lady – to whom I showed my children – went to the wood to join my daughters and went with them to the pier – afterwards returned – to say the rosary – the Council and to bed. The children healthy – in the morning the King went to town at the dock – after lunch fishing at the pier.

On Thursday May the 22nd, I got up at half past 7 – had breakfast – dressed – combed my hair – heard Mass – then read – wrote – later had lunch with the King – drew – read – I combed my hair – dressed – gave hearings like the Bishop of the ladies – then to say the rosary – afterwards kept the King company – ⊗ – later to the conversation in the marchioness 's house where I played with Belmonte – Micheli and Gravina and then home. The King did not go out in the morning – afternoon – he walked outside a little – the children healthy.

On Friday May the 23rd, I got up at 7 o'clock – had breakfast – dressed – combed my hair – heard Holy Mass – read – wrote – worked on my affairs – had lunch with the King – looked at some engravings – read – drew – saw Acton – then drew – the rosary – both Councils and to bed. The children well – the King did not go out in the morning – after lunch he went to town by dray and returned in the same way.

On Saturday May the 24th, I got up at half past 7 – had breakfast – dressed – combed my hair – heard Holy Mass – read – wrote – devoted myself – had lunch with the King – drew – read – worked on my affairs – to say the rosary – saw my children – in the evening saw Hamilton who talked about the misfortunes of Calabria – and then to bed. The children healthy. The King went a little afternoon for a walk in the grove.

On Sunday May 25th, I got up at 7 o'clock – had breakfast – curled my hair – dressed – hear Holy Mass – then the King came with Acton to talk about business – later had lunch – drew – saw some engravings – dressed – read – wrote – worked on my affairs – went to visit the King downtown – picked him up by one horse carriage – went to the blessing at Sant'Agostino – then came back – had a coffee with milk – saw the Archbishop and went down to the Marchioness' house – there played with Belmonte – Gravina and the lady – and then to bed. In the morning the King went riding – and after lunch down to shoot quails.

On Monday May the 26th, I got up at half past 7 – had breakfast – dressed – combed my hair – heard Holy Mass – <u>read</u> – wrote – arranged my books – papers – had lunch with my three daughters – and then stayed with them – cut – saw some engravings – read – wrote – worked on my affairs – and then came the King – I unpacked things [wich had] arrived from Vienna – the King came and talked with Acton – later to say the rosary – the Council and to bed. The children healthy – the King went in the morning to town to [visit] the dock – dined there – went to Posillipo by sea and returned by sea.

<u>On Tuesday May the 27th,</u> I got up at half past 7 – had breakfast – dressed – combed my hair – a horrible storm forced us to be in the dark with the King in the room – then I dressed – went to church – started to draw – I had lunch with the King and then kept him company – we saw prints – ☉ – then cut-up [some things] – saw some engravings – drew – arranged my things – wrote the post, and then I went to say the rosary – took care of my children and read – afterwards to bed. The children were healthy – the King was all day at home because of bad weather.

<u>On Wednesday May the 28th,</u> I got up at 7 o'clock – had breakfast – combed my hair – dressed – heard Holy Mass with Mimi – and then left with the King for Naples where we arrived at half past ten – saw my children – arranged my business papers – had lunch with the King – and read – kept the King company – ☉ – unpacked my papers – books – drawings – all arranged – read – wrote – saw my children – in the evening to the Council – after that I saw my children – wrote and to bed. The children healthy – the King went only at the lugger and in the evening went out at the rehearsal in the theatre.

<u>On Thursday May 29th,</u> I got up at 7 o'clock – had breakfasted – dressed – combed my hair – heard Holy Mass – Council – after drew – then Acton introduced the Spanish General to me – and had lunch with R. – read – wrote – drew – saw the wife of the Spanish General – pregnant women – later the Council – then saw my children – the opera at the Florentines and to bed. The children healthy – the King did go out all day from the house.

On Friday May the 30th, I got up at half past 7 – heard Holy Mass – had breakfast – brought the children to the King – combed my hair – dressed – then went to the hand-kissing – public table – and undressed – had lunch – read – wrote – kept the King company – ⊙ – then read – wrote – saw Sambuca – changed my dress – saw Lady Didier[267] received the hand-kissing by the ladies – undressed and went to the opera with my girls – and then to bed. The children healthy. The King went after lunch to the lugger.

<u>On Saturday May the 31st,</u> I got up in the morning – had breakfast – combed my hair – dressed – heard Holy Mass – went to the wardrobe to do the inspection for my people – then went down to see the children – had lunch – read – slept – drew – wrote my post – saw Acton – then the King returned – spruced myself up – gave some hearings – finished my business – went to San Carlo without the children for an act. The children healthy – the King after lunch went fishing in Strone.

On Sunday June the 1st, I got up at half past 7 – dressed – combed my hair – had breakfast – heard Holy Mass – made some small arrangements – drew – had lunch with the King – saw our children – drew – cut-up – saw Marchioness San Marco, Sambuca, and afterwards the children – made my toilette again and went to the San Carlo theatre without the children. The children healthy – the King after lunch went to the pier and the lugger.

On Monday June the 2nd, I got up at half past seven – had breakfast – dressed – combed my hair – Holy Mass – then the Council – later kept myself busy – afterwards saw the children – had lunch with the King – drew – read – wrote – kept myself busy – gave some hearings – then in the evening to an act at the Florentines and at home. The children healthy – the King could not go out because of bad weather.

<u>On Tuesday June the 3rd,</u> I got up – wrote the post – combed my hair – dressed – heard Holy Mass – read – wrote – worked on my affairs – then talked with Tarsia – Count Michele – Sambuca – de Marco – had lunch with my children – drew – kept myself busy – read – wrote – saw my children – walked with them on the terrace – then gave some hearings – finally undressed and sung with the King in his room. The children healthy – the King went in the morning on horseback at Strone – dined in Posillipo and returned by galliots.

On Wednesday June the 4th, I got up at 8 o'clock – had breakfast – dressed – combed my hair – heard Holy Mass – read – wrote – worked on my affairs – had lunch with the children – talked with Sambuca – drew – read – saw old Salandra – combed my hair – dressed – there was the Justice

Council – kept the King company – ⊗ and went to San Carlo – the children healthy – the King went out about 10 o'clock to try the lugger – dined at Molosiglio and came back at half past 3.

On Thursday June the 5th, I got up at 7 am – had breakfast – dressed – combed my hair – heard Holy Mass – afterwards read – saw my children – had lunch with the King – drew – read – wrote – worked on my affairs – saw my children – predicated a sermon to Theresa – saw Cariati, Patrizio, Sangro, there was Council of Finance – then my business and went to bed – the children healthy. The King went to ride in the morning – afternoon at 3 o'clock [he went to] Capo di Monte.

On Friday June the 6th, I got up at 7 o'clock and went to the Mass of my Theresa who received communion for the first time – which affected me a lot – afterwards I had breakfast with her and Louise – then there was the War and Navy Council – then I was with Mimi at Mass – afterwards I made my toilette – then went out to see the ladies – at the public table – then I undressed and kept the King company – ☉ – then I changed my dress – wrote – worked on my affairs – then I quickly went out with my three daughters to the house where I gave them a snack – afterwards I sent back Mimi and Louise and went with Theresa [to participate] in the fourty hours benediction at San Nicola alla Carità – from there I came back – saw the children – worked on my affairs and then to the theatre where during the first act we had the Elector Palatine of Bavaria[268] who is a great person – and then I went to sleep. The children healthy – Januarius had and expelled a worm. The King went to the afternoon to the lugger and the porcelain factory.

On Saturday June the 7th, I got up at half past 7 – had breakfast – dressed – heard the Holy Mass – attended to the first reading lesson – wrote – devoted myself – had lunch with the King – drew – wrote my post – took care of my children – saw the King – worked on my affairs and to bed. The children healthy – the King went to *tonnara*[269] in Posillipo – after-dinner at Portici.

On Sunday June the 8th, I got up at half past 7 – had breakfast – dressed – combed my hair – heard two Holy Masses – was present at Mimi's lesson – then saw my children – then had a big lunch for 24 people with the Elector of Bavaria – his two knights – to whom I introduced my children – showed the terrace – accompanied them to the porcelain factory – I returned to my room to read – write – do my affairs – at (2 3) o'clock Lamberg accompanied me to baron Didier who listened to Teresa play the harpsichord and she played – afterwards with the King – talked with him – later to the theatre. The children healthy – the King went in the afternoon to Posillipo by sea and returned by dray.

On Monday June the 9th, I got up at half past 7 – had breakfast – dressed – combed my hair – heard Holy Mass – read – wrote – worked on my affairs – had lunch with the children – ◣◢ – drew – read – wrote – worked – worked on my affairs – then gave some hearings – afterwards the Councils and then to bed – the King came in the morning to try the lugger and returned around 6 o'clock + children healthy.

On Tuesday June the 10th, I got up at half past 7 – had breakfast – dressed – heard Holy Mass – worked on my affairs – read – wrote – saw Vacher[270] who had arrived the evening before – had lunch with my children – drew – wrote – did my post – saw Madame Sangro – later audiences – then to the theatre to a first performance of a comedy in prose, the children healthy – the King went to have lunch at pier on galliots of Marsico and returned at 5 o'clock.

On Wednesday the 11th, I got up at half past 7 – dressed – heard hoy Mass – went to the Council – and read – wrote – worked on my affairs – had lunch with my two eldest daughters – kept them with me during the afternoon – and draw – then was painted – the King came – kept him company – + ☉ – then made my toilette – went to the San Carlo theatre for an act and saw the Elector. The children healthy – the King went to have lunch with Elector in Posillipo and returned at 5 o'clock.

On Thursday June the 12th, I got up at half past 7 – had breakfast – dressed – heard Holy Mass – was painted by Marsilli – saw Canuti[271] consulted him for Januarius – saw Vacher and his family, Carlo de Marco – had lunch with the children – kept them with me – drew – cut up – read +++ wrote – kept myself busy – gave hearings – saw my children – presided over the Council – then [put] curlers and went to bed – the children healthy – at 7 o'clock in the morning the King went to Caserta and returned at eight in the evening.

On Friday June the 13th, I got up at half past 7 – had breakfast – dressed – combed my hair – heard Holy Mass – presided over the Council – then had lunch with the King – kept him company – ☉ – later read – drew – kept myself busy – wrote – worked on my affairs – saw my children – went to the Lombards theatre or San Carlino[272] which played Florentine – the children healthy – the King went afternoon by boat to Posillipo and returned by boat.

On Saturday June the 14th, I got up at half past 7 – had breakfast – dressed – combed my hair – heard Holy Mass – read – wrote – worked on my affairs – talked with my children – had lunch with the eldest – stayed with them in the afternoon – read – drew – wrote my post – saw Princess Caramanico Sambuca – gave audiences to LadyTripalda and Scaletta – combed my hair – dressed – saw the Elector – after the first act we left. The children well. In the morning the King went to Posillipo and lunched on the galiots and did not return until evening.

<u>On Sunday June the 15th,</u> I got up at 8 o'clock – had breakfast – dressed – combed my hair – heard Holy Mass – saw my children – was busy reading – writing – then at half past eleven we had a visit of the Elector of Bavaria, who came to take leave of us – then public table – then kept the King company – ⊗ – then undressed – read – drew – read – wrote – worked on my affairs – the King came back – I gave some hearings – in the evening at the theatre where we remained for both acts and ballet – the King well – in the afternoon he crossed the sea by the lugger and galliots to Posillipo and returned by sea – the children well.

<u>On Monday June the 16th,</u> I got up at 8 o'clock – had breakfast – combed my hair – dressed – heard Holy Mass – drew – worked on my affairs – saw my children – had lunch with the King – then read – drew and read – wrote – gave some hearings to the wife of Conradino and others – afterwards the Sambuca's Council – then I went to Mimi's room she went to sleep without having supper, which worried me – then I bled myself and went to have dinner in bed – afternoon the King went by land to Posillipo – to the house – and thence returned by sea the same evening – he went to a comedy by Gian Colla[273] – I remained at home to bleed. I sent the children to my garden – they were fine.

<u>On Tuesday June 17,</u> I got up at 8 o'clock – had breakfast – dressed – heard Holy Mass – went to Mimi's room – saw Acton – then returned to Mimi's room – saw my children – had lunch with the King – drew – wrote my post – went to Mimi – took leave of Count Micheli who will be ambassador to Paris – then prepared for confession and confessed – from there to Mimi's room – had dinner and to bed. Mimi was sick – she was purged and her fever diminished – the King was in Posillipo – in the evening at Giancolla's comedy.

<u>On Wednesday June the 18th,</u> I got up at 7 o'clock – went to church took communion – went to see the children – then spoke with the King and Sambuca of the donation and project for Calabria – then saw the children – had lunch – afterwards kept the King company – ⊙ – then

drew – devoted myself – saw Princess Belmonte – then other hearings – started the de Marco 's Council that I could not continue feeling so bad that I had to go to bed The children healthy – in the morning Mimi took an emetic – 4 roots of ipecacuanha and she was much better – the King inthe afternoon went to Posillipo.

On Thursday June the 19th, I got up in the morning – had breakfast – dressed – made my toilette – combed my hair – heard Holy Mass – read – wrote – worked on my affairs – went to the chapel where I received the blessing of the Blessed Sacrament – afterwards had lunch with the King – saw Acton who brought the news of the conquest – then drew – later went out with Teresa and Louise to the blessing of San Francesco of Paola – then see my little garden of Santa Lucia – returned and went to the theatre in the evening. The children healthy – Mimi recovered, in the morning the King went to the quarter – later to the procession – afternoon he went out by the lugger to fish at Posillipo.

On Friday June the 20th, I got up in the morning – had breakfast – dressed – heard Holy Mass – presided over two Councils – dined with the King – then kept him company – ⊗ – drew – then read – wrote – worked on my affairs – gave audiences – later saw my children – at 9 o'clock had dinner and to bed, the children healthy – the King went to Posillipo by sea.

On Saturday the June the 21st, I got up at half past 7 – had breakfast – dressed – wrote – <u>read</u> – heard Holy Mass – went to the chapel – the exhibition – had lunch with my children – saw de Marco – Sambuca – Marchioness San Marco – Feligineri – wrote my post – <u>read</u> + – wrote – worked on my affairs – talked with ladies – saw Mimi asleep – sung and went to bed. The children healthy – the King went at 4 toCaserta – from there to Cacciabella to go to sleep and did not return.

On Sunday the 22nd, I got up in the morning – had breakfast with Louise – made my toilette – saw my children – drew – wrote – heard two Holy Masses – went to the chapel – saw de Marco – had lunch with my children – kept them with me – then I saw Sambuca – Acton – then some hearings – the King returned – I kept him company – ⊙ – then to the theatre – to both acts.The children healthy – the King went from Cacciabella where he had slept to Nola – where he saw the feast and returned in the evening.

<u>On Monday the 23rd,</u> I got up at half past 7 – had breakfast – dressed – heard Holy Mass – drew – wrote – worked on my affairs – and then went to the chapel – had lunch with the King – drew – saw my children – wrote – saw young Salandra in connection with her affairs, and then to the

Council and to bed – the children healthy – afternoon the King went to the *tonnara* at Posillipo.

On Tuesday the 24th, I got up at half past 7 – had breakfast – dressed – combed my hair – heard Holy Mass – wrote – read – kept myself busy – saw de Marco – then went to the chapel to take the blessing – had lunch with my children – stayed with them – talked with Sambuca – drew – saw Acton – later some hearings – drew and went to bed. The children healthy – in the mornig the King went to Caserta – saw the [wheat] being cut and returned in the evening

On Wednesday the 25th, I got up in the morning – breakfast – dressed – combed my hair – heard Holy Mass – presided over the Council – later to the chapel – took the blessing – had lunch with the King – drew – kept him company – kept myself busy – read – wrote – gave audiences to a lady from Messina – to Lady Mahoni[274] – to Ladu Althan – then changed my dress and went to the San Carlo Theatre – the children healthy – the King went to the sea to take the lugger to the pier.

On Thursday the 26th, I got up at half past 7 – had breakfast – wore dressing gown and went go take the Holy Viaticum to old Striker – then combed my hair – dressed – went to the chapel – attended Mass and procession – from there went with Lady Gravina and Acton to the pier[to go on board] the lugger – we had lunch there at a table of 12 people – afternoon we drove it a little – then we returned – I kept the King company – ⊙ – then to the porcelain factory [where we] went to see the great procession of 4 altars – and home – undressed – made my toilette – saw Acton for a moment – then went by one horse carriage with the same people that lunched with us to the little house in Santa Lucia to have dinner – the children healthy – the King early in the morning went to prepare the procession – he went to throw[275] in Posillipo and came to the little house – where I joined him.

On Friday the 27th, I got up at half past 7 – had breakfast – combed my hair – dressed and heard Holy Mass – then presided over the two Councils – had lunch with the King – drew and devoted myself – read – wrote – talked with Cimitile – kept the King company and went to unworhy comedy in prose – and at home. The children well – King went in the afternoon [went] to Capo di Monte.

On Saturday June the 28th, I got up at 8 o'clock – had breakfast – dressed and combed my hair – heard Holy Mass – wrote some letters – worked on my affairs – saw de Marco – then had lunch with my children – took care of them – saw Sambuca – Teresina Sangro – Acton – then dressed – combed my hair – went to the Fondo when the King came and after first the act home. The children healthy – in the morning the King went to Caserta and returned in the evening and joined me at the Fondo.

On Sunday the 29th, I got up at half past 7 – had breakfast – dressed – combed my hair – heard Holy Mass – drew – saw my children – went to the public table – kept the King company – ☉ – afterwards undressed – drew for Princess Belmonte – my children – I changed my dress – did little affairs and to the San Carlo theatre. The children healthy – the King went out later – because of the storm – to the pier to see his lugger.

On Monday the 30th, I got up at half past 7 – had breakfast – dressed – combed my hair – heard Holy Mass – then was present at the Council – then drew – wrote – worked on my affairs – had lunch with my two eldest daughters – afterwasrds stayed with them – drew – saw the Regent of the vicarship[276] – Carlo de Marco – Acton – all to inform me about case of the Cadets – then combed my hair – dressed – the King returned – I saw my children later made some of my affairs and then to the Fondo. The children healthy – the King went to lunch on the lugger with the officers – then Portici and returned in the evening.

On Tuesday July the 1st, I got up at half past 7 – had breakfast – dressed – combed my hair – heard Holy Mass – wrote my post – had lunch with the King – drew all day – then played music with him – then had some hearings such as Mayo Ostuni and Latilla[277] then finished writing – saw Sambuca and to bed. The children were well – The King could not go out all day because of the weather – in the evening he went to the theatre toG iancolla's play – I stayed at home.

On Wednesday July the 2nd, I got up at half past 7 – had breakfast – dressed – combed my hair – heard Holy Mass – presided over Carlo de Marco's Council – was present to the lunch at the King – then worked on my affairs – saw my children – had lunch with them – drew – read – wrote – saw Acton – gave hearings – later prayed – read – devoted myself – at 10 o'clock I went with my two eldest daughters to the theatre where – after the second act – I left. The King went at noon to Castellamare – where he stayed all day and night. The news from Spain is that their only son had died.[278]

On Thursday July the 3rd, I got up in the morning – had breakfast – combed my hair – dressed – heard Holy Mass – read – wrote – did my duties – then had breakfast with the children upstairs – a visit to the good Bohminin – went down – drew – kept the King company after hi return – ☉ – then combed my hair – dressed and went to [see] one act at Fondo – I received some hearings of ladies. The children healthy – the King returned at 4 o'clock from Castellamare.

On Friday July the 4th, I got up at half past 8 – had breakfast – combed my hair – dressed – heard Holy Mass – went to Acton's Council of – had lunch with the King – drew – worked on my affairs – read – wrote – I combed my hair – dressed – went to the Council and in the evening a terrible comedy of Gian Colla, the children healthy – the King could go out because of the bad weather and went for a short time to the pier.

On Saturday July the 5th, I got up at 8 am – had breakfast – combed my hair – dressed – saw my children – wrote my letters – heard Holy Mass – read – wrote – had lunch with the children – saw Sambuca – Marchioness San Marco – Acton – later hearings – changed dress – then wrote – did my affairs and saw my children – the King came back – went to bed early. The children healthy – the King was in Caserta all day.

On Sunday July the 6th, I got up early at eight o'clock – had breakfast – combed my hair – curled – heard Holy Mass – saw my children – drew – dressed – went with Lady Termoli – del Monte and Fragnito[279] to the little house in Santa Lucia where I waited for the King who came with Gravina – Marsico – Migliano – Corleto – Vasto – Acton – Rasoumouski – Danish commander Molek – we had lunch – walked – conversed – at 4 o'clock I came back home – I undressed – read – wrote – drew – worked on my affairs – went to scold and punish Theresa – then wait for the King + then changed my dress and to the San Carlo theatre. The children healthy – the King went early in the morning to a (Chiuserano) in Portici – came to dress – went on the Danish ship – and then to have dinner at (…) and thence to Posillipo by sea.

On Monday July the 7th, I got up at 8 o'clock – dressed – had breakfast – dressed – heard Holy Mass – saw my children – went to Sambuca's Council, which lasted 2 hours – and then had lunch with the King – drew – saw samples – read – wrote – saw my children – did in advance my post and went to bed – the children healthy – the King in the afternoon went to Portici and returned by sea only at 9 in the evening.

On Tuesday July the 8th, I got up at 8 o'clock – had breakfast – dressed – heard Holy Mass – saw de Marco – and Sambuca – then wrote – had lunch with my children – drew – read – wrote – worked on my affairs – saw my children – talked with Lamberg and to bed – the children were well – in the morning the King went to Caserta and returned at 10 in the evening.

On Wednesday July the 9th, I got up at 7 o'clock – dressed – heard Mass at 8 o'clock – there was the Carlo de Marco's Council – then drew – spoke to Garcia – to the confessor – had lunch with my children – read – wrote – drew – kept myself busy – worked on my affairs – read – + – then saw my children – afterwards devoted myself and to bed. The children healthy – the King went at 10 o'clock on the lugger to go out to sea.

On Thursday July the 10th, I got up at 7 o'clock – saw my children – had breakfast – put curlers – curled my hair – dressed – heard Mass – whished happy birthday to the smallest girl in the court – read – wrote – had lunch with my children – drew – kept myself busy – read – was present at Mimi's school – was painted – then the King came back – I kept him company – ☉ – then dressed and went to the well illuminated San Carlo Theatre. The children healthy – the King was all day at the sea and returned from Capri at 7 o'clock in the evening.

On Friday July the 11th, I got up at 8 o'clock – had breakfast – dressed – heard Holy Mass – presided over the Cimitile 's Council – kept the King company at lunch and then – ☉ – drew – read – wrote – worked on my affairs – the Council of War – then by dray to the Gian Cola's comedy – then to the promenade at Chiaia and to bed – the children well – the King went to Capo di Monte at half past 4 in the afternoon.

On Saturday July the 12th, I got up at half past 7 – had breakfast – combed my hair – dressed – heard Holy Mass – read – wrote my post – saw Sambuca – had lunch with my children – kept them company – talked with old Salandra – read – wrote – drew – worked on my affairs and went to bed early. The children healthy – in the morning the King went to Caserta and returned in the evening.

On Sunday July the 13th, I got up at 8 o'clock – dressed – had breakfast – heard Holy Mass – saw my children – read – wrote – worked on my affairs – drew – had lunch at 3 o'clock – and drew – saw Princess Belmonte – dressed – combed my hair – worked on my affairs – went to the San Carlo's theatre – afterwards to the fair by dray and had dinner at the little house in Santa Lucia – from there home. The children healthy – the King gave a dinner on the lugger for a Danish General – then went to Portici – from there he returned at nine o'clock.

On Monday July the 14th, I got up at half past 7 – had breakfast – dressed – heard Holy Mass – presided over the Council – had lunch with the King – drew – kept the King company – ☉ – then read – wrote – worked on my affairs – dressed – went to an act at the Fondo theatre – and then went to bed. The children healthy – the King in the afternoon went for a short time to Posillipo.

On Tuesday July the 15th, I got up at 8 o'clock – had breakfast – combed my hair – dressed – heard Holy Mass – saw Sambuca – had lunch with my children – talked with them – wrote all my post – read + – write – drew – saw Acton – many hearings for ladies – then came the King and to bed. The children well – I spoke to Louise about the future marriage of Frendel[280] – she cried a lot. The King was in Caserta all day.

On Wednesday July the 16th, I got up at half past 7 – had breakfast – dressed – heard Holy Mass – presided over the Council – then read – wrote – worked on my affairs – saw the ladies – had lunch with my children – drew – spoke to my confessor – took care of my children – made my toilette – then prayed – worked on my affairs – went to San Carlo theatre with my girls – and then a bit to the fair and from there home. The children healthy – King went – after the Council – to Castellamare by sea and stayed there.

On Thursday July the 17, I got up at 8 o'clock – had breakfast – combed my hair – dressed – heard Holy Mass – spoke to Rocella – had lunch with my children – spent the afternoon with them – spoke to Sambuca – drew – read + – wrote – worked on my affairs – talked with Acton – gave my hearings – Countess Gaetani with her daughter bride – the young Caravita for her father-in – law – then wrote – saw my children and to bed The children healthy – the King still remained all day at Castellamare – fishing.

On Friday July the 18th,[281] I got up at half past 7 – had breakfast – dressed – combed my hair – heard Holy Mass – wrote the post – saw Sambuca – at midday received the King on hir return from Castellamare – had lunch with him – drew – kept him company – saw my children – dressed – combed my hair and went to the two Councils of finance and War – from there feeling not well – I undressed and confessed my sins – after that I began to bleed and have the miscarriage that ended at three thirty in the morning. The children healthy – the King returned at noon from Castelfamare and did not go out all day.

On Saturday the19th, I saw my children in the morning and all day stayed in darkness, lying without talking, the children well. The King did not go out all day.

On Sunday the 20th, I heard Holy Mass and was in bed all day lying in darkness the children well – the King went in the morning with the children to the Te Deum – then had the hand-kissing and public table – in the afternoon the King went to the *tonnara* to Posillipo to fish tuna and in the evening to the theatre San Carlo.

On July 21, I heard Mass, saw my children, and the rest of the day – quiet in bed. The children healthy, the King went to lunch at Posillipo and spent the day and evening to throwing.

On the 22nd, I heard Mass, saw my children, and was in bed all day The children healthy, the King in the afternoon went to Portici and returned in the evening.

On the 23rd, I heard the Mass – saw my children and stayed in bed, the children healthy – King afternoon went to Capodimonte and to the Fondo in the evening.

On the 24th, I had breakfast with the children – in honour of Mimi Christine's name day, heard Mass and stayed in bed all day, the children healthy, King went to Caserta in the morning – returned in the evening, went to the opera at the fair and afterwards to the little house in Santa Lucia in Pompei.

On Friday July 25, I heard Holy Mass and stayed in bed all day, in the evening I saw the Great Maîtresse and the lady guard – the children well, the King in the evening went for a short time to the pier by the sea, then the comedy by Jean Golo.[282]

On Saturday the 26th, I heard Holy Mass and stayed in bed, in the evening I saw the lady, the children well, the King afternoon went by dray to Posillipo and in the evening to the San Carlo theatre.

On Sunday the 27th, I had lunch with my daughters in Honor of the Infanta Louise – I saw Frendel who married Filingieri[283] this morning and left for Cava. I heard Holy Mass, I spoke to Lisette of my children – made my toilette and – by the grace of God – at midday I got up from my bed,[284] I saw Sambuca, Count Lamberg was present during my lunch, and at 2 o'clock I went to bed – afterwards had lunch ♥ my children – in the evening I saw the lady guard and went to sleep. The children were healthy – the King went to lunch at Posillipo and made the (Chiuserana) – where he brought the four eldest children – to whom he gave the snack at home – then he returned and went in the evening to the San Carlo Theatre.

On Monday the 28th, I was in bed until 11 o'clock – then I got up for a little while – then came back to bed – afterwards in the evening I saw the lady guard and spent as the usual to bed between my children and doing nothing.The children healthy – the King afternoon went for a while to the pier – in the evening he went to the new theatre to [see] a new performance.

On Tuesday the 29th, I got up around 11 o'clock – had lunch with my two eldest daughters – saw Count Lamberg – Sambuca – Lord Belmonte – Acton – then spent the afternoon with my girls – about 5 o'clock I returned to bed and saw the lady guard and went to sleep, the children healthy – the King went to Caserta – there was a downpour and he returned at half past 11 in the evening.

<u>On Wednesday the 30th,</u> I got up at 11 o'clock – had lunch with the King – and then back to bed – afterwards at 4 o'clock got up again – worked on my affairs – read – then at half past 6 to bed – saw the lady, the children and went to sleep.The children healthy – the King in the afternoon went to Capodimonte – in the evening to [see] the first act of the rehearsal of the opera.

On Thursday the 31st, I got up at midday – lunched with the King – later returned to bed – got up at 4 o'clock – saw Carlo de Marco – my ladies and went to bed again – the children healthy – King afternoon went to Portici – in the evening to the fair – to the promenade.

<u>On Friday the 1st,</u> I got up for a while in the morning – retuned to bed again – then got uo at four o'clock – I saw Sambuca – later my ladies – then went to bed – <u>I confessed</u> my sins and went to sleep – the children healthy – the King – after the Council in the morning – where the promotion of Marsico was announced, in the afternoon went out to sea on the lugger – then returned home and did not go out anymore.

<u>On Saturday August the 2nd,</u> I woke up at half past 6 in the morning and received communion – later got up from bed – had lunch with my girls – spoke to St. Esilia Pignatelli, to Acton – then saw the ladies – my children and to bed. The children healthy – the King went to receive the indulgences at half past 10 with the girls – and then went to have lunch on the lugger and went to Ischia – where he remained day and night.

On Sunday August the 3rd, I got up in the morning – had lunch with my children – saw Count Lamberg – Acton – Sambuca – my children – Gengano – the ladies and in the evening went back and to bed. The children healthy – the King remained all day in Ischia – and did not return.

<u>On Monday August the 4th,</u> I got up for lunch – after having taken an ounce of salt of England to purify myself – I lunched at one o'clock – then called my daughters – afterwards the King came – he kept me company all day – then I presided Sambuca's Council in my room and went to <u>bed</u> where I prayed – dined and went to sleep – the children healthy – the King returned from Ischia at half past [3] – and in the evening went to a new Italian comic opera at the Florentines.

On Tuesday August the 5th, I got up late – lunched with the King – saw the children – <u>read</u> – wrote – worked on my affairs – saw the King – the children and to bed. The children well – the King afternoon went to Capo di Monte and in the evening to the Florentines theatre.

<u>On Wednesday August the 6th,</u> I got up in the morning – lunched with the King – saw my children – all day devoted myself to several

things – in the evening I went to bed – I saw Princess Caramanico – my ladies – Lamberg. The children well – the King in the afternoon went to Posillipo – in the evening to the Florentines theatre.

On Thursday August the 7th, I got up late – had lunch with the King – saw my children – then Gengano – Lord Sambuca – ladies – Acton – then to bed. The children well – the King after – lunch went to Portici – where he remained I went to sleep.

On Friday August the 8th, I got up late – heard Mass – worked on my affairs – read – wrote – the King returned – I had lunch with him – then in the evening I kept myself busy – I was present at both Councils – Finance and War – and then to bed. The children healthy – Francis had a slight sore throat – but it is finished when he went out from the house – Mimi had the runs – without any consequences – at midday the King returned from the hunting at Portici – from the mountain where he had stayed the night before – in the afternoon he went to the little house in Santa Lucia – in the evening after the Councils he went to sleep.

On Saturday August the 9th, I got up late – wrote my post – read – worked on my affairs – had lunch with Teresa – kept her with me – kept myself busy – talked with Cicio Pignatelli – kept the King company – saw ladies – my children and went to bed – the children healthy – the King went out at half past 4 in the morning – with Migliano – to fish (…) at Portici and returned at half past 5 – afternoon having sailed on the lugger – in the evening to the Fondo di Lucro theatre.

On Sunday August the 10th, I got up – worked on my affairs – spoke to Sambuca – had lunch with the children – then stayed with them – kept myself busy – read – wrote – received my letters – talked with Vacher – in the evening talked with the King – sent [letters] courrier of Parma and sent – read – wrote and to bed – the children healthy – the King lunched on lugger with foreign ministers – and then went to Posillipo – returned by land – went to the Florentines theatre and to the fair where there was a cavalry ball

On Monday August the 11th, I got up in the morning – heard Holy Mass – started writing my post – then we presided over Sambuca's Council – I had lunch with the King – then read – ◇ – devoted myself – read – then saw my children and to bed. The children healthy – the at five o'clock the King went to Portici – and spent the night there – to go hunt up the Mountain – in the evening my people organised a big ball and party for my recovery[285] – le Vacher – to my regret – left for Parma – with his wife and daughter.

<u>On Tuesday August the 12th,</u> I got up – heard two Masses – lunched with the King – saw my children – read – wrote – devoted my self – saw my children – went to bed early – and so I spent my day – the children healthy – the King returned by sea at ten in the morning from Portici – did go out until the evening – to the concert at San Carlo.

On Wednesday August the 13th,[286] I had breakfast in the morning with the children and the King – then I got up – heard two Masses – saw the whole court – then I had lunch with my children – kept the King company – ⊙ – then I lay down until 4 o'clock – I got up – kept myself busy – then there was Carlo de Marco's Council – afterwards I gave a great snack and dance sort of plenty of toys to 21 little children in the company of my dear ones – at half past eight everything was over – I began to read – to do my business and to bed. The children healthy – the King had hang-kissing and the public table – did not go out all day – in the evening to New Opera – to the big theatre.

<u>On Thursday August 14th,</u> I got up late in the morning – heard Holy Mass – had lunch with my children – saw Sambuca – then Marchioness San Marco – then the children – read – wrote – kept myself busy – the King came and I went to bed, the children healthy – in the morning the King went to Caserta – from there he returned in the evening he went to the big theatre.

<u>On Friday August 15th,</u> I got up – to my chapel the first time – heard Holy Mass – had lunch with the King – read – wrote – kept myself busy – saw my children a long time – baron Didier – then the Great Maîtresse and lady guard – afterwards read – wrote – devoted myself and to bed – in the morning we had the two Councils. The children well – the King in the afternoon went to Posillipo – to the house in Santa Lucia – where he played – supped and returned.

<u>On Saturday August the 16th,</u> I got up in the morning – had breakfast – dressed – heard Holy Mass – had lunch with the King – read – wrote – kept myself busy – saw my children – hearings – Count Lamberg – and went to bed. The children healthy – the King in the morning went to the *tonnara* in Posillipo – in the afternoon to the pier – in the evening to the Florentines theatre.

<u>On Sunday August the 17th,</u> I got up – went to Mass – had lunch with the children – saw Sambuca – read the letters – stayed with the children – then walked on the terrace – read – wrote – worked on my affairs – the King came back – I saw my ladies – my children – worked on my affairs* – and then to bed – the children well – in the morning the King went to

Posillipo where he fished – he lunched at *tonnara* – continued fishing – came back by dray at the time of promenade – gave hearings – and left again to have dinner on the lugger – with the Commandants of our vessels and frigate – and went to Procida during the night.

On Monday August the 18th, I got up – heard Holy Mass – had lunch with my children – then saw Sambuca – afterwards I was with my children – then I spoke to Lady Belmonte – then King came back and kept me company – ⊙ – after the Council and to bed, the children helthy – the King – who during the night went to Procida – returned at 4 o'clock in the afternoon and did not go out anymore.

On Thursday August the 19th, I got up – dressed – heard – saw all the courtiers – being the birthday of my son – then I had lunch with all my children – then kept the King company – ⊙ – stayed in bed all afternoon – saw lady Sangro for the case of Salandra – wrote my post – saw my children – Lamberg and went to bed, the children healthy – the King in the morning had hand-kissing and public table – did not go out all day and in the evening he went to the San Carlo theatre.

On Wednesday August the 20th, I got up the morning – heard Holy Mass – worked on my affairs – had lunch with my children – stayed with them – spoke to Sambuca – then wrote – read – worked on my affairs – saw old Corigliano[287] – San Marco – read * again – saw my children and went to bed – the children healthy – the King at two o'clock went to Castellamare by sea – where he stayed all day and all night.

On Thursday August the 21st, I got up – heard Holy Mass – had breakfast – worked on my affairs – had lunch with my children – then spoketo Sambuca – afterwards the King returned – I kept him company – worked on my affairs – started packing – arranged my books – al that was necessary for going to Castellamare – then I spoke to Donna Teresina Sangro – then I confessed my sins and went to bed – the children healthy – the King returned at two o'clock from Castellamare and went at midnight by dry to Posillipo – where he threw in the evening and returned at 10 o'clock.

On Friday August the 22nd, I got up at 7 o'clock – went to church – performed my devotions – then had breakfast – combed my hair – dressed – then I went with Teresa Louise to St.Januarius to the Cathedral – to give thanks for my recovery – then I came back – undressed – saw the children – had lunch with the King – worked on my affairs – saw Carlo de Marco – Acton – Gengano – Termoli – Simonetti[288] and all kinds of people – then to bed – the children healthy – the King in the afternoon went to Capo di Monte – in the evening to Gian Colla.

On Saturday August the 23rd, I got up at 7 o'clock – had breakfast with my girls – heard Holy Mass – finished my post – worked on my affairs – saw the Spanish General Rocas[289] and then went down with Gravina – Montalto – the lady and Diomede to the lugger – where I embarked – we had lunch very comfortably upstairs and at half past three we arrived at Castellamare – I went home by one horse carriage – where I had a rest – then I arranged my papers – said the rosary – kept myself busy until 8 o'clock – I went outside – stayed there until nine o'clock – I came back home and went to bed – the children healthy – the King came and stayed with me all day.

On Sunday August the 24th, I got up in the morning – dressed – combed my hair – wrote – heard two Masses – directed the conversation – had lunch – read – wrote – walked with the gentlemen – then talked – in the evening kept myself busy and went to bed. The King in the morning went to the sea – to shooting bonitos – in the afternoon he walked.

On Monday August the 25th, I got up – dressed – had breakfast – combed my hair – saw my daughters – I walked with them – we heard Mass – I had lunch with my girls at the big table – then read – wrote – went for a long walk round with my daughters and their ladies – then gave them a snack and returned to Naples – in the evening the Sambucsa' Council – after that I went to bed – the children healthy – in the morning the King went to kill bonitos – in the afternoon to Scafati to see the plain of the quails.

On Tuesday August the 26th, I got up at 7 o'clock – at 8 o'clock I walked with Sambuca – then I combed my hair – dressed and started to write my letters – then heard Mass – saw Count Lamberg – Prince Belmonte and his second son – Count Giusepe – all those had lunch with us – later drew – read – wrote – kept myself busy until evening – I kept the King company – ☉ – then read +++ – wrote – prayed – in the evening went out to play a match and had dinner out. The children healthy – in the morning the King went to kill bonitos but in the afternoon he did not go out anymore.

On Wednesday August the 27th, I got up in the morning – had breakfast – dressed – combed my hair – read – drew – devoted myself – heard Holy Mass – then had lunch with the King – then read – drew – kept myself busy – a long walk with our people – and then wrote – devoted myself – played some music – prayed – had supper and to bed. The children healthy – the King in the morning did not go out – in the afternoon he went to see [Mauro] Vincenzo – the hairdresser – came from his trip to Vienna very pleased with the Emperor and the graces that he had received.

On Thursday August the 28th, I got up in the morning – wrote – read – had breakfast – combed my hair – dressed – heard Holy Mass – I lunched with Rasoumowski and Breme – more in the afternoon – I went to a game table where little Marchioness Gravina Montalto and Onorato played – then I walked with all these gentlemen – I came back and then I waited for the King, who came at one o'clock at night with Acton – there was the Council – then had dinner and later to bed. The children well – the King left at 4 o'clock in the morning – went to Naples by sea – saw the children – the secretaries – went to the *tonnara* in Posillipo and then returned.

On Friday August the 29th, I got up – went for a walk with Acton – had breakfast – made my toilette – then went to Mass – kept the King company – ⊙ – then had lunch – drew – read – wrote – worked on my affairs – at half past five I went down by one horse carriage to the pier – I returned with the King – worked on my affairs – went to play reversis – had dinner and went to bed. The children healthy – in the morning the King went fishing – afternoon he went to the pier and came back with me.

On Saturday August the 30th, I got up and went for a walk with Acton – I had breakfast – combed my hair – dressed – kept myself busy – read – wrote – I saw the con… [290] – then I had lunch – then I started reading – writing – the King came back – I finished my letters – saw Sambuca – Count Lamberg – who had come and left in the evening – Acton went in the afternoon – after having seen the King – and then the King and I [spoke] to the adviser of Sicily for more than one hour and a half – to Simonetti – later feeling fever I went to bed I went to sleep. I had news from Naples that the children were well – except beloved Mimi who had fever – cold – headache – vomit – in the evening I knew that she was already better. The King went out in the morning to the sea – met the three [ships] accompanied by galliots and brought them back – at three o'clock he was at home.

On Sunday the 31st, I got up at nine o'clock in the morning after having had fever all night – I had breakfast – dressed – worked on my affairs – heard Holy Mass – then drew – had lunch – drew again – read – wrote these were my occupations +++ – then went out – had dinner and went to sleep – in the morning the King went fishing at the pier – afternoon he went out again to the pier. He wrote to me from Naples that Mimi was getting better – the others healthy.

On September the 1st, I got up – had breakfast – dressed – wrote – I combed my hair – drew – heard Holy Mass – had lunch – Rasoumowski came from Naples and dined here – then kept the King company – ⊙ – drew – wrote – read – kept myself busy – in the afternoon saw Sambuca – I walked with him and then he spoke to me – then wrote, the Council and – afterwards – wrote again – had dinner and to bed – the children well – the King in the morning did not go out – in the afternoon he [walked].

On Tuesday September the 2nd, I got up – had breakfast – dressed – combed my hair – heard Holy Mass – read – wrote – kept myself busy – had lunch – later drew – read – wrote – kept myself busy – talked with Sambuca – afterwards kept company with foreigners – went out with Lamberg and Rasoumouski – and Lady Altavilla – afterwards came back home – read – wrote – prayed and went out – to play a match of reversis and to bed. The children healthy – the King at midday went to hunt quails – returned to the pier and came up here.

On Wednesday September the 3rd, I got up – had breakfast – combed my hair – dressed – heard Holy Mass – drew – read ++++++ – worked on my affairs – walked to the pier – where I saw the pirates and the Turks – and then got on one horse carriage – wrote – prayed – worked on my affairs – so ended the day, the children well – the King went for a while to the pier before me and returned on horseback.

On Thursday September the 4th, I got up in the morning and went out on a donkey and then walked on foot – then I returned – had breakfast – combed my hair – prayed – dressed – heard Holy Mass – kept myself busy – had lunch – drew – read – wrote and then I went to the blessing – then I saw the marriage of the son of Bologna – afterwards to the Council – I played reversis and to bed. The children healthy – the King went to the pier to see the launch of the ship – then did not go out anymore.

On Friday September the 5th, I got up – had breakfast – dressed – wrote – read – went out to Mass – I had lunch with the King – and then drew – Acton came and spoke to the King – afterwards I kept myself busy – then I went out – I walked on the pier – and then returned to make my packages – played reversis – had supper and to bed – the children well – the King in the morning went walking for a while and in the evening to the pier.

On Saturday the 6th, I got up – had breakfast – dressed – heard Holy Mass – at 8 o'clock I went by carriage to Castellamare with the King – Marsico – Gravina – at half past 10 we arrived – I found my children very well – except Mimi who was tired and had a cold – I took care of them – at half past 11 we went to the blessing at the Court church – then lunched with the King – wrote – kept myself busy – combed my hair – curled – dressed – had hearings – young Geraci,[291] Marquise Simeri – Duchess de la Tripalda – from there to the Florentines theatre to [see] two acts – afterwards tired – bored at home – the children well – the King did not go out all day.

On Sunday September 7, I got up – heard Holy Mass – had breakfast with my children – scolded them – then combed my hair – dressed – went to the chapel – then public table where the bailiff Loras[292] was introduced to me – then I undressed – read – kep myself busy ++++ – afterwards kept the King company – ☉ – then started endless hearings – young Salandra for her affair – Montalto to take leave – Ferolito for her affair – S. Lorenzo – Gallucci[293] for their problems – Monsignor Onesti[294] – introduction of Cariati 's daughter – introduction of Lord Tarsia and his lady in connection with the marriage broken – Tripalda's daughter for the same reason – Belmonte – Butera for the party – from there I went to one act to the theatre – then at the fair by dray – from there to the little house – to have supper and to bed. The children well – the King in the morning went to Posillipo – the rest of the day he did not go out – I saw the two Germans ladies who had arrived the day before.

On Monday September 8, I got up – had breakfast – dressed – heard Holy Mass – made my toilette – read – wrote – then went down to the porcelain factory with Acton – Pignatelli – the two Spanish Generals – to the porcelain factory – where there were all the Liparoti – had lunch with them – then went home – wrote – then saw the troops parade – saw my children – dressed and went in splendid form to Pie di Grotta – returned – undressed – worked on myaffairs and went to the San Carlo theatre. The children well – the King in the morning went to see Liparoti and then did not go out anymore.

On Tuesday the 9th, I got up – dressed – had breakfast with my children – heard Holy Mass – I packed – at eleven o'clock I saw the new room valet arrive and saw all my children – I left at eleven o'clock on the xebec – *lo vigilante* – captained by Lardosa – then – at three o'clock – we arrived at Castellamare – I had dinner in my room and was busy reading – wrote – until 9 o'clock. I went to have supper and to bed. The children healthy – the King came with me and walked for a while in the evening.

On Wednesday the 10th, I got up – had breakfast – dressed – wrote – Holy Mass – finished the courier – at one o'clock had lunch – saw Baron and Baroness Didier – lunched with them and Lamberg – afternoon Baroness kept me company until half past 5 – we all went for a walk – I took leave of them – returned and I saw them leave with regret – she is an extremely nice person and he is a worthy man – kept writing and kept myself busy until dinner time – I had supper and went to bed. The children healthy – the King went out in the morning at 6 o'clock – the whole day went out by sea – in the afternoon [he went] hunting in Mortella and came back at 8 o'clock in the evening.

On Thursday the 11th, I got up in the morning and went for a ride on a donkey – I had breakfast – dressed – heard Holy Mass – drew – had lunch – there were Rasoumouski and Saa[295] – afternoon – I drew – kept myself busy – and then went for a short walk – I came and worked on my affairs – read – wrote – kept myself busy – afterwards the Council – had dinner and to bed. The children healthy – the King in the morning went fishing in the afternoon to the pier.

On Friday the 12th, I got up and walked with Acton – then I had breakfast – dressed – read – wrote – worked on my affairs – heard Holy Mass – had lunch – and then kept myself busy – read – wrote until half past 5 – I walked for a while and returned to read – wrote – kept myself busy – the King came back – we played the game of pool (white) with air rifles – and then some music – supper and to bed. The children healthy – the King in the morning went fishing and then went to Naples – afterwards to Mortella and then returned in the evening.

On Saturday the 13th, I got up in the morning – had breakfast – combed my hair – went for a walk – came back home – read – wrote – worked on my affairs – heard Holy Mass – had lunch – then drew – kept myself busy – wrote – went for a walk to the pier to see two galliots being captured – a little galliot – then went up to keep the King company – ☉ – afterwards worked on my affairs – had dinner and went to bed. The children healthy – the King went fishing in the morning and afternoon to the pier.

On Sunday the 14th, having had severe abdominal cramps for all the night – with nausea – and being upset – I remained in bed until half past 9 – when I got up – went to church, and then I took an ounce of salt of England – I was busy writing – reading – drawing – at one o'clock I had lunch in my room – then I kept myself busy – played music – then the King came back – we had supper and to bed. The children well – the King – and everyone from Castellamare – left at 6 o'clock in the morning for Sorrento and returned in the evening – in the afternoon there was a terrible storm.

On Monday September the 15th, I got up – coefois – combed my hair – heard Holy Mass – had breakfast – worked on my affairs – then I had lunch – afterwards kept myself busy – drawing – reading – writing – and then I went down to the pier with Lamberg and Breme – then I went by carriage – the King came back – we presided over the Sambuca's Council + – ⊙ – after had supper and to bed, the children well – the King went at half past nine to hunt quails and came back at 6 o'clock.

On Tuesday September 16th, I got up – had breakfast – combed my hair – heard Holy Mass – wrote – kept the King company – ⊙ – then had dinner – later – drew – read – wrote – kept myself busy until dinner time. The children healthy – the King did not go out all day.

On Wednesday September the 17th, I got up in the morning – went out on a donkey and on foot – then combed my hair – worked on my affairs – had lunch – drew – was in company with people – then I ent for a walk at the pier with Saa and Rasoumouski – we returned in a one horse carriage – I worked on my affairs – I kept myself busy – had dinner and to bed, thel children well – the King at half past 9 went to hunt quails and returned in the evening.

On September 18th, I got up at 7 o'clock – had breakfast – heard Holy Mass – and then I went with the lady and Marsico to Naples – when I arrived I saw all my children – worked on my affairs – I kept myself busy – had lunch with the children – then I spoke to Sambuca – Marchioness San Marco – Acton – I gave hearings to Delfino – a Lady from Turin[296] – who was introduced to me by Ferolito and Celedei with her daughters – then saw the children – read – wrote – the King returned – the Council and to bed. The children well – the King went to Salerno to the fair and did not return until evening.

On September the 19th, I got up – had breakfast – with my children – went to Holy Mass – combed my hair – dressed – at half past 2 I was with my children at St. Januarius chapel – had hand-kissing of Knights – then half gala dress – changed dress – had lunch with the King – kept him company – ⊙ – read +++ – wrote – and then dressed – went with the King to the cathedral – to venerate St. Januarius – returned presided over the Council – afterwards saw Countess Althan – Salandra – Sangro – Belmonte – then saw my children – read – wrote – undressed had dinner and to bed – the children well – the King after the Council went to throw in Posillipo – from there he returned at 10 o'clock.

On Saturday the 20th, I got up in the morning – had breakfast – dressed – heard Holy Mass – went to a public *Te Deum* – then hand-kissing for the birth of twin boys who were born of Princess of Asturias[297] – then public table – kept the King company – ⊗ – and undressed – had lunch in my room – saw my children – packed – saw Don Inocentio Pignatelli take leave and then left for Castellamare by carriage [with] – the King – Marsico and Altavilla – we arrived around 7 o'clock – settled in – worked on my affairs – had dinner and went to bed. The children healthy – in the morning the King made preparations for the gala and came with me to Castellamare.

On Sunday September the 21st, I got up at 6 o'clock – had breakfast – dressed – combed my hair – heard Holy Mass – at 8 o'clock we left – by a one horse carriage [with] – the King – Lady Marsico and Altavilla – for Salerno – at the first stop in Scafati the King went on horseback and galopped as far as Salerno – we arrived there – walked around to have a look there – all that there was of cattle – then we lunched in the wood carriage – which had the shape of a little house – in the afternnon we saw several goods – then I played piquet with the Prior – afterwards we came back in a one horse carriage – I undressed – I removed the dust and I stayed in my room lay down without going to dinner, the children well – the King was with me all day.

On Monday September the 22nd, I got up in the morning – had break-fast – combed my hair – dressed – wrote – drew – heard Holy Mass – had lunch – later read – wrote – drew until 7 o'clock – when the Council took place – then wrote again and kept myself busy until eleven o'clock – we went to have dinner – the children healthy – the King in the morning at half past 5 went to hunt quails and came back at 6 o'clock.

On Tuesday September the 23rd, I got up – took an ounce of salt of England – I trotted on a donkey – then on foot – dressed – heard Holy Mass – wrote – had lunch – saw Sambuca – drew – wrote – kept myself busy until supper time. The children well – from Naples I received the news that Francis had had indigestion – but without consequences – the King at half past 9 went to hunt quails and returned at 6 o'clock in the evening.

On Wednesday September the 24th, I got up in the morning and went on foot to the pier – on the return jouney on a donkey – combed my hair – dressed – heard Holy Mass – kept myself busy – ⊙ – then had lunch – drew – read – wrote – I ket myself busy – went out with Saa Lamberg and others – met Rasoumovski – went to the pier – returned by one horse carriage – wrote – kept myself busy – had dinner – the King in the afternoon went to Mauro to hunt hares and returned at 7 o'clock The children well.

On September the 25th, I got up at 7 o'clock – had breakfast and went on foot to the Madonna di Pugliano – returned later in a one horse carriage – combed my hair – dressed – had lunch – read the letters – drew – at half past 4 went out in company – then read – wrote – kept myself busy – the King came back – there was the Council and I kept myself busy until dinner time – the children well – in the morning the King went hunting at Mortella – and returned at 6 o'clock

On Friday September the 26th, I got up – had breakfast – went for a long ride on a donkey and then on foot – then returned – dressed – combed my hair – read + – wrote – heard Mass – had lunch – read again – kept myself busy – drew – went down to the pier – saw Farina's ships[298] – up – saw Sambuca – talked – kept myself busy until dinner time – the children well – the King at half past 9 went to hunt quails and returned at 7 o'clock.

On Saturday September the 27th, I got up in the morning – had breakfast and waited for the King's orders in connection with fishing – was busy reading – writing – at 2 o'clock I went to comb my hair – dressed – heard Holy Mass – had lunch – drew – read – wrote my letters – went to the pier – after having sent Acton there – to the pier – was present at a copious catch of 2 tanuta fish and 57 rotoli[299] – then returned – kept the King company – ⊙ – afterwards read – wrote – kept myself busy – had dinner and to bed – the children well – the King in the morning went prepared to go fishing – after – lunch he went down – an hour before me – settled everything and returned with me.

On Sunday September the 28th, I got up at 7 o'clock – had breakfast – combed my hair – dressed – at 9 o'clock heard Holy Mass – then went by galliot to Sorrento – we arrived at Meta – where M ° Saa received us – I went up by sedan chair – to the little house of Serra Capriola – then we went to the cathedral – afterwards a ride by one horse carriage to see the countryside – afterwards we lunched to the big house of Serra Capriola […] by M ° Saa – then we went to Sorrento by one horse carriage – we went to have the blessing in the cathedral – afterwards we went to visit the convents of women – from there we returned to Meta – embarked on a speed boat, and at 7 o'clock we were at Castellamare – I kept the King company – ⊙ – then let my hair loose – undressed – read – letters – wrote to Naples – wrote and to bed. The children healthy – the King at 7 o'clock went on the lugger – arrived at midday at Sorrento – in the afternoon he went riding with the nephew of Madame de Saa – to a hill – to shoot garden warblers returned before me – by a few minutes – by boat.

On Monday September the 29th, I got up – dressed – combed my hair – had breakfast – heard Holy Mass – read – wrote – kept the King company – ☉ – then dinner – afterwards drew – read – wrote – kept myself busy – the Sambuca's Council – had dinner and to bed, the children well – King went in the afternoon for a short walk.

On Wednesday September the 30th, I got up – had breakfast and went by the longest way – partly on foot – partly on a donkey – to Madonna della Libera[300] – there I heard Mass – returned home – made my toilette – then spoke to Mrs Monier[301] – afterwards lunched at a table of 17 people – all officers of galliots – Lamberg – Rasoumouski – Sambuca and our officier on duty – finished lunch – I spoke to Sambuca – then wrote my post – kept myself busy – read – wrote – the King came back and we played music – we heard tenor singing very well – then had dinner and went to bed. The children well – King at half past 9 went to hunt quails and came back at six o'clock.

On Wednesday October the 1st, I got up at 7 o'clock – had breakfast – dressed – combed my hair – heard Mass – at 8 o'clock I went down – I met the King who told me that he was going to the sea – I arrived at half past ten – saw my children – then read – wrote – kept myself busy – had lunch with my two eldest daughters – took care of them – and then unpacked – wrote – worked on my affairs – chose the bottom drawer for Wolersfeld[302] – afterwards saw the ladies who will invite me to the party – the King came back – there was the Carlo de Marco's Council – then King went to throw – I read – wrote – undressed – he came back early, the children well – the King went to the sea – returned at three o'clock – went out again at 8 o'clock and returned at half past nine.

On Thursday October the 2nd, I got up – combed my hair – had breakfast – dressed – heard Mass – then had lunch – kept the King company – then washed – dressed – saw the children washing – at one o'clock in the morning of night I went with the King and my children to the serenade which was beautiful – it was sung by 75 ladies for my recovery – the entire floor was full of nobility – my children were in their box – after the singing we returned – I kept the King company to – ☉ – then we went to havve dinner – in the theatre then there was the masked ball – very brilliant – we stayed there until one o'clock – afterwards [we came back]. The children well – in the morning the King went to trawl at sea.

On Friday the 3rd, I got up at 8 o'clock – had breakfast – combed my hair – dressed – went with my eldest two daughters – heard Mass at the

Madonna dei Fiorentini – was present at both Councils – then saw my children – had lunch – kept the king company – undressed – saw the paintings – the children – afterwards read – wrote – packed – then saw the ladies of the ball – later Lady Termoli with her daughter bride, – Monterotondo with her married niece – old Salandra – the wife of Coradino – Faggiano – wrote – undressed – had dinner and to bed – the children well – the King went to Portici at two o'clock and came back in the evening.

On Saturday October the 4th, I got up at half past 5 – walked on the terrace – and then wrote – made my toilette – had breakfast – heard Mass – went out in a big gala [dress] – the hand-kising in black court dress – with my children – then the public table – later – had lunch – changed my dress – kept the King company – ⊙ – read – then toilette again – the hand-kissing of the ladies – changed my dress and went to the theatre – where I brought my two daughters – I had the day before the pleasant news that the Grand Duchess had given to a son. My children well – in the morning the King went fishing at Portici – came back early and did not go out anymore.

On Sunday October the 5th, I got up the morning – unpacked – worked on my affairs – combed my hair – dressed – had breakfast – at ten o'clock I went with Theresa to hear Mass at St. Francesco di Paola – then on return I spoke with Stigliano the issue regarding the trial of Great Maîtresse – about the infamous hassle with Pignatelli – de Marco – with Tripalda – then I had lunch with my children – then I spoke to Sambuca to Lady San Marco – then read + – wrote – kept myself busy – started my audiences – Scigliano – Albito[303] – Roffia[304] – Casabuona – Regina for her problems – with the Countess Gaetani with her husband Conversano[305] – from there I was present at the marriage of Wolennsfeld with Vicenzo Goysueta[306] – afterwards I saw my children – kept myself busy and afterwards to the theatre – and then to bed. The children well – the King at nine o'clock went to Posillipo and [Chiuserano] – and from there rode to Strone whence he came back at half past six.

On Monday October the 6th, I got up at seven o'clock – had breakfast – heard Holy Mass – combed my hair – then arranged my affairs – read – took leave of the children – and at ten o'clock – I went with my three daughters to Caserta – I arrived at midday – made my arangements – had lunch in company – then worked on my affairs all day – the Council and to bed – the children healthy – the King after lunch went for a while to San Leucio.

On Tuesday October the 7th, I got up at 8 o'clock – had breakfast – combed my hair – dressed – heard Mass – saw my children – finished putting my house in order – wrote my letters – had lunch – kept the King company – ran with him up and down all the stairs – then finished writing my post – at half past 4 I went out with Vasto – Montalto and the lady and two daughters – I went up to the Mountain of Eboli and returned on foot – I began to write the instructions for Louise's ladies – then spoke to them and that lasted until half past 9 – where I undressed and went to bed. The children well – the King after lunch went for a little while to San Leucio.

On Wednesday October the 8, I got up – had breakfast – and then went for a walk in the woods – later heard Mass – introduced Blind and Bartheki to Louise – afterwards dressed – combed my hair – then spoke to Sambuca – showed him the apartements – saw Princess Caramanico – then to my children who arrived in Caserta – had lunch with the King – kept him company – drew – saw Don Inocenzio Pignatelli in connection with his business – and Cicio Pignatelli in connection with Calabria – then saw the children – kept the King company – ⊙ – the Council – worked on my affairs and to bed, the children well – I gave Louise some new ladies in waiting – the King in the morning went to Carbone – after lunch at San Leucio – both my son and Amelia came here.

On Thursday October the 9, I got up in the morning – had breakfast and out for a walk – on return I saw my children – heard Mass – combed my hair – dressed – read – wrote – I kept myself busy – had lunch with my children – walked through the apartements – saw them playing together – read the letters – wrote for the courrier of Tuscany – then listened to Theresa play the harpsichord and the King play the lyre – then kept myself busy – had dinner and to bed – the children well – the King at 7 o'clock in the morning went to Longano to hunt and returned at half past five in the afternoon.

On Friday October the 10th, I got up in the morning at 7 o'clock – had breakfast – dressed – write – drew – heard Holy Mass – kept the King company – saw my children – dinner with the King – and draw – read – wrote stayed a long time with my children – then the two Councils and to bed – the children fine – in the morning the King purged himself – after-dinner went to St. Leucy whence he returned in the evening.

On Saturday October the 11th, I got up in the morning – had breakfast – dressed – heard Mass – saw my children – read – wrote – kept myself busy – had lunch with the King – drew – wrote my post – read+ – wrote – saw a wife named Coreale[307] with Mastrilli – the widow of Frontone[308] with her daughters and the widow of counsellor Ferdinando[309] – then the

King returned – I kept myself busy and played the harpsichord for a while and then to bed. The children healthy – the King in the morning went to Carditello – came back at lunch time and after lunch [he went] to St. Nicola to hunt for partridge whence returned in the evening.

On Sunday October the 12th, I got up in the morning – had breakfast – dressed – heard Mass – saw my children – wrote – drew – had lunch with the King – kept him company – ⊙ – then <u>read</u> + – wrote – drew – saw Acton – played the harpsichord – then kept myself busy – and to bed – the children healthy – the King was at home in the morning because of bad weather – after lunch he went to San Leucio.

On Monday October the 13th, I got up at 7 o'clock – breakfasted – dressed – combed my hair – heard Mass – wrote – kept myself busy – had lunch with all my six children – then went to the library – chose some books – spoke to Lady Belmonte – to Castelpagano[310] – Avellino – then the King returned – the Council and to bed. The children all healthy – the King at 7 o'clock went to Venafro and returned at six o'clock in the evening. During the night Krottendorf[311] came to visit me.

On Tuesday October the 14th, I got up in the morning – had breakfast – dressed – combed my hair – wrote – saw my children – talked with Sambuca – had lunch with the children – drew – played the harpsichord – saw Monteleone for business – the Marchioness of Sambuca – then the King came – I saw my children and then went to prepare myself and to go to confession, the children well – the King went to hunt boars to Piedimonte.

On Wednesday October the 15th, I got up at half past 6 and went to church and performed my devotions – then had breakfast with my girls – combed my hair – dressed – read – wrote – talked with Sambuca – drew – had lunch with my children – stayed with them until half past three – then arranged my books – saw Carlo de Marco – wrote – presided over the Council and to bed. The children healthy – the King in the morning [went hunting] larks at Carditello – lunched there and in the evening made played *palumbelli*.

Followed by two blank pages

On Thursday October the 16th, I got up at 7 o'clock – had breakfast – combed my hair – dressed – heard Mass – spoke to Tarsia – Marsico – then unpacked books – drew – had dinner with the children – kept them with me after lunch – then drew – read – saw Foveno – Father Sterzingher[312] – a person with a letter from my sister Amelia[313] – then went out – walked with lady Marsico and Gravina – back to my affairs – the King returned – I kept him company for a while – then I heard Theresa play the harpsichord – and to bed – the children were healthy – the King went into town to take a lots of tuna at Posillipo – then had lunch at Molosiglio – afterwards he saw a frigate launched happily and successfully into the sea – then he listened to a concert of a comic opera – afterwards he returned.

On Friday October the 17th, I got up – had breakfast – dressed – combed my hair – heard Mass – spoke a long time with Gravina – saw my children – heard Mass – had lunch with the King – kept him company – ⊙ – and <u>read</u> – wrote – worked on my affairs – drew – presided over the two Councils and to bed. The children healthy – the King in the morning went [to hunt] larks at Carditello – after lunch he made the revisit of the Liparoti in the wood.

On Saturday October the 18th, I got up in the morning – had breakfast – dressed – combed my hair – heard Mass – read – wrote – kept myself busy – saw my children – had lunch with the King – then read – kept him company – read – wrote my post – drew – the King returned – I said my prayers and took care of my children all evening. The children well – the King went in the morning [to hunt] larks at Carditello – after lunch to shoot woodcock in San Leucio then in the evening to bed.

On Sunday the 19th, I got up at 7 o'clock – had breakfast – curled [and] combed my hair – dressed – heard Mass – then wrote – read – kept myself busy – saw the children – read – drew – read the post – later saw two Roman ladies – Rocca Fiorita – Cari – afterwards saw the children – kept the King company – ⊙ – then I undrressed – prayed – kept myself busy and to bed. The children well – the King went in the morning to the pheasant farm – after lunch to the wood.

On the 20th Monday I got up at 6 o'clock – had breakfast – dressed – heard Mass and at half past six – I went in a carriage with Marsico – Salandra – the King and I – to hunt al Forgillo which is three stations away – there I went to hunt – I shot once in the morning and once in the afternoon and I missed both – we lunched in the open air – at half past 4 we left and returned home – I changed dress – went to the Council and to bed – the children well – the King went and returned to the hunt with me.

On Tuesday the 21st, I got up at 6 o'clock – had breakfast – dressed and went out to walkthrough the wood – and then I came back and made my toilette – then Mass – and afterwards wrote my post – saw my children – had lunch with the King – drew – saw Madame San Marco – two Sicilian women – then Lord Feroleto – then wrote – afterwards called

Marchioness Altavilla – Sambuca – Marsico and Vasto – there Theresa played the harpsichord – then I wanted to play – but the King undressed and I too and went to bed – the children well – the King in the morning went [to hunt] larks at Carditello – after lunch in San Leucio.

On Wednesday October the 22nd, I got up at 6 o'clock – dressed – prayed – made some notes – had breakfast – combed my hair – heard Mass – talked with my confessor – drew – saw Sambuca – talked with Princess Caramanico – with Lord Belmonte – had lunch with the children – drew – saw Lady Belmonte – the Princess Jacy – afterwards an audience with the wife and sister – in – law of Secondo for her husband – then I went out with Gravina – Marsico to Canalone – I met my son and I returned with him – I kept my children in my room until the return of the King – then the Council and to bed. The children well – the King in the morning went to Carditello – lunched there and spent the whole day there.

On Tuesday the 23rd, I got up at 6 o'clock – said my prayers – had breakfast – dressed and walked out – I went to see the water tank on Trapeto – the mills – afterwards walked to Belvedere – then I heard Mass and returned on foot – at half past 10 – I made my toilette – and then wrote for a while – saw my children – had lunch with the King + then kept myself busy – drew – read – wrote – kept myself busy until it was time to go to bed – the children well – the King in the morning went to [hunt] larks – after lunch he [took] exercise.

On Friday the 24th, I got up at 7 o'clock – had breakfast – dressed – heard Holy Mass combed my hair – saw my children – <u>read</u>+ – wrote – kept myself busy – the King returned – had lunch with me then I kept him company – then read – wrote – I saw Tuperio[314] – the bishop of Troya[315] and Paterno – afterwards I saw Prince Charles Lichtenstein,[316] who was introduced by Lamberg – the King spoke to him a lot of hunting – and then we presided over the two Councils – as I felt my breathing was impeded and had a sharp pain in my right side – I called the doctor who, diagnosing me with fever – made me bleed. The children well – the King in the morning went to Carditello and after lunch took exercise.

<u>On Saturday the 25th,</u> I spent a very bad night with a big spasm and pain – I took – at every hour of the day – a Sambuca's flower tisane and honey poultices on the [sore] and enemas and plasters on the part and enemas – I saw my children – the governess – read for a while in the morning and in the afternnon – did not get up from bed – the children well – the King in the morning went to Carditello – in the afternoon to the pheasant farm.

On Sunday October the 26th, I spent a quiet night – still had the second fever – saw my children – hear Holy Mass – <u>read</u> + – worked on my affairs – saw the King – kept him company – ☉ – then changed my bed – saw Princess Caramanico – read* – saw Altavilla – my children and went to sleep – I was all day in bed. The children well – the King in the morning went to Caivano – after lunch to San Leucio.

On Monday October the 27th, I got up at 7 o'clock in the morning – took an ounce of salt of England in three times – heard Holy Mass – read – combed my hair – dressed – read – wrote – saw my children – had lunch with the King – kept him company + – then saw Madame de Sangro – Belmonte – San Marco – spoke with the King – my children – the Council and to bed. The children healthy – the King in the morning went to Carditello – in the afternnon [took] exercise.

On Tuesday the 28th I got up – had breakfast – dressed – drew – heard Holy Mass – wrote my post – had lunch with the King – kept him company – ☉ – then some audiences – afterwards saw Lady Althan – Madame de Sambuca – then saw my children – wrote and went to bed – the children well – the King in the morning went [to hunt] larks to Carditello in the afternoon to San Leucio.

On Wednesday the 29th, I got up – took my medicine – had breakfast – heard Mass – dressed – went out to walk with my three daughters – then returned – talked with Sambuca – then had lunch with my girls – saw a wax statue of Benedetto Labre[317] – then drew – saw Marsico – Princess of Jacy – de Marco – presided over the Council and to bed – the children healthy – the King in the morning went to Carditello – lunched there and after lunch went to Zingaro.

On Thursday the 30th, I got up at 7 am – took my medecine – then went out in a carriage and on a donkey – afterwards returned – dressed – combed my hair – drew – had lunch – drew – saw Gravina – Cuto[318] – Misilmeri[319] – Angio[320] – then read – wrote – saw Prince Charles – the children – worked on my affairs and to bed. The children healthy – the King in the morning went to [hunt larks Cuciardi – in the afternoon to the pheasant farm.

On Friday October the 31st, I got up in the morning – took my medicine – went out on foot and on a donkey for my health – returned – had breakfast – combed my hair – heard Holy Mass – saw Prince Charles for a moment – <u>read</u> – wrote – worked on my affairs – had lunch with my girls – then drew – <u>read</u>* – wrote – kept myself busy – the Councils and to bed. The children healthy – the King in the morning went to San Leucio and hunted there and stayed all day with Prince Lichtenstein – they killed 39 wild boars.

On November the 1st, I got up – took my medicine – heard Mass and went out – both on foot and on donkey – I returned – had breakfast – saw my children – made my toilette – read – wrote – kept myself busy – had lunch with all my children – drew – kept myself busy – read – wrote my post – saw a poor lady – in the evening kept myself busy – saw Prince Charles – Lamberg – Gravina – Vasto – Acton – I made Theresa play the harpsichord and then went to sleep – the children healthy – the King went to hunt (birds) at Calvi – all day with Prince Charles.

On Sunday November the 2nd, I woke up at 7 o'clock in the morning – had breakfast – heard Holy Mass – combed my hair – made my toilette – saw my children – read – wrote – had lunch with my girls – took care of them – drew – read+ – wrote – saw Acton – then my children – also my boys – the King returned – I kept him company – ☉ – then there was a great concert – everyone was present there – Ministers – Prince Charles and all the inhabitants of Caserta – Theresa played the harpsichord very well – after the music to bed. The children healthy – the King went at 9 in the morning with Prince Charles – to hunt pheasant – where they killed 551 pheasants.

On Monday November the 3rd, I got up in the morning at 7 o'clock – had breakfast – heard Holy Mass – combed my hair – dressed – saw my children – arranged my papers – wrote in advance my post – had lunch with children – took care of them – arranged my papers – at 4 o'clock I left Caserta with lady Altavilla – Gravina and Marsico and we came into town – I settled there – saw Sambuca for a moment – the King returned – there was the Council – after that I had colic – which kept me from being able to confess my sins in the evening and went to bed.The children were all healthy – the King in the morning went [to hunt] larks at Carditello – in the evening to the opera rehearsal.

On Tuesday November the 4th, day of my party[321] and that of a dear son I will not forget for all my life and who is always present for me – I got up at 6 o'clock – confessed – received communion – returned – after two Masses – had lunch – spoke to the King who made me a present of a court dress – afterwards I made my toilette and went out to for the hand-kissing – public table – many foreigners were introduced to us – and Commodore Curtis[322] – a man of merit – afterwards undressed – had dinner in my room – read – drew – kept myself busy – prayed – then the hand-kissing of the ladies – afterwards changed dress and went to the theatre – where Prince Charles came after the first act with us – after the second we went home. The children healthy – the King remained all day at home.

On Wednesday November the 5th, I got up in the morning at half past 6 – heard Mass – took my medicine – walked on the terrace – then to the riding stables on a donkey – afterwards came back – had breakfast – took part in the Council – then look for a bottom drower for Mauritio – afterwards made my toilette – had lunch with the King – kept him company – ☉ – then kept myself busy – talked with Pignatelli of Calabrian issues – read – wrote – the King returned – then I saw Duchess of Gravina in connection with her brother – then Castelpagano for the wedding of her daughter – afterwards Santo Stefano for a dowry – afterwards we went to the Fondo theatre – to *the chinese idol* – where Prince Charles came into our loge. The children healthy – except Francis – indigestion for which the doctor gave him an emetic – the King went out after lunch – from two until 5 o'clock he stayed in Strone.

On Thursday November the 6th, I got up early – took medicine – worked on my affairs – saw de Marco – heard Mass – made my toilette – saw Sambuca – Salandra – old Butera – Lady Pignatelli – had lunch – drew – saw Acton gave audience to Ferolito – Cariati – Bajard[323] – Mr amd Mrs Belmonte – Caramanico – prayed and went to the San Carlo theatre – at the second act the King returned – we remained until the second ballet, and then went home I went to sleep – the children well – the King at five o'clock in the morning went to Persano[324] and returned at half past 8 in the evening.

On Friday November the 7th, I got up at 7 o'clock – had breakfast – combed my hair – dressed – heard Holy Mass – at 8 o'clock there was the Cimitile's Council – then I kept the King company – ☉ – then I came back to Caserta – I did the first half way in a carriage and the second by dray with the King – on arrival I saw all my children – had lunch with the King – read – wrote – drew – in the evening to the Acton's Council – then prayed – undressed and to bed – the children well – the King returned in the morning with me – after lunch he went to San Leucio.

On Sturday November the 8th, I got up at 7 o'clock – had breakfast – combed my hair – dressed – heard Holy Mass – read++ – wrote my post – saw my children – drew – had lunch with the King – drew – read – wrote – saw young Serignano[325] – prayed for her husband – then saw Acton – my children – the King returned – wrote – prayed – kept myself busy – in the evening Theresa played the harpsichord and there I had some people – Acton – Gravina – Marsico – and Vasto – then went to sleep – the children healthy – the King in the morning went to Carditello – after lunch to San Leucio.

On Sunday November the 9th, I got up at 7 o'clock – had breakfast – dressed – heard Holy Mass – read+ – wrote – kept myself busy – finished my toilette – heard the second Mass – saw my children – had lunch with the King – kept him company – ⊙ – and read – wrote – saw the children – Marchioness Ferante for her son, Acton who returned to town – Gravina for his brother – then the King returned – had his coffeee – I took care of my daughters read my letters and went to bed.The children well – the King went in the morning to Calabria Citra – after lunch to the wood and to San Leucio.

On Monday November the 10th, I got up in the morning – took one ounce of salt of England and walked – then saw my children – hear Mass – breakfasted – made my toilette – then read the papers concerning Sicily – then saw the consultor Simonetti – talked with him – then read – devoted myself – had lunch with my two eldest daughters – read – talked with a man who knows the technique of making porcelain – then had a snack – later wrote – read – afterwards talked with Cattolica[326] – with the wife of Colonel Macdonald[327] – with the wife of Ciconi[328] – then saw the children – presided over the Council – saw the children again – undressed – wrote – prayed – had supper and to bed – the children well – the King at 9 o' clock in the morning went to Calabria Citra Ulteriore and returned in the evening.

On Tuesday November the 11th, I got up at 7 o'clock – had breakfast – dressed – wrote my post – saw my children – heard Mass – had lunch with the children – then wrote – saw Sambuca – afterwards some audiences – the widow of Vargas[329] – widow of Vico[330] – the wife of Soriento and others – then I spoke to the King – worked on my affairs – and then saw a juggler of mugs with my children who then played in my room – made a lot of noise – I undressed and went to bed – the children well – the King went at eleven o'clock to San Leucio – whence he returned in the evening.

On Wednesday November the 12th, I got up at 7 o'clock – combed my hair – dressed – heard Holy Mass – had lunch – then saw the children – worked on my affairs – saw Sambuca – then with my children with whom I had lunch – saw the Filingeris husband and wife – then arranged my affair – at 3 o'clock I went with the lady and Gravina to Naples – on my arrival Lady San Marco recomended me her brother – the King returned – there was the Carlo de Marco's Council and to the San Carlo theatre – after the first ballet – Prince Charles came to me in the loge and he remained during the second act and ballet. The children well – the King went with Lichtenstein to hunt woodcocks at Carditello – Krottendorf came to visit me at midday and it comforted me.

On Thursday November 13, I got up in the morning – had breakfast – heard Holy Mass – saw with Belmonte the apartements for my sister – spoke to Cicio Pignatelli, Rosina Maurizio – to Lady Belmonte – at ten o'clock I went with the King to Caserta – on arrival we found all our children – we lunched – read – drew – gave some audiences – and so I spent my day – in the evening I heard a serenade sung by two small children Laure and Carolinella – after that I worked and I went to bed. The children healthy. The King saw the rehearsal of *the barber of Seville* – in the morning he returned with me to Caserta and after lunch went to San Leucio.

On Friday the 14th, I got up in the morning – had breakfast – heard Mass – dressed – combed my hair – drew – read – saw my children – had lunch with the King – drew – spoke – read – wrote – kept myself busy – in the evening the two Councils and to bed – the children well – the King in the morning went riding at St. Arcangelo – after lunch [took] exercise.

On Saturday November the 15, I got up – dressed – had breakfast – heard Mass – saw my children – read – wrote – I kept myself busy – had lunch with the children – went to library with the girls – then Wolersfeld – read+ – wrote – kept myself busy – saw the King – the children – finished my post – kept myself busy and went to sleep – the children well – the King in the morning went to hunt wild boar and returned in the evening.

On Sunday November the 16th, I got up – had breakfast – heard Mass – dressed – combed my hair – saw my children – read – wrote – kept myself busy – had lunch with my children – kept myself busy – saw father Rugilo[331] – Acton – then read – kept myself busy – the King returned – even Lady Althan – then looked engravings – read letters – undressed me – kept myself busy and to bed – the children well – the King went from morning until evening to Carditello.

On Monday November the 17th, I got up in the morning – had breakfast – dressed – heard Holy Mass – wrote – kept myself busy – kept the King company – ⊙ – then had lunch with him – afterwards read – wrote – kept myself busy – saw Casa Buono wife – Bishop Monsignor Sisto[332] – then went to town with little Altavilla – Gravina and Corleto – on my arrival I saw the ladies – then Sambuca – afterwards we went to the Florentines theatre to [see] a new comic opera – we had Prince Charles with us and afterwards [went] home – the children well – the King in the morning played roral tennis – after lunch he went to Carbone – killed snipe and then came back to town.

On Tuesday November the 18th, I got up at 7 o'clock – heard Mass – combed my hair – then preside over the Sambuca's Council – afterwards dressed – read+ – wrote the post – saw the ladies – afterwards had lunch with the King – kept him company – at 4 o'clock with him in a carriage – on return – saw the children – kept him company – ⊙ – then heard the report on the fire which burned during the night the parish church of Caserta – undressed and kept myself busy the rest of the evening, the children healthy – except Amelia a slight fever because of her teeth, the King after the Council in the morning went to Strone and came back to have lunch – the rest of the day he was with me.

On Wednesday the 19th, I got up – had breakfast – dressed – combed my hair – heard Holy Mass – wrote – worked – arranged my papers – saw Sambuca – went to see my little girl – then had lunch with the children – made an unexpected visit to all my children – arranged my library – wrote – spoke with Madame Sangro – then four audiences – the wife of Vechione[333] for her husband – judge D'Anna with his beautiful daughter (pension) – Carafa with her unmarried daughter and Crespo for her husband – the rest of the evening [with] my children and took care of them, the children well – except Amelia a slight fever because of her teeth – the King in the morning went to Monteragone and returned in the evening.

On Thursday the 20th, I got up – had breakfast – dressed – heard Holy Mass – went to Amelia's room – twice in eldest daughters'room – then wrote – arranged my papers – talked with Marsico – then had lunch with the King – afterwards kept him company – read the letters – wrote – saw de Marco – arranged my papers – presided over the Council – and to bed, the children well – except Amelia a slight fever because of teeth – the King in the morning went to Cavalerizia [*sic*] in the afternoon at Carditello.

On Friday November the 21st, I got up in the morning – had breakfast – dressed – heard Holy Mass – saw Amelia – read+ – wrote – saw Monsignor on his return from abbey – Belmonte – had lunch with the children – read – went to take St. Viaticum to a poor dying lady – then read * – wrote – kept myself busy – saw a French lady – the young Franca Villa – Belmonte – then the two Councils and to the theatre to se the rehearsal of the theatre, the children well – the King went to a horse race at Carditello.

On Saturday November the 22nd, I got up at 7 o'clock – received the news that my sister Amelia – would come today – curled [and] combed my hair – dressed – had breakfast – read+ – wrote – arranged – saw Acton – Sambuca – Belmonte – Lamberg – had lunch – arranged my house – at three o'clock I went in a carriage with the lady and Altavilla – I went out from Capua where I waited for my sister – the King arrived and shortly after my sister with lady San Vitale[334] – the knight Virieux[335] and the exempt Saint Severin[336] – we took my sister in a carriage and arrived at Caserta – where I introduced her to the people who live there and to my children – at eight we had supper, and then – everybody was tired and we went to bed. The children healthy – except little Amelia, who continued to have fever and to deteriorate – the King in the morning went to hunt woodcocks with Charles Lichtenstein – afterwards he met me in Carditello and came back with me.

On Sunday the 23rd, I got up at 7 o'clock – had breakfast – dressed – heard Holy Mass with my sister who kept me company – then I read for a while and then I had to close all the shutters because of a terrible headache that tormented me – and I forced myself and had lunch – or rather – I took part at a lunch with 16 people – then my children came – Theresa played the harpsichord – afterwards the King – from there read until 5 o'clock – afterwards we retired for a while – at 6 o'clock we went to the theatre to see *Barber of Seville* – my children went to a another lodge. The King in the morning went to pheasant farm to make preparations – he did not got out – the children healthy – except Amelia still suffering.

On Monday the 24th, I got up early – wrote – had breakfast – read – heard Holy Mass with my sister – then went with her – Gravina and Virieux to the aqueducts – as the wind was very strong – she saw those only on return – we lunched together – then saw the children – talked – we walked to the garden – where I made a ride in a carriage to Canalone – then together until the King came back – I kept him company – ⊙ – then the Council – afterwards went to play pool with Belmonte – Gravina and my sister [played] reversis – had dinner and to bed. The children well – except Amelia suffering from her teeth – the King in the morning went until the evening to prepare the hunt at Caivano.

On Tuesday November the 25th, I got up in the morning – had breakfast – dressed – heard Holy Mass – saw my children – then went with my sister – Prince Charles and Sambuca in a carriage to hunt at Caivano – there I was with King at the crossing place – they killed many deers – female deer – wild boars – and home – where I wrote my post and undressed – took coffeee with milk – then wrote my post, afterwards we went to hear music where we heard the tenor of San Carlo – Cottelini – bassoon and singer Morelli[337] – afterwards had dinner and to bed, the children healthy – except Mimi a slight – King went at 8 o'clock to St. Arcangelo – to prepare everything and we took part.

On Wednesday November the 26th, I got up at 7 o'clock – I combed my hair – dressed – heard Holy Mass – saw my children – around 11 o'clock we went by one horse carriage to the waterfall – where there were a lot of people – we stopped to see it – and then we went to have dinner with 10 people at Belvedere – saw the house – after lunch we went to hunt wild boars – I was alone with the service hunters – the cold was terrific – we came back and we went to change – afterwards the Council – then we went to the pool hall where I played reversis with my sister – then the king took my place and I saw them play – afterwards had dinner and to bed – the children healthy – tonight also Amelia was successfully weaned. The King in the morning went ou for a while to prepare everything for thr hunt and stayed the rest of the day with us.

On Thursday November the 27th, I got up – combed my hair – dressed – had breakfast – at half past 8 we heard Mass – then we went out – with the King – my sister – Prince Charles – the two gentlemen of my sister, Onorato and Prior – to Carditello – here we got on a one horse carriage – visited all different possesions – pastures that make this place – we saw horse breeding centers – buffalos – cows – then lunched – afterwards there was the the marking of foals – afterwards we retired – we made our toilette and went to the performance of *The Barber of Seville* – then had dinner and to bed – before going to the theatre I had introduced several ladies to my sister who wished to know them – Butera – Cattolica – Althan. The children healthy – Amelia was successfully weaned thankfully the world – the King went out and stayed all day with us.

On November the 28th, I got up – dressed – had breakfast – combed my hair – saw my children – at half past 9 heard Holy Mass – then went with my sister and the King – and Prince Charles – to the pheasant farm – then went shooting with my sister to shoot a quantity of pheasants – we killed over 300 – we had lunch there and back to hunt – afterwards we returned – I changed my dress – took part in the 2 Councils – then accompanied my sister to the pool halland went to prepare for confession and combed my hair then to bed, the children well – the King was out all day with us.

On Sturday November the 29th, I got up at 6 o'clock – waited for my sister – at half past 6 we went to church – received communion and prayed for our adorable mother – afterwards we had breakfast together – talked – and then heard two other Masses – washed – dressed – afterwards read – wrote – then saw my children – at 1 o'clock I had lunch with my sister who kept me company until 4 o'clock – then read – wrote – kept myself busy – at 7 o'clock the King came back – I kept him company – ⊙ – then we prayed the office of the dead for the sad anniversary will be painful for the whole of my life and then went to bed. The children healthy – the King in the morning went to Zingaro to prepare everything.

On Sunday November the 30th, I got up – dressed – had breakfast – at half past 8 heard Holy Mass – then went with my sister – Belmonte and Tirienca in a carriage to Zingaro – there we found foreign ministers – many Sicilian ladies and men – there was a great hunt that was a great success – except a terrible fall on the part of Diomede – which frightened me a lot – and took away all the pleasure – then we had lunch at different tables with 128 persons – afterwards I returned with – my sister – King – Belmonte – and – I saw my children – made my toilette and went to the theatre – afterwards I kept the King company – ⊙ and went to sleep. The children healthy. The King went an hour before us to arrange everything and the rest of time was with us.

On Monday December the 1st, I got up at 6 o'clock and began to write – had breakfast – combed my hair – read + – dressed – saw my children – heard Holy Mass – at 11 o'clock I went in a carriage with my sister and 2 gentlemen to Carditello – we had lunch there – they made the cattle brand of buffalo cows – then returned – I arranged – presided over the Council and went to bed with the fever – the children healthy – the King went to 7 o'clock [to hunt] woodcocks and the rest of the day was with us.

On Tuesday December the 2nd, I got up – took an ounce of salts of England – walked – saw my children – heard Mass – afterwards my sister and the King went to San Leucio – dressed – wrote my post – had lunch – lay on the bed – fever came – then I saw Hackert – arranged my affairs – wrote – saw Sambuca – the King came back – I kept him company – saw my children – my post – prayed – saw my sister and to bed. The children healthy – I had fever – the King went by dray with my sister to San Leucio – where there was a hunt and came back with her.

On Wednesday December the 3rd, I got up – dressed – combed my hair – had breakfast with the children – heard Mass – then went to Carditello with Gravina and Prince Charles and lady – there we saw the wild boar hunting – afterwards we had lunch and we returned to Naples – where we saw courtiers – made toilette and then to the San Carlo theatre which was very well lit – returned from the theatre – at home – the children healthy – I left them with difficulty, I still have fever – the King went at 7 o'clock in the morning with my sister to Carditello – saw buffalo cows – and then I went there – we spent the rest of the day together.

On Thursday December the 4th, I got up – had breakfast – dressed – heard Holy Mass – presided over the Carlo de Marco's Council – then put some papers in order – then had lunch with my sister and the King – kept him company – after lunch read – wrote – made my toilette for the evening and went to the ball at the palace – where there was everybody – I saw people dance for a while, and then started to play reversis with Belmonte – Prince Charles and Gravina – at 11 o'clock to bed, the children well – the King in the morning after the Council went to the dock – then after lunch to Strone for a couple of hours, my sister went out in the morning with her people to see the churches – after lunch she went to Poggio Reale and to the enclosures of animals – in the evening she danced at the beginning with the King then with Corleto.

On Friday December the 5th, I got up – dressed – heard Holy Mass – all early in the morning – because we had to go to Castellamare – it was impossible because of bad weather – we retired – combed – then to the two Councils – then to the chapel to receive the blessing – after lunch – then we were together – I kept the King company – ⊙ – afterwards I went with my sister in Vivenzio's room – to see the machines then the armory – then made toilette and afterwards a bad play at the new theatre – my children were healthy – the King and my sister could not go out because of bad weather it rained heavily.

On Saturday the 6th, I got up at 6 o'clock – took one ounce of salts of England and (…) – then I had breakfast – combed my hair – dressed – I began to read + – wrote the post and kept myself busy – then I went to the chapel – [received] the blessing – later saw my ladies – I lunched alone – then kept myself busy – spoke to Sambuca – Acton – read ++ – worked on my job – had audiences – the King returned – I made my toilette and we went to San Carlo theatre – where after the second act I went to the home. The children healthy – the King at 7 o'clock in the morning went fishing with my sister and 10 people to Castellamare – whence he returned only in the evening.

On Sunday December the 7th, I got up at 7 o'clock – had breakfast – dressed – combed my hair – I went at 9 o'clock with my sister to Annunziata – there we heard Mass – saw the convent – the children and the hospital – I took 3 children – on return we went to porcelain factory and to see the Liparoti – then had lunch – then kept the King and my sister company and afterwards put up the unfortunate 3 poor people that I took at Anunziata – then undressed – read – wrote – gave audiences – kept the King company – ☉ – then made my toilette – went to Florentines [theatre] – and afterwards to the theatre ball – where there were more than 5000 masks and I was bored to death until 12 o'clock the children well – the King in the morning went to take exercise – after lunch at 2 o'clock [he went to] Capo di Monte

On Monday December the 8th, I got up at 8 o'clock – had breakfast – combed my hair – dressed – wrote – put a few things in order – went to Holy Mass – at half past 11 I went with my sister aboard the lugger – we found the King who took us on board the ship – we had dinner down there – and then went to see the frigates – the time was not good – we returned – saw the terrace – at home afterwards for Sambuca's Council of – I gave some audiences, and then a new performace at the Fondo theatre of Lucro – opera music – and afterwards to bed. The children were healthy – according to what they wrote to me – the King went on board at 8 o'clock and was the rest of the day with us – my sister went out in the morning to see some churches and then was with us.

On Tuesday December the 9, I got up in the morning – wrote – combed my hair – had breakfast – dressed – at 9 o'clock went to with my sister – Prince Charles and Virieux to Portici – we descended to marine guards where Acton showed us the building – schools and all – and then we went to see the Herculaneum – paintings – home – then we lunched at a table of 10 persons – afterwards I wrote – my sister saw the museum – and then we came back and we made our toilette – after we went to Belmonte Pignatelli's house where there was music and a wonderful dance – at 11 o'clock we returned – I kept the King company – ☉ – and to bed, the children healthy – except Louise with some fever and inflammation, the King went to the Fusaro from 9 o'clock until 4 o'clock and at 4 o'clock we returned – my sister was with me and danced at the party – I didn't do anything there.

On Wednesday December the 10th, I got up at 7 o'clock – dressed – combed my hair – heard Holy Mass – took part in the de Marco's Council – then kept myself busy – read+ – wrote – saw Madame San Marco and had lunch at 3 o'clock because of the fever that I had – afterwards kept myself busy – saw the King – ☉ – kept him company – dressed – gave audiences – went to the San Carlo theatre – and then to bed, the children well, the

King went to prepare everuthing for the hunt at Strone – my sister went to Pozzuoli with Lamberg and two gentlemen.

On Thursday December the 11th, I got up at 7 o'clock – dressed – had breakfast – heard Holy Mass – at 9 o'clock we went by one horse carriage with my sister – Prince Charles – Marsico – King – Onorato – to my little house in Santa Lucia – where we had breakfast with coffeee – and then we went to Strone – where we hunted and shot running wild boars – where we were in a box – afterwards we came back – we had lunch at home – and then read my letters and to the San Carlo theatre, the children healthy – the King and sister went out and returned with me.

On Friday December the 12th, I got up at 7 o'clock – had breakfast – dressed – combed my hair – heard Holy Mass – took part in the two Councils – then had lunch with my sister and the King – then was busy – reading – writing – giving audiences – keeping the King company on his return – $\odot$ – then Krotendorf – at six o'clock in the evening – made her well-received visit – I made my toilette and went with my sister to the of the Academy ball – there was music and the ball and everything was very beautiful – the children were healthy. The King after lunch went to Portici – in the morning my sister went to Grotta del cane with her men and after lunch to public places – in the evening with us.

On December the 13th, Saturday I got up – had breakfast – combed my hair – heard Holy Mass – read + – wrote – kept myself busy – had lunch – saw Pignatelli – and Carlo de Marco gave audiences – saw my sister again and made my toilette again – affertwards to the Florentines theatre where in the evening Cottelini performed, the children well – the King in the morning went to Torre Annunziata to the arms factory – lunched with my sister at the castle in the wood and we returned together – at 8 o'clock my sister went to Pompei – afterwards she was with the King.

On Sunday December the 14th, I got up – had breakfast – dressed – Holy Mass – worked on some affairs – at half past 11 I went with my sister for a walk at the promenade at Chiaia – we made three times the walk – then lunched at Posillipo – where the King joined us – and then we went to my big house – then home where kept myself busy – made my toilette and went to a wonderful party given by Sambuca, where there was music and ball – we stayed until half past 10 and from there went home. The children healthy – the King in the morning went to Agnano – afterwards was all day with us – my sister in the morning went to San Francesco di Paola – then to San Martino – to the chartreuse – afterwards the rest of the day with me.

On Monday December the 15th, I got up – dressed – had breakfast – combed my hair – heard Holy Mass – then talked with my confessor – afterwards wrote and saw Virieux – talked with him – then Sambuca – afterwards Acton – then the King came back – I kept him company – gave audiences – then to the comedy *Ariane and Thésée* to the Florentines theatre – from there home – the children healthy – the King and my sister at 7 o'clock in the morning went to Fusaro – there was hunting – fishing and then they returned together.

On Thursday December the 16th, I got up – had breakfast – dressed – combed my hair – wrote my post – talked with Marsico – Sambuca – [went] to the chapel of the church of – to [receive] the blessing – and then spoke to Countess Althann – afterwards Donna Teresina – San Marco – Brentano[338] – then had lunch – afterwards read – wrote – saw Acton – then some audiences – saw Sambuca – spent the evening with my sister – until the return of the King – where we had dinner and to bed, the children healthy – the King at 6 o'clock in the morning went to Persano – my sister went to Vesuvius – lunched in Portici int Lamberg's house and then at 4 o'clock returned and spent the evening with me.

On Wednesday December the 17th, it's for me the fifth year of the strongest pain I've ever felt – I got up – dressed – had breakfast – heard Holy Mass – presided over the Carlo de Marco's Council – then I returned with my sister and the King to Caserta – I saw my children – we three had lunch – then we talked – afterwards worked on my affairs – devoted myself – read – wrote ++++ – afterwards dressed – saw my children – kept the King company – ⊙ – then the Council ++++ – then with my sister to the pool hall – played reversis and to bed. The children healthy – the King came with us in the morning – after lunch went to shoot wild boars with my sister in San Leucio.

On Thursday December the 18th, I got up in the morning – had breakfast – saw my children – combed my hair – dressed – heard Holy Mass – went in a carriage to Carditello with my sister – knight Virieux and saw the prior – we were 10 at lunch – afterwards saw all day the cattle brand of buffalo cows – of horses – then at home made my toilette – kept the King company – ⊙ – then saw the children and at pool hall with my sister. The children well – the King in the morning went to Carditello – we joined him – had lunch and returned with him.

On Friday December the 19th, I got up in the morning – had breakfast – dressed – combed my hair – heard Holy Mass – had breakfast – wrote – read – kept myself busy – at half past 11 lunched with my sister – the King and hunters – then I was busy reading + – [and] writing – my children – the King came back – we presided over the two Councils – went for a while to the pool hall and then to bed, the children well – the King at midday went with my sister to Carbone – killed ducks and returned in the evening.

On Saturday December the 20th, I got up – had breakfast – dressed – heard Holy Mass – then wrote – read + – kept myself – saw my children – took part in their dinner – wrote my post – kept myself busy – the King came back – we had lunch – he kept me company – ☉ – I went to the pool hall and then was there during my sister's match, the children well – King at 9 o'clock went to hunt wild boar with my sister at Matalone and returned at 5 o'clock.

On Sunday December the 21, I got up – had breakfast – dressed – combed my hair – heard Holy Mass with my sister and children who had breakfast with me – then read – wrote – kept myself busy – had lunch with my children – read – kept myself busy – saw Madame S. Vital – read – wrote – and then the King came – we read letters from the Spanish courrier – I went into my sister's room – talked with her – afterwards I returned to my room and in the evening [went] to the pool hall. The children well – the King at 8 o'clock went to prepare the hunt at Carditello – my sister at half past 9 joined him and returned at 5 o'clock.

On Monday December the 22nd, I got up – had breakfast – combed my hair – dressed – wrote my post – kept myself busy – saw my children – heard Holy Mass – had lunch with my sister – kept her company – worked on my affairs – read – wrote my post +++++ – then saw my children – the King came back – there was the Council++++++++ – then I prepared for confession and went out with my sister to the pool hall – had dinner and to bed, the children well – as it rained the King could not go out in the morning – after lunch he went with my sister to San Leucio – to shoot wild boars.

On Tuesday December the 23rd, I got up in the morning at half past 6 – I went to the church to perform my devotions – afterwards had breakfast – dressed – combed my hair – heard Holy Mass – wrote my post – had lunch with the children – worked – kept myelf busy – worked on my affair – prayed – saw the children – then saw Sambuca – the King came back – I finished my post – went with my sister to the pool hall and to bed, the children well – the King went to the swamp at S. andrea – but could not hunt because of the rain – he killed several boars instead of ducks, my sister went with her people in town to Reclusorio – to *Chinese* – to the dock to see the carriages – stables and then returned.

On Wednesday December the 24th, I got up in the morning – had breakfast – went to de Marco's Council – then I spoke to the King – afterwards I curled my hair and [went] to Mass – then I saw my children – I had lunch with the King and my sister kept me company – I wrote – worked on my affairs – prayed God – I saw my children and made my toilette – the King came back – I kept him company – ☉ then I heard a sermon of Don Ferdinando Strina[339] to my children – I saw my sister give the presents and to all my children – then we went to the pool hall [and] played reversis – then I took a little chocolate with my sister – then there was music – Madam Balduci and the tenor Milico[340] sung – everyone – ladies and knights who live in Caserta were invited – afterwards we went to the three night Masses and then a big dinner with 60 persons ended the long evening.

On December the 25th Christmas Day, I got up at 8 o'clock – had breakfast – combed my hair – dressed – saw my children – went to Mass – at the second one Lamberg brought me the news that a Guard courrier had arrived and that the Emperor was coming – I went to write, and then I went with my sister to San Leucio – we heard a sung Mass and lytanie – afterwards had lunch in Belvedere and then I asked permission to return – Onorato accompanied me – I went home – read – wrote – spruced myself up – I made my toilette again – the King returned – I kept him company – ☉ – then I saw the ladies – went to pool hall and to bed The children well – the King at 8 o'clock went to San Leucio – prepared everything – my sister went there with me – hunted with the King and returned with him.

On Friday December the 26th, I got up at 7 o'clock – had breakfast – dressed and heard Holy Mass – read – wrote – kept myself busy – saw my children – Belmonte – Sambuca – had lunch with my girls – arranged everything at home – saw Acton who spoke to me about the revolt – escape of 228 convicts from prison + – then kept myself busy – the King returned – two Councils after which I undressed and kept myself busy until the King came to bed – the children well – the King at 10 o'clock went to hunt pheasants – in the evening my sister started to suffer from of migraine – lay down.

On Saturday December the 27th, I got up – combed my hair – dressed – had breakfast – heard Holy Mass with my sister – kept her company – read – wrote – had lunch with my sister and the children – then stayed with them – saw dancing the two eldest – and read – wrote – kept myself busy – in the evening went to the pool hall, the children well – the King went to Carbone and Carditello my sister went.[341]

On Sunday the 28th, I got up in the morning – had breakfast with the children and my sister – then dressed – combed my hair – heard Holy Masses – read – wrote – kept myself busy – saw Sambuca – had lunch with the children – talked to Loras – wrote – read – kept myself busy – went to the King's meeting – kept him company ⊙ – afterwards kept myself busy – in the evening to the pool hall – the children well – the King went to Carditello with my sister for a running hunt.

On Monday the 29th, I got up – dressed – had breakfast – wrote – kept myself busy – talked to Sambuca – read – wrote – kept myself busy – and then had lunch with my sister – stayed with her – saw Princess Belmonte – afterwards the Council and to bed. The children healthy – I had a big pain in one side which made me undergo three times electric treatment and is getting better – the King went to the swamp in S. andrea and killed many ducks – my sister stayed at home.

On Thursday December the 30th, I got up – When I woke up I was told about the courrier who brought the news that His Majesty the Emperor had slept in Gaeta and hoped to leave again at 7 o'clock – had breakfast – dressed – I heard Holy Mass – I wrote my post at ten thirty went with my sister – Gravina and Virieux – we met outside S. Maria Capua His Majesty the Emperor – was with the King – I went down and hugged him then went home in a carriage I showed my children the house – then had lunch – ke kept me company – later wrote my post and from there his Majesty the Emperor returned for a moment – went to the pool hall – then attended a big concert where all the best singers of the theatre sung – from there had dinner and to bed – children well the King in the morning went to Carditello to meet the Emperor and in the afternoon for a while in the wood, my sister was always with me.

On Wednesday December the 31st, I got up at 7 o'clock – combed my hair – dressed – His Majesty the Emperor came to breakfast with me and kept me company – then I saw my children – went to church and then my brother and my sister came with me to the aqueduct – from there to home to make the toilet – the departure of my sister was scheduled for Sunday, we had lunch at a table of 16 seats – Belmonte Sambuca Gravina Marsico and Migliano everything else came with my sister or His Majesty the Emperor – afterwards Teresa played the harpsichord – then his Majesty had me the grace to stay with me – afterwards we went to the Florentines theatre that had been made to come to this small theatre and then home, – the children well – the King went in the afternoon to St. Leucio with my sister to kill wild boar, and so ended the year 1783. A year in which I had infinite pains [:] those of the public sorrows of Calabria and Messina were terrible – the losses and the scale of this frightful catastrophe almost filled the whole year – I also lost a son whom I warmly loved and who – for the pain – it cost me to raise him and his precocious spirit nearly was my consolation, I had a bad birth that reduced me to death having received all the Holy sacraments – I had the misfortune to give birth to a dead child – Briefly that is the result of much deep anguish which has caused me great pain. The consolations were the arrival of my brother Maximilian and that of my sister from Parma and especially that of His Majesty the Emperor with whom I had the happiness to start the new year, I dare to hope that under these auspices it will be happier in my pain and sorrow I can only give thanks to the divine Providence that has supported me – and invoke it so that [I] use the life which he has given me, well.

JOURNAL 1784

On Thursday January the 1st 1784
I got up at six in the morning – had breakfast – combed my hair – dressed – arranged my papers – affairs for going into town – saw my children – heard Holy Mass and at nine o'clock we went out – His Majesty the Emperor – my sister Amelie – The King and I in a carriage to Carditello – there we had breakfast coffee with milk – and then saw from a one horse carriage a horse race where the two Majesties rode to kill boars – after the race we had lunch and then we all four went in a carriage to Naples where we left his Majesty the Emperor at his apartments – and then I went to my room made my toilette – afterwards we introduced the whole court to his Majesty went to the San Carlo theatre, I had a very bad headache in that day, my children – taht I left in Casrrta – were healthy – the King was everyday with us.

On Friday January 2nd, I got up – had breakfast – dressed – combed my hair – read + – wrote – heard Holy Mass – His Majesty the Emperor came to lunch – my children arrived at midday – the three daughters of Caserta – I had lunch with my sister and Her Majesty – and we talked for a while – afterwards we went for a walk to Strada Nova – to the pier – Chiaia – Posillipo and to the house of Santa Lucia – where we made our toilette and at half past six we went to the Academy – where we sung – danced – I spoke together with His Majesty the Emperor to the society – my sister danced – at nine o'clock we returned – I undressed twice – His Majesty the Emperor kept me company – remained some time with me and then I went to bed after having visited my sister for a moment. The children were healthy – the three girls came from Caserta to town. The King in the morning went early to Mondragone where he stayed until night.

On Saturday January the 3rd, I got up in the morning – had breakfast with my sister – then dressed – combed my hair – saw Sambuca – Acton – then Holy Mass – read – wrote – saw my children – we went for lunch with His Majesty the Emperor – my sister and I to Posillipo – there we saw the house and then His Majesty offered us a German lunch made by his people – afterwards – after not being able to go by sea – we came back by land and we went to see the big garden – afterwards we returned – I took leave of all my poor sistes entourage and we went to the theatre for an act at the Fondo – on our return we waited for the King who came – we had dinner – I kept him company and made a report of the two day – ⊙ – then I went to sleep, the children were fine – the King was in Mondragone all day and returned in the evening.

On Sunday January the 4th, I woke up early to see my sister who had promised me to have breakfast together – was given to me a letter from her with the news that she had left – this irked me – I got up – had breakfast – heard Holy Mass – His Majesty came to have dinner – three of us had lunch together – and then went to see the Liparoti quarter – the college of cadets – the library and machines room – then walked – on our return there was Council presided over by Sambuca + – and afterwards went to the Florentines theatre and then to the theater's ball without going down, the children well – the King was at home all day and went out with us.

On Monday January the 5th, I got up – had breakfast – dressed – combed my hair – heard Holy Mass – read – wrote – afterwards all my other children arrived from Caserta – I had lunch with His Majesty the Emperor and the children – they kept me company – we went to see the machinery of Don Giovani – in the evening to the big theatre – after that I kept the King company ⊙ and slept, the children well – the King in the morning went to the pheasant farm to kill wolves and returned in the evening.

On Tuesday January the 6th, I got up – dressed – had breakfast – heard Holy Mass – wrote my post – I lunched with His Majesty the Emperor and the children – we spent the day together – in the evening we went to an abominable [performance] of Gian Colla *Empéreur du Mogol* – then to the Academy where they sung and danced. The children well. The King went to the swamp of Acerra to shoot snipes.

On the 7th, I got up – had breakfast – dressed – heard Holy Mass – and then had lunch with the King and His Majesty the Emperor – then we went to see porcelain – the riding stables, the armory – back home – in the evening there was music of a dozen people – four women – eight men – they played – and home and to bed ⊙ – the children well – the King stayed at home because of bad weather.

On Thursday January the 8th, I woke up – dressed – had breakfast – heard Holy Mass – then spoke to Prince Charles – after lunch with the Emperor and children – to spend my day with them – in the evening to the new opera at the new theatre – His Majesty decided to stay some more days and came with us to Persano – I kept the King company ⊙ and to bed, the children well – the King went hunting at Fusaro.

On Friday January the 9th, I got up – had breakfast – dressed – at nine o'clock heard Holy Mass – I went with His Majesty the Emperor to see the exercise of the Liparoti – then passed through the porcelain [factory] and we got into a carriage – we went to the bridge to see the new store of wheat – of wood – of so many things that are beautiful – from there to the Navy guards – then to the castle – had lunch at the table that rises and falls – and then I went to show the garden and house of Jacy to the Emperor – the palaces all around – then we returned with the King – in the evening there was the Council which announced all the promotions – and afterwards we went to the Academy. The children healthy – the King went hunting in the meanwhile we saw the gardens.

On Saturday January 10, I got up – had breakfast – dressed – heard Holy Mass – then read + – wrote – had lunch with His Majesty and the children – spent the day with them – wrote my post – read – then made my toilette – went to a concert at the Belmonte's house – beloved Krotendorf came to visit me, the children well – the King went hunting all day.

On Sunday January the 11th, I got up – had breakfast – dressed – heard Holy Mass – and at midday – we went with His Majesty the Emperor to promenade at Chiaia – then had lunch at my little house in Santa Lucia – afterwards we stayed together – in the afternoon [went] for a walk – in the evening to the new opera at the Fondo – and then to the ball – when I went down for a moment with His Majesty the Emperor. The children well – the King spent his day with us.

On Monday January the 12th, had a strong colic during the night – I remained in my room – in the morning I saw the Emperor leave and the King to go fishing – saw my children – heard Holy Mass – saw Sambuca – read+ – wrote – kept myself busy – made a big toilette – received the King who was dressed up and went in the evening – with my two daughters – to the theatre – the new opera – and then to bed. I felt very weak because colic violently attacked me – the children well – the King went with the Emperor took some mackerel in Fusaro – had lunch at the new house and came back.

On Thursday January the 13th, I got up – had breakfast – heard Holy Mass – saw my children – then Acton – later wrote my post – I had lunch with His Majesty the Emperor and my children – then – finished the lunch – we went by boat – with Acton to Posillipo – saw the cavern in the wood – this took all the afternoon – we returned in a carriage – and I remained with His Majesty – gave several hearings – packed my bags for the journey – in the evening to the Florentines theatre – then undressed – saw Sambuca – arragend my affairs – made my payments – and then to bed. The children well – the King in the morning went to Persano until 4 o'clock.

On Wednesday January the 14th, I get up at six o'clock – had breakfast – dressed – heard Holy Mass – saw Pignatelli – Acton – all the people of His Majesty the Emperor – then my children – at ten o'clock – after having seen all the court – we left – His Majesty – Lady Gravina and me in a carriage to Persano – we had a very happy journey and arrived at a quarter past 3 – we stayed together for a while – afterwards we had dinner and in the evening music and conversation.

On Thursday January the 15th, I had breakfast with the Emperor – we spent the morning together – dressed – heard Holy Mass – then hunting with the Emperor – returned – I changed dress – I kept the King company ⊙ Serio[342] improvised and had dinner where Serio prepared a toast, in the main the children healthy – the King early in the morning went hunting.

On Friday January the 16th, I got up at 5 o'clock – dressed – heard Holy Mass – and then at 6 o'clock – went to Pestum in a carriage with His Majesty the Emperor – there we saw the ruins and returned – had breakfast and went hunting for six hours – on return we undressed and heard Molla improvise – had dinner and to bed – I kept the King company – ⊙ – they killed 28 boars at the Trinità and the day before 30 boars at the Piana di Mercurio. The children were fine – the King in the morning went to prepare everything for the hunt.

On Saturday January the 17th, I got up – had breakfast – saw and spent the morning with His Majesty the Emperor – then heard Mass – wrote – after lunch – at o'clock His Majesty – after having embraced us – assured us his of friendship – and left, I remained sad and kept myself busy all day, at six o'clock I had the coffee with milk – not having lunched – I kept the King company – ⊙ – then I spoke to Prince Charles and went out for dinner, the children well – the King did not go out at all because of the weather.

On Sunday January the 18th, I got up – dressed – had breakfast – heard Holy Mass – at 9 o'clock we went hunting – where it rained all time – awful weather – notwithstanding this they killed eight wild boars – we returned – at one o'clock I made my toilette again – dried myself – had lunch and then worked on throughout the day and evening to regain lost time – I went out at dinner time and to bed, my children well – I received from them the news of the arrival of His Majesty the Emperor, the King was hunting with me.

On Monday January the 19th, I got up – dressed – lunch – combed my hair – heard Holy Mass – saw hunters during their breakfast – then read – wrote – kept myself busy – after lunch at three o'clock – returned with hunters – read the letters – answered – then the Sambuca's Council – then kept myself busy – stayed in company for a while and had dinner and to bed – I had news that the children behaved well – the King went to mena nuova where he killed 32 wild boars.

On Tuesday January the 20th, I got up – had breakfast – made a big toilette – heard Holy Mass – then kept myself busy – talked with Sambuca – then wrote – afterwards wrote – at 2 o'clock had lunch – then heard Serio improvise – saw an hot-air balloon flying – then wrote – ⊙ afterwards played reversis – had dinnet and to bed, the children well – the King in the morning went hunting in a bad weather and killed three wild boars.

On Wednesday January the 21st, I got up – had breakfast – combed my hair – dressed – heard Holy Mass – kept the King company – ⊗ – then read – wrote – drew – I kept myself busy – had lunch – afterwards the wife of land agent Persano – drew with Hackert – then saw [the children] playing, [say] the rosary – afterwards talked – was in society – heard Serio improvise – had dinner and then to bed, the children well, the King went out only for a moment – because of the bad weather.

On Thursday January the 22nd, I got up – had breakfast – combed my hair – dressed – heard Holy Mass – read – wrote – kept myself busy – had lunch – then kept myself busy – the King went hunting for a while and killed two wild boars – then kept myself busy – went to the blessing – played music – played – had dinner and to bed, the children were fine – the King went out on foot for a moment owing to the bad weather.

On Friday January the 23rd, I got up – had breakfast – dressed – combed my hair – heard Holy Mass – kept myself busy – read – wrote – lunched – went to say the rosary – in the evening played reversis – had dinner and then to bed. The children well, the King went hunting for a while.

On Sturday January the 24th, I got up – dressed – heard Holy Mass – had breakfast – went hunting in Mena della Casa Fondata where 40 wild boars were killed – then returned – dried myself – dressed again – having rained – wind – hail – went to the chapel – and then kept myself busy and played, the children well – the King went hunting with us.

On Sunday January the 25th, I got up – dressed – had breakfast – heard Holy Mass – took part in the hunter's breakfast – spoke to Tarsia – wrote+ – read – kept myself busy – and then had lunch with the lady who was the one who remained at home – then I paraded and afterwards I went in a carriage – met the King – then I came back home – made my toilette – went to say the rosary – spoke to Prince Charles and went out for dinner, the children well – the King went hunting [and] killed 17 wild boars.

On Monday January the 26th, in the morning I dressed – heard Holy Mass – saw two hot-air baloon flying – then had breakfast – afterwards went hunting the Cigarella where 41 wild boars were killed – afterwards returned – undressed – dressed again – had lunch in my room – went to say the rosary – kept company to[343] – ⊙ – then saw Prince Charles – afterwards played reversis and had dinner – then I took leave with regret of the honest and well esteemed Prince Charles and went to have dinner – the children well – the King went hunting and returned with me

On Tuesday January the 27th, I got up – dressed – had breakfast – heard Holy Mass – read – wrote my letters +++++ – then had lunch – then talked to Sambuca – kept myself busy – went to say the rosary – then presided over the Sambuca's Council – afterwards I confessed my sins and went to bed. The children healthy – the King went hunting.

On Wednesday January the 28th, I got up – I had the joy of making my devotions – then kept myself busy – talked with Sambuca – had lunch – worked all day and evening that I went to bed. The children fine – the King went hunting all day – ⊙.

On Thursday January the 29th, I got up – dressed – combed my hair – worked on my affairs – heard Holy Mass – spoke to Gravina – lunched – the King returned – then I spoke to the chairman of Salerno Dentice – then Marsico – then worked – packed – went to say the rosary – had dinner and to bed, the children well – King went hunting all day.

On Friday January the 30th, I got up at six o'clock – combed my hair – dressed – heard Holy Mass – then at half past six I left [with] – Gravina – Marsico – and the lady – at midday arrived Naples – I found my children healthy thanks to God – I saw Sambuca – de Marco – I lunched – afterwards I unpacked – arranged my things – saw Acton – read + – kept myself busy – saw my children – presided over the Council and to bed I found all the children healthy – the King at 7 o'clock returned in good shape from Persano.

On Saturday January the 31st, I got up at 7 o'clock – dressed – had breakfast – heard Holy Mass – saw my children – wrote my post – I kept myself busy – at midday the King of Sweden – under the name of the Count of Haga[344] – came to surprise us – he dined with us and stayed there until 4 o'clock – then I kept myself busy – I had an introduction to many foreign ladies – afterwards I went to the San Carlo theatre where I saw the King of Sweden twice – and then to bed – the children well – the King did not go out all day.

On February Sunday the 1st, I got up at 7 o'clock – dressed – combed my hair – had breakfast with my girls – heard Holy Mass – worked on my affairs – at midday the King of Sweden – with nine of his knights – came to introduce himself in Swedish dress – we lunched at a ceremony of 40 seats – and I made my children come – we conversed for a while – after I retired to my room – I was sad so at 20 past 9 I undressed and went to bed ⊙, the children well – the King in the morning went for a while to the dock and remained the rest of the day at home.

On Monday February the 2nd, I got up in the morning – combed my hair – dressed – had breakfast with Francis – took part with affection in Teresa's communion – then Mass – read – wrote – kept myself busy – talked with St. Nicola – with Belmonte – had lunch with my girls – saw Sambuca – Acton – gave numerous hearings – two brides [came] to introduce themselves, a certain Simone to put his niece in a convent – Ferrante for his brother – then the Council – afterwards the opera where the Count of Haga came to visit us – then I went to sleep – ⊙, the children well – the King at 7 o'clock went to Caserta and returned at six in the evening.

On Tuesday February the 3rd, I got up – dressed – had breakfast – combed my hair – heard Holy Mass – wrote the post – then lunched – afterwards kept the King company – drew – then combed my hair – made my toilette – went to the court ball – where I played blackjack with the King of Sweden – afterwards to a dinner of 40 people – then to bed – ⊙, the children well – the King could not go out – because of the bad day – and stayed at home.

On Wednesday February the 4th, I got up – dressed – had breakfast – combed my hair – heard Holy Mass – went to the Council – then saw my children – kept myself busy – then had lunch with the King – kept him company – drew together – dressed – gave audiences and went to the Florentines theatre – at the end of the second act the King of Sweden came – then home.

On Thursday February the 5th I got up – dressed – had breakfast – combed my hair – attended the King' s breakfast – and then talked with Pignatelli regarding the Calabrian issue[345] – then Mass – spoke to Tarsia – after lunch with my children – saw some paintings – then read + – wrote – afterwards the Marcolini[346] came to whom I introduced my daughters – then at half past two the King of Sweden was with us – afterwards read and kept myself busy – then to bed – the children fine – the King at ten in the morning left for Mondragone.

On Friday February the 6th, I got up – dressed – had breakfast – combed my hair – heard Holy Mass – read[+] – wrote – talked with San Marco – then Sambuca – lunched – saw a nice drawing table – then read + – wrote – saw Acton – then had a number of audiences Marchioness Rugi[347] for her son and so many others – then made my toilette and waited for the King of Sweden for an hour – I went to the Academy – where there was music and a ball – I spoke and got bored – at eleven I went home where there was a great dinner with the King – all these Swedes – and some ladies and horse-men – at one o'clock dinner ended and I went to bed, the children were well – the King remained all day in Mondragone.

On Saturday February the 7th, I got up – dressed – lunch – combed my hair – heard the Holy Mass – saw San Nicola – talked to him – then with my children – lunched – afterwards spent my day with them – saw Acton – kept myself busy – read – wrote – the King returned – I kept him company – ☉ – afterwards gave many audiences – then made my toilette and to San Carlo – where the King of Sweden came for a moment to see us – from there to bed, the children well – the King at 5 o'clock returned with awful weather at Carditello – we were forced to sleep in another room as the wind was too violent.

On Sunday February the 8th, I got up – dressed – combed my hair – had breakfast with my four children – heard Holy Mass – presided over the Cimitino Council[348] – Acton was sick and could not presided his own – after lunch – then drew – kept the King company – ☉ – then gave audiences – saw Gatti – afterwards made my toilette – then went to the opera at new theatre that was very bad – then the ball where the King of Sweden came to dine with us in particular – and I did not go down and before one o'clock – I went to bed, the children well – the King did not go out all day because of bad weather.

On Monday February the 9th, I got up in the morning – had breakfast – dressed – combed my hair – heard Holy Mass – presided over the Council – saw my children – and then had lunch with the King – drew – read – wrote +++ – then kept myself busy – made my toilette – ⊙ – had audiences – afterwards saw the children – went to opera at San Carlo – then to bed. The children well – the King at two o'clock went to take some exercise with the Liparoti.

On Tuesday February the 10th, I got up in the morning – had breakfast – dressed – combed my hair – heard Holy Mass – and then talked to Brentano – later to de Marco – then saw the ladies – my children – then Sambuca – afterwards lunched – then stayed with my children – later saw Acton – wrote my post – kept myself busy – read – wrote – the King returned and we went to the opera at San Carlo where the King of Sweden came for a while to visit us, the children well – the King went to Caserta for the whole day.

On Wednesday February the 11th, I got up – had breakfast – dressed – combed my hair – presided over the Council – then heard Holy Mass – had lunch with the King – kept him company – ⊙ – later kept myself busy – read – wrote – drew – dressed and went to the San Carlo theatre where I went with the Count of Haga into the Grand Lodge – to see ballets – then I went to sleep, the children well – the King went out only for a while to take exercise.

On Thursday February the 12th, I got up – dressed – had breakfast – combed my hair – heard Holy Mass – read – wrote – saw my children – kept myself busy – saw the courrier – lunched with the King – walked on the terrace – finished my post – kept myself busy – gave hearings – dressed – then to the Florentines – from there – on return – to the San Carlo theatre where I did not go down from my lodge – the children well – the King remained all day at home – in the morning he only took a little exercise.

On Friday February the 13th, I got up – dressed – had breakfast – combed my hair – heard Holy Mass – presided over the two Councils – then lunch with the King – kept him company – ⊙ – then Krottendorf came to visit me – afterwards I was busy and then I dressed – then to a particularly poor comedy of *Pulcinella* – then at the Academy where I saw dancing – afterwards to bed. The children fine – the King did not go out all day.

On Saturday the 14th,in the morning – just got up – I went to take part in the entire toilette and breakfast of little Januarius – then dressed – combed my hair – went to church – wrote my post – afterwards lunch with the King – kept him company – walked for a moment on the terrace – then kept mysef busy – gave audiences – dressed – went to the San Carlo theatre and from there home, the children well – the King did not go out all day because of the weather.

On Sunday February the 15th, I got up – combed my hair – dressed – had breakfast with my children – then Mass – read – wrote – kept myself busy – lunched with the King – kept him company – saw masks passing through – stayed all day with my children – saw Count Lamberg's paintings – then dressed – went to the Florentines theatre – then to the masked ball where I went disguised as a bat and domino and no one recognized me, the children had a masked ball and they were fine – the King went in the morning to the Strone – after-lunch to the parade of the masks.

On Monday February the 16th, I dressed – had breakfast – combed my hair – heard Holy Mass – presided over the Council – then kept myself busy – lunched with the King – saw my children – walked on the terrace – read – wrote – kept myself busy – the King of Sweden came to see me – in the evening we went to the San Carlo theatre, where I took my two eldest daughters.The children well – the King could not go out all day because of bad weather.

On Tuesday February the 17th, I got up – dressed – heard Holy Mass – read – wrote – kept myself busy – talked with many people – lunched with the children – wrote my post – read + – kept myself busy – made my children make thir toilette – I did the same – and then had a ball in the apartment of the King of Sweden for 300 people – where my children came in Swedish dress and were lovely – there were three of us at dinner including the King of Sweden and we came back after midnight – I kept the King company – ⊙ – and then to bed, the children well – the King in the morning went to San Leucio to participate in a wedding and came back in the evening.

On Wednesday February 18, I got up at 7 o'clock – had breakfast – dressed – heard Holy Mass – presided over the de Marco's Council – then kept myself busy – wrote – afterwards lunch with the King – read – wrote – kept myself busy – saw the children – gave audiences – in the evening to the San Carlo theatre, the children well – except Francis with a cold and a slight fever – the King went after lunch to Portici.

On Thursday February the 19th, I got up at 7 o'clock – dressed – had breakfast – combed my hair – heard Holy Mass – read – wrote – kept myself busy – then went to the Florentines [theatre] – from there to a ball at the San Carlo theatre – where I went with old man's wig – there was a very pretty contradance of Pulcinella by the company of Cassano – the children fine – the King did not go out all day – except [went] to the parade of masks for a while – the children well except Fran[is] with his [cold].

On Friday February the 20th, I got up – dressed – had breakfast – combed my hair – heard Holy Mass – then lunched with the King – after lunch read+ – wrote – kept myself busy – saw my children – made my toilette – took part in the two Councils – ☉-to the comedy in prose at the Florentines[theatre] – afterwards to Academy to see the King of Sweden and from there home, the children well – Francis still with a cold – but up – the King in the morning took exercise – after lunch at the Strone for a couple of hours.

On Saturday February the 21st, I got up – had breakfast – dressed – heard Holy Mass – wrote my post – kept myself busy – lunched with the King – kept myself busy – read – wrote – made my toilette – participated in the court ball with over 300 people – where – after I having got bored a lot – we went to sleep, the children well – Francis better – the King after lunch went out to Strone for a while.

On Sunday February the 22nd, I got up – dressed – had breakfast – combed my hair – heard Holy Mass – went to see my children – took care of them – then had lunch with the two Kings – spending my afternoon together – then went out with the King of Sweden and Gravina to the masquerade parade – then made my toilette – saw my children's ball, went to a comic opera to the Florentines [theatre] – then at San Carlo ball where I took my two eldest daughters – Then there was a beautiful contra dance and paintings of the young Salandra and afterwards to bed, the children better – the King went out and then was always with us.

On Monday February the 23rd, I got up – dressed – had breakfast – presided over the Council – heard Holy Mass – and then rehearsed a contradance – lunched with the King – presided over the Sambuca's Council – kept the King company – ☉ – and then returned to the rehearsal – made my toilette – and the palace ball where there were 300 people – where I danced a contra dance e and a minuet then – there was a wonderful dinner – 12 tables with 20 seats each and one with 150 – and then to bed, the children well – they went to the ball as Swedes dressed – the King did not go out all day.

On Tuesday February the 24th, I got up – had breakfast – dressed – combed my hair – heard Holy Mass – saw my children – rehearsed a contradance – had lunch with the King – at three went out domino dressed – in a one horse carriage – to see a hot-air balloon flying very well with a masquerade – walked by one horse carriage – went down to the theatre to rehearse – then made my toilette – saw the ball and dinner of my children – kept my children company – then went to the theatre – performed a contra dance and pantomime in honor of the King of Sweden – then went to undress at home – ⊙ afterwards returned dressed as domino and bat to the theatre and then I went to sleep, the children well – the King went only out for the masquerade parade and in the evening to the Florentines – for the rest of the day he was home – he introduced me also a mask of rabbit – the children well – they had their little ball – ended very cheerfully their carnival.

On February the 25th, Ash Wednesday I got up – dressed – combed my hair – heard Holy Mass – took the ashes – received a visit from the King of Sweden – lunched with the King – read+ – wrote – kept myself busy – presided over the Council – gave numerous audiences and at nine o'clock went to bed – the children fine – the King after lunch at two o'clock went to Strone and returned at five o'clock.

On Thursday February the 26th, I got up at half past 6 – had breakfast – combed my hair – dressed – read – heard Holy Mass – at ten o'clock I went to the place to pick the King of Sweden up and he came with me to Strone – where there was an exercise of the Liparoti – then two hunts – afterwards a big dinner with all the foreigners – then I returned with Belmonte – the King of Sweden and Darmfeld[349] – afterwards having left them at their house – I returned home – undressed and went to bed, the children well – the King went early in the morning with the Liparoti to Strone and came back with us.

On Friday February the 27th, I got up – dressed – had breakfast – combed my hair – heard Holy Mass – the sermon – then lunched with the King – kept him company – ⊙ – then dressed – went out with the King of Sweden and my King to the porcelain [factory] – then to the house to Posillipo that we have all covered – then we left the King at home and went to the house where – after the two Councils – I undressed and went to bed, the children well – King went out only with me all day.

On Saturday February the 28th, I got up in the morning – dressed – had breakfast – combed my hair – heard Holy Mass – saw my children – then went with the two Kings to the College of Navy guards – afterwards to the groves of Portici – then lunched at the table of the castle with 12 people – then went to the arms factory – to Torre Annunziata – then home – gave audiences – undressed – wrote – kept myself busy and went to sleep, the children well – the King went everywhere with me and the King of Sweden – went from Torre Annuziata to [Portici].

On Sunday February the 29th, I got up – had breakfast with my children – dressed – made the King buy watches – went to Mass – the sermon – then with Theresa – Louise – Francis – I walked the Chiaia promenade twice and then w in a carriage – on my return I spoke to lady San Marco – Marco Carlo – Lady Tyuchi[350] – then I lunched with my children – then read ++ – wrote – kept myself busy – gave audiences – afterwards made my toilette – went to the Academy where I got bored doing nothing – afterwards to bed. The children well – the King went to Carditello for the whole day.

On Monday March the 1st, I got up at 7 o'clock – had breakfast – dressed – combed my hair – heard Holy Mass – went to the Sambuca's Council – then spoke to Sambuca, went with Gravina – Vanvitelli[351] – to see all the apartements to choose one for my son – then spoke to Loras – to Calsatigi[352] – then lunched alone – afterwards saw Acton – then walked on the terrace – later wrote – saw the King – Minister of Spain Hereria[353] – then the King of Sweden – then wrote – afterwards saw the Princess of Jacy – Tanuci[354] – then Regina[355] – Poulet[356][Josueta] – then undressed – curled my hair and confessed my sins, the children well – the King in the morning went to the dock – and then to Positano with the King of Sweden.

On Tuesday March the 2nd, I got up in the morning – had breakfast – dressed – I had the pleasure of going to church perform my devotions – then dressed – wrote – at 9 o'clock I went with my three daughters to the hurch San Francesco di Paola – afterwards I sent them to Caserta and I returned to arrange my affairs – dressed – saw Lady Hereria – then took leave of the children – went with the King of Sweden to my house – and then to the dock – there I got on a launch – we went sailimg for a short time – the sea was rough – and went down to my little house where – after a walk we lunched and at half past three we left – the King – Belmonte – Darmfeld and I – in a carriage to Caserta where – on my arrival – I worked on my affairs and spruced myself a little – then prayed – the King of Sweden came – conversed with me for a while – and then we went to the pool hall and from there – at ten o'clock went to sleep, the children were healthy – the King in the morning went to Caserta – at half past 7 in the morning – and in the evening we met there.

On Wednesday March the 3rd, I got up at 7 o'clock – combed my hair – dressed – saw my dear Mimi – had breakfast – I saw my eldest daughters – heard Holy Mass – then arranged home – papers – gave orders to Belmonte – spoke to Tarsia – at eleven o'clock I went to pick up the King of Sweden and went to the acqueduct – at two o'clock we returned – I left him at the apartment and went home – I made my toilette again – wrote for a while – at three o'clock he returned with all Swedes – I showed them the house – offered lunch – afterwards saw the house again – and then went by carriage to the waterfalls and returned – left him at apartment – went home – presided over the Council – undressed – prayed – wrote and went to bed, the children were fine – the King [went] to Carditello to prepare for the tomorrow's hunt – he was there all day.

On Thursday March the 4th, I got up at 7 o'clock – dressed – had breakfast – heard Holy Mass – then saw my children – wrote – worked on some affairs – at eleven I went to pick up the King of Sweden – who preceded me and came to my carriage – we went to Carditello – then saw a wild boars hunt – then lunched – then we returned – I made my toilette – had a long conversation with the King +⊙ – then I introduced the Spanish Minister's wife to him – Lady Hereira[357] – afterwards we went to a tragedy entitled [*Gelmine*] – I was with the King of Sweden in the lodge, and then to bed, the children well – the King in the morning went early to prepare everything and came back by dray.

On Friday March the 5th, I got up – dressed – combed my hair – had breakfast – heard Holy Mass – stayed with my dear Mimi – at a quater to eleven Gatti inoculated her in the left arm with two bites of smallpox – God bless this operation, which cost me a lot – loving this little girl with passion – I put her into the hands of divine Providence – the kind – sweet and good little girl acted as if nothing had happened – played as usual – I spent the morning in her room – at midday the King of Sweden came – I took him to Belvedere – we lunched there – then I took him back – he left to see the race in Naples and I read – wrote – I kept myself busy – kept my King company on his return – ⊙ – then the two Councils – afterwards the King of Sweden – I conversed with him – Acton and Belmonte. The King went out before us and returned after us from Belvedere – the children well – my dear Mimi was with a sweet and delicious joy all day.

On Saturday March the 6th, I got up at 7 o'clock – went to my dear Mimi, who had slept very well – had breakfast – dressed – wrote – heard Holy Mass – went for a walk with my dear Mimi and Gatti – then read – wrote – had lunch with my two eldest daughters – read+ – write the post – kept myself busy – made my toilette – prayed – saw my children – the King of Sweden came – he went with me to the theatre at *the tragedy of Tancred*, which was performed very badly – from there went to sleep, the children well – the Kingat half past 8 went with the King of Sweden to hunt at Calvi and returned in the evening – my beloved Mimi in the morning went out to walkwith me in the grove – the after lunch she went out in a carriage to Belvedere and was joyful and quiet all day.

On Sunday March the 7th, I got up – had breakfast – dressed – heard Holy Mass – took care of my children – read – then went to pick up the King of Sweden and went by one horse carriage to the pheasant farm – then there was a running horse hunt where they killed 130 [hares] – then I retuned – left the King of Sweden and the company had lunch at the fatal San Leucio and returned with the lady – saw my children – had dinner – wrote – I dressed again – combed my hair – saw my children and went to the tragedy of Semiramis – then to bed – the children were well – my dear Mimi went out in the morning and in the evening and was very happy – the King went early to prepare the hunt – lunched at San Leucio and returned with the whole company.

On Monday March the 8th, I got up at 6 o'clock – had breakfast – dressed – saw dear Mimi – heard Holy Mass – read – wrote – went out to stroll with Mimi – and then spoke at San Nicola – then wrote the post in advance – at two o'clock the King of Sweden came – I had lunch with him face to face – and then we talked – then I made my daughters come – they talked about stories – geography – at half past 4 I went to walk with the King of Sweden at Canalone – then we returned in a carriage – I wrote to the King – went in my dear Mimi's room – saw Lady San Marco – then the King of Sweden came back and I had a little concert where there were Baron Darmfeld – Belmonte – Gravina – Marsico – Sambuca and Lamberg – my daughter played the harpsichord – then we saw being printed[358] and afterwards he left – I remained talking to Sambuca – arranged my papers and to bed. The King in the morning went to Venafro[359] and he did not return – the children well – my dear Mimi was happy – well and went out morning and evening.

On Tuesday March the 9th, I got up at half past 5 – had breakfast – dressed – combed my hair – heard Holy Mass – saw dear Mimi who had slept rather badly – I left at 7 o'clock with the King of Sweden – Belmonte Darmfeld – in a carriage for Venafro – we arrived there and went down to *baracone* – at eleven o'clock they started a running hunt in a circle – they took 25 boars – I saw it from a kind of lodge that was for this purpose made – afterwards we had lunch under a tent and then I returned with the King of Sweden – the lady and Darmfeld – I left the King to his apartments and returned home – I saw my children – made my toilet and went to Mimi's room – then the King of Sweden came back with Darmfeld – [Gerson] – Belmonte – Sambuca – Gravina – Marsico and my lady – at nine o'clock I took leave of all these people and after a brief standing conversation – I took leave of the King of Sweden, who left – I spoke to Sambuca – then wrote – prayed – undressed and to bed

March Wednesday the 10th, I got up – dressed – had breakfast – heard Holy Mass – went to my dear Mimi's room – spent the morning with her – went out with her – then saw Sambuca – afterwards had lunch – then once again in Mimi's room until the time the King came back – I kept him company during his lunch – then – ⊙ – afterwards I went to the Council ++++++ – then I went to Mimi's room – had dinner and to bed. The children well – the King – who had spent the night in Venafro – returned at five o'clock – in the afternoon my dear Mimi was happy and went out in the morning and in afternoon.

On Thursday March the 11th, I got up at 7 o' clock – had breakfast – combed my hair – dressed – heard Holy Mass – confessed my sins – afterwards heard another Holy Mass – went to my dear Mimi's room – went out – walked with her – retired – had lunch – wrote – in my my dear Mimi's room – saw San Teodora – then went to trot towards Capua – afterwards whole evening with my little girl – kept myself busy and to bed. The children well – dear Mimi started to have trouble under her armpit and spots started to suppurate – she was purged in the evening with 8 grains of sweet mercury and she was happy and cheer – King went to Carditello all day.

On Friday March the 12th, I got up early – to my child'sroom – kept the King company – ⊙ – then heard Holy Mass – went out and spent all morning with my child, lunched with the King, kept him company, read – wrote – kept myself busy – stayed in the children's room – presided over both Councils and to bed – the children well – dear Mimi – after a pained night vomiting and purging – was fine all day – she walked – played – was happy and smallpox seemed to be completely [vanished] and do its regular course, the King in the morning went to listen to the sermon and at two o'clock at the pheasant farm.

On Saturday March the 13th, I got up at 7'oclock – went to my little one's room – dressed – breakfast – combed my hair – heard Holy Mass – read+ – wrote – I kept myself busy – saw two Swedes – took them to Mimi's room – saw my ladies – lunched with my eldest girls – spen the day with Mimi – read – wrote – kept myself busy and to bed. My beloved

Mimi was fine – after lunch a little weaker and fell asleep early – the two spots were fully developped and she had no other spot her whole body, the other children well – the King went to Carditello for the whole day.

On Sunday March the 14th, I got up at 6 o'clock – received the visit of beloved Krotendorf – then took care of my child – heard Holy Mass – had lunch in my room – read – wrote – kept myself busy – went to Mimi's room and spent all day, the King in the morning went [to listen] to sermon, and from there to Carditello to lunch whence he returned in the evening – dear Mimi cried a lot because of her armpit – in the morning [she] was all day with her head down in bed – until five-thirty when she had dreadful convulsions – that lasted over an hour – it was terrible this was so irritated prostrated sick all evening when her pulse is recovered from the convulsion – the fever was very strong all night and she was often uneasy asking to drink so she spent the day and took place the irruption.

On Monday the 15th, I did not go to bed at all – at six o'clock I dressed – combed my hair – heard Holy Mass – had breakfast – spent the whole morning with my children – lunched with my girls – then spent all day with my little girl – Marchioness San Marco came to enquire about my child – also Sambuca – I stayed [there] until the time of the Council – after that I went straight to bed. The children well, dear Mimi in the morning was better – after lunch she had a high fever – and [having] all the symptoms that presaged convulsions but they did not appear at all – in the evening had a great evacuation which relieved her. The King was at the pheasant farm all day.

On Tuesday March the 16th, I got up in the morning and went to [see] the little one – dressed – combed my hair – had breakfast – heard Holy Mass – took care of my little girl who was completely full of spots – then saw Sambuca – afterwards the rest of the gentlemen – lunched with my girls – then wrote my post – saw Lady Belmonte – Caramanico – then my child – wrote – devoted myself and to bed, the children well, dear Mimi got up – was well as if she had not been sick – played – was quiet until the evening – the amount of the spots – especially in the feminine parts – unnerved her a little – but for the remainder she was fine – other children well – the King went to Naples to see the launching of the lugger – lunched at the little house and came back at five o'clock.

On Wednesday March the 17th, I got up at 6 o'clock – dressed – had breakfast – combed my hair – heard Holy Mass – looked after my child the whole morning without moving [from her] – had lunch with the King – chose books for the library then stayed with my child – Lady Didier came – talked with her – then stayed with my child – afterwards went to the Council – from there saw Cardinal Orsini[360] and Gravina – then until midnight with my child. The children fine – my dear Mimi still continued to have eruptions – which made her worry and suffer – especially at night in bed – the King remained all the morning at home and went out only at two o'clock to Carbone – to return at six o'clock.

On Thursday the 18th, I got up at 7 o'clock – had breakfast – dressed – saw my little sick child – heard Holy Mass – saw my children – spent the whole morning with my little one – had lunch with the King – went to the library – then read – wrote – undressed – went to Mimi's room – read my letters +++++++ +++++ – then saw Lady Didier – her husband and senator – later saw my child sleep and calm down – kept myself busy until 8 o'clock – Lady Didier came to keep me company, and then I went to bed. The children well – poor Mimi suffered a lot and got in a very bad mood because of the suppuration of spots, the King after lunch went to Carditello and returned at four o'clock.

On Friday March the 19th, I got up at 7 o'clock – dressed – had breakfast – combed my hair – heard Holy Mass – kept myself busy – stayed with my child – lunched with the King – kept him company – saw a hot-air balloon fly – read – wrote – was with my little one – saw Lady Didier – Corigliano[361] with her child – Donna Pepa Carafa for her husband – then the two Councils – afterwards the King bled for fullness of blood – I undressed and [went] to bed, the children well – my dear Mimi was very dejected all day because all the spots – of which there were many – were suppurating, in the morning the King was [to listen] to the sermon – after lunch to the swamp of Acerra.

On Saturday March the 20th, I got up at 7 o'clock – dressed – combed my hair – had breakfast – heard Holy Mass – read – wrote – saw my children – [with] my dear Mimi – kept myself busy – lunched with the King – saw some engravings – read + – wrote – I kept myself busy – the King returned – I saw him in the evening – he kept me company – ⊙ – then I saw Lady Didier – of whom I took leave with a lot of sadness because I was fond of her – then to bed – the children well – my dear Mimi was all day happy and well as usual, the King was in San Leucio all day.

On Sunday March the 21st, I got up – dressed – had breakfast – heard Holy Mass – saw my child – read+ – wrote – kept myself busy – had lunch with my eldest daughters – saw Loras who was taking leave – read – went to the library – kept myself busy – stayed with my children – the King returned – then I saw Cardinal Orsini and Gravina at the soiree and from there to bed, the children well – dear Mimi as usual – quiet, well – the spots supurated and partly dried, in the morning the King went fishing at Fusaro and returned in the evening.

On Monday March the 22nd, I got up at 7 o'clock – dressed – had breakfast – combed my hair – heard Holy Mass – wrote – kept myself busy – at eleven o'clock I went to Belvedere with the King by dray, and then – to the waterfall – I came back on foot with him – we saw our children – I kept him company – ☉ – then we lunched – read – worked – at 4 o'clock he went out – I wrote for a while – spoke to Prince Belmonte – to Lady San Marco – to Princess Satriano – then I saw my children – afterwards to the Council – kept mysel busy for a while and to bed. The children fine – my dear Mimi completely healthy – the King at 4 o'clock went – for one hour and a half – to San Leucio.

On Tuesday March the 23rd, I got up – dressed – had breakfast – combed my hair – heard Holy Mass – wrote – had lunch with my children – saw some books – finished writing – talked with Sambuca – the Princess of Jacy – then devoted myself – kept myself busy – saw my children and to bed – the children well – my dear Mimi was in top shape – the King went to Carditello for the whole day.

On March 24, I got up in the morning at 7 o'clock – dressed – had breakfast – combed my hair – heard Holy Mass – was busy at eleven o'clock – I went out with my dear Mimi for the first time since her inoculation – then lunched with the King – read – kept myself busy – talked with Cicio Pignatelli – with Princess Belmonte – with Ferolito – another lady – then Misilmeri – then to the Council and afterwards to bed – the children well – in the morning the King went to San Leucio – after lunch to Calabria Citra.

On Thursday March the 25th, I got up at 7 o'clock – dressed – combed my hair – had breakfast – heard – with my dear Mimi – Holy Mass to thank God for her recovery – then spent the morning with my children – then with the King [to listen] to the sermon – on my return kept him company – ☉ – undressed – had lunch – read – wrote – kept myself busy – talked with [Curi] – with the wife of Casabuona[362] – then the King came back – I was with my children – kept myself busy and to bed, the children well – dear Mimi after lunch went out by carriage – the King after lunch went – for a couple of hours – to the bridge at Carbonaro.

On Friday March the 26th, I got up at 7 o'clock – dressed – had breakfast – heard Holy Mass – then went with the King – Salandra and Cassano in town – we went uprightly to the dock – when I saw the two new brigantines – *Minerva* and then dutch vessel was at the harbor and maneuvered – The commander gave us snack – and then we went by boat to my little house in Santa Lucia where we had lunch – after lunch we worked four hours of meeting on Calabrian issue and decided the crucial point – in the meeting were Sambuca – Acton – Pignatelli – King and I – there I returned – face to face with King + then I kept him company – ⊙ – then I undressed – there were the Councils and I went to bed. The children well – dear Mimi went out in morning and evening – the King was with me all day.

On Saturday March the 27th, I got up at 7 o'clock – dressed – had breakfast – heard Holy Mass – kept myself busy – wrote – read – Prior spoke to me – then had dinner with the King – kept him company – saw my children – read+ – wrote – kept myself busy – saw Valignani – Countess Ventimiglia with her brother in law – then wrote – kept myself busy and to bed, the children fine – my dear Mimi went out in morning and evening – the King went for a walk in the morning – after lunch he went to Carditello and returned in the evening.

On Sunday March the 28th, I got up in the morning – had breakfast – dressed – heard Holy Mass – saw my children – read some papers – at eleven o'clock went to listen to the sermon – from there saw the big painting of Kaufmann – then had lunch – kept the King company – read – wrote – saw Pignatelli who is going to Rome – then kept myself busu and to bed – the children well – dear Mimi was purged and was worse than other days – the King after lunch went walking to the woods.

On Monday March the 29th, I got up in the morning – had breakfast – dressed – heard Holy Mass – arranged my papers – saw my children – had lunch with the King – kept him company – ⊙ – then kept myself busy – saw San Marco – then kept myself busy all evening – to the Council and to bed – the children well – the King – owing to bad weather – could not go out all day.

On Tuesday March the 30th, I got up – dressed – had breakfast – heard Holy Mass – saw my children – wrote the post – stayed a long time with Theresa – then had lunch with the King – kept him company – ⊙ – then kept myself busy – saw Gagliani – Prince [Retian] – Duchess Castelpagano[363] – Mr. Hereria – my children – kept myself busy the rest of the evening and to bed – the children well – the King after lunch went to Carditello for a while.

On Wednedsay March the 31st, I got up – dressed – had breakfast – saw my children – heard Holy Mass – wrote – talked with Father Lambini[364] – lunched with the King – kept him company – wrote – worked on my affairs – talked with Lady Belmonte – gave some hearings – then [went] to spiritual exercises – afterwards to the Council and to bed – the children well – the King could not go out all day because of terrible weather.

On Thursday April the 1st, I got up – dressed – had breakfast – combed my hair – heard Holy Mass – was busy with my papers – lunched with the King – kept him company – saw my children – kept myself busy – went to the spiritual exercises and from there to confession and to bed – the children well – the King – because of bad weather – did not go out all day.

On Friday April the 2nd, I got up at 7 o'clock – went to church – made my devotions – then had breakfast – saw my children – combed my hair – dressed – kept myself busy – at eleven o'clock I went with my two eldest daughters San Francesco di Paola to hear Mass and receive the blessing – then had lunch with the King – spent my day keeping him company and to arrage my library – my books – the children well – the King could not go out because of bad weather.

On Saturday April the 3rd, I got up – dressed – had breakfast – combed my hair – heard Holy Mass – saw my children – went to the library – arranged my books – lunched with the King – kept him company – read – wrote – kept myself busy – went to the spiritual exercises – then kept myself busy and to bed – the children well – in the morning the King went to San Leucio for a while – after lunch to Carditello.

On Sunday April the 4th, I got up – dressed – had breakfast – combed my hair – heard Holy Mass with Mimi – then went for a ride in a one horse carriage with Marchioness Acton and Diomede to San Silvestro – then went up to the waterfall and returned on foot – made my toilette – had lunch with my children – took care of them – read – wrote – I kept myself busy – in the evening went to the spiritual exercises ☉ – then kept myself busy and to bed, the children well – the King went to Carditello for lunch and returned in the evening.

On Monday April the 5th, I got up – dressed – had breakfast – heard Holy Mass – read – wrote – kept myself busy – had lunch with my children – then worked in the library – saw Marquise San Marco – then two English Women – one who lost her son – afterwards further hearings – and [went] to the exercises – then to the Council and to bed – the children well – the King went to Fusaro – to Portici – to the dock – saw the children in Naples and did not return until evening.

On Tuesday April the 6th, I got up – [made my]toilette – had break-fast – heard Mass – saw my children – wrote the post – lunched with the King – wrote – <u>read</u> – kept myself busy – gave hearings and went to the spiritual exercises – kept myself and then to bed – the children well – in the morning the King went for a ride in a dray – after lunch to Calabria Citra to see some hunting works.

On Wednesday April the 7th, I got up – dressed – had breakfast – combed my hair – heard Holy Mass – the Council – afterwards lunched with my children – kept myself busy – <u>read</u> – wrote – in the evening the King returned – talked with me + ☉ – and then we went to the exercises with my girls – received the blessing – then was busy with the library – then to bed – the children well – the King went to Portici – after the Council in the morning – from there to the dock – saw the children and returned home.

On April the 8th, Holy Thursday I got up – dressed – combed my hair – went to the function – to Carmine – then returned – lunched with the King – kept him company – ☉ – then washed the feet of twelve poor girls – afterwards <u>read</u> – then went to San Francesco di Paola – to the ecclesiastic of San Antonio – visited Holy Sepulchre – afterwards [went] to the parish – from there took back my children – afterwards returned with the King to listen to the sermon – after that went home to arrange my books – the children well – King went after lunch to Holy Sepulchre in Belvedere.

On Friday April the 9th, I got up – dressed – combed my hair – at 9 o'clock went to the parish of the Carmelites to attend the church functions – then at midday kept the King company – had lunch – then undressed – saw my children – <u>read</u> – wrote – kept myself busy and fin-ished arranging my library – then to bed – the children well – in the morn-ing the King was at church and then after lunch he went to Carditello.

On April Saturday the 10th, I got up – dressed – combed my hair – had breakfast – heard the church functions – talked with Lambini for a while – then had lunch with the King – kept him company – ☉ – then read – kept myself busy – saw the fiscal agent of Caserta, Sambuca, finished my job – then confessed my sins – put curlers and went to bed – the children well – in the morning the King went to the church functions and after lunch to pheasant farm

On April the 11th Easter Sunday, I got up at half past 6 – went at seven o'clock with the King to the public chapel – there received communion and performed my Easter duties – then returned – I had breakfast with the King and my children – heard Mass with my children – then talked a long time with Pignatelli who had returned from Rome – then combed my hair – dressed – went to the hand-kissing – then the public table – then changed dress and had lunch – afterwards kept the King company – then saw San Marco – then read.... [365] – afterwards saw Duchess la Vella[366] and my children – went with the last to the blessing of the parish – afterwards talked to Gravina abour my son – undressed – arranged my papers – had dinner and to bed. The children well – the King after lunch went to Carditello and returned after eight o'clock.

On April the 12th Easter Monday I got up at half past 6 – dressed – combed my hair – had breakfast – continued to arrange my affairs – heard two Masses – then at 9 o'clock went with the King to listen to the sermon – then the commander of Miquelets brought us the news that the two famous bandits Angiolello del Duca and Rosso[367] had been arrested half dead – after the sermon I went to take my children with me – then I got into a carriage with them and happily arrived at Portici – I settled my children – then had lunch with the King – then unpacked my papers and books – afterwards made my toilette for the ceremony in honour of Januarius – at six o'clock I went to Naples with the lady in a carriage – I saw my children again – very healthy – especially Francis – Januarius better and Amelia looking tired – I stayed with them and then kept the King company – ⊗ – then the *cantata* at the Florentines [theatre] where I was bored to death – afterwards half asleep – I returned with the King – the children well – in the morning the King went after the sermon to Portici – he arrived fifteen minutes before me – in the afternoon at three-thirty left and went by sea to Naples and returned with me.

On Tuesday April the 13th, I got up – dressed – had breakfast – combed my hair – heard two Holy Masses – saw my children – then at half past ten to the Sambuca's Council – afterward had lunch with the King – kept him company – catalogued – arranged my books – and then wrote my post – went [to say] the rosary and spent the rest of the evening with my children, the children well, the King after lunch at half past three went to Naples and returned at 8 o'clock.

On Wednesday April the 14th, I got up – dressed – had breakfast – combed my hair – heard Holy Mass – kept myself busy – lunched with the King – kept him company – ⊙ – then saw Lady San Marco – [went] to [say] the rosary and then – since I felt fever – to bed, the children well – the King after lunch went to town.

On Thursday April the 15th, I got up late – having had fever all day and evening I got up – heard Mass kept myself busy – lunched with the King – then saw Sangro – afterwards to bed where the fever was higher and at 3 o'clock at night a small throat abscess opened and gave me relief. The children well – the King went into town and stayed the evening at the theatre.

On Friday April the 16th, I got up – dragged myself all day – read – wrote – lunched with the King – kept him company – kept myself busy – in the evening to the two Councils and to bed. The children came from Naples healthy – the King could not go out all day because of bad weather.

On Saturday April the 17th, I got up – dressed – lunch – heard Holy Mass – saw my children – devoted myself – had lunch with the King – then read – kept myself busy – saw Mrs. Hereria for two hours – then San Marco – then the post – my children to and to bed – the children well – the King after lunch went to Naples and came back in the evening.

On Sunday April the 18th, I got up – dressed – had breakfast – heard two Masses – wrote for the courrier – saw my children – lunched with them – busy with the lessons of Francis – then went to the eldest [daughters] – afterwards returned to my room – read for a while – went to the blessing and played with my three eldest and to bed, the children fine – the King lunched at the castle, and then went to try the brigantine at sea.

On Monday April the 19th, I got up – dressed – had breakfast – heard Holy Mass – combed my hair – dressed – kept myself busy – wrote – had lunch with the King – read – kept myself busy – saw my children – Princess Butera, S. Clemente – [Cerisano] – the widow of Capecelatro[368] and then to the Crown and from there – to the the Council and to bed – the children well – in the morning the King went out a little – after lunch he was at home.

On Tuesday April the 20th, I got up – dressed – had breakfast – combed my hair – spoke to the governess – saw my children – went to Holy Mass – then wrote the post – kept myself busy – had lunch with the King – kept myself busy – read – wrote – talked with Sambuca – afterwards saw young Monteleone – then Capecelatro – afterwards [went to say] the rosary – then young Andria – afterwards the King returned – kept myself busy and to bed – the children well – in the morning the King went out a bit for a walk – after lunch he went to Naples and returned in the evening.

On Wednesday April the 21st, I got up at 7 am – curled [and] combed my hair – dressed – had breakfast – heard Holy Mass – saw my children – at half past nine I went with the Marchioness and Vasto to Naples – there

I met the Great Maîtresse who spoke to me – then I went with Belmonte – Gravina – the engineer and [Angesiolo] – to see apartments for the transfer of my son among men – afterwards I spoke to de Marco – then had lunch – kept myself busy – read++ – wrote – went to the terrace – then talked with Acton – after lunch made my toilette – the Council – prayed God and went to the theatre – there – where I was bored a lot – [in a carriage] – face to face with the King to Portici and to bed – the children well – the King went from Portici to Naples by sea and spent the evening with me.

On Thursday April the 22nd, I got up – dressed – had breakfast – combed my hair – saw my children – heard Holy Mass – worked on my affairs – afterwards lunched with the King – kept him company ++++++ – read – kept myself busy – saw Lady San Marco – Genzano – the rosary and some hearings – then kept myself busy and to bed – the children well – after lunch the King went to town – in the morning he went fishing.

On Friday April the 23rd, I got up – dressed – had breakfast – heard Holy Mass – made my affairs – saw my children – had lunch with the King – kept him company – then attended the meeting about Calabria with the King – Sambuca – Acton – Pignatelli and I – afterwards unpacked some things – then saw Duchess of Termoli – the sister of Lieto – Donna Pepa Carafa, Grimaldi – the Countess Althan – [went to say] the rosary – to both Councils and to bed. The children healthy – in the morning the King went out fishing for a while and then he stayed at home all day.

On Saturday April the 24th, I got up – dressed – had breakfast – read – wrote – heard Mass – kept myself busy – lunched with the King – kept him company – read – wrote – kept myself busy – went for a walk – with my two eldest girls – to the low wood – then by one horse carriage to St. Forio – then home – kept myself busy with the rosary – my children – and to bed, the children well – in the morning the King went fishing, to see a cannon being tested on the bridge and after lunch to Naples.

On Sunday April the 25th, I got up – dressed – had breakfast – heard Holy Mass – went to my childrens'room – kept myself busy – wrote – had lunch with my children – saw them play – attended their lessons – then kept myself busy – went out with my two daughters – for a walk to the pier – afterwards got in a one horse carriage with the three girls because Mimi had come too, and from there to the say the rosary and to bed.

On Monday April the 26th, I got up – dressed – had breakfast – combed my hair – heard Holy Mass – read – wrote – went to Amelia's room – wished her happy birthday – returned – kept the King company – ⊙ – then had lunch with him – read while he was sleeping – kept him company – kept myself busy – gave hearings – saw Lady Althan – went to say the rosary – then saw my children and to bed – the children well – the King went out a bit after lunch for a walk.

On Tuesday April the 27th, I got up – dressed – had breakfast – heard Holy Mass – read – wrote my post – I kept myself busy – had lunch with the King – read – devoted myself – saw the children – afterwards I went out with my three girls – for a ride in a one horse carriage to Naples – on return gave audiences – saw Castelpagano – talked with Sambuca – with Lamberg – saw my children and to bed – the children well – after lunch the King went to Naples to bring his brigantines and returned late in the evening.

On Wednesday thr 28th, I got up at 6 o'clock – dressed – went to church – I went down – with my two eldest daughters – at 7 o'clock down to the pier – acompanied by Vasto and Montalto – we went to the King's brigantine where we had breakfast – pulled some broadsides – then at half past two – by one horse carriage – the King took us back home – I made my toilette – saw my children – had lunch with the King – kept him company – ⊙ – then undressed – read and paraded – went to say the rosary – gave some hearings – then to the Council – to bed – the King got up early – he received us on the brigantine and then was all day at home

On Thursday April the 29th, I got up after 7 o'clock – dressed – had breakfast – combed my hair – heard Holy Mass – stayed with the children – wrote – read – kept myself busy – had lunch with the children – spent the afternoon with them – saw Marsico, San Marco, and then went to stroll with Louise – Francis – Mimi – to the countryside – trotted – afterwards some audiences Villafranca,[369] Caperano, Sanchez, a Flemish Count Merode[370] – then saw Butera – Genzano :: [371] afterwards with my children – the King returned and I went to bed – my children well – the King was all day at Caserta – in the morning I sent [a letter] to him and received his answer at six o clock.

On Friday April the 30th, I got up – dressed – combed my hair – heard Holy Mass – kept myself busy – read – wrote – saw my children – saw the ships that arrived – the two frigates and xebec – then read – wrote kept myself – lunched with the King – presided over the two Councils – kept him company – ⊙ – then saw him leaving – then read + – wrote – kept myself busy – saw my children and in bed. The children well – in the morning the King went to town to see frigates arrive – then after lunch he went out again and left at 9 o'clock for Capri where he spent the night.

On Saturday May the 1st, I got up at 7 o'clock – had breakfast – dressed – combed my hair – heard two Masses – spoke to Luchesi[372] – had my girls' teeth fixed and also mine – spoke to Belmonte – had lunch with my children – took care of them – spoke with Safatta – then wrote my post – kept myself busy – saw Princess Belmonte – Butera – Countess Ventimiglia – received a letter from the King – answered him – went to say the rosary and then to the puppets theatre with all whom has children – like us – to Caserta. My children well – the King stayed in Capri all day – since yesterday evening – though the weather is bad.

On Sunday May the 2nd, I got up in the morning – had breakfast – dressed – combed my hair – heard two Holy Masses – saw my children – read – wrote – saw Sambuca – Acton – everyone who was outside in the antechamber – lunched with my children – read+ – wrote – kept myself busy all day – saw and talked with Lady Markof[373] – then with the wife of Galatolo and then with ladies – then undressed – saw my children – I kept myself busy – the children well – the King stayed all day in Capri and wrote to me.

On Monday May the 3rd, I got up at 7 o'clock – dressed – had breakfast – combed my hair – heard Holy Mass – spoke to Gagliano who had returned from Rome – was present at a long row involving Mimi during her lesson – then had lunch with my eldest daughters – afterwards talked to an old man (… …) – then took part in the lessons of Francis and Mimi – then saw San Marco – went to the woods to the castle where I saw a ball launched [Cari] which went well – then [had] a snack with the children – at the table which goes up and down – and then went with the children by one horse carriage to Ricia's house – then returned – I had several hearings – Gravina – Termoli – Sangro – then the wife of Casa Buona – that of judge Crispo and of Blanco afterwards my children danced round a tree decorated with toys and had lunch – I continued to talk with Madame de Sangro and went to bed – the children well – the King stayed in Capri all day.

On Tuesday May the 4th, I got up – dressed – had breakfast – combed my hair – heard Holy Mass – wrote my post – scolded Theresa – saw de Marco – Sambuca – then had lunch – saw Ventapane[374] – then wrote – saw Acton – a sharp pain forced me to lie down – then read ++ – wrote – kept myself busy – went to [say] the rosary – finished my post +++ – talked with Sambuca and to bed – the children well – the King stayed in Capri.

On Wednesday May the 5th, I got up at 7 o'clock – dressed – had breakfast – combed my hair – heard Holy Mass – always with my lorgnette – undecided about what to do – saw the King – did not move from Capri – saw my children – at one hour o' clock I finally decided and to go to town with

Salandra – Rocafiorita and the lady – in town I had lunch – worked on my affairs – read – wrote – saw the King coming – at three-thirty he came – I sat in a carriage with lady Altavilla and went to the pier – the King arrived – I took him in my carriage and returned – I kept him company – ☉ – and then I went with him – Acton and Fragnito – to the pier by boat – there I went on board two vessels – then we went back – I worked on some affairs – the Council and to bed – the children well – the King returned from Capri after lunch – after a stay of 4 days and two half days in good health.

On Thursday May the 6th, I got up in the morning – had breakfast – dressed – heard Holy Mass – read – wrote – kept myself busy – had lunch with the King – kept him company – ☉ – read +++++++ – then dressed – went with the King to St. Januarius – then took him to the pier – where he embarked and I returned to Portici – saw my children – took care of them and to bed – the children well – in the morning the King went to Portici – after lunch he stayed with me.

On Friday May the 7th, I got up – had breakfast – combed my hair – heard Holy Mass – then read – wrote – kept myself busy – saw my children – had lunch with them – kept them with me – ☉⊗ – read – wrote – kept myself busy – gave hearings – both Councils and to bed – the children well – the King went to the Councils [and] to Mortella for the whole day.

On Saturday May the 8th, I got up – dressed – had breakfast – combed my hair – heard Holy Mass – read – wrote – kept myself busy – had lunch with my children – read – wrote the post – and then went to Acerra with my children – gave them a snack – all alone with the four of them and Montalto who drove the carriage – on returning I spoke to Lady Herreira – and then to bed – the children well – the King went at Mortella for the whole day.

On Sunday May the 9th, I got up – – dressed – combed my hair – heard Holy Mass – kept myself busy – had lunch with my children – then took care of them – after lunch I went to the high garden for a walk with the children – then to the pier – trotted and afterwards saw Countess Althan – [gave] hearings – the King came back and in the evening I went to the house of the Marchioness Altavilla – where we saw a lot of people – and then to bed – the children well – the King went to hunt quails to Mortella all day.

On Monday May the 10th, I got up – dressed – had breakfast – combed my hair – heard Holy Mass – took care of my children – had their teeth extracted – then kept them with me at breakfast – we had lunch with the King whom I kept company – ☉ – he then went o town ++++++ – I kept myself busy a bit and then went to the pier with my three daughters and walked – from there home – [went] to the Council and to bed – the children well – the King went to town to see the troops.

On Tuesday May the 11th, I got up in the morning – had breakfast – dressed – heard Holy Mass – saw my children – wrote all my post – arranged my packages – talked with Sambuca and his sister – in – law – went to Naples – lunched – worked on my affairs – talked with Acton – de Marco – read+ – wrote – kept busy during the evening – saw Cardinal Bernis[375] – introduced my daughters to him – then waited for the King – see him and went to bed – the children well – three girls after lunch came to visit me in town – the King was at Caserta all day.

On Wednesday May the 12th, I got up – dressed – had breakfast – combed my hair – heard Holy Mass – read – wrote – kept myself busy – had lunch with my girls – gave hearings – then talked with Pignatelli of Calabrian affairs – after lunch read again+ – went out with my three daughters to the little house at Fiatamone[376] – where ew had a snack – there we met the King – our family stayed together – I returned by dray with the King and kept him company – ⊙ – then [went] to the Council and to bed – the children well – the King lunched on board and was at the seaside all day.

On Thursday May the 13th, I got up – dressed – had breakfast – had breakfast – combed my hair – heard Holy Mass – then worked on my affairs – afterwards offered a table to Cardinal Bernis where there were the two Hererias – Belmonte – Sambuca – Acton – Gravina – Pignatelli – San Nicola and the ladies guard – I showed him the apartments – the terrace – then [with] my children – whom already knew[377] – after Sambuca remained to talk with me – then Acton – later I gave hearings – saw my children and to bed – the children well – the King was on board all day and on his return kept me company – ⊙.

On Friday May the 14th, I got up – dressed – had breakfast – combed my hair – heard Holy Mass – read – wrote – kept myself busy – talked with Sambuca – then went on board – the King's brigantine – with Belmonte where we had a table for 12 people we endured a terrible storm and the completed table [378] – a long time we stood idly – on our return the King accompanied me and kept me company – ⊙ – Princess Belmonte talked to me – more hearings again – then [went] to the two Councils and to bed – the children well – in the morning the King went on board and returned with me.

On Saturday May the 15th, I got up in the morning – had breakfast – dressed – heard Holy Mass – read – wrote – kept myself busy – talked with Sambuca – then wrote my post – lunched with the children – read + – wrote – kept myself busy – in the evening saw Cardinal Bernis and talked to him – at nine o'clock went on board the King's brigantine with Acton and had lunch at a table of 8 people – afterwards saw [signals] of night. The King was all day on board – children well.

On Sunday May the 16th, I got up – dressed – combed my hair – had breakfast – heard Holy Mass – saw my children – read – wrote – about eleven o'clock I went with a large following – in more than a dozen boats – to see the squadron that was all decked and superb – I went on board all ten ships – and then – with the same pomp and ceremony – we went to have the lunch at my little house – where all officers – commanders and private citizens were invited – my children came there later – also Cardinal Bernis – at 5 o'clock we went in great fanfare but without cannon rounds – to see the King two vessels – the frigate and brigantine – where we offered a snack and ice cream to the children – at 8 o'clock we returned – I kept the King company ⊙ then to bed – the children well – the King was at sea all day.

On Monday May the 17th, I got up – dressed – had breakfast – combed my hair – at eight there was the Sambuca's Council – then a meeting for Calabria – ⊙ – then I heard Mass – afterwards I went down with Belmonte – had lunch on board the King's brigantine – then I returned – kept myself busy – and then at 12 o'clock I went down with Sambuca once again and went on board the brigantine – then undressed and remained to read + – wrote – saw my children and to bed – the children well – King half day on board.

On Tuesday May the 18th, I got up – dressed – had breakfast – combed my hair – heard Holy Mass – wrote my post – saw de Marco – Sambuca – lunched with my children – saw San Marco – read – wrote – kept myself busy – saw my children – in the evening Cardinal Bernis [stayed] until eleven – afterwards to bed – the children well – the King was all day in the Gulf with the squadron.

On Wednesday May the 19th, I got up – dressed – had breakfast – combed my hair – heard Holy Mass – saw my children – at eleven o'clock the King came back – I kept him company – ⊙ – then had lunch with him – read while he was sleeping – strolled on the terrace and saw engravings with him – wrote – spoke to Sangro who warded – the Council and to bed, the children well – the King returned at eleven in the morning and did not go out.

On Thursday May the 20th, Ascension Day I got up – dressed – had breakfast – heard Holy Mass – wrote a lot – then saw Pignatelli who leaves for Calabria to remove the monks – then saw Sambuca – lunched with my children – saw apartments destined for the Hauss brothers[379] – then talked with the lady – afterwards read+ – wrote – kept myself busy – dressed – saw

Cardinal Bernis – gave hearings and went to get bored by an act to the Florentines theatre – and then to bed – the children well, in the morning the King went to Posillipo at [two] to Portici by sea – saw the passage of people of Scafati and at [24] home.

On Friday May the 21st, I got up at 7 o'clock – arranged my packages – combed my hair – dressed – had breakfast with my children – heard Mass and went with my 3 children to Portici – there I met my three other children – I took care of them – arranged my packages – then lunched with them – afterwards read +++ – then kept myself busy +++++ – afterwards to [say] the rosary – [went] to the Councils and to bed – the children well – King returned in the evening after he had been all day at the sea.

On Saturday May the 22nd, I got up at 7 o'clock – had breakfast – read – wrote – kept myself busy – lunched with my children – talked with Lamberg – with N. – with San Marco – then with Sambuca – went to [say] the rosary – listened to Don Ciro Uloa – Conradini – then again Sambuca – finished my post – affairs and to bed. The children well – in the morning the King went and stayed at Castellamare.

On Sunday May the 23rd, I got up – dressed – had breakfast – combed my hair – read – wrote – heard Holy Mass – dressed – went to lunch at a table for 15 people – then finished lunch I remained to converse with Cardinal Bernis – afterwards I went to the pier with my 4 children and then onto the King's ship – where they had a big snack – on returning I kept the King company – ☉ – kept myself busy and went to bed. The children well – in the morning the King returned from Castellamare – remained on board all day and returned in the evening.

On Monday May the 24th, I dressed – had breakfast – heard Holy Mass – went to have myself painted – saw my children – arranged my affairs – lunched with the King – read – kept myself busy – saw Lady Hereria – then finished my letters – saw my children – went to [say] the rosary – Council and sent the courrier – the children well – the King went fishing a little in the morning and after lunch.

On Tuesday May the 25th, I got up – dressed – had breakfast – combed my hair – heard Holy Mass – wrote my post – then had lunch with the King – read – then finished my post – saw San Marco – Belmonte – the Bishop of Rovella[380] – other hearings – went to [say] the rosary – prepared to make my confession and to bed – the children well – the King went fishing at Portici for a while – same thing in the morning and evening.

On Wednesday May the 26th, I got up at 6½ – went to church – performed my devotions – had breakfast – dressed – combed my hair – heard

Holy Mass – had myself painted – packed my bags for Naples – saw the children – lunched with the King – then read – ⊙ – afterwards went out with 4 children in a one horse carriage and Montalto who drove – the King and Salandra on horseback – we went to see a rose tree – then Chiaromonte garden where the children had a snack – from there home – [to say the] rosary – many hearings and to bed – the children well – the King went fishing in the morning – after lunch he came with me.

On Thursday May the 27th, I got up – dressed – combed my hair – had breakfast – heard Holy Mass – had breakfast with my three daughters and heard Mass in St. Pasqual – then Caravita – at home I met Breme who spoke to me – then arranged my affairs – went to Naples with my three daughters – on arrival – settled – arranged – talked with Acton – saw my children – talked with Lamberg – with San Marco – gave audiences and went to bed – the children well – in the morning the King went to Caserta and returned in the evening.

On Friday May the 28th, I got up – had breakfast – dressed – combed my hair – heard Holy Mass – went to both Councils – then kept myself busy – went to lunch with my children – took care of them – read – wrote – saw my children – Lady Sangro – Genzano – Belmonte – gave audiences – and then to bed – the children well – the King went at eleven on board a ship and there he spent the night.

On Saturday May the 29th, I got up – dressed – had breakfast – combed my hair – heard Holy Mass – spoke to Acton – Sambuca – then came the King – then I lunched with King – read during his light sleep – then wrote the post – kept myself busy – gave some hearings – I put curlers and to bed – I especially suffered during the day as result of my pregnancy, the children were well – the King returned from Castellamare at eleven o'clock and went in the evening to the concert at the opera house.

On Sunday May the 30th – the King's nameday[381] – I got up at 7 o'clock – had breakfast with my three girls – took them to wish their father [happy nameday] – and then I made all our great toilettes – heard two Masses and went to the hand-kissing – then the public table – afterwards I undressed – lunched – read – kept the King company – ⊙ – then kept myself busy – played with the children – dressed again in court dress – had my hands kissed by ladies – then undressed – went with my four children to the performance – the children Francis and Mimi were there for the first time – the first was [serious] – the little girl was happy – in the evening the King went to the pier – before the hand-kissing of the ladies.

On Monday the 31st, I woke up – dressed – had breakfast – combed my hair – heard Holy Mass – saw my children – heard the lesson of Theresa and Louise regarding geography – history – I was very satisfied for the first one – then I had lunch – read – kept myself busy – saw all […] – then strolled – kept myself busy and went to the opera – then slept – the King did not go out all day – the children well.

On Tuesday June the 1st, I got up at 7 o'clock – dressed – had breakfast – heard Holy Mass – combed my hair – presided over de Marco's Council – then lunched with the King – read – kept him company – wrote my post – kept myself busy – ⊙ – then gave audiences – saw my children play – had dinner with them – and to bed – the children well – in the evening the King went to the pier for a while.

On Wednesday June the 2nd, I got up – dressed – had breakfast – combed my hair – heard Holy Mass – had some of my children's teeth extracted – then had breakfast with them – after talked with Tarsia – Brentano – San Marco – after the lunch [stayed] with my children – then kept myself busy – saw Acton Sambuca + – afterwards the King returned – [went] to the opera and after the first act home – the children well – the King went to Caserta all day and returned in the evening.

On Thursday June the 3rd, I got up – dressed – had breakfast – combed my hair – heard Holy Mass – chose some fabrics – had myself painted – then saw my children – had lunch with the King – read during his light sleep ++++ – kept him company – ⊙ – then took care of my children – dressed – afterwards saw Azaro[382] who had to hurry to Rome because of Hereria's illness – then stayed with the King and then to Florentines (theatre) – the children well – the King was home all day.

On Friday June the 4th, I got up – dressed – had breakfast – heard Holy Mass – then presided over [two] Councils – after lunch [stayed] with the children – kept them company – read – wrote – kept myself busy – in the evening gave audiences, and then listened to good clarinet and violin music with my girls – Acton – Marsico – Vasto – Sangro – then had dinner with the children and to bed – the children well – at eleven o'clock the King went to Castellamare by sea and stayed there all day and night.

On Saturday June the 5th, The King came back early – I woke up at 7 o'clock – I got up – dressed – had breakfast – heard Holy Mass – kept the King company – ⊙ – then wrote my post – saw people – talked with San Marco – lunched with my children – took care of them – read ++ – wrote – gave 7 hearings – strolled on the terrace – saw my children – talked with

Rocella – kept myself busy and went to bed – the children well – in the morning King went out again at ten to Castellamare and remained there.

On Sunday June the 6th, my Theresa's birthday she has entered in her 13th year – I got up – made a short toilette – saw my daughter receive communion with great tenderness – I prepared her presents – then wrote to the King and charged Acton [to deliver] this letter – then I had breakfast with my three girls – took care of them – made a long toilette – then hand-kissing – saw the whole court – lunched with my children – took care of them – talked with San Marco – Belmonte – San Nicola – then went out with my three daughters to the public promenade at Chiaia – went down and up again – then went in a carriage – afterwards went back – gave audience to Lady Villarosa[383] – to Mahoni – then went to the theatre with my three girls – at theatre started with the chinese performance – there was an act and another ballet – afterwards I went out with my eldest girls and went to the little house in Santa Lucia at dinner – there was a good lighting and music – Rocella – Gravina – Marsico – Vasto – Montalto – Leonessa[384] – San Nicola and the lady guard supper there – at one o'clock we returned and went to bed – the children well – the King remained all day at Castellamare and he wrote that he was well.

On Monday June the 7th, I got up at half past 7 – dressed – had breakfast – combed my hair – spoke to Sambuca – saw Rasownousky whom the King sent to me – then Mass – looked after Mimi – saw my children – at midday the King returned – lunched with me – then during his light sleep I began to read ++++ – afterwards I kept him company – then looked after sick Mimi – had to talk a long time with Lisette regarding her fatal marriage – afterwards looked after beloved Mimi – kept the King company – ☉ – then the Council – took a little chocolate – kept myself busy and to bed. The children fine – except my dear Mimi who at 9 o'clock had fever with a headache – she went to bed – dejected – about 5 o'clock she had an emetic infusion – then suffered – in the evening she was given a bit of lemon ice-cream and she seemed to get better. At midday the King returned from Castellamare and did not go out anymore.

On Tuesday June the 8th, I got up at 7 o'clock – dressed – combed my hair – heard Holy Mass – had breakfast – saw Mimi better – wrote my post – lunched with the King – kept him company – read – wrote – I kept myself busy – finished my job – went to Mimi's room – saw my other children and presided over de Marco's Council – after that I had a little chocolate – kept myself busy and to bed, the children well – dear Mimi took another emetic in the morning – was dejected during the day – in the evening she ate an ice cream but very little. The King went in the morning to fish at Posillipo – and in the afternoon to the riding stables to see young horses being hooded.

On Wednesday June the 9th, I got up at 7 o'clock – had breakfast – combed my hair – dressed – heard Holy Mass – stayed a long time with my beloved Mimi – then saw Sambuca – lunched with the children – took care of them – read + – wrote – kept myself busy – walked on the terrace – talked with Castelpagano – Belmonte – then got ready – to confess my sins and went to bed – the children well – my dear Mimi was better but had fever – she asked for macaroni and ate them with appetite – in the morning the King went to Caserta and returned in the evening.

On Thursday June the 10th, I got up at 6 o'clock – went to perform my devotions in church – had breakfast – dressed – heard and saw my children – Gravina talked with my son – then went to the chapel – heard another mass – lunched with the King – ☉ kept him company and read during his light sleep – made my accounts – scolded my children – pre-sided over my two Councils and wnt to get bored at San Carlo – then to bed – the children well – thanks to God – my dear Mimi walked through all the rooms – the King in the morning at the procession of Corpus – then after lunch at the riding stable to see mules being hooded.

On Friday June the 11th, I got up at 7 o'clock – had breakfast – dressed – heard Holy Mass – saw my children – talked with Don Vincenzo Corasi – with Simonetti – then went to the chapel to receive the blessing – talked with Sambuca – Ferdinando Luchesi – lunched with the children – kept myself busy – saw Acton – strolled on the terrace – saw Princess Caramanico – Tarsia – San Marco – kept myself busy and to bed – the children well – dear Mimi is still convalescencing – but fine – the King in the morning went to Caserta and remained there.

On Saturday June the 12th, I got up at 7 o'clock – dressed – had breakfast – combed my hair – heard Holy Mass – went to visit ill Blend and Seraphina[385] [Chancellor] who are ill – then I talked with de Marco – I went to the chapel to receive the blessing – saw Princess Belmonte – then lunched with the children – kept them company – kept myself busy – saw Acton – then a Milady – Duchess San Clemente[386] and her sister and Casarano – then gave 9 hearings – afterwards talked to Lord Belmonte and then Gravina – kept myself busy and to bed – the children well – the King remained another day at Caserta.

On Sunday June the 13th, I got up at 7 o'clock – dressed – had break-fast – combed my hair – heard Mass – spoke to Simoneti – and then went to the chapel – from there talked with Sambuca – Lady Belmonte – lunched with the children – kept them company – read my letters – kept myself busy – read+ – wrote – saw Acton – went onto terrace and then to the Fondo theatre – where I was bored to death – the King came there and we came back at one o'clock – the children well – the King came back at the time of the theatre from his trip to Caserta.

On Monday June the 14th, I got up at 7 o'clock – dressed – had breakfast – combed my hair – heard Holy Mass – presided over the Council – then went to the chapel – afterwards kept the King company – ☉ – lunched with the King – read – slept – kept myself busy – then at half past 6 went out with my three daughters to Posillipo – went down home – gave them a snack and then returned – talked with Teresina – read+++ – wrote and went to bed – the children well – the King went at 6 o'clock after lunch once again to Caserta and stayed there.

On Tuesday June the 15th, I got up at 7 o'clock – dressed – had breakfast – combed my hair – heard Holy Mass – wrote my post – went to the chapel – lunched with my children – spoke to San Marco – <u>read</u> +++ – wrote – kept myself busy – saw my children – gave hearings to Malaspina – Omignano – a widow and daughter – Corigliano – kept Lady Hereria company – finished my post and talked with Sambuca – and then to bed, the children well – the King remained all day at Caserta.

On Wednesday June the 16th, I got up at 7 o'clock – had breakfast – dressed – combed my hair – took Holy Viaticum to a poor sick person – then talked with de Marco – Countess Althan – afterwards went to the chapel – talked with Belmonte – Gravina – San Nicola – Marsico – lunched with the children – took care of them – read + – wrote – kept myself busy – saw Acton – Monsignor Saluzi[387] – kept myself busy – then spoke to Gravina – saw the King – presided over the Council + – then slept – the children well – the King at 9 o'clock returned from Caserta healthy.

On Thursday June the 17th, I got up at 7 am – had breakfast – dressed – heard Holy Mass – then kept myself busy – afterwards went [to receive] the blessing in the chapel – saw my children – lunched with the King – read while he was sleeping – kept him company – ☉ – afterwards made my toilette again – went to see the procession – then by dray to Chiaia – a trot and home – afterwards [went] to the San Carlo theatre – the children well – in the morning the King went fishing and after lunch stayed with me.

On Friday June the 18th, I got up – dressed – had breakfast – heard Holy Mass – kept myself busy with my children – read – wrote – had lunch with the children – saw Count Lamberg, Belmonte – Sambuca – read – kept myself busy – walked to the terrace with the children – the King went back and we presided over the two Councils and to bed – the children well – the King was all day by the sea – to see the English squadron.

On Saturday June the 19th, I got up at 7 o'clock – dressed – had breakfast – combed my hair – heard Holy Mass – saw my children – wrote my post – worked on my affairs – lunched with the King – kept him company – ⊙ – then read +++ – wrote – I kept myself busy – gave 16 hearings – saw my children and went to the San Carlo theatre – the children well – the King went after lunch to Capo di monte.

On Sunday June the 20th, I got up at 7 o'clock – had breakfast – combed my hair – dressed – heard Holy Mass – made my toilette – kept myself busy – then lunched in public – afterwards saw some machines – undressed – kept the King company – ⊙ – then with the children and him – afterwards dressed – [went] to Chiaia – to go for a ride in a dray with the King – then saw Ferolito – Triglia – Pepa Carafa – afterwards to the opera and to bed – the children went out – the three girls [went out] after me to Chiaia and in the evening the two eldest went to an act at the theatre.

On Monday June the 21st, I got up – dressed – had breakfast – heard Holy Mass – presided over the Council – then kept myself busy – Dinner with the children – take care of them – saw de Marco – Acton – read +++ – saw Ruoti – then San Nicola who was nominated vicar of regent – later the Marquis Fuscaldo[388] – afterwards [with] the children – kept myself busy and to bed – the children well – the King at eleven o'clock went to Castellamare by sea and stayed there.

On Tuesday June the 22nd, I got up at 4 o'clock – wrote my post – walked on the terrace – and combed my hair – dressed – slept for an hour – saw Sambuca – then [with] the children – stayed with them – saw engravings – read – slept – wrote – talked with Fuscaldo – with Rocella – dressed – then went for a walk with the three girls in my garden where I gave them a snack – from there with them by one horse carriage to the farthest fountain at Chiaia – then home – spoke to Lord Belmonte and to his lady – then saw Acton – Sambuca – sent letters for Spain and to bed – the children well – the King remained all day at Castellamare.

On Wednesday June the 23rd, I got up at 7 o'clock – had breakfast – combed my hair – dressed – heard Holy Mass – saw my children – kept myself busy – saw de Marco – Sambuca – had lunch with the children – stayed with them – read – kept myself busy – the King returned – I stayed with him – spoke to San Marco – scolded Louise – strolled with the King –

then saw Lady Hereria and presided over the Council and to bed – the children well – the King returned from Castellamare at 5 o'clock and did not go out anymore.

On Thursday June the 24th, I got up – dressed – had breakfast – combed my hair – heard Holy Mass – saw my children – then went on board English commandant Trosty – commanded by Lord Lindsay[389] – then after having seen everything and the King [having visited] the other four ships – we went to the little house at Santa Lucia – where we offered them a lunch and afterwards we returned – kept the King company to – ☉ – and undressed – read – kept myself busy – saw my children – spent the day between reading my letters – saw Sambuca – kept myself busy – then dressed again for the opera – the children well – the King went with me on board English ships – then in the evening to the pier for a while.

On Friday June the 25th, I got up at 7 o'clock – dressed – had breakfast – combed my hair – heard Holy Mass – presided over the two Councils – then lunched with the King – read – kept him company – ☉ – afterwards read – wrote – saw Marsico – Belmonte – stayed with my children – had dinner and went to bed – the children well – after lunch the King went to Portici and returned only at 10 o'clock in the evening.

On Saturday June the 26th, I got up at 7 o'clock – dressed – had breakfast – combed my hair – heard Holy Mass – combed my hair [sic] – read – wrote my post – saw my children at ten o'clock I went with Prince Belmonte to Molosiglio – I went on board the brigantine – at one o'clock the English commander came there with his captain – we lunched at a table for nine people – then at half past 4 I went back – I undressed – had a rest – saw de Marco – San Marco – then dressed – gave 21 hearings and went to the theatre – I had a bad day and suffered a lot – in the morning the King was on the brigantine where I lunched – after lunch to Posillipo where he returned at midnight.

On Sunday June the 27th, I got up – dressed – lunch – combed my hair – heard Holy Mass – kept myself busy – read – wrote – lunched with the King – read ++++ – kept myself busy – read my letters +++ – afterwards my children – finished my affairs – received audience Malaspina – Monterotondo – dressed – went to the opera – from there by dray with the King and other people – to have dinner at the little house in Santa Lucia – and Baron d'hier[390] there and then walked to Chiaia – on walk was the first sunny day, the children well – after lunch the King went to Posillipo by sea to play music.

On Monday June the 28th, I got up at 7 o'clock – had breakfast – dressed – heard Holy Mass – saw my children – at 10 o'clock the Council – then kept the King company – ☉ after lunch – <u>read</u> +++++++ – afterwards wrote – kept myself busy – <u>read</u> + – afterwards went to the terrace with my children – then went to the opera and to the Fondo for an act – from there home – the children well – after lunch the King went to Portici and returned in the evening.

On Tuesday June the 29th, I got up at 7 o' clock – dressed – had breakfast – combed my hair – heard Holy Mass – wrote – read – saw my children – talked with de Marco – Prince Tarsia – Marsico – lunched with my children – talked with San Marco – then with a Sicilian regarding a problem – with Sangro – Sambuca – dressed and went out with my three daughters by one horse carriage – went to the pier and to the Chiaia promenade – afterwards returned to talk to Vasto – walked and then gave the letters to Sambuca – stayed with my girls on the terrace – read and then to bed – the children well – the King at eleven o'clock went to Castellamare and remained there all day.

On Wednesday June the 30th, I got up at 7 o'clock – had breakfast – dressed – combed my hair – heard Holy Mass – worked on my affairs – read – wrote – kept myself busy – saw my children – saw Sambuca – lunched with the children – then read – the King returned and went to sleep and so did – I kept him company – ☉ – afterwards walked on the terrace – dressed – went to the Council – after that at 10 o'clock I went with the King by dray to trot as far as the point of Posillipo – and then a promenade to Chiaia – and at midnight home – the children well – the King returned at 4 o'clock in the afternoon from Castellamare and spent the rest of the time at home.

On Thursday July the 1st, I got up at 7 o'clock – dressed – had breakfast – combed my hair – went out – attended Louise who had two teeth extracted – had breakfast with her – heard Holy Mass – kept myself busy wrote and worked on my affairs[391] – Gagliani then Tarsia – Onorato – read my letters – had lunch with the children – took care of them – then talked to San Marco – gave some hearings – spent the whole evening with my children and my dear husband on the terrace – the children well – the King went to have dinner and perform manœuvres with the English squadron.

On Friday July the 2nd, I got up – dressed – had breakfast – combed my hair – heard Holy Mass – took part to the two Councils – had lunch with the King – read – slept – kept busy all day between my children [and my] – husband – in the evening [made] my toilette and went to the Academy, where there was music and I played reversis with Belmonte – Gravina and Caramanico – the children well – the King did not go out all day.

On Saturday July the 3rd, I got up – dressed – had breakfast – combed my hair – heard Holy Mass – was busy – spoke to my confessor – lunched with the King – read – kept myself busy – kept him company – ☉ – then wrote my post + – afterwards made my toilette – then went to hearings of which there were 27 – then to the Fondo [theatre] for an act, the children well – the King remained all day at home.

On Sunday July the 4th, I got up – dressed – combed my hair – heard Holy Mass – worked on my affairs – spoke to San Nicola – lunched with my children – read – wrote – kept myself busy – saw San Marco – made my toilette – then went to the San Carlo theatre and from there to the [fair] – the children well – the King lunched on his brigantine and did not return until evening.

On Monday July the 5th, I got up – dressed – had breakfast – combed my hair – heard Holy Mass – and then talked with Sambuca – then lunched with the King – kept him company – after read + – wrote for the courrier – kept myself busy and to bed – the children well – the King at 4 o'clock went to walk by the sea and remained there.

On Tuesday July the 6th, I got up – dressed – had breakfast – combed my hair – heard Holy Mass – saw Acton – then de Marco – [with] my children – lunched with them – kept myself busy – read – wrote – talked with San Nicola – the King came back – I kept him company – ☉ – then the Council – kept myself busy and to bed – the children well – the King – who had been since the day before by the sea – at 3 ½ returned home and did not go out anymore.

On Wednesday July the 7th, I got up – dressed – had breakfast – heard Holy Mass – was busy reading – writing then had lunch with the King – read – wrote – took care of my children – saw Countess Althan – combed my hair – presided over the Council – as I felt strongly unwell – I did not go out and went to bed – the children well – in the morning the King validated the lance – in the evening he went to Florentines and to the promenade at Chiaia.

On Thursday July the 8th, I got up – dressed – went to Amelia's room to let her try a wet nurse – was withheld [from her] – afterwards I bled – then I lay down – saw my children – afterwards Mass – had lunch – read – took care of my children – took them to the drawing lesson – combed my hair – dressed – stayed with the children and [went] to the theatre to [see] one act – and then to bed the King sailed all morning – went with me to the theatre – then went to the promenade at Chiaia and had dinner in the little house at Santa Lucia.

On Friday July the 9th, I got up at 7 o'clock – dressed – had breakfast – combed my hair – heard Holy Mass – read – wrote – saw my ladies – kept myself busy – settled all with my children – at half past 9 the King came to have lunch – then I read +++ – afterwards kept myself busy – worked on my affairs and presided over the two Councils – took care of my children and to bed The King in the morning went to have breakfast at sea on a English lifeboat – came back at 3 o'clock for lunch and did no go out – my children fine – except little Amelia with a frightening thinness and with a kind of marasmus for which one would like to give her the milk of the wet nurse, but this will be impossible.

On Saturday July the 10th, I got up at 7 o'clock – dressed – combed my hair – went up to Amelia's room – I did all I could to breastfeed her – then stayed with the children – had breakfast with Francis – heard Mass – combed my hair – had lunch with the King – read ++++ – then kept the King company – ⊙ – took care of my children – I dressed – gave 30 hearings – and then to the opera with my two eldest daughters. The King after lunch went by boat – the children fine – except Amelia did not want take breast – despite several attempts it was necessary to feed her with donkey milk for feeding.

On Sunday July the 11th, I woke up – had breakfast with Theresa – dressed – heard Holy Mass – took care of my children – read my letters – spoke with the regent – lunched with my children – took care of them – read + wrote – kept myself busy – received the Council – combed my hair – dressed – went with my three girls by one horse carriage to Posillipo – met the King – returned by dray – went to the San Carlo theatre – from there to the promenade at Chiaia – he had dinner at the little house in Santa Lucia. The children well – the King went at eleven by lifeboat to Posillipo and returned in the evening with me.

On Monday July the 12th, I got up at 8 o'clock – had breakfast – combed my hair – heard Holy Mass – presided over the Council – saw my children – read – wrote – kept myself busy – talked with Marsico – lunched with the children – talked with the regent – with Cavi – then – read – wrote – kept myself busy – gave some hearings – spoke to Lady Sangro – then went out by one horse carriage with Theresa – Sangro – Rocella and Spinelli – to Posillipo to [take] breath of air – but in vain – then returned through Santa Lucia – undressed – had supper and went to bed – the children well – the King at elen o'clock went Castellamare by sea and stayed there.

On Tuesday July the 13th, mardy I got up at half past 2 in the morning – having had a strong blaze throughout the body that did not allow me to rest – I began to write – to walk on the terrace – then dressed – combed my hair – heard Holy Mass – had breakfast – kept myself busy – wrote my post – saw Marsico – San Nicola – then in the morning I had … p. ar.........[392] – after lunch with the children – took care of them – read – wrote – saw Acton – took care of the children – gave audiences – recorded my letters – saw Sangro and to bed – the children well – the King remained all night and all day to Castellamare.

On Wednesday July the 14th, I got up at 8 o'clock – after a terrible storm that there was during the night that I could not sleep – I dressed – had breakfast – heard Holy Mass – the King returned – I stayed with him – with my children – then spoke to San Marco – lunched with the King – kept him company – ☉ – read ++++ – slept for a while – changed – kept myself busy ++++ – stayed with the children – gave some hearings and went to the Council and to bed, the children well – in the morning the King went back and did not go out for all the day.

On Thursday July the 15th, I got up at 7 o'clock – had breakfast – dressed – heard Holy Mass – spoke to Sambuca – to Viceroy Caraciolo – lunched with my children and saw the wife and children of Troya – talked with Conradino – then read – wrote – kept myself busy – dressed – combed my hair – saw the King – in the evening to the opera at San Carlo, and then to bed – the children well – in the morning the King went to Caserta and returned in the evening.

On Friday July the 16th, I got up in the morning – had breakfast – dressed – went to Mass – presided the two Councils – then had lunch with the King – kept him company – ☉ – afterwards reading – kept myself busy – stayed with my children – at half past 6 I went with the King to the Carmelites in public – received the blessing – on return I changed – saw Caraciolo for a moment – then read – talked with Vacher – at half past eleven the King came to me and I went with him to the promenade at Chiaia – at one hour o'clock after having seen him embark – I went back – the children well – the King went at one o'clock [at night] to see the acrobats to the Fondo theatre – then he picked me up – afterwards he embarked.

On Saturday July the 17th, I got up – dressed – lunch – spoke to Marsico – heard Holy Mass – read – wrote – kept myself busy – had lunch with my children – kept myself busy – read – saw San Nicola – talked with

Sambuca – with San Marco – dressed – saw Lady Hereria – 23 hearings and then to the Florentines [theatre] to get bored myself and to bed – the children well – the King – who left during night – at midday came back at the pier – he came back at midnight.

On Sunday July the 18th, that year which I was dying – nobody remember that – and I with a General unconsciousness which stil increases – I got up – dressed – had breakfast – combed my hair – heard Holy Mass – took care of my children – wrote – worked on my affairs – had lunch with the King – read – slept – kept myself busy – wrote – saw my children – made my toilette – saw the Hungarian Guards – went to the opera to San Carlo theatre – then to the promenade at Chiaia and then home – the children well – after lunch the King went to Posillipo by boat and returned by land.

On Monday July the 19th, woke up at half past 6 with the news Mimi had a strong paroxysm – I jumped out of bed and ran – then dressed – had breakfast – went to the children's room – presided over the Council – had lunch with the King – read ++ – kept him company – ⊙ – then took care of my child – busy with my affairs – in the evening dressed – wrote – talked with Sambuca – then the King picked me up and I went with him to the promenade at Chiaia – and then to bed – the children fine – Mimi had a paroxysm – then came the fever – tried to purge her – after lunch she got up – came to me – was happy – then she lay down again – fever was quite strong – she did not eat for all the day – the King was at the sea for a while – in the evening he went to see the acrobats and then to stroll.

On Tuesday July the 20th, I got up at 7 o'clock – went to Mimi's room – saw her health – had breakfast – dressed – combed my hair – heard Holy Mass – wrote my letters – worked on my affairs – had lunch with the King – read +++ – wrote – kept myself busy – stayed with the sick child – took care – read and had lunch with Theresa and to bed – the children well – my dear Mimi during night had a second fever which debilitated her a lot – she was purged – vomited everything and had a terrible doziness – this indicated that she needed an emetic – which she took [19] times and which took effect – but which prostrated her a lot – especially because of the ice and water – finally was always dozing.The King went out only at night to see a play at the Florentine [theatre].

On Wednesday July the 21st, I got up at 7 o'clock and had Theresa's molar extracted and Louise's bandages removed – I had breakfast and took care of them and was with Mimi – I dressed – at 10 o'clock [went] to the Council – then lunched with the King – read+++ – wrote – kept myself busy – stayed with the sick child – read – saw the ladies – spoke to San Marco – Policastro[393] and then dressed – to the promenade at Chiaia with the King and thence to bed – the children well – dear Mimi during the night had her third fever – she was purged with sweet mercury – was very dejected but less than the previous day – she wanted to eat and took a bit of broth with soup which undigested she vomited after two hours – she was prostrated and approximately at midnight forced by taking the enemas we caused her such [flatulence] which gave her a little relief. The King after lunch went to Portici for a while and went back – then went to Florentines and afterwards picked me up to go to the promenade at Chiaia.

On Thursday July the 22nd, I got up at 7 o'clock – dressed – had breakfast – combed my hair – went to Mimi's room and with her I went to the porcelain [factory] – stayed home – dressed – went to Mass – kept myself busy – saw my child – had lunch with the King – read+++ – wrote – took care of my little patient – went to both Councils and then to the promenade at Chiaia – the children fine – Mimi was getting better – she still had a fever – she asked to be able to get up and was out of bed for three times – but was still very weak – she was purged with four doses of policrest salt, the other children well – the King did not go out all day – only with me for a promenade at Chiaia – whence he went to sleep on board the brigantine at the pier.

On Saturday July the 23rd, I got up at 7 o'clock – had breakfast – dressed – combed my hair – saw my little sick child – took care – saw the King who could not leave – kept myself busy – had lunch with the King – read – kept him company – ⊙ – then saw my children – kept myself busy – dressed – read – had dinner with my daughters and to bed – in the morning the King could not leave – the children fine – the little sick child better but still with fever.

On Saturday July the 24th, dear Mimi's birthday – I went to wish her [happy birthday] – she was better – I had breakfast with my eldest daughters – toilette – hand-kissing – Mass – kept the King company – ⊗ – and undressed – had dinner – read + +++ – dressed again – read – gave 31 hearings – went with my daughters to see one act of the opera – the children well – my dear Mimi had almost no fever and was up all day. The King went at 7 o'clock to Ischia.

On Sunday July the 25th, I got up at 7 o'clock – dressed – had breakfast – combed my hair – spoke to de Marco – to Count Pignatelli – took care of my children – had lunch with them – took care of them – talked with Sambuca – read – wrote – kept myself busy – then talked with Viceroy Caracciolo – afterwards [went] with the two eldest girls to the theatre – and then with them to the fair – where they went one and a half times around the promenade – at midnight I was at home and [went] to bed – the children well – the King remained in Ischia all day and wrote to me.

On Monday July the 26th, I got up at 7 o' clock – dressed – had breakfast – combed my hair – heard Holy Mass – spoke to Gagliano – Calabrito[394] – Caracciolo – Marsico – lunched with my children – took care of them – then read – wrote – kept myself busy – talked with Rocella – Lady Belmonte – Lord Gravina and to bed – the children well the King remained in Ischia all day.

On Tuesday July the 27th, I got up early to write my letters – had breakfast with Louise to whom I wished happy birthday – I took care of my children – made my toilette – heard Mass – saw Sambuca – the whole court – undressed – had lunch with the children – took care of them – talked with Acton – read++ – wrote – kept myself busy – saw Ostumi – Casa buona – went to the opera with my two eldest girls and from there to bed – the children well – the King stayed all day in Ischia.

On Wednesday July the 28th, I got up – dressed – breakfasted – combed my hair – saw San Nicola – heard Mass – spoke to Sambuca – lunched with my children – read – kept myself busy – saw the King – kept him company – ⊙ then walked on the terrace – read+++ – wrote – kept myself busy – in the evening to the Council – then went to the fair – to the promenade at Chiaia – the children well – the King [came] from Ischia at 3 o'clock and did not leave.

On Thursday July the 29th, I got up – dressed – had breakfast – combed my hair – heard Holy Mass – went to Sambuca's Council – lunched with the King – read+++ – wrote – kept myself busy – read – dressed – saw Princess Caramanico – [with] my children – went at a tragedy to the new theatre and then to Chiaia – from there to bed – the children well – the King after lunch went to Portici for a couple of hours.

On Friday July the 30th, I got up at 8:00 – dressed – had breakfast – combed my hair – heard Holy Mass – presided over the two Councils – which saved the problem of Cimitile's retirement – then had lunch – read – kept myself busy – saw my children – dressed – saw Sangro – not feeling well I could not go out and lay on a sofa lying – at half past 10 I went to bed – the children well – the King went to Capo di monte after lunch – in the evening to the play and to the promenade at Chiaia.

On Saturday July the 31st, I got up at half past 7 – dressed – had breakfast – heard Holy Mass – busy – wrote my letters – had lunch with the children – took care of them – then saw and talked with Sambuca, Lady San Marco, Count Michele Pignatelli – talked with Butera – gave 29 hearings – then confessed [my sins] – the children well – the King at 9 o'clock went to Portici and came back at eleven.

On Sunday August the 1st, I got up at half past 6 and had the joy of going to church to perform my devotions – then made my toilette – dressed – had myself painted – had lunch with the children – talked with Sambuca – kept myself busy – read – wrote – made my toilette – went to Posillipo – picked the King up and went with him to receive indulgences at San Pasquale – on returning kept him company – ⊗ – then undressed – packed my papers – then dressed again and went to the promenade at Chiaia, which – with the full moon and lots of people – was superb – we stayed there until half past one – the children well – the King went to lunch at Posillipo and returned with me – he went to the Florentines theatre and then came to take me for a walk

On Monday August the 2nd, I got up – dressed – had breakfast – combed my hair – worked on my affairs – heard Holy Mass – went with Theresa to Ospedaletto[395] – received indulgences – and then lunched with the King – read – wrote the letters – kept myself busy – talked with Gravina – read – dressed – saw a lot of ladies – then to the Council – worked on my affairs and to bed – the children well – King went to the dock to fish and then to the promenade at Chiaia.

On Tuesday August the 3rd, I got up at 7 o'clock – arranged my affairs – had breakfast with my children – dressed – heard Holy Mass – at 9 o'clock we went – my three daughters and I – on the brigantine – we had lunch there and the trip was very pleasant – at half past 1 we arrived at Castellamare – I got in a horse carriage with my children – settled the house and my affairs and was busy all day with the children and my affairs – at half past 9 I had supper with the little company that we have here and [went] to bed – the children fine – the little girl performed her devotions – the King came with us – remained to have lunch on board and then.[396]

On Wednesday August the 4th, I got up at 7 o'clock – strolled with my daughters for a while – had breakfast with my children down in the cavern – then dressed – combed my hair – attended to the lessons of my childen – heard Holy Mass – ☉ – busy – had lunch in company – read – slept – took care of my children – saw Vespoli who was director of finances – then walked with my children and came back at home – took care of them – had dinner and to bed – the children well – little Mimi followed with her devotions – the King in the morning went down and after lunch [went] to the building site.

On Thursday August the 5th, I got up – dressed – had breakfast – went to walk for a while – saw my children – heard Holy Mass – read – wrote – kept myself busy – had lunch with the King – read the letters – busy with my children – my affairs until evening – walked with the children – Ardore, Popoli – who each informed me that their wives have given birth to a son [Caivane] – Cimitile – Cimitile who were appointed to the post of State directors – came to thank me in the evening – on returning – the Spanish courrier came to ruin [my day] – he brought me the news that a boat was blown with our two brave young men and also brought mere bad news – spent a bad night – did not have dinner and went to bed – the children fine – the King went in the morning and in the evening to the building site.

On Friday August the 6th, I got up – dressed – had breakfast – combed my hair – kept myself busy – heard Holy Mass – busy – dejected – after lunch with Acton – Belmonte and Abbott Ricci[397] who brought the order of diana to the King – then read – kept myself busy – at 6 o'clock went with my eldest children to the building site – came back – presided over the Council – had dinner and to bed – the children well – the King went to swimm in the morning and in the evening went to the building site.

On Saturday 7 August the 7th, I got up – dressed – had breakfast – combed my hair – heard Holy Mass – busy – spoke with the King + – and then combed my hair and dressed again – then lunched – read – kept myself busy – walked with my children for a while – kept busy in my room – afterwards had supper and to bed – the children well – the King went to the building site in the morning – after lunch strolled.

On Sunday August the 8th, I got up in the morning – had breakfast – walked – read – kept myself busy – talked with the King and Acton – made my toilette – heard Holy Mass – had lunch – kept the King company – ⊙ – then read +++++ – wrote – I kept myself busy – walked – kept busy and to bed – the children well – the King in the morning went fishing for a while and after lunch went for a walk.

On Monday August the 9th, I got up – dressed – had breakfast – combed my hair – heard Holy Mass – secretly confessed [my sins] – spoke to my people – wrote – read – kept myself busy – lunched – talked with Rasoumovski – then with Sambuca – afterwards walked – then the Council where the King told Sambuca some hard truths – had dinner and then to bed – the children well – the King at 4 o'clock went to Posillipo by land – lunched in Naples with the children, and then came back at 7 o'clock.

On Tuesday August the 10th, I got up – dressed – had breakfast – combed my hair – combed my hair – kept the King company – ⊙ – then wrote my letters – lunched – slept – talked with Sambuca – then walked and went to [receive] the blessing in the little chapel – on returning read and kept busy – then went to have supper and to bed – the children well – the King was at home and did not go out after lunch [went to] Mortela on horseback.

On Wednesday August the 11th, I got up – dressed – had breakfast – wrote – kept myself busy – presided over the Council – lunched – and then to bed – took care of the children – wrote – to the second Council – talked to de Marco – Pignatelli – Marsico – took care of my children and went to bed – the children well – except Mimi who vomited and was purged all day and was not too well – the King after lunch went to the building site for a while and came back right away.

On Thursday August the 12th, I woke up – dressed – had breakfast – combed my hair – heard Holy Mass – took an ounce of epsom salt to purge myself and spent the whole day suffering – then lunched – there was count Michele who came to thank me and Gravina – then read – kept myself busy – wrote – in the evening to bed without having lunched – not feeling too well + the children well – the King after lunch went to Mauro and returned in the evening.

On Friday August the 13th, I woke up at 7 o'clock – got up – dressed – had breakfast with my children – made my toilette – heard Holy Mass – saw those who had come to wish me [happy birthday] – lunched with the world – and then read +++ kept myself busy – kept the King company – ⊙ – afterwards saw a little dance performed by my children – Princess Caramanico came to thank me on behalf of her husband who has been appointed ambassador to France – afterwards looked after my children – the King played music – and afterwards had supper and to bed – the children well – the King in the morning went fishing – returned at nine o'clock and did not go out for the rest of the day.

On Saturday August the 14th, I got up – dressed – had breakfast – combed my hair – heard Holy Mass – saw my children – wrote all my letters – kept myself busy – had lunch with the King – read+++ – wrote – kept busy all day – in the evening went with the King to receive the blessing and all day in my room until supper time – the children well – the King in the morning went to the building site and did not go out for the rest of the day.

On Sunday August the 15th, I got up early – heard the second Mass of the King – then breakfasted – read – wrote – dressed – heard Mass – afflicted myself – strolled around – lunched – read – kept myself busy – went for a walk – with the King to receive the blessing – on returning in the evening with the children [went] to puppets theatre and to bed – the children well – in the morning the King went for a walk.

On Monday August the 16th, I got up in the morning at 7 o'clock – dressed – had breakfast – combed my hair – heard Holy Mass – strolled – dressed – kept the King company – ⊙ – then dinner – read ++++ – wrote – kept myself busy – arranged my papers to go downtown to the Council and to bed – the children well – the King in the morning went out and after lunch to walk.

On Tuesday August the 17th, I got up at half past 3 in the morning – dressed and went down by one horse carriage to the port – embarked on the lugger – lunched – heard Mass – at Portici I had to put myself in a boat – the sea was calm – at half past 9 I arrived – rest – arranged my affairs – saw my children – talked with San Marco – dinner with the King – read – slept – finished my post – made my toilette – saw Belmonte – Sangro – then went to the new theatre and from there I went home – slept – [wrote] the children – both those I left in Castellamare – and also those I met in Naples – – the King well – after having taken me as far as Portici – where I got into a rowingboat – [he]got into another one and went at Posillipo – he returned for lunch and in the afternoon went back for a couple of hours – in the evening he went with me to the theatre.

On Wednesday August 18, I got up at 7 o'clock – dressed – had reak-fast – combed my hair – heard Holy Mass – then saw Acton – San Nicola – Caracciolo – Cattolica – Luchesi – Marsico – ladies – saw my children – had lunch with the King – read + wrote – kept myself busy – presided over the Council – kept the King company to – ⊙ – afterwards gave hearings – talked with Althan – Sangro – Caramanico and others – then went to the opera – the King went there – after the first act both finished we went home and to bed – the children well – the King in the morning went fishing at Portici – in the evening [went to] launch.

On Thursday August the 19th, my son Francis is eight years – I got up – dressed – had breakfast with him – heard Holy Mass – dressed – combed my hair – [went to] important hand-kissing – public table – I felt sick – I went to bed – then had lunch only at three o'clock – read – kept myself busy – at five o'clock [there was] the Council – then dressed – made toilette – saw Lady Hereria – hand-kissing of the ladies – afterwards undressed – went to the opera at San Carlo – kept the King company – ⊙ – then [went to] sleep – the children well – the King because of the Gala could not go out at all today.

On Friday August the 20th, I woke up at 7 o'clock – dressed – had breakfast – heard Holy Mass – kept myself busy – arranged my affairs – saw my children – went to see vicar Pignatelli[398] who has returned from Calabria – then read letters from Spain – at ten o'clock I went onto the brigantine – where reports of Algir were read by Acton – spoke – lunched at half past at 2 – we arrived at Castellamare – read – wrote – unpacked – saw my children – spruced myself up – [went to] the Council – had supper and to bed – the children fine – the King went with me and remained until the evening with me.

On Saturday August the 21st, I got up – dressed – had breakfast – combed my hair – heard Holy Mass – busy writing – reading – seeing my children – had lunch together – read + – slept – [made my] toilette again – saw my children – kept myself busy and then to bed – the children well – the King went out and in evening to the building site for a while.

On Sunday August the 22nd, I got up at 7 o'clock – dressed – had breakfast – combed my hair – heard Holy Mass – saw my children – kept myself busy – kept the King company – ⊙ – then had lunch – read – slept – dressed again – wrote – read+ – stayed with my children – kept myself busy +++ – and then to bed – the children well – the King went out only at half pasr 6 to sleep at Portici.

On Monday August the 23rd, I woke up with a bit of colic – dressed – had breakfast – combed my hair – heard Mass – spoke to Marsico – wrote – kept myself busy – saw my children – lunched with them – stayed with people – talked with Rasoumowsky – wrote – read – kept myself busy – strolled with Corleto – Rasoumowsky and Montalto – then kept myself busy – at 8 o'clock the King came back – the Council – had supper and to bed – the children well – the King – who had slept at Portici – went to San Leonardo – killed 200 quails – then went to have lunch at Posillipo – afterwards to the *tonara* and from there back home.

On Tuesday August the 24th, I got up at 7 o'clock – dressed – had breakfast – combed my hair – heard Holy Mass – wrote my letters – took care of my children – lunched – talked with the King – read – slept – talked with Lamberg – General Pignatelli – and Madam Cirillo[399] – afterwards took care of my children – to the Council and to bed – the children well – the King went to the building site in the morning and in the evening.

On Wednesday August the 25th, I got up in the morning – celebrated Louise's birthday – had breakfast with my children – then made my toilette – heard Mass – wrote – kept myself busy – talked with Viceroy

Caracciolo – lunched – kept the King company – ⊙ – then undressed – read +++ – kept myself busy – aftewards dressed again – went with my two eldest girls and the King by one horse carriage – to [see] the nuns – received the blessing – then to the convent – scolded Theresa – dinner and to bed – the children well – the King in the morning went fishing – after lunch he went out with me.

On Thursday August the 26th, I got up at 8 o'clock – dressed – had breakfast – cobed my hair – heard Holy Mass – kept my self busy – wrote – saw my children – had lunch with the King – was on guard while I read[400] – wrote – kept my self busy – saw my children – walked – gave few hearings and to bed – the children well – the King went in the morning and after lunch to the building site – in the evening he remained at the puppets theatre.

On Friday August 27, I got up at 7 o'clock – had breakfast – dressed – combed my hair – heard Holy Mass – ⊙ – kept myself busy – read – wrote – had lunch with the King – read – kept my self busy – read – walked – [went to] the Council and had supper in bed – the children well – the King in the morning went to the building site – in the afternoon on horseback to Mortella.

On Saturday August the 28th, I got up in the morning – had breakfast – dressed – wrote my post – read + – then dressed – heard Holy Mass – kept myself busy – lunched with the King – read – strolled to the pier with Acton – San Nicola and Montalto – saw the building site and returned with the King – talked about the Messina affair and to bed. The children well – the King in the morning went out for a walk and after lunch went fishing.

On Sunday August the 29th, I got up at 7 o'clock – had breakfast – combed my hair – read+ – wrote – arranged my affairs – dressed – heard Mass – kept myself busy – had lunch with the King – read+ – wrote – talked with Rasoumowsky – kept the King company – ⊙ – arranged my affairs and to bed – the children fine – the King in the morning went fishing – after lunch he went at 2 o'clock to [same] and came back at 7 o' clock from hare hunting.

On Monday August the 30th, I got up at 4 o'clock – made a short toilette and went down by one horse carriage to embark on the brigantine – we got into a rowingboat because of the calm in Torre del Greco and arrived in Naples – fortunately I saw my children – there worked on my affairs – arranged my papers – sent my letters – saw de Marco – the King came back – I went with him and Acton to the terrace – and had dinner – read – slept – worked on my affairs – the Council – [made my] toilette and then [went to see] a comic opera at the Florentine theatre – whence home – the children well – the King went with me until the Torre[401] – from there he went to the *tonara* at Posillipo – to kill a lot of tuna – returned at one o'clock for lunch and only went out in the evening to the theatre with me.

On Tuesday August the 31st, I got up at 7 o'clock – dressed – had breakfast – combed my hair – heard Holy Mass – worked on my affairs – kept myself busy – the arrival of the [naval] squadron – or at least – the news that it was coming worried me – I went to church to receive the blessing with the King – and then read letters – after dinner – Read – kept myself busy – read – and gave hearing Torre and his daughter – [went] to listen to letters being read – Gabriele – S. Cipriano[402] Donna Pepa – to Ottajano – Malaspina – then to Lady Sambuca – Avelino – Tursis – Lord Sambuca – to Sangro and from there to bed – the children well – the King went fishing in the morning – came back to lunch and left at 3 o'clock to meet the [naval] squadron.

On Wednesday September the 1st, I got up at 7 o'clock – dressed – had breakfast – combed my hair – heard Holy Mass – then talked with Tarsia and Vasto and kept myself busy – then talked with Gravina – went with my children to [receive] the blessing into church and then had lunch with them – took care of them – read – wrote – read + – then stayed with the children – saw them having dinner – and then kept myself busy +++ and to bed – the children well – the King remained all day in Procida whence he wrote to me healthy.

On Thursday September the 2nd, I got up at 7 o'clock – dressed – had breakfast – combed my hair – heard Holy Mass – spoke to Dom Cicio Pignatelli – San Nicola – Cattolica – San Marco – went to church with my children – lunched with them – saw Sambuca with letters from Spain – then Acton – at half past 3 our squadron which appeared – acompanied by the King – returned from Algir[403] – it was beautiful to see it – I was out all day to see it with Acton – then dressed – saw the King and to the theatre – the children well – the King remained all day at sea and returned with the squadron.

On Friday September the 3rd, I got up at 7 o'clock – dressed – had breakfast – combed my hair – heard Holy Mass – went to the Council – then to the chapel to the blessing – saw my children – lunched with the King – slept – read – wrote – I kept myself busy – Read + – then kept the King company – ☉ – afterwards another Council – saw the children and to bed The children well – the King went on board in the morning – after lunch [went] to Volla [to hunt] quails.

<u>On Saturday September the 4th,</u> I got up – dressed – had breakfast – combed my hair – heard Holy Mass – the Council – then to the chapel – saw my children – afterwards went with Belmonte on board the brigantine and lunched with the naval officiers that had returned from Algir – at half past 4 I went back – took a rest – <u>read</u> – kept myself busy – wrote my letters – gave 22 hearings – then to the Florentines theatre. The children well – the King went with me on board – then – after having acompanied me – he went to Portici [to] the flood and took 5000 sparrows and from there to the Florentine [theatre] to see both acts.

On Sunday September the 5th, I got up – dressed – lunch – combed my hair – saw and talked about the promotion with the King and Acton – went to the chapel and heard Mass – kept the King company – ⊙ – then spruced myself up and went to the dock – then embarked on the brigantine with Acton – where we had lunch with the rest of the naval Captain who have returned from Algir – then after lunch we went to see St. John – St. Joachim and Minerva[404] – then home – had a rest and afterwards various hearings – I went to the theatre where the children – or rather the two eldest girls – went with me – the children well – the King was with me all day.

<u>On Monday September the 6th,</u> I got up – dressed – had breakfast – combed my hair – worked on my affairs – took part in the Council – and then went to the chapel and was blessed – heard Holy Mass with the King – saw my children – dinner – talked to San Marco – the tax [lawyer] Vivenzio[405] – then read – kept myself busy – walked on my terrace – made toilette – the King returned tired from hunting – I undressed and went to bed – the children well – the King went at half past twelve in San Leonardo hunting quail and came back at half past 8.

<u>On Tuesday September the 7th,</u> I got up at 7 o'clock – dressed – combed my hair – heard Holy Mass – then bled 6 ounces of blood – after lunch – rest – saw my children – had lunch with the King – read ++++ – and wrote – kept myself busy in the evening – dessed again and go to play, the children well – the King was at home.

<u>On Wednesday September the 8th,</u> the day of Pie di Grotta – I got up – dressed – combed my hair – had breakfast – heard Holy Mass – presided over the Council – then lunched with the King – kept him company while we watched the troops parading – saw my children combed and spruced – made my toilette – at half past 4 we went out in public with all our children

to Pie di Grotta – I kept the King company – ☉ – then had a rest – dressed again and to the San Carlo theatre – after the first ballet we went to the promenade at Chiaia which was lit – and after a bit we came home – the children fine – the King only went out in public and always with me.

On Thursday September 9, I got up at 7 o'clock – dressed – had breakfast – combed my hair – heard Holy Mass – kept myself busy – worked on my affairs – spoke to the King – my confessor – took care of the children – lunched with the King – read – talked with Cari – then <u>read</u> + – then spoke to de Marco – Lady Belmonte – made my toilette and went to the San Carlo theatre and from there [went] to sleep – the children well – the King went after lunch went to shoot quails at Volla.

On Friday September 10, I got up at 7 o'clock – dressed – had breakfast – combed my hair – heard Holy Mass – presided over the Council – then kept myself busy – lunched with the King – read – slept – <u>read</u> – wrote – kept myself busy – talked with Lady San Marco – kept myself busy and to bed – the children well – the King went after lunch to Posillipo and remained there in the evening to launch.

<u>On Saturday September the 11th,</u> I got up – dressed – had breakfast – heard Holy Mass – spoke to Lady Filingieri for a long time and then had lunch with my children – read – I kept myself busy – chose the trousseau for Lisette – then gave 40 hearings and kept myself busy and to bed – the children well – the King went in the morning and after lunch to Posillipo – in the evening he was at home.

<u>On Sunday September the 12th,</u> I got up at 7 o'clock – dressed – had breakfast – combed my hair – heard Holy Mass – kept myself busy – spoke to San Nicola – lunched with my children – <u>read</u> – wrote – talked with Caracciolo, in the evening saw Countess Althan – Lady Belmonte and to bed – the children well – the King went fishing – had lunch and was all day at Posillipo – he returned at midnight and did not go out anymore.

<u>On Monday September the 13th,</u> I got up at 7 o'clock – dressed – had breakfast – combed my hair – heard Holy Mass – then saw the two Hauss brothers who had come to be preceptors of my son – then the Council – kept the King company – ☉ – lunched – read – wrote – saw San Marco – read – then saw Gravina – my children – introduced the Hauss brothers to them – and then to bed – the children well – the King went after lunch to St. Leonardo to shoot quails and returned in the evening.

On Tuesday September the 14th, I got up – dressed – had breakfast – combed my hair – heard Holy Mass – wrote my letter – read + – and then had lunch with my children – read – kept myself busy – talked with a Sicilian called Fidoto – walked – took care of my children +++ and to bed – the children well – the King in the morning went fishing at Portici – lunched here and returned only at midnight without leaving anymore.

On Wednesday September the 15th, I got up at 7 oclock – dressed – had breakfast – combed my hair – heard Holy Mass – presided over the Council – discussed some matters with the King – had lunch – read – kept the King company – ⊙ – had a rest – read – ket myself busy – saw the Herzans[406] husband and wife – then went with Marsico – Migliano – Corleto – picked the King up at Posillipo – got in a dray with him and returned – the children well – the King after lunch went fishing – throwing – to the *tonara* – at Posillipo.

On Thursday September the 16th, I got up – dressed – had breakfast – combed my hair – heard Holy Mass – kept myself busy – spoke to Hauss – lead them to my son's room – lunched with the King – read – wrote – I kept myself busy – read – and in the evening went with the King at the academy – where there was music – on returning kept ther King company – ⊙ – then to bed – the children well – the King went after lunch to Volla – to shoot quails and in the evening to the academy.

On Friday September the 17th, I got up – dressed – had breakfast – combed my hair – heard Holy Mass – busy – lunched with my children – spoke to several persons – read + – wrote – I kept myself busy – walked – talked with San Marco – saw my children – to the Council and to bed – the children fine – the King in the morning fished at Portici – and after lunch went [to hunt] quails – in the evening he was at home.

On Saturday September the 18th, I got up – dressed – had breakfast – combed my hair – heard Holy Mass – kept myself busy – saw Acton – read + + – wrote – I kept myself busy – lunched with my children – took care of them – talked with San Marco – with Luchesi – the Countess Herzan to whom I showed my children and my house – then gave 40 hearings – put curlers and [went] to bed – the children well – the King in the morning went to the mountains to hunt – after lunch [went] fishing and was at Portici all day and did not return until night.

On Sunday September the 19th, I got up – dressed – had breakfast with the King and Theresa – combed my hair – dressed – heard Holy Mass – went to the chapel – took part in the function – saw people – undressed – had lunch with my children – read + + + + – wrote – I kept myself busy – toilette again – then went to the academy where – after having heard music – I started to play a match – for a while – and then went to sleep. The children well – the King went out with me.

On Monday September the 20th, I got up – dressed – lunch – had breakfast – heard Holy Mass – spoke to Luchesi – Sambuca – Gravina – Viceroy Caracciolo – lunched with the children – then kept myself busy – read – spoke to de Marco – Belmonte – kept myself busy and to bed – afterwards the Council – the children well – the King in the morning went to the fair at Salerno and returned in the evening.

On Tuesday September the 21st, I got up at 7 o'clock – and went to perform my devotions unworthily in church – then had breakfast – dressed – combed my hair – heard Holy Mass – wrote then lunched with the King – read – kept myself busy – dressed – went for a ride at Posillipo with the King in a dray – kept him company – undressed – gave several hearings and to bed – the children well – the King went out with me for a walk.

On Wednesday September the 22nd, I got up – dressed – had breakfast – combed my hair – heard Holy Mass – presided over the Council – then had lunch with my children – kept myself busy – read – wrote – kept myself busy – afterwards talked with Hauss and to bed – the children well – the King in the morning went on board the *Minerva* – after lunch to Volla – I had fever all day.

On Thursday September the 23rd, I dressed – up at 7 o'clock – took an ounce of epsom salt – then walked – saw my children – heard Mass – took care of my children – lunched with the King – read – wrote – kept myself busy – read – spoke to Sambuca – then made my toilette and went to the academy – at half past ten home – the children well – the King went to St. Leonardo [to hunt]quails.

On Friday September the 24th, I got up in the morning – dressed – had breakfast – combed my hair – heard Holy Mass – went to the Council – then read – kept myself busy – lunched with the King – read – kept myself busy – then in the evening saw a girl singing and playing the harp with my children, the children well – the King [went hunting] quails at Volla.

On Saturday September the 25th, I got up – dressed – had breakfast – combed my hair heard Holy Mass – then kept myself busy – at eleven went with my three daughters to Madonna dei Fiorentini to hear Mass – then went to have lunch with the King – read – wrote – kept myself busy – saw people and gave 53 hearings – then to bed – the children well – the King went for a short time at Volla.

On Sunday September the 26th, I got up – dressed – had breakfast – combed my hair – heard Holy Mass – spoke to Marsico – then Vespoli – then General Pignatelli – after lunch [stayed] with my children – then talked with San Marco – with Fidotto – with Herzan – afterwards I dressed – saw Princess Gerace[407] – Monsignor Spinelli[408] and to the big theatre – the King went there – we were present at two acts and then to bed – the children well – the King was all day at Caserta and returned in the evening.

On Monday September the 27, I got up at 8 o'clock – dressed – had breakfast – combed my hair – heard Holy Mass – and the Council – then kept myself busy – lunched with the King – read – afterwards saw Acton – at half past three he was called because of a fire at the pier – I ran onto the terrace – and in a moment with great grief I saw that the beautiful vessel *San Giovanni* was going up in flames – they only thought saving the rest – I thought all day of this painful disaster in the evening – I spent the evening with the King ⊙ – then to bed – the children well – the King after lunch went to Volla.

On Tuesday the 28th, I got up – dressed – had breakfast – combed my hair – began to write letters – lunched with the King – read – kept him company – ⊙ – then kept myself busy – dressed and in the evening saw Lady Althan – afterwards [went to] a bad play at the Fondo theatre and to bed – the children well – the King went with me to the theatre and did not go out all day.

On Wednesday September the 29th, I got up at 8 o'clock – had breakfast – dressed – heard Holy Mass – presided over the Council – I kept myself busy – had lunch with the King – read – wrote – kept myself busy – made my toilette – at 5 o'clock I went with my three daughters to San Gaetano to receive the blessing – then by *Strada Nuova* at house and afterwards to the San Carlo theatre – the children well – the King went to Posillipo for a while.

On Thursday September the 30th, I got up – dressed – had breakfast – dressed – heard Holy Mass – <u>read</u> – wrote – I kept myself busy – had lunch with the King – read – kept myself busy – talked with Lady San Marco – then made toilette – gave hearings – and then went to the opera at San Carlo – afterwards home – the children well – the King after lunch went fishing at Posillipo.

On Friday August [sic] the 1st, I got up in the morning – had breakfast – dressed – combed my hair – heard Holy Mass – presided over the Council – then had lunch – read – kept myself busy – <u>read</u> – saw my children – made my toilette – went to the academy where I listened to music – and at home the children well – the King went to hunt at Volla.

On Saturday October the 2nd, I got up – dressed – dressed – and then I bled – had breakfast – had a rest – after bleeding wrote a little – read – kept myself busy – had lunch with the King – kept myself busy – a Swedish lady and 30 hearings – later to the theatre and frm there home – the children well – the King went a little to hear the rehearsal to the theatre and did not go out for the rest of the day.

On Sunday October the 3rd, I got up – dressed – had breakfast – combed my hair – heard Holy Mass – took care of my children – my affairs – lunched with the King – read+ – wrote – kept myself busy – then gave hearings and afterwards went to the theatre – ⊙ – the children well – the King went to hunt quails.

On Monday October the 4th, I got up – dressed – had breakfast with my son for his day[409] – heard Mass – afterwards the Council – then toilette – the hand-kissing – public table – had lunch privately – had a rest – kept the King company – ⊙ – afterwards kept myself busy – dressed again – hand-kissing of the ladies and to the theatre with Theresa – the children well – the King was all day at home there was a gala.

On Tuesday October the 5th, I got up – dressed – had breakfast – combed my hair – heard Holy Mass – began to write my letters – kept busy – then dinner with the children – took care [of them] – read – wrote – in the evening participated in the fateful wedding of Lisette[410] that I cried a lot – she cried with me as also my Theresa and married the officier [Sanchez] – then talked to several persons – made toilette and went to the academy – the children well – King went to St. Leonardo [to hunt]quails.

On Wednesday October the 6th, I got up – dressed – had breakfast – combed my hair – heard Holy Mass – spoke a long time with Gravina – then to Princess Torella – afterwards lunched with the King – kept him company – read – wrote – presided over the Council – then several audiences and to the theatre – where the King came to visit me – the children well – the King in the morning went to the swamp and in the evening diluvio of the sparrows at Portici.

On Thursday October the 7th, I got up – dressed – had breakfast – combed my hair – heard Holy Mass – busy – spoke with Caracciolo – Count Lamberg 2. □ – then read my letters – lunched with my children – read+ – wrote – kept myself busy – gave several hearings – made my toilette and went to the Florentines theatre – the children well – the King went to lunch at Fusaro and fished there.

On Friday October the 8th, I got up – dressed – had breakfast – combed my hair – went to the Councils – as I felt unwell I went to bed – then heard Mass – worked on my affairs – then lunched with the King – kept him company – saw Ladies Hereria – Althan – Belmonte – other ladies – made my toilette and went to the Academy – then home to keep the King company – ☉ – and then to bed – the children well – the King did not go out all day.

On Saturday October the 9th, I got up – dressed – had breakfast – combed my hair – heard Holy Mass – saw the King leaving – talked with de Marco – Acton – arranged my affairs – saw my children – before 10 o'clock I left with my three girls in a carriage with a very hard weather – at half past twelve we arrived at Caserta – then I had a rest – lunched in the company of the King and my children – said the rosary – arranged all my papers – saw my children – kept myself busy all evening and at 9 o'clock [went] to bed – the children well – the King after lunch went to San Leucio for a while.

On Sunday October the 10th, I got up at 7 o'clock – dressed – had breakfast – combed my hair – heard Holy Masses – then saw my children – devotted myself – read – wrote ++++++ – lunched with the King – kept myself busy – arranged my books – my papers – kept the King company – then saw my children – at half past nine undressed and went to bed – the children well – the King went after lunch to the pheasant farm.

On Monday October the 11th, I got up – dressed – had breakfast – combed my hair – heard Holy Mass – saw my children – wrote letters for some ladies – at three o'clock lunched with the King – read – kept him company – ☉ – then wrote – made my affairs – saw Gravina – went with him to the my son's apartment – talked to him – spoke to the King – saw my children – presided over the Council and went to bed, the children well – the King in the morning went to Belvedere – in the afternoon he walked.

On Tuesday October the 12th, I got up – dressed – had breakfast – combed my hair – heard Holy Mass – read – wrote – kept myself busy – saw canon Rossi[411] – my confessor – read ++++++ – then saw my children – on their arrival in Naples lunched with the King – read ++++ – then wrote – I walked through the rooms – read – wrote ++++ afterwards devoted myself – prayed – presided over de Marco's Council and went to bed – the children well – the King after lunch went to Carditello.

On Wednesday October the 13th, I got up at 7 o'clock – dressed – had breakfast – combed my hair – heard Holy Mass – read – wrote – kept myself busy – talked with Gravina – took care of my children – had lunch with the King – read – kept myself busy – saw my son's trousseau – had it stored – talked with Pignatelli – heard Theresa play the harpsichord – kept myself busy – stayed with my children and went to bed – the children well – the King went hunting in the morning – could not go to Pie di Monte because of the bad weather and came back at lunch time – after lunch he strolled.

On Thursday October the 14th, I got up – dressed – had breakfast – combed my hair – heard Holy Mass – saw my children – busy writing instructions for my son – saw Marsico – lunched with my children – took care of them – read – wrote – talked with Fedotto – then Princess Belmonte – busy praying – reading – saw the King – my children – kept myself busy and to bed, the children well – the King hunted all day to Piedimonte.

On Friday October the 15th, I got up at 7 o'clock – combed my hair – dressed – had breakfast with my four eldest children for Theresa's nameday – then heard two Masses – then went for a walk in the wood at Canalone with Francis – Theresa and Mimi – then I returned – changed – lunched with King – kept him company – ☉ – then read – wrote – kept myself busy – went to see Louise who is sick – presided over the Council – returned to Louise and to bed – the children well – except Louise with diarrohea and vomiting – the King in the morning rode to Caivano – after lunch he went to San Leucio.

On Saturday October the 16th, I got up – dressed – had breakfast – combed my hair – heard Holy Mass – read+ – wrote – kept myself busy – had lunch with my children – took care of them – saw the Spanish General – Countess Althan – then went with the King to my children' room – talked with him and Acton – then kept myself busy and to bed – the children well – the King in the morning went to Carditello […] on […] and after lunch to San Leucio – Theresa had a slight fever and cold – Louise a little trouble and stomach disorders – but both out of bed and without consequences.

On Sunday October the 17th, I got up at 7 o'clock – dressed – had breakfast – combed my hair – heard Holy Mass – read+ – wrote – kept myself busy – saw my children – talked with Orlando – then read – wrote – Acton came – before going to the city – took leave of me – I kept being busy until it was time to go to bed and I only interrupted [my activities] to see my children. The children were healthy – the two eldest already out – the King was all day hunting to Carditello – in the morning [went to hunt] larks-after lunch he galloped.

On Monday October the 18th, I got up at 7 o'clock – dressed – had breakfast – combed my hair – heard Holy Mass – read – wrote – kept myself busy – saw my children – kept the King company – ☉ – then lunched with him – read – kept myself busy – saw Lady San Marco – Don Carlo de Marco – Gravina – another hearing for ladies – went up to my children's room – presided over the Council and went to bed, the children well – except Francis, who complained of some cold and trouble, the King in the morning was at the Carditello [hunting] larks – after lunch he was at the pheasant farm.

On Tuesday October the 19th, I got up at 7 o'clock – as I still felt fever I had a bad night – Vacher suggested that I bleed – I obeyed and bled – then had breakfast – saw my children – I read – had myself taken to my children's room to see Francis – afterwards lunched with the King and began to read ++++ – afterwards wrote – kept myself busy – I saw Moinsignor Spinelli – Positano and Paesiello – read several papers – kept myself busy – then saw my children and to bed, the children well – except Francis to whom dom Felice gave an emetic – for fear of small pox – although some symptoms seemed to me very weak, the King in the morning went to Carditello [to hunt] larks – after lunch to San Leucio.

On Wednesday October the 20th, I got up at 7 o'clock – dressed – had breakfast combed my hair – heard Holy Mass – saw my children – had myself taken to Francis' room where I spent two hours – then went down – kept myself busy – lunched with my children – arranged my affairs to my will – then talked with Lady Belmonte – Casa bona – Sangro – a priest – de Marco – talked with the governess – on the King's return we went together to see Francis – then to the Council – finished my affairs and to bed. The children well – we continued to suspect that Francis had small-pox – although all the symptoms were of a cold – Louise also had a slight fever and cold, the King in the morning went to hunt larks to Carditello – stayed there for lunch – after lunch hunted there on horseback.

On Thursday October the 21st, I got up at 8 o'clock – dressed – had breakfast – combed my hair – heard Holy Mass – went to Francis's room and to those of my other children – kept myself busy – talked with Count Micheli[412] – lunched with the King – read – kept myself busy – arranged my books – kept myself busy – stayed with my children – gave hearings to two ladies – then kept myself busy all evening and to bed – the children well – Francis undoubtedly had a cold – the King in the morning went to hunt larks-after lunch to the pheasant farm.

On Friday October the 22nd, I got up at 7 o'clock – dressed – had breakfast combed my hair – heard Holy Mass – saw my children – kept the King company – ⊙ – then arranged my books in the library – had lunch with the King – read – saw Acton – Gravina – Father Fegnara – teacher of Latin – then Hackert with these pictures – kept myself busy – presided over the Council and to bed+ the children well – Francis was up throughout the day – the King could not go out in the morning – but after lunch he went to partridge hunting.

On Saturday October the 23rd, I got up at 7 o'clock – dressed – had breakfast – combed my hair – heard Holy Mass – read – wrote – kept myself busy – had lunch with the King – read – talked with Caracciolo – read + – lunched – saw my children – listened to Theresa play the harpsichord – conversed with Acton – Caraciolo Gravina and to bed – the children well – Francis – Mimi has a cold and a slight fever – the King in the morning went to hunt larks – after lunch to hunt partridges.

On Sunday October the 24th, I got up at 7 o'clock – dressed – had breakfast – combed my hair – heard Holy Mass – went to Francis' room – read – wrote – spoke to Caracciolo – showed him all the apartments – had lunch with my two eldest girls and Januarius – then took care of them – read – wrote – talked with Brissac – went to Francis's room – kept busy – wrote until the time to go to bed, the children almost all with cold – Theresa – Louise and Mimi – Francis' turned into a nasty fever and he was very dejected, the King in the morning went to hunt larks and after lunch he wanted to hunt but could not do so because of bad weather.

On Monday October the 25th, I got up at 7 o'clock – dressed – had breakfast – combed my hair – heard Holy Mass – wrote – went to see Francis – saw my children – had lunch with the King – read – kept myself busy – saw Monsignor Carafa[413] – Misilmeri – went to my son's room – read – presided over the Council – went to my son's room and to bed – the children with cold – my son Francis with a nasty fever – and dejected. The King – in the morning was at home – after lunch he went to San Leucio.

On Tuesday October 26th, I got up at 7 o'clock – dressed – had breakfast – combed my hair – heard Holy Mass – kept the King company – read – wrote – went to my son's room – then had lunch – read – devoted myself + and – went to my son's room – afterwards toTheresa's room – devoted myself and went to my son – the King went out after lunch to stroll a bit – in the morning my son better – but after lunch ninth fever of the day came violently – prevented him from breathing – it was necessay to bleed him – put him in plasters – the day was bad – the other well – Theresa some fever and cold.

On Wednesday October the 27th, I got up at half past twelve at night and went up to see my son until two o'clock, then I returned to my room – at 7 o'clock I returned there – had breakfast there – then went down to dress – combed my hair – heard Mass – then to my my son's room – after lunch with the King – went to my son's room – saw San Marco – Belmonte – went to Mimi's room – to Theresa's – then went to my son's room and at nine o'clock – feeling very exhausted and dejected – I went to bed. My son had the new bout of fever at ten o'clock – in the opinion of doctor Cotugno[414] and [...] two doctors gave a double dose of china herb to herself – epsom salt and a grain [Kermes] – many enemas and the day was fair – still very dificult breathing, Theresa had also to purge with the epsom salt, Mimi also had great pain in the ear and a little agitation.

On Thursday October the 28th, I got up at 7 o'clock – went to my son's room – then went down – dressed – combed my hair – had breakfast – heard Holy Mass – went to my son's room – lunched with the King – read – was nervous – went to my son's room – spent all afternoon – then to Teresa's room – to Mimi's room – worked on some little affairs – [with] my son and went to my room to bed. My son had the eleventh fever without any symptom of illness – quite well although very hot and dejected – kept giving him china herb – Salt camomile and Kermes – they also began to give him goat's milk – he was very weak – Theresa had fever and a cold – Mimi was better. The King went out a little after lunch to San Leucio.

On Friday October the 29th, I got up at 7 o'clock – dressed – had breakfast – went to my son – combed my hair – heard Holy Mass – read – wrote ++ – devoted myself – went to my son's room – had lunch with the King – read – wrote – saw Belmonte – went to my son's room – presided over the Council – then my affairs and to bed +. The King in the morning went to Carditello – after lunch he strolled for a while – my son had less fever but was very weak – dejected – they continued the same medicines and the child appeared to be better.

On Saturday October the 30th, I got up at 7 o'clock – went to my son's room – had breakfast – dressed – heard Holy Mass – read – wrote – kept myself busy – went to my son's room – lunched with the King – kept him company – read – wrote – went to the children – talked with lady Sangro – stayed with the children – then finished my post and returned to the child until midnight. The King in the morning did not go out and after lunch went to Carditello, my son had the thirteenth fever as always – punctually at ten o'clock it seemed less – at two o'clock he had a large evacuation which denoted a crisis he was better but in the evening got worse prodigiously – prostration – drowsiness – dizziness and a fever among the most violent that everyone feared for his life.

On Sunday October the 31st, I got up at 5 o'clock – dressed – went up to my son's room – then had breakfast – combed my hair – saw my other children – read – returned to my son – had lunch alone – read – wrote+ – kept myself busy – went to my son – read +++ – kept myself busy and [went] to my son – then to bed – the King was to Carditello all the day hunting larks. My son is getting better – they strongly attacked from all sorts of remedies – fever came at the same time – but without increasing.

On Monday November the 1st, I got up at 7 o'clock – dressed – had breakfast – combed my hair – heard Holy Mass – went to my son's room – wrote – kept myself busy – had lunch with the King – read+++ – wrote – kept myself busy – saw my children – Lady San Marco – went to my son's room – presided over the Council – kept myself busy and confessed my sins – then with my son and to bed – the King – because of the bad weather could not go out all day – my son had a fairly quiet night – fever came at the same time – but light – the weakness was notable – we also noted that the strength of the disease had attacked the ear and he heard only with difficulty.

On Tuesday November the 2nd, I got up at half past 6 and went to perform my unworthy devotions – had breakfast – dressed – combed my hair – heard Holy Masses – I had myself taken to my son's room – then wrote my letters – lunched with the King – read – kept myself busy – talked with Pignatelli – Genzano – went to my son's room – then kept the King company – finished my post then prayed and to bed – the King went to San Leucio in the morning and after lunch, my son was getting better – fever was less – all his symptoms better but his weakness excessive – all other children well.

On Wednesday November the 3rd, I got up – dressed – combed my hair – heard Holy Mass – wrote – kept myself busy – went to my son's room – talked with de Marco – lunched with my children – talked with Lamberg – kept myself busy – worked – talked with Lady Gravina – Lady Hereria – afterwards [went to] the Council – prayed and [went] to bed – the King went to Carditello in the morning and returned in the evening, my son was better – had fever for less than five hours but [he was] very deaf and extremely weak – the others well.

On Thursday November the 4th, I got up at 7 o'clock – dressed – had breakfast with my daughters – had two Holy Masses – combed my hair – went to see my son – dressed – received the hand-kissing – public table – then undressed – kept the King company – ⊙ – then saw Lady San Marco – <u>read</u> – afterwards saw Belmonte – Sangro and Cattolica – saw my children – dressed again and went to the theatre to [see] a comic opera – and then to bed – The King went in the morning and after lunch to the grove, my son was better – took an egg – the milk fever struck him punctually at two o'clock in the afternoon – but it was weaker – the other children well.

On Friday November the 5th, I got up at 8 o'clock – dressed – had breakfast – combed my hair – heard Holy Mass – devoted myself – read – wrote – kept myself busy – had lunch with the King – saw my children – <u>read</u> – wrote – kept myself busy – the Council – kept myself busy and [went] to bed The children healthy – my son had a fever – but it was less intense – the weakness always excessive – the King went after lunch to the revisit of Liparoti – trotted to San Leucio and then at home.

On November Saturday the 6th, I got up at 7 ½ o'clock – had breakfast – combed my hair – dressed – heard Holy Mass – read – wrote – kept myself busy – went to my son's room – had lunch with the King – read – kept myself busy – wrote – read – at 7 o'clock I went with the King to see a very good performance of a play entitled *la Colombe de madame de Gintis* with a little ballet that my three girls performed after the show – which caused me great pleasure – considering their attention and their good will I remained conversing with Acton Marsico Migliano – and then to bed – the children well – my son was slowly improving – the King in the morning went to Calabra Citra – in the afternoon to San Leucio.

On Sunday November the 7th, I got up at 7 o'clock – dressed – had breakfast – combed my hair – devoted myself – heard Holy Masses – busy all morning – lunched with the King – kept him company – ⊗ – then read for a while – I kept myself busy – talked with the King – Acton and Pignatelli regarding Calabrian affairs – then again to hear the my children' comedy – Lady Caramanico – Gravina – Marsico and Acton remained with me – afterwards to bed – the children well – my son wanted stand up for a few minutes and was better – the King because of the bad weather could go out only a little on foot.

On Monday November the 8th, I got up – dressed – had breakfast – combed my hair – heard Holy Mass – saw my children – busy with my affairs – read – wrote – arranged my papers – then had lunch with the

King – read – kept myself busy – talked with knight Virieux – saw my children – presided over the Council and kept myself busy – and then to bed, the children well – my son had indigestion caused by milk – but slight – the King in the morning went to Carditello – after lunch to San Leucio.

On Tuesday November the 9th, I got up at half past 7 – dressed – combed my hair – took an ounce of salt from England as medicine – walked through all the rooms – had breakfast – heard Holy Mass – took care of my children – wrote my letters – read – wrote – had lunch with my two eldest daughters – then kept myself busy – talked with San Marco – with Countess Althan – with my confessor – saw my children – then finished my letters and to bed – the children healthy – Francis miraculously better but weak. The King went to Carditello the morning and was there all day.

On Wednesday November the 10th, I got up – dressed – had breakfast – heard the Holy Mass – read – wrote – kept myself busy – had lunch with the King – saw Lady Belmonte – [fons] de Vala – Scordia – Cari – then Richecourt – presided over the Council and went to bed – the children healthy – my son better – I had seen him in the morning – the King went to the after lunch Royal e and returned in the evening.

On Thursday November the 11th, I got up in the morning at 7 o'clock – dressed – combed my hair – had breakfast – heard Holy Mass – read – wrote – I kept myself busy – had lunch with my children – took care of them – read – wrote – saw the King – kept myself busy and to bed – the children well – the King spent whole San Martin's day at San Leucio.

On Friday November the 12th, I got up – dressed – combed my hair – bled – then lay on a couch – talked with my confessor – hear Holy Mass – kept myself busy – had lunch with my children – <u>read</u> – wrote – kept myself busy – saw the doctors – presided over the Council and went to bed, the children well – my son was recovering very slowly – the King went to the pheasant farm for the whole day.

On Saturday November the 13th, I got up in the morning at 7 o'clock – dressed – had breakfast – combed my hair – heard Holy Mass – read – wrote – saw and spoke to Richecourt – then had lunch with my children – read – kept myself busy – saw Acton with his brother – wrote my post – talked with the doctors – kept myself busy and to bed – the children fine – the King went to San Vito and was out all day – my son was recovering very slowly.

On Sunday November the 14th, I got up at 7 o'clock – dressed – had breakfast – combed my hair – heard Holy Mass – spoke – read – wrote – had lunch with my children – took care of them – read – wrote – saw Lamberg – Lord Belmonte … [415] then kept myself busy – talked – saw the King – my children and to bed – the children well – except my son who is wasting away and feels me with fear – the King went to Calabria Citra to hunt all day.

On Monday November the 15th, I got up – dressed – combed my hair – heard Holy Mass – read – wrote – kept myself busy – kept the King company – ⊗ – and then talked with the doctor – had lunch with the King – read – talked with San Marco – Viceroy – other hearings for ladies – the Council – worked on my affairs and to bed – the children fine – only my son continues with this languor that makes me tremble – the King was at home in the morning and after lunch went hunting at Carbone.

On Tuesday November the 16th, I got up at 7 o'clock – had tea – having had a strong indigestion all night – I dressed – combed my hair – heard Holy Mass – read – wrote – went to my son's room – then had lunch with my children – took care of them – talked with Lamberg – then read – wrote – then talked with Princess Belmonte – with Richecourt – Vacher – finished my post – saw Lamberg and to bed – the children well – except Francis who is langwishing continuously, the King went to Carditello to hunt wild boars and was there all day.

On Wednesday November the 17th, I got up at 7 o'clock – dressed – had breakfast – combed my hair – heard Holy Mass – read – devoted myself – wrote – talked with Prince Tarsia – then Rocella – Lady Caramanico-had lunch with my children – took care of them – talked with Brissac – wrote – saw Mrs. Sangro – Butera – then [went] to the Council and to bed – the children well – my son a little better – the King was S. Giovanni hunting site all day.

On Thursday November the 18th, I got up – dressed – had breakfast – combed my hair – heard Holy Mass – read – wrote – kept myself busy – went to my son's room – talked with Marsico – had lunch with my girls – talked with Lamberg – read – wrote – devoted myself – went to my son's room – kept myself busy and to bed. In the morning I found my son greatly improved – at eleven o'clock he caught a cold – he had again fever with scary symptoms – at 5 o'clock he calmed down – the other children well except Teresa with a stomach disorder – the King went to hunt common snipes at Calvi.

On Friday November the 19th, I got up in the morning at 7 o'clock – dressed – had breakfast – combed my hair – heard Holy Mass – read – wrote – kept myself busy – went to my son's room – kept the King company – ⊗ – had lunch with the King – read – kept myself busy – saw Acton's sister-in law – then kept myself busy – [went to] the Council and to bed – the children well – at nine in the evening my son had a new fever – which lasted him all night with the symptoms of a terrible cough – the other children well – the King could not go out in the morning and after lunch went for a while to San Leucio.

On Saturday November the 20th, I got up – dressed – had breakfast – combed my hair – heard Holy Mass – read – wrote – kept myself busy – went to my son's room – lunched with the King – took care of my children – read – wrote – sent my letters – talked – in the evening conversed with Richecourt – Hamilton – Belmonte and Acton – then [went] to bed – the children well – my son did not have a new attack of fever but the previous one still persisted,the King after lunch walked for a while in the wood.

On Sunday November the 21st, I got up – dressed – had breakfast – combed my hair – heard Holy Masses – went to my son's room – read – wrote – had lunch with my children – read my letters – kept myself busy – then saw Duchess Noya[416] and Cimitile's daughter – Luperano's wife[417] – then went to my son's room – came back – read – saw my children – wrote – kept myself busy and to bed – the children well – Francis with fever and a convulsive cough which is consuming him-the King went to have lunch at San Leucio in the company of Diana the huntress.

On Monday the 22nd, I got up – dressed – had breakfast – heard Holy Mass – saw my children – went to my son's room – spoke to...... [418] – then had lunch with my children – read – kept myself busy – talked and saw six wet nurses – spoke to Pignatelli – then with the King – the children – the Council – kept myself busy and to bed, the children well – Francis had fever – a cough which is consuming him – the King went all day to San Arcangelo.

On Tuesday November the 23rd, I got up at 7o'clock – dressed – had breakfast – combed my hair – heard Holy Mass – read – wrote – kept myself busy – went to see my son – lunched with my children – took care of them – then saw San Marco – kept myself busy and [went] to bed + the children well – Francis a little better – the King was all day at Carditello.

On Wednesday November the 24th, I got up at 7 o'clock – dressed – had breakfast – combed my hair – heard Holy Mass – read – wrote – kept myself busy – went to my son's room – had lunch with my children – talked with Sambuca – with Lamberg – then kept myself busy – saw Lady Belmonte – DonnaTeresina – went to [see] my son – kept the King company – ⊗ – afterwards kept myself busy and [went] to bed – the children fine – Francis still with his convulsive cough and a slight fever – the King was at San Leucio and the pheasant farm all day.

On Thursday November the 25th, I got up – dressed – had breakfast – combed my hair – heard Holy Mass – read – wrote – kept myself busy – talked with...... [419] – then had lunch with my children – took care of them – read – wrote – kept myself busy – went to my son's room – kept myself busy in my room and [went] to bed. The Children well – my son Francis had cow's milk – but neither the cough nor the fever went away – the King went at three in the morning to Mondragone and returned at 7 o'clock in the evening.

On Friday November the 26th, I got up at 7 o'clock – dressed – had breakfast – combed my hair – heard Holy Mass – read – wrote – kept myself busy – went to my son's room – lunched with the King – saw my children – read – wrote – kept myself busy – went to my son's room – [went to] the Council and to bed The children well – Francis as usual with his convulsive cough which causes pain – the King in the morning strolled in the grove – after lunch he went to Carditello.

On Saturday November the 27th, I got up – dressed – had breakfast – combed my hair – heard Holy Mass – read+ – wrote – I kept myself busy – had lunch with my children – took care of them – read + – wrote – kept myself busy – talked with the doctors – kept the King company – ⊗ – then saw Richecourt – was my children's play – and then stayed with Hamilton and Acton and afterwards to bed – the children well – Francis is convalescing slowly – the King was all day to the pheasant farm.

On Sunday November the 28th, I got up – dressed – combed my hair – heard Holy Mass – read – wrote – kept myself busy – talked with Gravina – Brancacio[420] – Lady Caramanico – afterwards had lunch with my children – read – wrote – kept myself busy – went to my son's room – kept the King company – read my letters – prepared my confession and then confessed my sins – and then to bed – the children well – Francis is recovering slowly – the King was at a hunt at Carditello all day.

On Monday November the 29th, I got up at half past 6 – went to church – performed my devotions – then had breakfast – dressed – combed my hair – heard two Masses – kept myself busy – lunched with my children – took care of them – read – wrote – saw Lady San Marco – went to my son's room – kept the King company – saw my children – presided over the Council – then said the office of the dead it being the anniversary of the best mother and to bed – the children well – Francis is improving slowly – the King was at lunch, and [also] at San Leucio.

On Tuesday November the 30th, I got up at 7 o'clock – dressed – had breakfast – combed my hair – heard Holy Mass – wrote my post – went with my children to San Francesco di Paola – lunched with the King – read – kept myself busy – spoke to Lady Althan – kept myself busy and [went to] bed, the children well – Francis slowly is recovering – the King in the afternoon went to Carbone and returned in the evening.

On Wednesday December the 1st, I got up – dressed – had breakfast – combed my hair – heard Holy Mass – read – wrote – kept myself busy – had lunch with my children – spoke to Madame Feydeau – lay on my bed – because I had some pains – spoke to General Pignatelli – r...... [421] – then wrote – took care of my children – saw them – had dinner – kept myself busy and to bed – the children healthy – Francis is slowly getting better – the King in the morning went fishing at Castellamare – in the evening to the opera to San Carlo – whence he returned at ten in the evening.

On Thursday December the 2nd, I got up at 7 o'clock – dressed – combed my hair – heard Holy Mass – then bled – saw my children – lunched – paraded – then heard the second Holy Mass – had lunch with the King – read – kept myself busy – paraded – stayed with my children – saw the Duchess of Tursis with her daughter bride – then the library – read my letters – kept myself busy and to bed. the children well – Francis much better – thanks to God – the King went after lunch to a hunt near San Leucio.

On Friday December the 3rd, I got up at 7 o'clock and took an ounce of epsom salt four times – I walked – got dressed – had breakfast – combed my hair – heard Holy Mass – wrote – kept myself busy – went to Holy Mass – lunched with my children – took care of them – read – wrote – went to my son whom – thanks to God – I found better and then the Council and to bed – the children well – Francis is recovering – the King went to have dinner and spend the day at Carditello.

On Saturday December the 4th, I got up – dressed – lunch – combed my hair – heard Holy Mass – read – wrote – kept myself busy – heard the second Mass – had lunch with my children – read – wrote – saw Acton's sister-in-law whom I showed the house – then Princess Belmonte – then my children – kept myself busy and [went to] bed – the children well – Francis is slowly recovering – the King went to lunch at San Leucio and stayed there to hunt wild boars.

On Sunday December the 5th, I got up at 7 o'clock – after having had a sleepless night – combed my hair – had breakfast – dressed – heard Holy Mass – read – wrote – at eleven o'clock another Mass – lunched with my children – saw Acton – Lady Belmonte – went to [see] my son – talked with the King who pained me – I put myself back in order – kept myself busy and to bed – the children well – Francis is recovering – the King went to Carditello to hunt wild boars all day.

On Monday December the 6th, I got up at half past 7 – dressed – had breakfast – combed my hair – heard Holy Mass – read – wrote – kept myself busy – talked with Vasto – r…… [422] – then Marsico – lunched with my children – took care of them – read – kept myself busy – went with my two eldest daughters to my son's room – saw the wet nurses – kept the King company – kept myself busy – saw Lady Belmonte – my children – went to bed – the children well – Francis very upset – he was finishing his snack – stood up – the King was present at the branding of horses at Carditello.

On Tuesday December the 7th, I got up at 7 o'clock – dressed – had breakfast – combed my hair – heard Holy Mass – read – wrote – I kept myself busy – had lunch with the King – kept him company – ⊗ – then talked with Lady San Marco – whose daughter I confirmed in the morning – then kept myself busy – worked on my affairs – wrote my post – worked on my affairs and [went] to bed. The children well – Francis recovered slowly – the King after lunch walked for a while.

On Wednesday December the 8th, I got up at half past 7 – dressed – had breakfast – combed my hair – heard Holy Mass – read – wrote – kept myself busy – talked with Cattolica – saw my children – had lunch with them – kept myself busy – read – saw my son – who thank God is better – then saw Richecourt – Count Lamberg – then kept myself busy and to bed – the children well – Francis slowly getting better – the King was all day at Carditello.

On Thursday December the 9th, I got up at half past 7 – had breakfasted – dressed – combed my hair – heard Holy Mass – kept the King company – ⊗ – then went to arrange the library – afterwards heard another Mass – had lunch with the King – saw Lamberg – kept myself busy – read – talked with … [423] – then kept myself busy and went to bed – the children well – Francis better – the King after lunch went to the pheasant farm.

On Friday Decembe the 10th, I got up – after a good night – dressed – had breakfast – combed my hair – heard Holy Mass – read – went to arrange the library – heard another Holy Mass – lunched with the children – kept myself busy – read – went to my son's room – presided over the Council – kept myself busy and saw Belmonte and to bed – the children well – Francis is slowly gettting better – the King went hunting at Sant Leucio all day

On Saturday December the 11th, I got up – had breakfast – combed my hair – heard Holy Mass – read – wrote – kept myself busy – had lunch with my children – took care of them – went to the library – then read – wrote – went to my son's room – went down with Belmonte husband and wife, Acton's brother and his wife went my children's play – then stayed with Lady Belmonte and to bed – Francis is recovering at a snail'space and faces a terribly long convalescence – the King was all day to Jerusalem the place where the pheasant are shot.

On Sunday December the 12th, I got up at 7 o'clock – dressed – had breakfast – combed my hair – spoke to the doctor – to Braya[424] – to Vacher – saw my children – heard two Masses – kept myself busy – wrote – heard another Mass – kept the King company – ⊗ – lunched – saw my children – read – wrote – kept myself busy – saw Lady Belmonte – had Theresa play music – and then to bed – the children well – Francis is slowly recovering, in the afternnoon the King went to Carditello.

On Monday December the 13th, I got up at 1 o'clock – dressed – combed my hair, heard two Masses – spoke to Vasto to … [425] – went to lunch with the children, kept myself busy read and wrote, saw and spoke to Vicscountess Hereria with Princess Belmonte and General Richecourt and prepared for confession – then to bed, the children well, Francis continues his slow recovery, the King was at Carditello all day.

On Tuesday the 14th, after having felt slight pains all night, the labour began at half past 6 in the morning and after ten past gave birth to a healthy robust daughter, who will called Antoinette.[426] I spent the whole day receiving care and seeing my children, and in the evening [saw] Sambuca [for] a moment, the children well – the King went out for a walk only in the afterrnoon.

On Wednesday the 15th, after a good night, I woke up – had my breakfast – heard Mass – saw my children – then Acton and de Marco – I spent the rest of the day in bed with my children – I saw Princess Belmonte – at 6 o'clock breastfed the little child for the first time, and I went to sleep, the children well, Francis – who the day before had stopped taking milk and resumed eating was better, the King in the morning went to the *Te Deum* of the Carmelites, hand-kissing, public table could not go out for the rest of the day owing to bad weather.

On Thursday the 16th I woke up – had breakfast – heard mass, took care of my children, saw Princess Caramanico – had lunch, saw Count Lamberg – remained in bed, took care of my children, in the evening I saw Richecourt and afterwards [went]to sleep. The children well, Francis is slowly getting better, the King could not go out all day owing to bad weather.

On Friday the 17th, I woke up, had breakfast heard Mass, took care of my children. Prince Belmonte – [saw] – Gravina, lunched – then saw Acton – afterwards Lady Belmonte and my children and [went] to sleep.

On Saturday the 18th Mass, had breakfast, read – saw Altavilla – Richecourt and my children – still in bed – the children well – the King went to Carditello.

On Sunday the 19th, Mass – my children – read for a while in the morning and after lunch saw Belmonte – Richecourt and my children – still in bed – the children well – the King had lunch with our eldest daughters at the pheasant farm.

On Monday the 20th, Mass – children – wrote a little and still in bed – the King could not go out because of bad weather.

On Tuesday the 21st, Mass – saw my children – wrote the post – saw Lady Belmonte and to bed – the children well – the King was all day at Carditello.

On Wednesday the 22nd, I had a headache and spent the morning in the dark – my children – after lunch spoke to.... [427] – to Butera – to Genzano and then to the governess – to the doctors and was still in bed – the children well – the King was all day fishing at Fusaro.

On Thursday the 23rd, I woke up – had breakfast – heard Holy Mass – had lunch – saw my children – old Salandra and Ardore – then lunched – afterwards got up – thanks to God – from the bed – for the first time at half past 2 – then saw San Marco – my children – in the evening Richecourt – Belmonte and [went] to sleep – the children well – the King could go out a little only in the morning because of bad weather.

On Friday the 24th, I woke up – saw the doctors – the governess – the children – heard Mass – got up for lunch – then saw thanks to Divine Mercy my son Francis, who has come from the pit – I took care of him and amused him – then in the morning I saw Gravina – Montalto – Lamberg – in the evening Tarsia – Marsico – Richecourt and Belmonte – afterwards [went]to sleep – the children well – the King went to lunch at the fish farm and fished with our three daughters.

On Saturday December the 25, Christmas Day I woke up at 8 o'clock – had breakfast with my children – got up – heard 3 Holy Masses – saw Pignatelli – San Nicola – Lady Sambuca – Sangro – then had lunch with my children – then kept myself busy – read – saw Lady Hereria – having seen her husband in the morning – Lady Cattolica – and Sangro – then Richecourt and Belmonte – afterwards [went] to sleep – the children well – the King in the morning went to *Te deum* in the new chapel – hand-kissing – public table and after lunch [went] hunting at San Leucio – the children well.

On Sunday December the 26th, I got up – dressed – heard Masses – read – saw Lamberg – read letters and [went] to bed – with a big headache – saw Caramanico – Richecourt – Belmonte and then [went] to sleep – the children well – the King was at Carditello all day.

On Monday December the 27th, I got up at eleven – dressed – heard Mass – had breakfast – spent the day with my children and kept myself busy in the evening – saw Belmonte and Richecourt – in the morning saw Lamberg – the children well – the King was all day at the pheasant farm.

On Tuesday December the 28th, I got up at eleven – dressed – heard Mass – had breakfast with Theresa – then saw San Marco – spoke to…. [428] then Belmonte – Richecourt and [went] to bed – the children fine – the King at eleven o'clock went to Mondragone and spent all day and night there.

On Wednesday December the 29th, I got up at eleven o'clock – dressed – heard Mass – had breakfast – saw Lord Hereria afterwards spoke to … [429] to Gravina – to my children – to Princess Belmonte then [went] to bed – the children well the King remained at Mondragone.

On Thursday December the 30th, I got up at eleven – heard the Mass – saw my children – had breakfast – saw Lamberg – talked with…. [430] – then read the letters – afterwards kept myself busy – stayed with my children – saw the King on his return from Mondragone – saw Princess Belmonte – looked after my little child who was restless and in bed – the children healthy – the King in the evening returned from Mondragone.

On Friday December the 31 st – the last day of the year – I got up at 9 o'clock – dressed – combed my hair – had myself blessed by my confessor – me and my child – then heard Holy Mass – and – by the grace of God – out of the bedroom which I had cleaned – swept – afterwards I saw my son Francis – who is still very weak – then all the other children – lunched with the King – kept myself busy – presided over the first Council – once again [went] to my room – saw Richecourt – Princess Belmonte, and then to bed – the children well – the King walked for a while in the grove.

and so ended 1784 – I began it with the Emperor – [and] my sister – they left the same month – the King of Sweden came to visit us, and there were months of quiet – I happily had Mimi inoculated – I was pregnant – later I had sudden and intense sorrows from Spain – a deadly disease for my eldest son and then a happy birth. May God grant me a happier year.

JOURNAL 1785

On January 1, 1785

Saturday January the first, I woke at 7 o'clock – had breakfast with my three daughters and the King – and then saw the governess – doctors – then got up – heard Holy Mass – and – read x – afterwards saw Francis – my other children – I stayed with them during their lunch, only had some broth – having a severe headache – I saw Gatti – then lay down on a sofa – I spoke to...... [431] – later read x – wrote the letters, took care of my children, talked with Richecourt and Princess Belmonte – heard some garden music – had lunch in the dining room instead of in bed, my beloved children well – the King was all day hunting common snipes at Acerra.

On Sunday the 2nd, I woke up early – heard Holy Mass – dressed – combed my hair – I had fever during the night – my nerves were irritated – I began to read – X – wrote and then had lunch with my children – then busy – reading – X – writing – saw Acton and his brother who had to leave .... then my children – kept myself busy – saw Donna Teresina Sangro – Richecourt – then Princess Belmonte and afterwards had dinner and [went] to bed – the children fine – the King went for the whole day to Carditello and in the evening went to see pantomimes which the ladies and knights are performing at the theatre at Anguissola's house, Rasoumowsky left at a quarter past 5 generally missed.

On Monday January the 3rd, I woke up at 7 o'clock – had breakfast and then wrote for the courrier until eleven o'clock – so I got up – had breakfast – dressed – went to church – had lunch with the King – saw my children – then Marchioness San Marco – afterwards read – wrote – kept myself busy – took part in the Council – then saw Princess Belmonte – had supper and [went] to bed. The children – thanks to God are fine, in the afternoon the King went hunting at Carbone.

On Tuesday January the 4 th, day of my dear and beloved Charles'birth – which would have been eleven and the day I had the greatest pleasure just as I had the greatest pain after his death, I awoke at 7 o'clock – had breakfast – saw the governess – the doctors and my children – I began to write until eleven o'clock – when I got up from bed – dressed and heard Mass – I had lunch with the King – after lunch I played piquet with him and – from 3 o'clock until half past 8 – I wrote without moving – then I saw the courriers who are leaving – then Richecourt – later Countess Althan then Belmonte and had supper and to bed. The children – thank God – fine – Amelia had a slight but harmless cold – Antoinette having had a little stomach pain – I purged her during the evening with a little rhubarb syrup. The King in the moining went out for an half hour to walk and after lunch – because of bad weather – he stayed at home.

On Wednesday January the 5th, I got up at 9 o'clock – arranged several affairs of the house – like those of my accounts – the wardrobe for Naples and several other affairs – then I heard Mass – saw my son, spoke to Sambuca – then I had lunch and went with my children – then I was busy reading – writing – talking with my confessor – saw Aprile – then the King returned – I played piquet with him – then I spoke to Princess Caramanico – I worked on my affairs – saw my children – spoke to Belmonte and went to bed. The children – thanks to God – healthy – Amelia still with her cold, the King went at ten o'clock to San Vito to hunt partridges and returned at 5 o'clock before lunch – the King sent me Lord Hamilton with Prince Belmonte to see a newly invented writing lamp.[432]

On Thursday January the 6th, I woke up at 7 o'clock – had breakfast in bed – saw the governess – the doctors – talked with Vacher a long time regarding my health – and then got up at 9 o'clock – dressed – combed my hair – had breakfast – went to Mass – worked on my affairs – saw my son – lunched with my children – took care of them – saw Princess Butera – Marchioness Tanucci – then read letters with the King – saw the governess – the doctors – then Princess Belmonte – worked on my affairs – prayed and went to bed. The children – thank God – well, Amelia still with a bit of a cold, Francis went out because of a beautiful day and is slowly getting better, the King in the morning went to Carditello and after lunch to Carbone – in the evening [went] to a French play.

On Friday January the 7th, I woke up at 7 o'clock – had breakfast – saw my children – the governess – then got up – dressed – combed my hair – heard Holy Mass – saw the doctors – decided with them to send my son Francis to Portici – aftewards saw this child – lunched with the others – was busy reading – writing – saw the King – [went] to the Council and kept myself busy – then went to bed – the children fine – the King went to hunt at Matalone and returned at midnight.

On Saturday January the 8th, I woke up at 7 o'clock – had breakfast – saw the doctors – the governess – then got up – dressed – heard Holy Mass – read – wrote – took care of my children – lunched with the King – played piquet with him – afterwards wrote my letters – I kept myself busy – took leave of honest Vacher with regret – then saw my children again – the governess – Princess Belmonte and then [went] to bed – the children healthy – little Antoinette has been constipated for three days and this worries me – in the morning the King went out a little to San Leucio – in the afternoon he did not go out at all.

On Sunday January the 9th, I woke up at 7 o'clock – had breakfast – then got up – dressed – combed my hair – heard Holy Mass – read – wrote ++ – kept myself busy – saw my children – had lunch with Francis – thank God – for the first time – afterwards saw my other children – then Acton came and took leave before going to town – then I played with my two little girls – I read my letters and those from Spain – was busy – saw Princess Belmonte – then went to bed. The children well – the little Toinette[433] was fine and quiet, the King was at Carditello all day.

On Monday January the 10th, I got up at 7 o'clock – had breakfast – dressed – combed my hair – heard Holy Mass – saw my children – was busy reading – writing – had lunch – with my children – took care of them – saw San Marco – then spoke to my confessor – then Gravina – Lady Teresina Sangro – afterwards the King came back – we presided over the Council and then kept myself busy – saw Belmonte and to bed. The children well, the King went to the swamp at Calvi to [hunt] mallards – from morning until night – afterwards [went] to the Council and went to the [theatre] to tragedy of the knights.

On Tuesday January the 11th, I woke up at 7 o'clock – had breakfast – saw the governess – the doctors – then got up – combed my hair – dressed – heard Holy Mass saw my children – kept the King company – read – wrote – I kept myself busy – had lunch with my children – talked with Lamberg – wrote my letters – stayed with the children – saw Countess Gaetani – who introduced me to her daughter – the wife of [Miseragua] – a charming young person – who was sacrificed to vile interest – and then the King came – I kept him company – afterwards I saw Madame Hereria – who came to thank the King for being her son godfather – from there I went to see the dress rehearsal of my children's play – with ballets entitled *l'isle hereuse* and *l'oracle*, on my return I saw Richecourt for a moment – then prepared for confession and confessed my sins – whence to bed, the children well – the King was at San Leucio all day – being the feast of his name day.

On January 12, I woke up at half past 6 – got up and went to perform my devotions unworthily – then I had breakfast with my children – afterwards made a big toilet – curled [and] combed my hair – dressed – heard the Mass with my children – prayed for their beloved father – afterwards saw Lord Hereria, Richecourt – Lamberg – had lunch with Francis – took care of my children – afterwards had lunch – read – wrote – kept myself busy – then the King returned – I went to meet him with both my sons and Amelia who brought the letters of their sister – then I went inside – kept the King company for the first time after the delivery – ⊗ – then I saw the ladies with the King and went to the performance of my children – who were very good – especially Theresa and they moved me a lot – made me very happy – then I dressed – went to see them have dinner – stayed with Lady Belmonte for a while, and then to bed, the children – thanks to God – healthy – the King took part in a big wild boar hunt at Calvi for the whole day.

On Thursday January the 13th, I woke up at 7 o'clock – had breakfast in bed – then got up – dressed – combed my hair – saw my son and Amelia leave for Portici – praying the Heavens that the air [over there] will be favorable for them – then heard Mass, kept myself busy – wrote, had lunch with my children – took care of them – then wrote – read – saw my confessor – kept the King company – read the letters – saw Richecourt – Princess Belmonte – then went with the King and our two eldest daughters to Corleto's house to see the tragedy of *Cesar*[434] which they perfomed very well, *les pantomines d'andromaque,* et *Ninette à la cour* – though well executed – I did not like them – the tragedy which having moved me a lot – from there I returned – said my prayers – waited for the King – ⊗ – had supper – undressed and [went] to bed. The children well. The King was at the pheasant farm and fell from the mule but thanks to God without any consequences..

On Friday January the 14th, I got up at 7 o'clock – dressed – had breakfast – combed my hair – heard Holy Mass – was busy reading – writing – had lunch with my children – took care of them – read – wrote – presided over the Council – then went to the play of my dear children – afterwards spoke to Belmonte and to bed, the children well – the King was all day at Carditello.

On Saturday January the 15th, I got up – dressed – had breakfast – combed my hair – saw my children – heard Holy Mass – read – wrote++ – kept myself busy – had lunch with my children – took care of them – talked with Gravina – saw Belmonte – read – saw Acton – then the King came back – later kept him company – ⊙ – afterwards spruced myself – dressed and went to the tragedy of *Cesar* and the two pantomimes which were better than previous time – afterwards [went] to bed. The children well the King spent the whole day hunting at the pheasant farm hunting all day – and took Count Hoyos with him.

On Sunday January the 16th, I got up at 7 o'clock – dressed – had breakfast – combed my hair – heard Holy Mass at the main chapel – which is beautiful but which I do not like for my devotions – and read ++ – wrote – kept myself busy – had lunch – saw my children – read – went to the comedy with my children – after that saw Lady Hoyos whom I took with me – afterwards wrote and [went] to bed – the children fine – the King went at half past 8 to see Calabrian regiment – then the (following day) – then [went] to sleep to Pagliare of Mondragone.

On Monday January the 17th, I got up at 7 o'clock – dressed – had breakfast – combed my hair – had breakfast with all my children – wished dear Mimi happy birthday – whom her 7th birthday – then went to Mass – worked on all my affairs – at a quarter to 10 I left with all my dear children – Januarius with his people – in the first carriage – then Theresa and Mimi – Louise – Antoniette with me – the journey – thanks to God – was very pleasant – we arrived at a quarter to twelve – saw everyone – anwered the King – who had written to me – spoke to Richecourt – had lunch with my children – took care of them – saw Marchioness San Marco – read ++ – unpacked – saw and visited with pleasure my new library – afterwards saw Vicenzo who returned from Paris – read – wrote ++++ – saw Don Domenico Spinelli – then had dinner and stayed with my children – saw Princess Belmonte – kept myself busy and went to bed – the children well – was assured the same things about my son Francis – my Mimi fell, down – the King was all day at Mondragone.

On Tuesday January the 18th, I got up at 7 o'clock – dressed – had breakfast – combed my hair – went to see my children – then heard Mass – afterwards spoke to my confessor – then heard another Mass – spoke to General Pignatelli – then read – wrote – had lunch – kept myself busy – saw Marchioness San Marco – made my toilette – and then I received Viscountess Hereira who introduced a French lady to me – Lady Gontaud[435] – then the wife of the Russian Minister – Lady Scavronsky[436] – later a Bolognese – Pepoli[437] – married Meza Capa – then a milanese – at the end Lady de Sangro – then I went with Gravina and Vasto to the French [theatre] – they acted *l'amant bouru et la fausse Agnes* – the King arrived half way trough performance – I returned with him – undressed – kept him company – ⊙ – then [went] to sleep. The children quite well – Theresa had the fever with a bad cold and sore throat – Louise also has a cold – the children [who are at] Portici are better – the King thanks to God came back healthy from Mondragone.

On Wednesday January the 19th, I got up at 7 o'clock – dressed – had breakfast – combed my hair – put on my curlers – heard Holy Mass – at ten o'clock there was de Marco's Council – then spoke to Lady Filingieri – after lunch with the King – then arranged my library – went to my daughters'room – afterwards at two o'clock went with the King to Portici – where I had the consolation to see my son healthy and much better – I took care of him and Amelia – afterwards returned with the King – where – on arrival I kept him company – ⊗ – after I made my toilette again – spoke to Belmonte and went with the the King to the French [theatre] – they acted *Jayce* et *les contrétémps amoureux de la maison* – had supper and [went] to bed – Theresa had fever and sore throat – she was already up – but with a nightcap and dressing gown – Louise has a cold – all three eldest daughters were purged as a precaution – the King went with me to Portici and spent the day with me.

On Thursday January the 20th, I got up around 8 in the morning – had breakfast – heard Holy Mass – saw my two little girls – then combed my hair – put on court dress – went to write for a while – then [went] to the hand-kissing – the public table – afterwards undressed – had lunch – kept the King company – at three o'clock presided over the Council – saw Hoyos – strolled with her on the terrace – then to the hand-kissing of the ladies – afterwards changed and went to the opera at the San Carlo theatre where we stayed for the whole opera, and then home to sleep. The King did not go out all day – the children – Theresa – Louise have a cold – Januarius has a mangled face – for me the first menstruation after delivery arrived in the morning at 10 o'clock.

On Friday January the 21st, I got up at 7 o'clock – had breakfast – combed my hair – heard Holy Mass – went out – chose and gave the trousseau for Giovanina – then read + – wrote – saw my sick daughters – Januarius – Mimi – then kept myself busy – went to the terrace – saw lady San Marco – then still busy – afterwards saw my children and went to the French [theatre] – they performed *le Bouru bienfesant, l'aveugle clairvoyant* and another little play of which I forgot the title – [were] all very good – afterwards we came back home, and I went to bed – the children better – Theresa's fever is passing – Louise spent the day in bed – Antoinette in the evening had abdominal cramp but it passed without any remedy – from Portici I had good news of my son and my daughter – the King in the morning took exercise and then went to fish at Fusaro whence he returned at 5 o'clock in the afternoon.

On Saturday January the 22nd, I got up at 7 o'clock – had breakfast – combed my hair – heard Holy Mass – read – wrote – kept my self busy – my son Francis came from Portici with Amelia – I called Januarius and Mimi and I enjoyed myself with all [my children] on the terrace – then they left – I still remained to take care – then I had lunch – Richecourt kept me company – I showed him my house – then I saw San Marco and afterwards the King came back – I went to gave many hearings – then to the Fondo theatre to see a comic opera performed by bad acting company – from there home – had supper and [went] to bed, I had vertigo – a [sensation of] weight on my head – which worries me – the children were fine the sick ones better – the King in the morning took exercise and then went to hunt wild boar at Strone.

On Sunday January the 23rd, I got up – dressed – had breakfast – combed my hair – heard Holy Mass – read – wrote – kept myself busy – saw my children – had lunch with the King – kep him company – then talked with the Marchioness – Belmonte – gave many hearings – afterwards at nine [went] to a new theatre to see a new bad and boring – play – whence to the theatre – to the masked ball in domino dress – there were 1600 masks – I did not went out of my loge with Gravina and Belmonte – I had supper with the King and then at half past midnight [went] to bed. The children well, in the morning the King took exercise and at two o'clock [went] to Portici – whence he returned at 5 o'clock in the afternoon.

On Monday January the 24th, I got up at 8 o'clock – dressed – had breakfast – combed my hair – heard Holy Mass – saw my children – read – wrote – I kept myself busy – spoke to Lord Belmonte – General Pignatelli – then had lunch with the King – kept him company – wrote – kept myself busy – saw five British ladies – then took part in Sambuca's Council – gave twelve hearings and then went to the opera at the San Carlo theatre – afterwards went to bed, the children well – the King after having taken exercise with the Liparoti [went] to shoot ducks in Agnano and came back to have lunch at home.

On Tuesday January the 25th, I got up – dressed – had breakfast – combed my hair – heard Holy Mass – read – wrote – kept myself busy – saw my children – took care of them – saw the Marchioness – wrote my post – made my toilette – saw Countess Hoyos – Lady Althan – then in the evening went to the French [theatre] where they performed *le jouéur* et *les précieuses ridicule* – from there home and to bed – the children well – the King at 10 in the morning went – after the exercise at Carbone – to shoot ducks and returned at midnight

On Wednesday January the 26th, I got up at 8 o'clock – dressed – had breakfast – combed my hair – heard Holy Mass – had myself painted – saw General Pignatelli – kept myself busy – read + – then had lunch – saw Count Lamberg – Marchioness Belmonte – many ladies introduced to me – then went to the Florentines theatre to a very bad concert and afterwards kept the King company – ⊗ then in domino dress went to get bored at the masked ball – where there were 850 masks – I bored myself to death – I did not go down and at one o'clock went to sleep. The children well – the King went to Carditello at eleven and returned at midnight.

On Thursday January the 27th, I got up at 7 o'clock in the morning – dressed – combed my hair – had breakfast – saw my children – then [went] to Mass – at half past 8 I went with the King to Fusaro by one horse carriage – in the morning we hunted boars – Belmonte – Hamilton – Marsico – Migliano – Salandra – Onorato – Priore – were our company – after the hunt we lunched on the island – then again hunting – afterwards we returned home – I undressed – made my toilette – kept the King company – ⊗ – then the Council – afterwards to the opera at the San Carlo theatre with my two eldest daughters – then had dinner and [went] to bed – the children well, the King stayed with me all day.

On Friday January the 28th, I got up – dressed – had breakfast – combed my hair – heard Holy Mass – presided over the Council – went out with Theresa and Mimi – to Chia for a short time – then went to lunch with the King – read – kept him company – saw the Marchioness – then several ladies – the mother and the wife of young Gaetani – to intercede for him – Casa Bona's wife and many others – then went to the French theatre – where they acted *le menteur et Crispin rival de son maître* – afterwards had supper and [went] to bed. The children well – the King after lunch went to Posillipo by dray for a short time.

On Saturday January the 29th, I got up – dressed – had breakfast – heard Holy Mass – read+ – wrote – saw Acton – Cattolica – Vasto – Pignatelli – my children – had lunch – saw Count Lamberg – then came the King – I kept him company – ⊙ – then was busy and gave 42 hearings – afterwards went to the San Carlo theatre and from there to sleep – the children well – the King went to take exercise at Posillipo and to fish whence he returned at half past three.

On Sunday January the 30th, I got up at 7 o'clock – dressed – had breakfast – combed my hair – heard Holy Mass – then had myself painted and Filingieri kept me company – then had lunch with the King – kept him company – ☉ – then read – saw Lady San Marco – then gave several hearings – afterwards saw my children's ball then [went] to a very good and interesting comedy played by cadets entitled *la subordination* – then domino dressed [went] to the masked ball – where I was acompanied by Marsico – then I went up again to take Theresa who was at the loge – at half past twelve [went] to bed – the children well – after lunch the King went out masked throw confetti.

On Monday January the 31st, I got up at 8 o'clock – had breakfast – combed my hair – saw my children – heard Holy Mass – then presided over the Council – then had dinner with the King – kept him company – read++ – wrote – saw the Marchioness – Donna Teresina – wrote – kept myself busy and went to the opera at the San Carlo theatre – the children well – the King – in the morning before the Council – took exercise – and after lunch went to Capo di Monte.

On Tuesday February the 1st, I got up at 7 o'clock – dressed – had breakfast – combed my hair – saw my children – went to Mass at a quarter to 9 – I left with my lady in a carriage – the lady was Palma – Lord Belmonte and Hamilton – and we went to Carditello – where we found the King with many foreigners – men and women – we had breakfast in the tent – I then got in a one horse carriage with my lady – the Hoyos and Miledy [....] – so we saw the hunt – and then we had lunch – we were close to 100 people – from there we returned – I with the King alone home – I made my toilette – saw my children and went to French Spedale[438] theatre where they performed *l'orphelin anglois et Henri quatre* – afterwards home – kept the King company – ☉ – had supper and [went] to bed – the children fine, the King left for Carditello one hour before me – the rest of the day we stayed together.

On Wednesday February the 2nd, I got up at 7 o'clock – dressed – had breakfast – combed my hair – heard Holy Mass – saw my children – presided over the Council – had lunch with the King – kept him company – played piquet with him – ☉ – then read – wrote – kept myself busy – saw my children – talked with Lady Belmonte – took leave of Lamberg – gave hearings to the ladies – afterwards went with my two eldest daughters to the comedy of cadets – then returned – domino dressed and went to a ball where there were 1,200 masks – I did a tour in a uncovered domino – afterwards went to my loge – where my children were and from there we went home at half past one – there was a figurative minuet and contra dance – with six children – of Lady de Amicis – very pretty and interesting – having been with children we [were lively] – my children well – the

King because of bad weather could not go out during the day – in the evening went to the Florentines theatre.

On February the 3rd Thursday before Lent, I got up at 8 o'clock – dressed – had breakfast – combed my hair – – heard Holy Mass – read – wrote – worked on my affairs – had myself painted – spoke to my confessor – to Richecourt – had lunch with the King – saw my children – was busy – reading – writing – gave hearings – saw my children's ball and went to San Carlo – from there to bed, The children well, the King did not go out all day.

On Friday February the 4th, I got up at 8 o' clock – dressed + – combed my hair – had breakfast – went to the Council – and to San Francesco di Paola with my girls – afterwards had lunch with the King – played piquet – kept him company – saw my children – gave hearings – saw Countess Althan – then the Duke and Duchess of Courland – as the Count and Countess Wartenberg[439] – who were introduced to me by Princess Belmonte – I kept them company, and then I went to the French theatre – where there was *the Barber of Seville* and *le mort marie* from there [went] home to sleep, the children well – the King did not go out all day.

On Saturday February the 5th, I got up at 7 o'clock – dressed – had breakfast – combed my hair – heard Holy Mass – saw my children – who went to visit Francis – who came from Portici – then saw Richecourt – afterwards had lunch with the King – kept him company – ⊙ – read – wrote my letters – gave my audiences – Richecourt introduced Manfredini[440] to me – in the evening [went] to the opera with my children and then home, the children healthy – the King did not go out all day.

On Sunday February the 6th, I got up – dressed – had breakfast – combed my hair – heard Holy Mass – kept myself busy – then at eleven o'clock I went with my three daughters to the Liparoti exercises commanded by the King – the exercises were without fire – there were all the garrison and foreigners – from there I returned home – saw the ladies – then had lunch – afterwards read – wrote – kept myself busy – saw Acton – then went out with my children for a walk at Toledo – from there home – took part in my children's ball – saw them have dinner – then in domino dress went to the ball at the theatre – until the moment of the King's masquerade – then I went up and it was really beautiful – they gave me the golden veil – we remaied there until two o'clock and so did my daughters – afterwards [went] to sleep – the children well – in the morning the King took exercise – lunched with his people – and then went out masked.

On Monday February the 7th, I got up at 8 o'clock – dressed – had breakfast – combed my hair – heard Holy Mass – read – wrote – at half past 10 presided over Sambuca's Council – then had lunch with the King – later played piquet – kept him company – ⊙ – then kept myself busy – stayed with my children – saw the ladies – made my toilette – at half past 7 I went to a court ball – to which were invited 450 people – then danced there – Theresa and Louise danced there – afterwards there was a general dinner and – at one hour after midnight – we went to sleep – the children well – the King did not go out all day.

On February the 8th ShroveTuesday, I got up at 8 o'clock – dressed – had breakfast – combed my hair – heard Holy Mass – read – wrote – kept myself busy – tried a mask with my children – saw my son Francis – Amelia – then had lunch with the children – read – wrote – kept myself busy – saw Lady San Marco – participated in the wedding of Giovanina with Vantitelli – to whom I wish every happiness – but I am very sad – because I loved her very much and was well served – after having violently grieved and saddened – I made my toilette – dressed as Venus – the girls as Graces – Mimi dressed as cupid and – and so dressed – I painted a picture to the King and presented sonnets to him – then I kept him company – ⊗ afterwards I kept myself busy – then domino dressed [went] to the ball at the theatre – at half past one from there home – the children well – the King went to the masked parade only after lunch for a short time.

On February 9 Ash Wednesday, I got up at 8 o'clock, dressed, had breakfast – combed my hair – heard Holy Mass – then arrangef my affairs – saw my children – had lunch with the King – played piquet – kept him company – ⊙ – then saw Madam Cottelini – kept myself busy, afterwards saw Princess Belmonte – [gave] several hearings to ladies – afterwards presided over the Council and went to bed, the children well – the King did not go out at all.

On Thursday February the 10th, I got up at 7 o'clock – dressed – had breakfast – combed my hair – heard Holy Mas – spoke to fiscal Vivenzio,[441] then the regent of vicarage[442] – and then went with my three daughters to San Gaetano – from there returned – talked with Pignatelli – then had lunch – afterwards read + – wrote – kept myself busy – then gave several hearings to ladies – whence had a meeting regarding Calabria with the King – Sambuca – de Marco – Acton – Pignatelli – Vespoli which lasted until half past10 and from there [went] to sleep, the children fine, the King was at Fusaro all day.

On Friday February the 11th, I got up at 7 o'clock – had breakfast – dressed – combed my hair – heard Holy Mass, <u>read</u> – wrote kept myself busy – talked with de Marco – several persons – went to listen to the sermon – had lunch with my children – took care of them – spoke to Lady San Marco – Belmonte – gave hearings to ladies – afterwards to private citizens – then the Council – then three hours of meeting regarding Calabria – afterwards [went] to sleep – the children well – the King was at Fusaro all day.

On Saturday February the 12th, I got up at 7 o'clock – dressed – had breakfast – combed my hair – heard Holy Mass, <u>read</u> – wrote kept myself busy – talked with Sambuca – Gravina – then went with my daughters to Madonna dei Fiorentini – on return spoke to Belmonte – Rocella – San Marco – Butera – had lunch – read – wrote – gave many hearings – kept myself busy – saw air balloon fly – very well – then kept myself busy – arranged my papers and then confessed my sins – afterwards went to sleep, the children well – the King went to Carditello and to Carbone and returned in the evening.

On Sunday February the 13th, I got up at 7 o'clock – shamefully performed my devotions – then had breakfast with my children – made my toilette – whence to listen to the sermon – on my return I saw Richecourt – and my children – went to lunch with the King – and then undressed – wrote – packed – saw Lady San Marco – worked on my affairs – read – saw Hoyos – read – heard my Theresa play the harpsichord – and then saw Lady Sangro – Belmonte – Butera, Lord Pignatelli – the General, Father Munter[443] – then made my toilette – went to the Academy – stayed there with foreigners – then played black jack with them – whence home – had supper and [went] to bed – the children well – the King after lunch went to shoot for a while at Agnano.

On Monday February the 14th, I got up at 6 o'clock – worked on a few domestic arrangements with my papers and affairs – then had breakfast with my children – dressed – heard Holy Mass – gave them my blessing – and at a quarter past 8 went by carriage with the King to Venafro – I left the bridge and arrived at half past twelve – where upon I lunched – arranged my affairs – kept Lady Hoyos company – then took part in the decree made by the King during the Council – later wrote to my children – I kept myself busy – took part in the Council and went to sleep – I left all my dear children – thanks to God – healthy – the King took part in a short wild boar hunt.

<u>On Tuesday February the 15th,</u> I got up at 7 o'clock – dressed – had breakfast – combed my hair – wrote my letters – head Holy Mass – had lunch with five people – Lord Hoyos – the Duchess Avelino – Montalto – Corleto – then kept myself busy – then kept the Hoyos company – from there saw the King return – kept him company – ⊗ – then kept myself busy – wrote – saw my papers – then played *loto dauphin*[444] with another six people – and from there had dinner and went to sleep – I am very cold with a slight fever, the children well – the King killed eleven wild boars and 28 deers, and was at Collo and Selvota.

On Wednesday February the 16th, I got up – dressed – combed my hair – had breakfast – kept myself busy – heard Holy Mass – at ten o'clock went to hunt at Cupa Marzi – where after a mile and a half after climbing the mountain for a mile and a half I arrived crossing place – I shot two boars – then at 5 o'clock we returned – I made my toilette – kept myself busy and then had supper – the children well – we took 35 boars in all.

On Thursday February the 17th, I woke up at 7 o'clock – after a restless night – dressed – combed my hair – then made a second toilette – heard Mass – read – wrote – had lunch at five o'clock – after lunch – wrote – then saw the Duke of Courland and kept him company – then read – kept myself busy – kept the King company – ⊗ – afterwards undressed and changed – then wrote to my children – went out – to attend a concert and a supper – and then [went] to bed – the children – according to my news – in good health – the King hunted 15 wild boars at the hunting site called Castellone.

<u>On Friday February 18</u>, I got up at 7 o'clock – dressed – had breakfast, combed my hair – heard Holy Mass – read – wrote – I kept myself bysy – had lunch with Lady Hoyos – the Duchess d'Avellino – talked with both – then played the harpsichord – sung – then kept the King company – wrote to my children – had supper and [went] to bed – the children well – the King went to Strone and shot 25 boars there.

<u>On Saturday February the 19th,</u> I woke up at 7 o'clock – dressed – had breakfast – combed my hair – heard Holy Mass – kept the King company – ⊙ – kept myself busy – had lunch with the King – played *loto dauphin* – then there was music – I kept myself busy – had supper and [went] to bed – the children well – the King could not go out because of bad weather – Krotendorf [visited me] in the evening.

<u>On Sunday February the 20th,</u> I got up – dressed – combed my hair – read my letters – wrote – heard Holy Mass – kept myself busy – had lunch at big table – then kept myself busy – talked with Lady Hoyos – saw and

bid farewell to the Duke of Courland – kept the King company – stayed with people – wrote to my children – played *loto dauphin* – had supper and [went] to bed – the children – according to my news – the King hunted for a short time – but the weather was very bad.

On Monday February the 21st, I got up – dressed – had breakfast – combed my hair – heard Holy Mass – kept myself busy – had lunch with Countess Caltanisetta and Montalto – then kept myself busy – kept the Countess company – read – worked – wrote my letters – then saw the Countess – who took keave – then went to have supper and sadly took leave from the Countess Hoyos and her husband – she is very good person – the children well – the King went hunting – but returned early owing to the bad weather.

On Tuesday February the 22nd, I got up at 8 o'clock – dressed – had breakfast – combed my hair – heard Holy Mass – read – wrote – kept myself busy – arranged my papers – had lunch, played music principally the harpsichord – later sung – then wrote – kept myself busy – had supper and [went] to bed – the children well – the King could only go out for a ride for an half hour after lunch – the weather was terrible.

On Wednesday February the 23rd, I got up at 8 o'clock – dressed – had breakfast – combed my hair – heard Holy Mass – read – wrote – kept myself busy – played the harpsichord – had lunch at a big table – wrote – kept myself busy – played the harpsichord – sung with Hadrava[445] – read – wrote – I kept myself busy – again saw the Duke of Courland who has returned – had supper and went to bed – the children fine – the King after lunch went hunting for a short time.

On Thursday February the 24th, I got up – dressed – had breakfast – combed my hair – heard Holy Mass – read – wrote – kept myself busy – had lunch with 4 people – kept myself busy – played the harpsichord – kept the King company – ⊗ – then kept myself busy – played the harpsichord – played *loto dauphin* – had supper and [went] to bed – the children well – the King went hunting all day.

On Friday February the 25th, I got up at 7 o'clock – dressed – had breakfast – combed my hair – went to Mass – at nine o'clock I went hunting with the Duke of Courland and Belmonte – I was hunting at the crossing place – I fired five shots – killed two wild boars one of which was very big and wounded another – we returned about six o'clock – made my toilette – kept the King company – ⊗ – then wrote – kept myself busy – had lunch – supper and [went] to bed – was informed that Antoinette was sick and with cold – which worried me a lot – the King went out a couple of hours before us and spent the rest of the day with us.

On Saturday February the 26th, I got up at 7 o'clock – dressed – had breakfast – combed my hair – heard Holy Mass – read – wrote – kept myself busy – had lunch face to face with Corleto – kept myself busy – played the harpsichord – wrote to my children – listened to Serio improvising on the theme of the gratitude of subjects towards their masters this was done to amuse the Duke of Courland – who had lunch and proposed a toast recited mediocre verses – then [went] to sleep, the children well – the King spent hunting all day.

On Sunday February the 27th, I got up at 7 o'clock – dressed – had breakfast – combed my hair – heard Holy Mass – worked – kept myself busy – had lunch with Corleto – Montalto e Caltanisetta – then kept myself busy – played the harpsichord – wrote to my [children] from Naples – started to pack – had supper and [went] to bed – the children well – the King came all day hunting.

On Monday February the 28th, I got up at 7 o'clock – dressed – had breakfast – kept myself busy – heard Holy Mass – saw some engravings with the King who went straight home because of the heavy snow – then kept him company – ⊙ – then had lunch – kept myself busy – played the harpsichord +++ – then played – saw the Council – kept myself busy – talked with my confessor – had dinner and [went] to bed. The children well – the King could not go out to hunt owing to the heavy snow – the courrier from Brussels went back here.

On Tuesday March the 1st, I woke up at 7 o'clock – dressed – had breakfast – combed my hair – heard Holy Mass – read – wrote – I kept myself busy – had lunch with Corleto – Montalto and Caltanisetta – then kept myself busy – played the harpsichord – arranged my affairs – played *loto dauphin* and went to bed, I received the news from Naples that Antoinette had tremors again – this worries me, the others fine – the King went hunting all day.

On Wednesday March the 2nd, I got up at half past 5 – dressed – had breakfast – heard Holy Mass – then at 7 o'clock went out by carriage with the King to Venafro – on the way we had snow wind and rain and luckily we arrived at eleven o'clock in the morning – I found all my dear children healthy and the girls charming – particularly Antoinette – we had lunch all together and – then I unpacked and played piquet with the King – then took care of my children – gave some hearings – and then went to the

Fondo theatre with the King to listen to the music of [...] – from there home – the children well – the King was all day at home.

On Tuesday March the 3rd, I got up – dressed – had breakfast – heard Holy Mass – at eleven o'clock we went to see the *Ceres* launched into the sea – a frigate of 44 guns – it was all a wonderful success – then came back home – where I had lunch with the King – played pinquet – kept him company – ⊗ – then kept myself busy – saw the ladies – my children – spent the evening with them playing *loto dauphin* – then had dinner and [went] to sleep – the children well – the King could not go out the whole day because of bad weather.

On Friday March the 4th, I got up – dressed – had breakfast – heard Holy Mass – was busy making my accounts – had kunch with the King – kept him company – played piquet with him – ⊗ – then kept myself busy – gave several audiences – later [wemt]to the Council – after that – in particular – the King and I talked with Acton – had supper and then [went] to bed – the children well – the King could not go out owing to bad weather.

On Saturday March the 5th, I got up – dressed – had breakfast – combed my hair – heard Holy Mass – spoke to Stigliano – had lunch with my children – took care of them – read + – wrote – kept myself busy – then dressed and in the evening went to the French cruel tragedy [*Rice*] – and home – the children well – the King at half past twelve went to Fusaro.

On March 6 Sunday I got up at 7 o'clock – dressed – had breakfast with Mimi – combed my hair – then heard Mass – arranged several small affairs – then at eleven – we went down to Molosiglio – where we went on board to see a big Dutch frigate called *the Tyyce* – commanded by English commander Bylan – then on a small one commanded by Cambel – after having seen those we went to have lunch at my little house with the three commander – Migliano – Acton – Corleto and lady – having finished I returned to [...] read – saw my children – gave endless hearings – went to the Fondo theatre with my two eldest daughters and the King – on returnng we found our ambassador to France – Prince Caramanico – who has returned after four years, the children well – the King went out with me all day – except after lunch [when he] went on a sailing boat for short time.

On Monday March the 7th, I got up – dressed – lunch – heard Holy Mass – then read – then at half past nine went with my lady guard to Caserta – where I packed – then I had lunch with the King and Migliano and then worked on my affairs – afterwards I went home with the King – I saw my children – unpacked trinkets from Paris – then presided over the Council – then went to bed – the children well – in the morning the King went to Carditello came to have lunch with me at Caserta and then went to San Leucio – where he picked me up and returned with me.

Tuesday March 8, I got up at 8 o'clock – dressed – had breakfast – combed my hair – heard Holy Mass – saw my children – at eleven o' clock showed all my children to Caramanico – then had lunch with the King – kept him company – ⊗ – then I played piquet – wrote my letters – kept myself busy – and then I made my toilette – in the evening I went to the Academy – where I stayed with the Duke of Courland – I came back home – and then to bed, the children well – the King did not go out all day.

On Wednesday March the 9, I got up – dressed – had breakfast – combed my hair – heard Holy Mass – presided over the Council – then saw the Duchess and Duke of Courland – with their retinues – I showed them the terrace and all my apartments – then we went by boat I – the King – the Duke – two gentlemen – Belmonte and Caramanico – to my little house where we found Salandra – Hamilton and Onorato – we had lunch – we talked – I then came home and spoke to Caramanico – then Acton – afterwards to several ladies – in the evening we went to French Spedale [theatre] [to see] – *l'home du jour* – and then went to sleep – the children – thank God in good health – the King spent the morning and had lunch with us – then drove the Duke to Strone to a wild boar hunt.

On Thursday March the 10th, I got up – dressed – had breakfast – saw my children – wrote – kept my self busy – talked with Stigliano – then saw people – made my affairs – talked with de Marco – had lunch with my children – read + – wrote – kept myself busy – strolled on the terrace and in the evening went to the French [theatre] – [to see] *la Veuve du Malabar*[446] – ⊙ then to bed – in the evening the new minister of Spain Las Casas[447] was introduced to us – the children well – the King went to hunt wild boars at Carditello all day.

On Friday March the 11th, I got up – dressed – combed my hair – took medicine – received the courrier fromVienna – busy – had lunch with the King and my children – read + – wrote – kept myself busy – gave many hearings – then presided over the Council – then went to bed – the children well – the King went for an hour to Fusaro to prepare to go fishing.

On Saturday March the 12th, I got up – dressed – had breakfast – combed my hair – heard Holy Mass – read – wrote – talked to Caramanico – [then] Gravina – had lunch with my children – took care of them – read

+ – wrote – kept myself busy – sent the Sardinian courrier – the post – [worked on] all my affairs and 20 hearings – then went to bed +++ – the children well – the King was at Caserta for the whole day.

On Sunday March the 13th, I got up – dressed – had breakfast – combed my hair – heard Holy Mass and at ten o'clock went with the King and my two eldest daughters – Theresa and Louise – to Fusaro – there we fished – then lunched – Acton – Caramanico – Migliano – Cervinara – Leonessa – afterwards we fished again and I returned – as I had gone – with the King and my children – I made my toilette – read the letters and went to the French [theatre] with my daughters – they performed *le Père de famille* and afterwards I sent them back [home], and then I saw the short play – from there home – ⊙ – then [went] to sleep – the children well – the King stayed with me all day

On Monday March the 14th, I got up – dressed – had breakfast – had my teeth cleaned – heard Holy Mass – presided over the Council – then worked on my affairs – talked with andria – Gravina – had lunch with my children – <u>read</u>+ – wrote – kept myself busy – saw the ladies – then made my accounts – arrangements – gave a lot of audiences – and [went] to bed – the children well – at eleven o'clock in the morning the King went to hunt common snipes at Carbone.

On Tuesday March the 15th, I got up – dressed – had breakfast – heard Holy Mass – wrote letters – talked with Caramanico – had lunch with my children – read – wrote – kept myself busy – saw all the people who came to take leave – I packed – then [made] my toilette – then saw the ladies – then went to the Academy – I played with Princess Belmonte – Salandra and Lord Marsico – and then I went with the King to Portici to spruce myself – ⊗ – afterwards had supper and [went] to sleep – the children well – the King was all day the pheasant farm – in the evening he returned and went with me to the Academy and to Portici.

On Wednesday March the 16th, I got up at 7 o'clock – had breakfast with my son Francis and little Amalia – then dressed – combed my hair – talked with the governess – then unpacked – put all my boxes – papers – writing in order – at eleven o'clock heard Mass – my daughters came from Naples – I took care of them – had lunch with the King – played piquet – kept myself busy – talked with Gravina – saw the apartments with him – and stayed with my children, went to listen to sermons – the spiritual exercises – then played with my children – kept myself busy and [went] to bed, the children well – in the morning the King went to Torre and after lunch strolled for a short time.

On Tuesday March the 17th, I got up at half past 7 – dressed – had breakfast – combed my hair – heard Holy Mass – heard all Mimi's lessons – and then went for a walk with my two daughters up to the wood – on returning saw all my children – I kept myself busy – had lunch with the King – worked – talked with Rocella – San Marco – saw my children – Countess Althan – went to [listen to] the sermon – said good evening to my children and went to the Council and to bed, the children well – in the morning the King went to town – then after lunch strolled in the grove.

On Friday March the 18th, I got up – dressed – had breakfast – combed my hair – heard Holy Mass – worked on my affairs – then had lunch with the King – worked – kept myself busy – talked with Virieux – Genzano – Belmonte – saw the King – kept him company – ⊗ – then went to listen to the sermon ++++ – from there to the Council – then [went] to bed – the children well – in the morning the King went to hunt curlews-to Torre – after lunch in town and returned by the promenade of the bridge.

On Saturday March the 19th, I got up at 7 o'clock – dressed – had breakfast – combed my hair – heard Holy. Mass – read+ – wrote – kept myself busy – saw the Minister of Spain – then had lunch with my children – took care of them – talked with Caramanico – then wrote – talked with Belmonte – [gave] hearings to ladies and kept myself busy – then went to listen to the sermon – from there gave hearings to a lady – then took care of my children all evening – then – ⊗ – [went] to bed, the children well – the King went to Carditello and returned early to kill the first little egret.

On Sunday March the 20th, I got up – dressed – had breakfast – combed my hair – heard Holy Mass – kept myself busy – stayed with my children – talked with Richecourt – had lunch with the King – read – kept myself busy – worked – talked with Lady Termoli – wrote – then went to [listen to] the sermon – took care of my children – then worked and went to bed – the children well – the King because of the bitter cold could only go for a short walk – Krotendorf consoled me doing his regular visit.

On Monday March the 21st, I got up – dressed – had breakfast – combed my hair – heard Holy Mass – kept myself busy – talked with Gravina – then had lunch – afterwards kept myself busy – then saw Hauss – my eldest – then the second Hauss – after Father Pignone[448] – then [listen to] the sermon – afterwards the Council and then went to bed – the children well – in the morning the King went to hunt curlews – at Torre – and after lunch in Naples – where he went by boat.

On Tuesday March the 22nd, I got up – dressed – lunch – had breakfast – heard Holy Mass – wrote my letters – then saw little Antoinette arrive – afterwards saw my other children – had lunch with the King – worked – kept myself busy – talked with my confessor – went to listen to the sermon – to [receive] the blessing – then with my children – afterwards to the Council and to bed – the children well – in the morning the King went to hunt curlews at Torre – after lunch he did not go out anymore.

On Wednesday March the 23rd, I woke up at 7 o'clock with the news that Louise was sick – I jumped ou of bed – put on a dressing gown – then I made my toilette – saw my children – heard Mass – arranged my affairs – spoke to Calabrito – acompanied by Gravina and Marsico – went to town – there I saw the apartment for my son – then spoke to Belmonte – afterwards had lunch with Januarius – I arranged several things – spoke to Acton – strolled on the terrace and then returned with the King – saw my daughter Louise – then unpacked trinkets from Paris – presided over the Council – and went to Louise's room and [went] to bed – the children fine – except Luisa that at half past four in the morning had a paroxysm – that lasted half an hour then a feeling of heaviness in my stomach but in the evening was better – the King went [to hunt] little egrets – then to fish at Fusaro – from there he picked me up at Naples and went back to Portici.

On Thursday March the 24th, I got up – made my toilette – busy – heard second Theresa's Mass – went to Louise's room – at ten o'clock went to church functions – at midday went out – received Richecourt's letters – had lunch with the King – worked – at half past two – performed a douching – then worked – saw my children – at midnight [went] to the sermon – then with the children – I kept myself busy – changed and [went] to Holy Sepulchre – but without paroxysm – in the morning the walked for a while – after lunch at home.

On Good Friday March the 25th, I got up – dressed – had breakfast – combed my hair – dressed – then at 9 o'clock went to the church functions – returned at midday – afterwards worked – stayed with my children – talked with Belmonte – the valet – then prayed – kept myself busy – stayed with my children – and went to bed – the children well – Louise better – but still has fever – the King went to and returned from Naples – after lunch – by sea.

On March the 26th, Holy Saturday I got up – dressed – had breakfast – combed my hair – worked on my affairs – went to church – then had lunch with the King – kept him company – ⊗ – after stayed with my

children – saw Marchioness San Marco – Hereria – then headr the harpsi-
chord play – my son who acompanied – then Theresa played – afterwads
I went to confess my sins – then [went] bed – the children well – better
Louise – after lunch the King went to Naples for a short time.

On March the 27th, Easter Sunday I got up – dressed – went with
the King to spend my Easter – then had breakfast with my children –
then made my toilette – then went to Mass – then [went] to the hand-
kissing – to the public table – undressed – kept the King company – ⊙
afterwards talked with Gravina – dressed – went to receive a blessing at
St. Augustine – then changed – went down to the lady's room there and
played reversis with Belmonte – Caramanico and Marsico – then to bed –
the children well – the King only went with me to the blessing

On Monday March the 28th, I got up at 6 o'clock – dressed – went to
my son's room – had breakfast – dressed – combed my hair – heard Holy
Mass – everybody with him – and then [went to listen] to the sermon –
afterwards walked with him and my daughters – on returning I entrusted
him into the hands of men – Ayo – Duke of Gravina – preceptor – the eldest Hauss – young Hauss – and Poli the preceptor – four valets of rooms –
finally the child behaved very well in everything – I was there until 4
o'clock when he left – I returned at six o'clock – he came back for the
blessing – then presided over the Council – kept myself busy and [went]
to bed – the children fine – the King went to lunch at castle – afterwards
to kill little egrets inthe wood several times.

On Tuesday March the 29th, I got up at 6 o'clock – dressed – had
breakfast – combed my hair – heard Holy Mass – [went] to my son's
room – at 8 o'clock I went and remained there until midday – I went back
to have lunch with the King – played piquet – wrote my letters – kept
myself busy, went to [receive] the blessing – talked with Richecourt – took
care of my children – and [went] to bed, the children well – after lunch the
King went to Naples by land.

On Wednesday March the 30th, I got up at 7 o'clock – dressed – had
breakfast – combed my hair – heard Holy Mass – went to my children's
room – then had lunch with the King – I kept busy – played piquet – kept
him company – ⊙ – then saw Lady San Marco – went [to receive] the
blessing – the Council and [went] to bed – the children well – Theresa still
with her cold – but without any consequences – the King could not go out
all day because of bad weather.

On Thursday March the 31st, I got up at half past 7:30 – dressed –
breakfasted – combed my hair – took care of my children – talked with

Marsico – wrote – I kept myself busy – painted – had lunch with Mimi – spoke to Caramanico – then kept myself busy – talked with Lady Althan – went to my son's room – then [to receive] the blessing – kept the King company while I read the letters – talked with Richecourt – kept myself busy and then went to bed – the children well – Theresa took medicine – Louise came to me – the King went to the swamp at Acerra though the weather was awful.

On Friday April the 1st, I got up at 7 o'clock – dressed – had breakfast – combed my hair – heard Holy Mass – went to my son's room – kept myself busy – went for a walk in high wood – then had lunch with the King – kept him company – played pinquet –talked with Lady San Marco – Acton – worked on my affairs – gave hearings – then the Council and [went] to bed – the children well – the King after lunch went to Naples by land.

On Saturday April the 2nd, I got up – dressed – had breakfast – combed my hair – heard Holy Mass – spoke to Acton – then Richecourt – afterwards lunched with my children – took care of them – made choices and travel preparations – then talked with B – afterwards had myself painted – spoke to Lady Belmonte – then to Lady Trana – Villafranca – later [went to say] the rosary – spoke to the King – wrote my letters and [went] to bed – the children well – the King was at Carditello all day.

On Sunday April the 3rd, I got up – dressed – had breakfast – combed my hair – heard Holy Mass – saw my children – made my toilette – then went with Princess Caramanico to town – at the *Strada Nova* we had to go down because the Viaticum was passing – afterwards I arrived – I saw my children – I spoke to Richecourt – then Acton – then I had lunch – kept myself busy – worked on my affairs – the King came back – I went with him to see the vessels – then returned to Portici – kept him company – ⊗ – afterwards saw my children – kept myself busy and [went] to bed – the children well – the King went to have lunch at the castle at Portici and then came to bed

On Monday April the 4th, I got up – dressed – lunch – had breakfast – heard Holy Mass – saw my children – saw Pignatelli and talked with him – then had lunch – spoke to Caramanico – went with him and Corleto to town – kept myself busy – saw the King – San Marco – Belmonte – Sambuca – Stigliano – Castropiano – Gaetana – then went to a new play at the new theatre – the concert was quite good – the play – stupid as usual returned with the King – ⊗ – then to bed – the children well – they went to eat at Pagliara – the King went to the swamp at Acerra.

On Tuesday April the 5th, I got up – took part in the King's bleeding which was a precautionary measure – then dressed – had breakfast – combed my hair – heard Holy Mass – presided over the Sambuca's Council – then had lunch with the King – played piquet – wrote my letters – went to say the rosary – kept myself busy – [went] to bed – the children well – the King all day at home because of bad weather and of rain and bleeding.

On Wednesday April the 6th, I got up at 7 o'clock – dressed – had breakfast – combed my hair – heard Holy Mass – was present at Mimi's lesson – arranged my papers – had lunch with the King and my children – played piquet – talked with Lady San Marco – General Pignatelli – with Butera – went to [say] the rosary – talked with Lady Casa Buona – with Lord Guarino and [went] to bed – the children – thanks to God – well – the King in the morning was purged and after lunch went to town and to see our vessels.

On Thursday April the 7th, the seventeenth year of my marriage and of the departure from Vienna – I got up at 7 o'clock – dressed – had breakfast – combed my hair – heard Holy Mass – was busy – at ten thirty went with Francis to town to see my children – had lunch with them – then kept myself busy – spoke to de Marco – Acton + – some ladies – then worked on my affairs and returned with Princess Caramanico – kept myself busy and went to bed – the children well – the King was at Carditello and Caserta all day.

On Friday April the 8th, I got up at 7 o'clock – dressed – had breakfast – combed my hair – heard Holy Mass – saw my children – wrote – I kept myself busy – had lunch with the King and my children – played piquet – kept the King company – ⊙ then wrote – took care ++++ went to the terrace of the Great Mistress – talked with Lady Sangro – with Richecourt – went to [say] the rosary – the Council + then [went] to sleep – the children well – the King did not leave home.

On Saturday April the 9th, I dressed – had breakfast – combed my hair – heard Holy Mass – made and saw arrangements – spoke to Acton – received the news of the happy chilbirth of the Queen[449] – which for me was a double pleasure as I am – had lunch with my children – talked with Vasto – an abbot Edlingen[450] – had him listen to the harpsichord played by my children – wrote – kept myself busy and [went] to bed – the children well – the King was all day at Carditello.

On Sunday April the 10th, I got up – dressed – had breakfast – heard Holy Mass – kept myself busy – went with the King and my three daughters to the castle – had lunch at the table that goes up and down – and then I came back and at half past three went with the King to the city – where

I took care of my children – saw Lady San Marco Belmonte – hearings to some ladies – and the Florentine theatre to see *le Roi Teodore* which bored enormously – and where I still reconized the nation by the crowd that there was – we returned – ⊗ – and I went to sleep – the children well – the King was with me all day.

On Monday April the 11th, I got up – dressed – had breakfast – combed my hair – heard Holy Mass – then kept myself busy – saw my children – had lunch with the King – read – wrote – I kept myself busy – 13 +++ – then [went to say] the rosary – to the Council and to bed – the children well – the King in the morning went to the city by sea and no in the afternoon he did not go out at all.

On Tuesday April the 12th, I got up – dressed – had breakfast – combed my hair – heard Holy Mass – kept myself busy – then went with my three girls to town – to see Januarius and wished him happy birthday – then I sent my daughters back home and spoke with Belmonte – Pignatelli – had lunch with my children – spoke to Acton – finished my letters – arranged many affairs – talked with Lady San Marco – Belmonte – other women and ladies in audience – then made my toilette and went to the Academy – I played with Lord Belmonte – Marsico and Carinola – and returned home with fever – went to bed – at Portici the children [are] well – the King had lunch at the castle and after lunch went to town.

On Wednesday April the 13th, I got up – dressed – had breakfast – combed my hair – heard Mass – worked with difficulty because I had fever – then I spoke to Tarsia – I had lunch – kept myself busy and went to bed early – the children well – in the morning the King went to town.

On Thursday April the 14th, I got up – dressed – took an ounce of salt from England – then walked – dressed – ocupé – spoke to Caramanico – dinner with my children – ocuper me with it – write – work – talked with San Marco – Richecourt in – then go to bed – the children well – the King went to the swamp at Acerra – for the whole day went to hunt snipes.

On Friday April the 15th, I got up – dressed – had breakfast – heard Holy Mass – worked on my affairs – had lunch with the King – worked – read – arranged my affairs – [went to say] the rosary – to the Council and to bed – the children well – the King after lunch went to town for a while

On Saturday April the 16th, I got up – dressed – had breakfast – combed my hair – heard Holy Mass – read+ – wrote – spoke to Acton – worked on my affairs – had lunch with my children – at half past 3 talked with

Las Casas for a long time – Minister of Spain – then with Richecourt – gave hearings and went to bed – in the morning Krottendorf came – the children fine – the King was at Carditello all day.

On Sunday April the 17th, I got up – dressed – had breakfast with my son – heard Mass – spoke to San Nicola – at midday I had to go to bed – feeling high fever – a great pain – I spent the whole day very debilitated – with a total interruption of Krottendorf – the children well – the King in the morning went to Naples.

On Monday April the 18th, I spent a bad night – I confessed my sins to have a good conscience – in the morning at midday was bled from my foot – that relieved me a bit – even though the day was insufferable – in the afternoon I read for a short time – in the evening heard Sambuca's Council – the children well – the King went to fishing at Castellamare.

On Tuesday the 19th I was better – but still in bed all day – my children – Richecourt – were the only people whom I saw – I presided over the Council and began to sleep – the children well – the King strolled by the sea all day.

On Wednesday April the 20th, I stayed in bed all day as a precaution but had no fever – I saw K – S. Marco Belmonte – presided over the Council – the children well – the King walked to the sea.

On Thursday April the 21st, King – in the evening saw some ladies – the Duke of Courland who returned from Rome and to bed – the children well – the King was at home all day.

On Friday April the 22nd, I got up – saw my children – worked on my affairs – saw the German abbots – then Richecourt – had lunch – spoke to Acton – presided over the Council and went to bed – the children well – the King went to town – had lunch on the brigatine and returned early.

On Saturday April the 23rd, I got up – dressed – had breakfast – combed my hair – heard Holy Mass – read + – kept myself busy – saw the envoy – shoewd him my children – then had lunch with Francis and Mimi – afterwards kept myself busy – spoke to Caramanico – to Marchioness San Marco – abbot Edlingen – arranged my affairs and to bed – the children well – except Theresa who is in bed with a slight fever and sore throat – the King was all day at Caserta.

On Sunday April the 24th, I got up – dressed – had breakfast – combed my hair – had breakfast with my children – heard Holy Mass – kept myself busy – had lunch with the King – had myself painted – then went with the King to the city – where I saw the porcelain [factory] – my children – worked on my affairs – saw the[dukes] of Curland – the duke with the child – then returned by the new carriage with the King – ⊗ – then [went to say] the rosary – saw my children – kept myself busy – heard musical garden and to bed – the children well – the King went and returned with me to the city not having gone out because of bad weather.

On Monday April the 25th, I got up – dressed – had breakfast with my children – had lunch.

The confusion has been so great these days – and the multiplicity of affairs – that I leave on Saturday the 30th,[451] without finishing my journal.

The diary of my journey will be written separately and it will be inserted here – I start again form the day of my arrival on September 7th.

On 7 September at midnight disembarked [among the crowd] arriving at Molosiglio I had the pleasure of embracing my dear children – which was a great consolation for me – after the first tenderness I went up and had myself brought to my room in a sedan chair – where all my ladies – everyone in the house was waiting for me – I went ot see my sick little girl – then come back to my room for a moment – made my toilette and went to San Carlo theatre – where they were performing an opera and first ballet very well – after an act […] [went] to sleep.

On September 8 I got up at 7 o'clock – saw my children – dressed – had breakfast – combed my hair – at 9 o'clock went to the Council – then to Holy Mass – after lunch [stayed] with the King and my children – after kept myself busy – wore court dresst and then – at half past 4 – went out in public with six my children to Pie di Grotta – on return made a second toilette and went to the Fondo theatre to see *le Capitaine Cok*[452] – afterwards [went to] the promenade at Chiaia – where after some tours – we returned home – had dinner and [went to] sleep – the children well – little sick one better – the King was all day with me.

On Friday September 9, I got up at 8 o'clock – dressed – had breakfast – combed my hair – heard Holy Mass – the Council – then saw the ambassador of France – had lunch with the King – kept him company – saw people – in the evening the wife of the ambassador – some hearings – we went to the Academy – the great hall has been painted – there was a sweltering heat – we stayed there for a short time and went home – had lunch and went to sleep – the children well – the little one is slowly recovering – the King after lunch went to Portici by sea and stayed for a couple of hours.

On Saturday September the 10th, I got up at 7 o'clock – saw my children – had breakfast – combed my hair – heard Holy Mass – spoke to General Pignatelli – to Marquis della Sambuca, to Lady Belmonte – to

San Marco and lunched with the children – saw General Acton – then kept myself busy – wrote – gave hearings – kept myself busy and afterwards – at 9 o'clock – went to bed – the children well – the King was at Caserta all day.

On Sunday September the 11th, I got up – dressed – had breakfast – combed my hair – heard Holy Mass – saw my children – worked on my affairs – at midday I went with the Princess of Jacy and the Prince Caramanico – to have lunch at Posillipo – I found the King – then all the commanders came to have lunch with us – Maltese – Dutch – English – after lunch I remained to converse for a short time – then I returned home – I spoke to the King a long time – + ⊗ – then gave hearings and afterwards went to sleep – the children well – the King went before me and returned after me because he wentfishing at Posillipo.

On Monday September the 12th, I got up at 8 o'clock – dressed – had breakfast – combed my hair – heard Holy Mass – dressed – went to see the wet nurse – then my son's school – then [listened to] my daughters's harpsichord – after lunch – then kept the King company – kept myself busy – gave hearings – [went] to the Council and to bed – the King went only in the afternoon to Portici.

On Tuesday September the 13th, I got up – dressed – had breakfast – combed my hair – heard Holy Mass – wrote my letters – busy – had lunch with the King – I kept myself busy – gave hearings – in the evening went to the promenade at Chiaia and to bed.

On the 14th, I got up – dressed – had breakfast – combed my hair – heard Holy Mass – had lunch with my children – I kept myself busy – gave hearings – in the evening [went] to the Council – and to bed – the King went to hunt quails.

On Thursday the 15th, I got up – dressed – had breakfast – busy – had lunch with my children – spoke to Marco – Sambuca – Acton – saw the ladies – and in the evening I prepared my confession and confessed my sins and then to bed – the King at eleven o'clock went to Castellamare70 – […] – […] +++++ – 155.[453]

On Friday the 16th, I got up and went to church – performed my devotions unworthily – then – returned – I stayed with my children – had breakfast – dressed – I saw the King arrive – had lunch with him – kept myself busy – saw people – gave hearings – [went] to the Council and then to bed. The King in the morning returned from Castellamare – then went to hunt quails at San Leonardo.

On Saturday the 17th, I got up – dressed – had breakfast – kept myself busy – went to Holy Mass – wrote – I kept myself busy – had lunch with the King – I kept myself busy – gave hearings – went for along the Chiaia promenade and bed – the King did not go out.

On Sunday the 18th, dressed – made my toilette – had breakfast – heard Holy Mass – had lunch with the King – kept myself busy – gave hearings – in the evening [went] to the promenade at Chiaia and to bed – the King did not go out.

On Monday September the 19, I got up – dressed – made my toilette – had breakfast – heard Holy Mass – and at eleven o'clock – went to the chapel with all my children, then dinner – was busy – at half past four I went out with the King and my four older children to the cathedral at St. Jan. where – after adoring the Blessed Sacrament – venerated St. Januarius – we returned – I took leave of Mr de Village – kept the King company – ⊗ – then some audiences – afterwards we had the Council – then went to the promenade at Chiaia – after lunch at the little house where the navy captains and in part our navy were called – then [went] to sleep.

On Tuesday September the 20th, I got up – dressed – had breakfast – combed my hair – heard Holy Mass – spoke to Duke Gravina – then had lunch with King – kept myself me – then I spoke with Cardinal Spinelli – afterwards gave hearings – and then to the promenade and to bed – the King in the morning went to the swamp – after lunch [went] to a review an exercise.

On Wednesday September the 21st, I got up – dressed – had breakfast – combed my hair – heard Holy Mass – lunched with the King – kept myself busy – <u>read</u> – gave hearings – went to the Council and to sleep – the King took exercise and did not go out at all.

On Thursday September the 22nd, I got up – dressed – had breakfast – combed my hair – heard Holy Mass – kept myself busy – saw my children – had lunch with the King – busy – <u>read</u> +++++ – gave hearings – talked with <u>my confessor</u> and to bed – the King went out to take exercise.

<u>On Friday September 23rd,</u> I got up – dressed – breakfasted – combed my hair – heard Holy Mass – busy – had lunch with the King – was busy – ⊗ – <u>read</u> – and gave hearings to several ladies – afterwards the Council and [went] to bed – the children well – the King after lunch went to Portici.

<u>On Saturday the 24th,</u> I got up – dressed – had breakfast – combed my hair – heard Holy Mass – was busy – had lunch with the King – worked – saw the ladies – [gave] a quantity of hearings – strolled and [went] to bed – the children fine – after lunch the King took exercise – in the presence of the Dutch.

The numerous affairs at the time of my return – the violent troubles I have had from the minister of Spain Mister de las Casas – I have dazed me the point that I have lost the faculty of doing anything and I have only been able to be absorbed by my pains here my cruel position that continues on October the 10th we went to Caserta and it is from there that I write about my constantly painful situation.

On Tuesday November 1st, I got up in the morning at 7 o'clock – had breakfast – dressed – saw my children – I went to Mass at the chapel – then I was busy – at eleven o'clock I went to my novena – had lunch with my children – saw Princess Belmonte – wrote my letters – in the evening went to the ball, and then to bed – after having seen and played pool [and] reversis.

On Wednesday November the 2nd, I got up at 7 o'clock – dressed – had breakfast – went to Mass – then kept my self busy – the courrier from Vienna arrived – Richecourt brought me the letters – the King came to have lunch – then I kept myself busy – in the evening there was a Council and then I confessed my sins and [went] to bed.

On Thursday November the 3rd, I got up in the morning at 6 o'clock – went unworthily to church – performed my devotions – and dressed – had breakfast – combed my hair – at eleven o'clock heard the last day of my *novena* – Dinner with my children – m kept myself busy – saw the French ambassador and his lady – went to the French show *le tambour nocturne* – which I get bored and then [went] to bed.

On November the 4th, I had lunch with my girls – made a long toilette – heard two Masses – received the whishes from everyone – and then fucks hands – Public table – how to King Company – ⊗ – then saw Marsico – San Marco – Belmonte – Sangro – Termoli – Cattolica – the regent – then to the comic opera at the new theatre – where I bored myself to death and then [went] to bed – ⊙.

On Saturday November the 5th, I got up – dressed – had breakfast – combed my hair – heard Holy Mass – was busy – wrote my letters – had lunch with my children – in the evening went to the French comedy *Dupui et Deronais*[454] which I liked a lot and aftwerwards [went] to bed.

On Sunday November the 6th, I got up – dressed – had breakfast – combed my hair – heard two Holy Masses – one in the main chapel – the other in the private chapel – was busy – put my papers in order – made my accounts – had lunch with my children – read +++ – played the harpsichord – at half past three I went with my three girls to the waterfall and returned on foot – in the evening [went to see] a beautiful tragedy called *Gaston et Bajard*[455] – then went to sleep – ⊙.

On Monday November the 7th, I got up and took an ounce of salt from England – afterwards dressed – had breakfast – heard Holy Mass – spoke to Richecourt – Marsico – had lunch with my children – read +++ – wrote – kept myself busy – then the Council and – not feeling well – in bed

On Tuesday November the 8th, I got up at 8 o'clock – having had a bad night – dressed – had breakfast – combed my hair – heard Holy Mass – wrote my letters – had lunch with the King – worked – wrote – talked with Lady San Marco, then with Tarsia – Roccafiorita – talked with the King when – feeling bad + I could not go to the comedy – finished my post – spoke to my confessor and went to bed.

On Wednesday November the 9th, I got up – dressed – had breakfast – combed my hair – heard Holy Mass – was busy – had lunch with the King – wrote – worked – saw Lady Belmonte – presided over the Council and [went] to bed.

On Thursday November the 10th, I got up – dressed – had breakfast – combed my hair – heard Holy Mass – had lunch with the King – then kept myself busy – talked with Sangro – other people – in the evening went [to see] the comedy entitled *Beverley.*

On Friday the 11th, I got up – dressed – had breakfast – combed my hair – heard Holy Mass – spoke to Acton – kept myself busy – had lunch with my children – talked with Caramanico – kept myself busy – in the evening [went to] the Council and to bed.

On the 12, I got up – dressed – had breakfast – combed my hairs – heard Holy Mass – read – wrote – talked with my children – had lunch with them – kept myself busy – after lunch saw the ambassador and his wife – then [went to see] the play of *Henry IV*[456] and [went] to bed.

On Sunday the 13th, I got up – dressed – had breakfast – combed my hair – heard Holy Mass – talked with my children – read – wrote – had lunch with the children – read ++++ – walked with them to Canalone – read +++ returned – afterwards [went to see] the comedy *la Veuve du malabar* and [went] to bed.

On Monday the 14th, I got up – dressed – had breakfast – combed my hair – heard Holy Mass – spoke to Caramanico – had lunch with the children – spoke to Lady San Marco – kept myself busy – [went] to the Council and to bed.

On Tuesday the 15th I got up – dressed – had breakfast – combed my hair – heard Holy Mass – spoke to Sambuca – had lunch with the children – spoke to Marsico, Cattolica, Sangro, wrote my post – went to the pool hall and to bed.

On the 16th Wednesday I got up – dressed – combed my hair – heard Holy Mass – afterwards kept myself busy – ++++ – saw Richecourt – had lunch with my children – saw Princess Belmonte – kept myself busy – [went] to the Council and to bed.

The confusion that reigned in my head and in all my actions after that fatal affair did not leave me the time to do anything – even to think – my head was confused and not capable of anything – it is only today the 29th that after being unworthily entrusted to God's Mercy that I performed my devotions and put everything into the hands of Divine Providence – I am starting again to put some order in my ideas and to start my diary.

On Tuesday the 29th, I got up at 6 o'clock – shamefully went to church – then had breakfast – had Mimi hair cut – attended Theresa's second Mass – then had breakfast with them – wrote for a short time – at ten o'clock went with Theresa to church – where there was a important Mass for the dead, for Her Majesty the Empress – then talked with Sambuca – then Richecourt – after lunch with my children – talked with Marsico – with Sangro – then went to [receive] the blessing – afterwards saw th Ambassador and his wife – wrote my letters – undressed and at 9 o'clock went to recite the office of the dead for the best and most respectable of mothers – afterwards [went] to sleep. My children are in good health – the King went to the pheasant farm – in the morning to Monte Grane[457] and returned at four o'clock.

On Wednesday November the 30th, I got up at 7 o'clock – after having had a bad night, dressed – had breakfast – combed my hair – saw my children – the governess – heard two Masses – spoke to Cattolica – Marsico – wrote – then saw de Marco – had lunch with my children – I kept myself busy – talked with Bressac – with Lady Belmonte – Countess Althan – took care of my children – went to the Council and kept myself busy – prayed and [went] to bed. The children well – the King went to Carditello in the morning and returned in the evening with the Prior.

On Thursday December the 1st, I got up at 8 o'clock – dressed – had breakfast – combed my hair – took care of with my children – went to Mass – wrote – saw my little one have soup – then saw Richecourt – had lunch with my children – saw Mimi who complained – talked with Marsico – mada my accounts – kept myself busy – went to [...] – saw the King – and then received the blessing in church – afterwards my children – and to the theatre – where they performed *Democrite amoureux* and *Le procureur arbitre*[458] pretty well – then went to sleep – the children fine – the King went on riding to hunt above Caserta Vechia[459] and returned early because of bad weather.

On Friday On December the 2nd, I got up at half past 7 – dressed – had breakfast – combed my hair – took care of my children – heard Mass – spoke to Acton – and then with Richecourt – had lunch with my children – took care of them – then wrote – talked with Prince Belmonte – afterwards saw the King – went with him to church – then kept him company – ☉ – then the Council – afterwards kept myself busy and went to bed. The children well – the King went to his estates at Carditello only with Cassano as his bodyguard.

On Saturday December 3rd, I got up at 8 o'clock – dressed – had breakfast – combed my hair – saw my children – heard Mass – spoke to Acton – then had lunch with my children – kept myself busy – read – wrote, spoke to Tarsia – later saw the King – in the evening went to the comedy *Maris corigées et du mort marié* – then [went to] sleep – the children well – the King went to Monte Calvo and Cerga Cupa to hunt wild boars.

On Sunday the 4th, I got up at 8 o'clock – went to have breakfast – dressed – combed my hair – saw my children – went to the chapel – acompanied St. Viaticum – [for] poor Don Angelo Baratelli[460] – then heard Mass – called my children – kept myself busy – talked with Acton – then had lunch with my children – kept myself busy – saw Lady San Marco – in the evening the King returned – we went to the French comedy *La legataire*[461] – followed by the Babiliard and then went to sleep.

On Monday the 5th, I got up at o'clock – dressed – had breakfast – combed my hair – heard Holy Mass – kept the King company – ☉ – then kept myself busy – had lunch with the King – worked – wrote – spoke to old Duchess of Monteleone – then Richecourt – then saw my children – kept the King company – presided over the Council – where the right to freedom of the city for 60 thousand ducats – the right escheat – and that of consulship were uncertain – prayed – talked with Marsico and [went] to bed – in the afternoon the King went to San Leucio – in the morning home.

On Tuesday December 6th, I got up at 7 o'clock – dressed – had breakfast – combed my hair – heard Mass – spoke to Sambuca – then Pignatelli – Count Michaeli – then Tarsia – had lunch with my children – took care of them – spoke to – Cattolica – Bressac – Marsico – Richecourt – stayed with my children – read – wrote – in the evening the King returned – afterwards kept him company – at eight o'clock I went to play pool – the King went to St. Prisco and [pernice].

On Wednesday December 7th, I got up at 8 o'clock – dressed – had breakfast – combed my hair – busy with my children – heard Mass – spoke to Caramanico – Belmonte – then had lunch with my children – spent the afternoon with them – wrote – kept myself busy – Lady Belmonte – Lady Sangro – a foreigner called Bevilaqua – then with the King [went] to the pool hall – the King was in San Vito.

On Thursday December the 8th, I got up at 8 o'clock – dressed – had breakfast – combed my hair – heard two Holy Masses – talked with my confessor – Prince Belmonte – had lunch with my children – took care of them – then talked with Galatalo – Duchess Monteleone – afterwards went to the comedy [entitled] *Montrose Amélie et les batus payent l'amende*[462] then [went] to bed, King was all day at Carditello.

On Friday December the 9th, I got up at 7 o'clock – dressed – had breakfast – combed my hair – heard Holy Mass – saw my children – busy – went to choose books in the library – had lunch with the King – kept him company – + ⊙ – then changed dress – in half gala [dress] – kept myself busy – stayed with my children – saw Richecourt – + + – then the Council – kept myself busy – and [went] to bed, the children well – the King owing to bad weather could not go out.

On Saturday December the 10th, I got up at 7 o'clock – dressed – had breakfast – combed my hair – heard Holy Mass – spoke to Tarsia – Acton – had lunch with my children – ++ – took care of them – spoke to the Duchess of andria – to Richecourt – then kept myself busy – in the evening went to the theatre – where they performed *Eugenie et la fête d'amour*[463] – afterwards talked with the King – ⊗ and [went] to sleep.

On Sunday December the 11th, I dressed – had breakfast – combed my hair – heard Holy Mass – then busy – spoke to Acton – had lunch with my children – ◈ – spoke to the Duchess of andria – played with my children – read – I kept myself busy +++++ – then talked with Richecourt – went with him to the rehearsal of the comedy and ballet of my daughters – had supper with them and then to bed. The children well – the King went to Fusaro and from there to see the opera at the San Carlo theatre.

On Monday December the 12th, I got up at 7 o'clock – combed my hair – dressed – had breakfast – heard Holy Mass – was busy reading – writing +++ – then had lunch with the King – + – kept myself busy – saw Lady San Marco – the ambassador with his wife, Termoli and Lady Spenser[464] – Richecourt – presided over the Council – saw my children and [went] to bed, the children well – in the morning the King rode for a short time – after lunch [he went] to the grove.

On Tuesday December the 13th, I got up at 7 o'clock in the morning – dressed – had breakfast – combed my hair – heard Holy Mass – I heard that poor Baratelli was dead – wrote my letters – read – ++ – kept myself busy – talked with Sambuca – had lunch with the children – then spoke to General Pignatelli – who has returned from Madrid – and then – to Sangro, Richecourt – the King returned – we spoke to Pignatelli again – I finished my letters – we went to the race of the children – then had supper and [went] to bed, the King went to hunt partridges.

On Wednesday December the 14th, I got up at 7 o'clock – dressed – had breakfast – combed my hair – heard Holy Mass – had breakfast with the children – spoke to Gravina – Tarsia and Cattolica – to Richecourt – then had lunch with the children – talked with Lady Belmonte – read – wrote – then saw the ambassadorand his wife, B[465]: Princess Caramanico – talked with the King – ⊗ – then with Richecourt – went to bed, the children fine – the King was at Carditello all day.

On Thursday December the 15th, I got up at 8 o'clock – spoke to the King – ⊙ – dressed – had breakfast – combed my hair – heard Holy Mass – read – wrote – talked with Cara…. [466] ⊙ – Belmonte – had lunch with the children – talked with Richecourt – to Lady San and Marco – then Altavilla – Cattolica – two ladies – with my children – then kept myself busy – after went to the comedy *les Menechmes*[467] and then *le Francis à Londres* – having seen before General Pignatelli – the King went to Carditello.

On December the 16th, I got up – dressed – had breakfast – combed my hair – heard Holy Mass – spoke to Acton – had lunch with my children – and then spoke to Sangro – wrote for courrier – in the evening the Council and [went] to bed – the children well – the King was at Carditello all day.

On Saturday December the 17th, I got up – dressed – had breakfast – combed my hair – heard Holy Mass – busy – then had lunch with the King – read – wrote – talked with Marsico – Prince Tarsia – read – then kept myself busy – went to receive the blessing – kept myself busy and [went] to sleep, the King went out only for a moment because of bad weather.

On Sunday December the 18th, I got up – dressed – had breakfast – combed my hair – heard two Masses – spoke to the King – ⊗ – then I was busy – had lunch – then read – kept myself busy ++ – talked with my confessor – went to [receive] the blessing + +++ – talked with several people – kept myself busy and [went] to bed, the children well – the King went for an hour to San Leucio.

On Monday December the 19th, I got up – dressed – combed my hair – heard Holy Mass – was busy reading – writing – had lunch with the King – was busy with Lady San Marco – with Genzano – and the blessing – the Council and bed, the children well – in the morning the King went for a moment to Carditello.

On Tuesday the 20th, I got up – dressed – had breakfast – dressed – spoke to Belmonte ++ to Pignatelli – had lunch with the children – spoke again to Belmonte – Pignatelli – to Sangro – wrote my letters – saw the children – the King and then went to sleep – the children well – the King went to the state property at Calvi to hunt wild boars ++.

On Wednesday the 21st, I got up – dressed – breakfasted – combed my hair – heard Holy Mass – busy – spoke to the King – had lunch with him – spoke again – ☉ – and then Countess Gaetani – the daughter of Castelpagano and Countess Althan – then kept the King company at 7 o'clock – bled myself at 8 o'clock – had supper and [went] to bed, after lunch the King could go out only for a short time.

On Thursday the 22nd, I got up at 8 o'clock – dressed – combed my hair – had breakfast – heard Holy-Mass – spoke to Caramanico – had lunch with my children – took care of them – read – talked to Br … s[468] – at 5 o'clock Princess Belmonte accompanied me to see Princess Lubomirsky[469] – with whom I conversed – until the return of the King – who had lunch – then the Council – where the King appointed the cordon to the two Generals – Acton and Pignatelli – with a pension of 1000 ducats – the children well – my little and beloved Antoinette new has two teeth sprouted – the King went to hunting patridges.

On Friday the 23rd, I got up – dressed – had breakfast – combed my hair – heard Holy Mass – saw Carlo de Marco – Acton – then had lunch with the children – read – kept myself busy – saw the children – saw the ambassador and his wife – later kept myself busy – confessed my sins and [went] to bed – the children well – the King was at Fusaro all day.

On Saturday the 24th, I got up at 6 o'clock – went unworthily to church – performed my devotions – then had breakfast – curled [and] combed my hair – dressed – saw my children – heard Holy Mass again – then talked with Acton – had lunch with my children – wrote my letters – kept myself busy – talked with the King – ⊗ – afterwards kept myself busy – stayed with the ambassador – took part in the Council – at the end the King appointed the cordon to a dignified General Acton – which I made me very happy – at 10 o'clock I had a little coffee – at half past 10 went out for a concert – Theresa played the harpsichord very well – at midnight we went to the chapel which was very beautiful – all lit – then there was a great supper at which everything that exists at Caserta was served – the children well – the King went in the morning to the […] and returned early in the afternoon.

On Sunday the 25th Christmas day, I got up at 8 o'clock – had breakfast with dear Mimi – made a full toilette – heard three Masses – saw all the children and went out – then [went] to the hand-kissing – where the King had already given the cordon to General Pignatelli – which also made me happy too – afterwards the public table – then I undressed – had lunch in my apartment – afterwards I saw Belmonte – San Marco – Sangro – Cattolica – Lord Pignatelli – Duchess of andria – then spruced myself and went to a silly comic opera – where I was bored me to death – from there [went] to sleep – the children well – the King after lunch went to a wild boar hunt at San Leucio.

On Monday December the 26th, I got up at 8 o'clock – dressed – had breakfast with my children – played for a while – took care of them – then went to two Masses – combed my hair – dressed – gave Mimi a lesson – had lunch with the children – took care of them – read – ⊗ – then gave Mimi a lesson – the Council – then saw the comedy of my children – who performed *la curieuse* and did an allegorical dance – for our return – all very well – fom there to bed, the children fine – after lunch the King went to the grove for a while.

On Tuesday December the 27th, I got up at 8 o'clock – had breakfast – dressed – combed my hair – heard two Masses – took care of my children – wrote – had lunch with the children – wrote – kept myself busy – saw the ambassador – my children – wrote and [went] to bed, the children well – the King from morning until night was at the pheasant farm.

On Wednesday December the 28th, I got up – dressed – had breakfast – combed my hair – heard Holy Mass – spoke to Sambuca – then had lunch with the children – spoke to Belmonte – kept myself busy – [went] to the Council and to bed, the children well – the King was at Carditello all day.

On Thursday December the 29th, I got up at 7 o'clock – dressed – had breakfast – spoke to de Marco – wrote – kept myself busy – talked with Caramanico – had lunch with my children – took care of them – talked with Lady Termoli – Bovino – San Marco – Richecourt – with a certain Richard – took care of my children – went to bed, the children well – the King went to Varcatura and in the evening to the opera at San Carlo theare – whence he returned in the evening at half past 10.

On Friday December the 30th, I got up – dressed – had breakfast – heard Holy Mass – kept the King company – ⊗ – then busy – stayed with the children – had lunch with the King – read – kept him company – saw Sangro – [went] to the Council – saw Marsico – went to bed, the children well – the King – owing to bad weather – could not go out at all.

On Saturday December the 31st, I got up at 8 o'clock – dressed – had breakfast – combed my hair – heard Holy Mass – kept myself busy – had lunch with the King – read – kept myself busy – wrote my letters – saw my children – in the evening we went to the chapel which was lit up – recited the *Te deum* – then I went back – finished some of my affairs and then [went to] the theatre – where they performed *Tom Jones* and *Fanfan* and *Colas* – especially the first [was] very nice – then [went] home – to sleep – the children well – the King could not go out at all day because of bad weather.

And so – by the grace of God – another year has ended – there is a long gap in my diary – it is that of my four-month journey – I wrote my brief considerations in a separate notebook – this year will be unforgettable – I had the violent sorrows which have greatly saddened me – the providence and goodness of God – for a very special grace – have considerably pre-served me – I had actions of grace with which to return the favour to the Divine Mercy – and I will try – with my conduct – in the new year to show my gratitude – I am seven months pregnant – after all the sorrows which have eaten my soul – I do not answer at all for the end of this pregnancy – whatever God's will – I submit myself with calm resignation – and not having anymore anything in the world right now and in the future – that binds me to the world except the desire to fulfill my duties and deserve a happy eternity – the purpose of all my desires. Amen.

NOTES

1. Mimi was the nickname which the Queen gave to her daughter, Maria Cristina.
2. This is a reference to Anton Lamberg-Sprinzenstein, Count Lamberg, Habsburg Ambassador to Naples between 1778 and 1784.
3. Here is a reference to Giuseppe Carlo Gennaro, the son of the Queen.
4. Donna Vittoria Guevara, a Lady of the court.
5. This is a reference to Domenico Grimaldi (1735–1805), a Calabrian economist.
6. Angelo Giuseppe Maria Gatti (1730–1798) was an eminent physician of the time known for the widespread innoculation of smallpox as a prophy-lactic and for this reason he was called to Naples in 1777 with a mandate to vaccinate the children of the Queen.
7. This is a reference to Maria Cristina Amelia, daughter of the Queen.
8. Diego Pignatelli, Prince of Marsiconuovo, in those years, was captain of the volunteer battalion of Marines, also known as the Liparoti (i.e. the natives of the island of Lipari). Gentleman of the chamber, had received

the cordon of San Gennaro. In 1784 he became the master of ceremonies of the Neapolitan "Victory" lodge of which Diego Naselli was grand master.

9. Don Filippo Orsini, Duke of Gravina (1742–1824) was at the time a Lieutenant general in the Neapolitan army and held the position of First Horseman of the Queen.

10. This is a reference to the French Ambassador Louis de Tayllerand-Périgord (1738–1799).

11. The Queen mentions here Marie Antoinette, the Queen of France and sister of Maria Carolina.

12. Princess Ferolito, a Neapolitan noblewoman.

13. Giuliana Falconieri, Princess of Santacroce, was a noblewoman of Florentine origin who soon became an entertainer in one of the most famous salons of Papal Rome in the late eighteenth century.

14. Teresa Montalto di Sangro (1735–1818), was at the time a Lady of the Court.

15. This is a reference to Maria Carolina's presence at the Teatro San Carlo in Naples.

16. Princess Maria Teresa (1772–1807) was the eldest daughter of the Queen.

17. Prince Francesco (1777–1830) was the second son of the Queen.

18. Giuseppe Beccadelli di Bologna e Gravina (1726–1813), Marquis of Sambuca, was a diplomat and politician in the service of the Kingdom of Naples and Sicily. In 1776, taking advantage of Minister Tanucci's fall from grace, he took over Tannuci's role and initiated a profound change in foreign policy based on the guidelines suggested by Maria Carolina.

19. The Queen had received news that on 22 October 1781 her sister, Marie Antoinette, had given birth to Louis Joseph.

20. This symbol seems to refer to the intimate moments of the Queen.

21. It should be noted here – and this applies to the rest of the diary – that the Queen used (though not frequently) signs, acronyms, numbers, vowels and consonants, the latter followed by an ellipsis. These were used to remind herself of certain details which she wanted to keep a secret.

22. Marquis Agostino Cardillo was at that time Commissioner of the *regio cedolario nella prima ruota della Sommaria*, was responsible of the cases relating to the verification of the feudal nature or bourgeois funds.

23. Francesco Loffredo, Prince of Migliano. In those years Francesco was the gentleman of the King's chamber and an officer in the battalion of Liparoti.

24. Anna Francesca Caracciolo, Princess of Melissano (1756–1836).

25. Chiara Spinelli, Princess of Belmonte (1744–1823) (1744–1823). In 1762 she became the second wife of General Antonio Pignatelli (for a brief outline of which see below, p …, n.…). The Princess was chambermaid, a close friend who was privy to the decision and confidence of the Queen.
26. Count Michele Pignatelli (1725–1803), of the Princes of Belmonte, was then envoy to the Embassy in Paris.
27. This is most likely Onofrio Perrone.
28. This is most likely a hint to Don Fabio Albertini, Prince of Faggiano, who was an officer in the Neapolitan army.
29. This is a reference to Count Giuseppe Sacco Pompeo (1708–1781) who was Minister of the Economy for the Duchy of Parma, Piacenza and Guastalla. In that year, owing to an intrigue at Court, his commission was withdrawn by the Duke of Parma.
30. Talleyrand has previously been mentioned, cited above p … n …
31. Prince Frederick William Hesenstein (1735–1808) was at the time in the service of the Swedish army with the rank of sergeant.
32. Here the Queen is referring to her daughters Maria Teresa, already cited above p. xxx, no. xxx, and Maria Luisa (1773–1802).
33. This is a reference to Donna Costanza Caetani (* ante 1717–1797), daughter of Don Michelangelo I, Duke of Sermoneta, and of Anna Maria from the marquises of Strozzi. In 1733 she married Don Bartolomeo V of Capua, Count of Altavilla.
34. Antonio Pignatelli (1722–1794), Prince of Belmonte, was the Head Horseman of the King and Queen, to whom he also became chief steward and chamberlain.
35. Vincenzo Moncada (1732–1805), Prince of Calvaruso, was the brother of the aforementioned Anna, and at the time, Senator of Messina.
36. Marquis Nicola Espluga was at the time Captain of the Royal Navy and temporary commander of the Royal Infantry Corps.
37. This is a reference to Palmira Vanvitelli, who was the daughter of the famous architect Luigi Vanvitelli. At the time, she enjoyed singing chamber music, and was a great success.
38. This is most likely referring to the wife of Nicola Sossi, who was at that time Royal Auditor – General of the Italian State, Stato de' Presidi.
39. The is a reference to the economist Abbot Ferdinando Galiani (1728–1787), who in January 1759 had received from Minister Bernardo Tanucci the post of Secretary of the Embassy in Paris, from where he returned in 1769 to become Secretary of the Supreme Commercial Court in 1770, then member of the Council of the Allodial Committee (1777). At the time, he was the first Commissioner of the Supreme Council of Finance (1782), who received, in 1784, the assignment of Commissioner of Superintendence of the "Fund of Separation" (1784).

40. This is most likely a reference to Giovanni Ruffo, Prince of Scaletta (1751–1808), hereditary peer of the Kingdom of Sicily, Senator of Messina.
41. Judge Giuseppe Maria Secondo (1715–1798) was the civil governor of the island of Capri. In those years he was Counselor of the Supreme Court of Justice in Naples.
42. This refers to lawyer Emanuele Del Giudice, at the time Secretary of Justice.
43. This could be the wife of Duke Gaetano Giordano, who belonged to the noble family of the same name, who moved from Rome to Naples.
44. Don Nicola Maria Vespoli (1718–1804) was at the time secretary of the State Council.
45. This could be Don Filippo Benedetto de Cordova who at the time was the abbot of the Benedectine abbey of San Martino delle Scale close to Palermo.
46. Fabrizio Spinelli (1738–1794), Prince of Tarsia, was at the time the King's Master of the Royal Hunt.
47. Knight Gaetano Ventimiglia was butler of the court.
48. Innocenzo Pignatelli, a diplomat in the service of the Court of Naples, was at the time appointed Minister Plenipotentiary to Malta.
49. This is the first reference to the well-known Sir John Francis Edward Acton (1736–1811), sixth Baronet also known by the Italianized name of Giovanni Acton, who had reorganized the navy of the Grand Duchy of Tuscany in the seventies and was called to the Court of Naples in 1778 at the express request of Maria Carolina, with the same mandate. During the eighties he became an influential figure at Court and, with the support of the Queen, was the instigator of the pro-Austrian turning point in the Kingdom's foreign policy. At the beginning of the nineties he represented the faction that, again with the support of the Queen, cut off the reformists in order to align the Kingdom of Naples with a political project which was completely different from that of revolutionary France.
50. During that time the Bishop of Aversa was Francesco Del Tufo (1726–1803).
51. This is a reference to the Duke of Toritto, Giuseppe Caravita (1710–1789), who was the son of the criminal lawyer, Tommaso, and of Felicia Sersale and had followed in his father's footsteps. The son of Caravita, referred to in the diary, is most likely the eldest son Filippo, who in turn became Magistrate of the Kingdom.
52. Don Mariano Arciero (1707–1788) was elder of a boarding school.
53. Maria Rosa Caracciolo (1707–1801), from the Dukes of Martina, Princess of Cariati, was Lady of the Court and governess to Crown prince Francesco and the infant Gennaro Carlo.

54. Giovanni Vincenzo Tommaso Revertera (1745–1810), Duke of Salandra, was in those years Chamberlain, Colonel of the navy fleet and first class Grandee of Spain.

55. This is a reference to the cult of child saints called Santolilli.

56. On 12 April 1780 at the Court of Naples was born the Prince Gennaro, who died at the age of nine.

57. The Milanese Lady Costanza Orrigoni (1759-1790), Duchess of Montalbo, was the wife of Antonino San Martino of Ramondetta, Duke of Montalbo, Colonel in the royal army, Praetor of Palermo in 1766 and gentleman of the King's chamber.

58. Stefania Monteaperto was one of the Queen's ladies in waiting.

59. Carlo de Marco (1711–1804). In October 1759 he was appointed by Charles de Bourbon, while on route to Spain, Secretary of State for Justice and Ecclesiastical Affairs. Thus, he held two positions continuously for more than thirty years, often combining them with other important tasks.

60. This refers to the first anniversary of the death of Empress Maria Teresa of Austria (1717–1780).

61. The Queen used to call her son Gennaro, Gennarino, cited above. n., p..

62. Giuseppe Spiriti (1757–1799) of Calabrian origin, was the nephew of Marquis Salvatore Spiriti, reformer, economist, scientist.

63. Here is mentioned Maddalena of the Barons de Martino, wife of lawyer Francesco Saverio Mancini (1760–1847).

64. Princess Ekaterina Romanovna Vorontsova Dashkova (1743–1810), was a Russian writer and publisher. Close associate of Catherine II, Dashkova was also the official representative of Russia abroad and had used enlightenment ideas to improve the image of her country.

65. This refers to Emilia of Gennaro, daughter and heir of Don Nicola of Gennaro, Prince of Sirignano. She married Marquis Tommaso Caravita, son of President Giuseppe Caravita.

66. Giuseppe Caravita (1715–1788) was at that time President of the Royal Chamber of Sommaria.

67. Giulia Carafa Cantelmo Stuart (1755–1841), was at the time one of the Queen's ladies in waiting.

68. Alfonso Maria Freda (1740–1817), versed in the theological sciences, became a doctor of civil and canon law. Later, in October 1797, on the proposal of King Ferdinand IV, he was consecrated Bishop of Lucera.

69. This is the wife of the Spanish Colonel Emanuele de Leon who had been Commander and Dean of the Royal Audience in the province of Teramo.

70. Here the diary mentions Donna Maria Eleonora Caracciolo Pisquizi, Princess of Villa Santa Maria and Duchess of Gesso, already cited n. p.

71. Stefano Patrizi (1715–1797), nephew of the Bishop of Gaeta, Francesco Patrizi, was at the time adviser to the Royal Chamber of Santa Chiara.
72. The great Count of Altavilla, Don Bartolomeo V of Capua (1716–1792), was at that time Lieutenant general in the Neapolitan Army.
73. The Marquis of Corleto, Don Nicola Riario Sforza (1743–1796), was then gentleman of the King's chamber.
74. In those years the Prior of the Court was Vincenzo IV Carafa, Prince of Roccella (1739–1814).
75. This most likely refers to Diomede Carafa, Duke of Maddaloni and Count of Cerreto Sannita, son of Count Filippo, already cited n. p..
76. This could be Donna Giovanna Pappacoda, Princess of Centola, the daughter of Don Giuseppe and Maria Anna Spinelli.
77. Here she mentions Sisto Sforza Cesarini (1730–1802), Count of Celano. The King of Spain had given him the majorat of Celano in the Kingdom of Naples.
78. This refers to Donna Maria Teresa Rervetera (1777–1851), daughter of the Dukes of Salandra.
79. This may allude to the Carafa family, from the Dukes of Maddaloni.
80. Jozèfa Amelia Potocka (1752–1798) was an amateur painter and collector of paintings. Jozèfa married Count Stanislaw Feliks Potocki, son of a Polish tycoon who was oriented toward a pro-Russian policy, who in 1785 became Grand Master of the Grand Orient lodge of the Polish Kingdom and the Grand Duchy of Tuscany.
81. Prince of Stigliano, Marcantonio Colonna (1724–1796), courtier.
82. This refers to Filippo Carafa (1761–1793), Count of Cerreto. The Carafa family had its possessions in two counties: the lower Early, with Maddaloni as its capital, and the upper early, with Cerreto Sannita as its early town. The Counts of Carafa periodically named for each of the two counties a governor or Vice Count who looked afterwards their interests and administered justice.
83. Francesco Valignani, Count of Miglianico, was at the time a knight of Jerusalem.
84. This could be a descendant of the noble Cantelli family, Counts of Rubbiano, already firmly placed at the top of the economic and social system of Parma in the second half of the Seventeenth century
85. Gaspare Mollo, Duke of Lusciano (1754–1823), was at the time a highly valued Court poet.
86. Nicola d'Ayello, President of the tax lawyers. In October 1782 he became Commissioner of the supervision of customs and excise in the Supreme Council of Finance.
87. Nicola Maria Caracciolo was advisor to the Supreme Magistrate of Trade.

88. Giuseppe Spinelli (1746–1805), Benedictine Father. At the time he was Archbishop of Catanzaro.
89. Placido Dentice (1725–1785) was executive officer in the Royal house at Court.
90. This refers to Donna Costanza Caetani, already cited.
91. Tomas d'Avalos (1752–1806), Marquis of Vasto. He was a diplomat who at the time held the position of President of the Academy of Sciences and Belles-Lettres.
92. The Teatro dei Fiorentini (which no longer exists because it was lost owing to the construction of the Charity Ward) took its name from the nearby church of San Giovanni dei Fiorentini.
93. Vincenzo Montalto was Bishop of the Sicilian cavalry regiment.
94. This could be the Austrian Johann Philip (1747–1803), Count of Hoyos, who was married to Marie Christine (1755–1821), Princess of Calry and Aldrigen. The counts of Hoyos were both pastelist artists.
95. Frederik Anton 'Fritz' von Wedel-Jarlsberg (1748–1811) was in those years Envoy Extraordinary at the Court of Denmark.
96. Francesco Marino III Caracciolo (1734–1784), Duke of Atripalda, was at that time Grand Chancellor of the Kingdom of Naples and Grandee of Spain, Court Steward.
97. This refers to the anniversary of the death of Prince Carlo Tito (1775–1778).
98. Heinrich Friedrich Füger (1751–1818) was a miniature painter, who became famous both in Vienna and Dresden. In 1776, Füger arrived in Rome, where he began to try his hand at historical paintings. He lived in Naples at the Bourbon court. Queen Maria Carolina gave him the commission to decorate the last room of the Palatine Library in Caserta. He returned to the imperial court, was appointed Director of the Academy of Vienna in 1783 and in 1806 he became the Director of the Imperial Gallery of Design.
99. This hearing could refer to the issue concerning the request which Carlo of Marco sent the Sicilian junta on 17 November 1781, asking it to pronounce in favour or against the abolition of the Holy Office.
100. Donna Caterina de' Medici (1747–1824), Marquess San Marco, was the daughter of Don Michele de' Medici, fifth Prince of Ottaiano and third Duke of Sarno, and Donna Carmela Filomarino of the princes of Rocca d'Aspro. In 1767, Caterina married Don Troiano Cavaniglia (1707–1780), Marquis of San Marco. The Marquess was then Lady of the Court and friend of the Queen.
    Like this in the text.
101. Vincenzo IV Carafa, Prince of Roccella, already cit n.p.

102. Marquis Filippo Malaspina was Lieutenant colonel in the service of the Kingdom of Naples.
103. This refers to Donna Geronima Spinelli Savelli (1758–1824), from the princes of Cariati and dukes of Seminara. She was the wife of the Royal Customs officer, Marquis Giuseppe Maria D'Anna (1754–1812).
104. Diego Naselli (1727–1830), Prince of Aragona, an army officer in the navy. In 1778 he was appointed Brigadier of the King's armies, and later held the rank of Lieutenant general. At that time he also held the post of Grand Master of the National Grand Lodge of Naples, where he had been elected on 2 June 1776.
105. Like so in the text. The Queen Maria Carolina does not specify what she devoted herself to.
106. This could be the abbreviation for Giuseppe Beccadelli of Bologna and Gravina, Marquis of Sambuca, already cited n.p.
107. Maria Giovanna Doria del Carretto (1743–1832), Duchess of Tursi, was at the time Lady of the Court.
108. A small town in the province of Naples.
109. General Francesco Pignatelli (1734–1812), Count of Laino, had lived in the Kingdom of Naples in the service of the Bourbons of Naples.
110. This is probably the abbreviation for John Acton, already cited.
111. The Swiss painter Angelika Kauffmann (1741–1807) specialized in portraits and historical subjects. In 1781, afterwards the death of her first husband, Angelika married the Venetian painter Antonio Zucchi. Together, from 1871 and 1872, they decided to move to Italy. Afterwards a short stay in Rome, in 1782, the couple settled in Naples, where the painter had received an offer, which she declined, to undertake the role of court painter. Angelika had painted a portrait of King Ferdinand IV (see Journal: 21 September 1782), which she finished the same year in Rome, and a group portrait of the royal family.
112. It alludes to Granatello, the Bourbon fort in Portici
113. Bartolomeo Capua (1716–1792), Prince of Riccia. At that time he was Lieutenant general.
114. It refers to Madame Böhme who was one of the three Austrian chambermaids of the Queen.
115. The Grand Master of the time was Diego Naselli, already cited.
116. The Marquis of Ruggiano, Nicola Macedonio (1727–1790), was in those years gentleman of the Chamber.
117. Marquis Juan Asenzio Goyzueta (–1782) had followed Charles of Bourbon in the reconquest of the Kingdom. Appointed company Secretary in 1761, he was then Secretary of State for the Department of Business and Trade and the Superintendent of the Royal Navy and the *Tribunale del Lotto di Napoli*, which was one of many different types of courts.

118. This probably refers to Bernardo Filingieri (1747–1803), Royal Councilor of Commerce, gentleman of the Chamberof the King of Sicily. He was Senator of Palermo from 1778 to 1781. Later, in 1785, he became Minister of the Giunta pretoria (Pretorian Council) in Palermo.

119. The Prince of Avellino, Giovanni Caracciolo (1741–1800), had at the time the post of Chancellor of the Kingdom.

120. Riccardo Carafa della Stadera, Duke of andria (1741–1797), was at that time gentleman of the Chamber.

121. Filippo Lopez y Royo (1728–1811) was Bishop of Nola for twenty-eight years, from 1768 to 1793.

122. Sir William Douglas Hamilton (1730–1803) was English ambassador to the court of Naples from 1764 to 1800. He soon became a widower on 25 August 1782. The British diplomat had become a close friend of the Bourbons. In particular, the ambassador had accompanied King Ferdinand on hunts. On 6 September 1791, the ambassador married Emma Lyon, who soon became a friend and confidante of the Queen.

123. Catherine Hamilton nee Barlow (1738–1782) was the daughter of the British MP Hugh Barlow. In 1758 Catherine was married to Sir William Hamilton.

124. The text is interrupted here. On the then page it resumes from 27 September.

125. Carlo Ramet, Knight of the Order of Constantine, was minister of Naples at the Papal Court

126. This is a reference to the request by General Francesco Pignatelli regarding a Cordon, or the highest degree of a knightly order.

127. This may be Caterina Branciforte e Pignatelli, who was the daughter of Salvatore Pignatelli, Prince of Butera, who had married the catholic Prince Francesco Antonio Bonanno e Borromeo.

128. Luise Marie-Thérèse Bathilde d'Orléans (1750–1822), Duchess of Chartres. She was the wife of Luigi Filippo Giuseppe d'Orléans and was appointed Grand Master of the Grand Orient of France in 1781. At the time the Duchess of Chartres was an assiduous patron of the court of Naples.

129. This probably refers to Marie Gabrielle Olive de Lamoignon, who was the wife of Charles Henry de Feydeau, Marquis of Brou (1754–1802), nephew of the State Councilor of the Council of Finance, Claude Henry Faydeau of Marville.

130. This could be an unidentified Sicilian lady belonging to the Tornabene family.

131. Here the diary mentionsCarlo Capecelatro, Marquis of Casabona (1743–1805).

132. Antonio Spinelli (1720–1790) Prince of Cariati.

133. This is a reference to Maria Antonia Spinelli (1735–1813), Princess of Tarsia, who was at the time one of the Queen's court ladies.
134. The Roman Abbot Onorato Caetani (1742–1797) of Saints Peter and Stephan in Valvisciolo. He was a clergyman, who in those years was a member of the Academy of Sciences and Fine Arts in Naples.
135. Count Andrej Rasoumovski (1752–1836) was a Russian diplomat for many years in the service of the court of Vienna. In January 1779 he was sent to the court of Naples. Descendant of the Cossack with the same name who had charmed the Russian Empress Elizabeth, he was good looking and had been suspected of amorous intrigue with the wife of his successor, Paul. This was the reason for the end of his friendship with the heir to the throne and the decision by Empress Catherine II to send him abroad. Although at first she was very cautious in Naples towards the young Russian diplomat, soon his presence was particularly pleasing to the Queen which she hoped would not only bring the Russian diplomatic closer, but would also lead to a possible marriage for one of her daughters with a Russian archduke. The confidential relationship between Rasoumovski and the Queen did not please King Charles, and in 1784 Rasoumovski was called back by the Empress of Russia.
136. Here the diary mentions Lucia Grifeo e Gravina, from the princes of Partanna, widow of the magistrate Filadelfio Artale (1716–1782). Baron Artale was Praetorian judge of the Consistory and of the High Court, a tax lawyer and Auditor General until 1774. In that year he was also promoted to consultant in the Royal Government of Sicily in Naples. He passed away in August of that year.
137. Here the diary mentionsone of the chambermaids of the Queen, the widow belonging to the bourgeois Palma family.
138. This may be Nicola Maria de Sungro (1756–1833), the son of Don Domenico and Donna Teresa Montalto. He held various positions at court: gentleman of the chamber, Knight of Justice in the Order of San Gennaro, but also Head Butler and First Horseman.
139. This probably refers to Giovanni andrea de Marinis, Marquis of Genzano (1755–1824). The marquis lived primarily in Naples at the well-known Genzano palace.
140. Italian in the text, (new street).
141. This may allude to Carlo de Marco, already cited n.p.
142. This is a hint to Anna Maria Marpacher, wife of the court surgeon Michele Troja (1747–1827). In 1779, Troja was appointed chief surgeon at the hospital of the Incurables in Naples and afterwards a professor of ophthalmology at the University of Naples. In 1780 he became the first surgeon of King Ferdinand, a member of the King's chamber, and accompanied the King on his hunting trips.

143. Maria Teresa Caracciolo, Duchess of Gravina (1738–1789), was in those years lady of the court.
144. Ludovico Giuseppe Arborio, Marquis of Breme (1754–1828). A diplomat, he represented the King of Sardinia in Naples (July 1782) and Vienna (1786). In 1784 he returned to Turin to prepare for the visit of the Neapolitan royal couple, which took place the then year, and which saw him in the role of director of festivities and guide during the state visit.
145. Don Domenico Spinelli Savelli (1744–1825) was gentleman of the Chamber to King Ferdinand IV.
146. Francesco Rodrigo Moncada, Count of Caltanissetta (1762–1816),was gentleman of the Chamber to King Ferdinand IV.
147. Princess Gonzaga could be Giulia Cavriani (1767–1846) who had married Prince and Marquis Don Francesco Luigi Gonzaga, Venetian patrician and Grandee of Spain.
148. This is probably a descendant of the noble Aflitto family, which is still unidentified. The particularity of this noble family is given by the predominant choice of the novitiate.
149. Here the diary mentionsDonna Ferdinanda Reggio from the princes of Aci, lady of the court of the Queen.
150. Widow of Juan Asenzio Goyzueta, already cited n.p.
151. This refers to Princess Maria Amelia (1782–1866), daughter of the Queen, who in 1809 married Louis Philippe d'Orléans, Duke of Orleans.
152. Here the diary mentionsAgata Branciforte, wife of the Prince of Paternò Francesco Moncada, who was at the time a gentleman of the King's chamber
153. It refers to the royal site of Carditello, which was south of Capua. During the reign of Ferdinand many farms were built to accommodate the court on hunting trips. In 1787 there was a royal hunting lodge with a special trail for horses.
154. On 19 October 1782 the *segreteria d'azienda* (secretary of the financial company) was removed and a Supremo Consiglio di Azienda (supreme council of the company) was established).
155. Donna Giulia di Capua, Duchess of Termoli (1729–1789). She was at that time a lady of the court.
156. Luigi Serra, Duke of Cassano (1747–1825). In those years he held the office of tax lawyer in the chamber of the royal heritage of Santa Chiara and was a member of the economic board.
157. Maria Luisa Fortunata de Molina (1764–1800) was the daughter of Don Pedro, a noble Spanish officer in the service of the army of Charles III. He arrived in Naples in 1733, in the role of Adjutant and then as Commander of the Bourbon army. In Naples he married the Genoese Salinero. In 1781, at the age of 17, Maria Luisa married her cousin, Andrea Delli Monti

Sanfelice, from the Dukes of Lauriano and Agropoli, with whom she had shared much of her childhood and later had two sons in a short period of time.

158. Maria Eleonora Caracciolo Pisquizi (1720–1798), Princess of Villa Santa Maria, Duchess of Gesso, was the daughter of Filippo Caracciolo, Duke of Gesso.

159. Ferdinando Corradini (1731–1801), former secretary of the Chamberof Santa Chiara, and judge of the Vicar. In October 1782, he was appointed to the Supremo Consiglio di Azienda (supreme council of the company).

160. Like this in the text.

161. Angelo Matteo Ferrante, nephew of Marquis Matteo Ferrante, was at the time the Kingdom's tax councillor.

162. Here the reference is to one Lady Wintersee who was of one the three Austrian chambermaids of the Queen.

163. Gaetano Pugnani (1731–1798) was composer and first violinist of the Royal Chapel in Turin, he belonged to the lodge of Turin.

164. The Ambassador of Morocco, Muhammad Ibn Uthmàn Al-Miknasi, was sent to Naples in August 1782 by Sultan Alawite, Muhammad Ibn Abd Allah to conclude a peace treaty with King Ferdinand, which was signed on 19 October 1782. In July 1780 they entered into trade agreements with Morocco.

165. Here the diary mentions Giovanni Giacomo Onorati, who in May 1777 was appointed Bishop of Troja and exercised his bishopric until 1793.

166. Maria Bertaldi, known as 'Balducci' (1758–? 1784), from Genoa, had become a singer famous for her exceptional range of voice. At the time, she sung for the Teatro San Carlo in Naples.

167. The young Francesco, Count of Thurn and Valassina (1748–1790), was the son of the steward who had been the Grand Duke Pietro Leopoldo. Count Thurn at the time was Major General in the service of the Grand Duchy.

168. Maria Francesca de Sangro (1747–1812), at that time lady of the court of the Queen, was the wife of Francesco Loffredo, Prince of Migliano.

169. This refers to the Herodotus' tragedy *the Lost army of Cambises.*

170. This refers to the illustrious Swiss physician Samuel Auguste Tissot (1728–1797). His early notoriety was based on a controversy regarding the importance of inoculation argued in one of his books, in which he condemned the method of bloodletting, promoting a series of natural ingredients and foods. In 1762, Tissot had received a gold medal from the Health House and was requested as a doctor by a number of European sovereigns. At the request of Emperor Joseph II, from October 1781 to June 1783, he occupied the Chair of Clinical Medicine at the University of Pavia.

171. Mars] Marsico.

172. Mig] Migliano.
173. The Prince of Cimitile, Giovan Battista Albertini (1717–1788), was a diplomat in the service of the Kingdom of Naples and an experienced gentleman of the Chamber. In 1763, he was Plenipotentiary Minister in Portugal and in 1775 Minister Plenipotentiary in Rome. Upon returning to Naples, he was appointed Superintendent General of the royal financial company and in 1782 Director of the Supreme Council of Finance and State Councilor.
174. Joseph II of Habsburg-Lorraine, (1741–1790), older brother of the Queen, was at that time Emperor of the Holy Roman Empire.
175. Like this in the text.
176. Maria Anna Caracciolo (1746–1785), wife of Francesco Marino III Caracciolo, Duke of Atripalda, was at that time lady of the court.
177. This refers to the Colonna family of Stigliano.
178. Jacob Philip Hackert (1737–1807) was a painter of European fame. At the Bourbon court he worked together with his brother engraver George Abraham (1755–1805). He was appointed first court painter with the commission to paint views dearest to the King, to advise on the purchase of works of art and take care of the artistic education of the princes. In addition, Hackert took care of the transportation of the King's Farnese collection from Rome to Naples, the restoration of the paintings in the art gallery and the decoration of the new royal sites of San Leucio and Carditello.
179. Charles Henry Dominique, Count of Nay and Richecourt (1730–1789), was Imperial Chamberlain and General of the Cavalry. At the time he was Minister Plenipotentiary to Naples.
180. Don Nicola Revertera (1778–1786) was the eldest son of the Duke of Salandra.
181. This probably refers to Nicola Pignatelli (1740–1804) who was a Jesuit of Spanish origin.
182. These could be the initials of Marquess San Marco, already cited n. p.
183. This could be an abbreviation for Prince Cimitile, already cited. n. p.
184. This could be Marianna Villapiana (1715–1799) who in December 1741 married the Neapolitan nobleman Giovanni Giuseppe Carafa della Stadera of the Counts of Montecalvo and princes of Sepino (1694–1760).
185. Catherine von Storm was the wife of the Danish diplomat Frederik Anton 'Friz' von Wedel, already cited n.p.
186. Maria Vincenza Caracciolo, from the princes of Avellino, Princess Ottajano (1745–1794), was the wife of Giuseppe de' Medici, Prince of Ottajano, founder of the lodge of English obedience also known as "Friendship".
187. A] John, Acton.

188. Marzio Mastrilli (1753–1805), known under the name of the Marquis de Gallo, was a diplomat in the service of the Bourbons. Nephew of Domenico Caracciolo, the Marquis's diplomatic career began in 1782 when he was appointed Minister Plenipotentiary to Turin, where he arrived in June 1783. Between June and July 1785, he hosted in his palace in Turin the Neopolitan royals, then went on a trip to the capital of the Italian States.

189. The French Marquess Marie Caroline Rosalie de Poyanne de Baylens (1760–1828) was the daughter of the Lieutenant-générale of the Royal Army, Charles Léonard de Baylens, Marquis of Poyanne. In 1778, Marie Caroline Rosalie married Hélie Charles of Talleyrand, Prince de Chalais (1754–1829), Lieutenant general of the army and Peer of France. At the time, Madame de Chalais was visiting the court of Naples.

190. This is a hint to Serafina Caracciolo (1731–1798), who was the wife of Pier Nicola Alvaro della Quadra Carafa, Prince of San Lorenzo (1730–1786). The Queen was aware that two months earlier, on 25 September 1782, San Lorenzo had lost his son Domenico Antonio Carafa (1756–1782).

191. See: Maria Luisa Fortunata of Molina San Felice, already cited. n. p.

192. Antonio Montaperto Massa, Duke of Santa Elisabetta, was a diplomatic representative of the Sicilies in Vienna.

193. Luigi Filippo II of Borbone, Duke of Chartres (1747–1793), was Grand Master of the French Freemasonry, who at that time was visiting the Court.

194. This refers to the Count of Genlis, Charles Alexis Brulart (1737–1793), who was descended from an ancient noble family. He was the grandson of a minister of Louis XV. Brulart was a sergeant in the King's army and a naval officer. He distinguished himself in China and India, and in 1760 earned the Cross of St. Louis. In 1780, he was discharged. In 1789 he became one of the first nobles to join the Third Estate, and became a member of the Jacobin Club.

195. Charles de Fitz-James, Duke of Fitz-James (1743–1805), was the son of the French Marshal Charles de Fitz-James, Governor of Limousine. Afterwards the resignation of his father, he took over as a Peer of France

196. This refers to Ignazio Lanza Branciforte, Prince of Trabia (1758–1784). His brother Pietro would become a Senator of the Kingdom of Sicily, Secretary of State and Court Master to the King of Naples and Sicily.

197. This could be Caterina Spinelli, Princess of Montacuto (1741–1797), who was the wife of the Neapolitan patrician Giovanbattista Spinelli, Prince of Cariati, and Duke of Seminara (1719–1792).

198. Francesca di Paola Caetani, known as Paulina, was the daughter of Gaetano Francesco Caetani, fourth Duke of Sermoneta, and of the Viennese Donna Maria Carlotta von Rappach. In 1730, Donna Paolina

married Don Stefano Marini, Prince of Striano, whose stronghold was located in the countryside of Nola. In Naples, the Countess was Vicar General and looked after the interests of her nephew Francesco, eleventh Duke of Sermoneta, Senator of Rome.

199. In the second half of the Eighteenth century, hats were a very fashionable accessory. There were two primary models: The first was fanciful, its size was often important and it was rich with ornaments. The second was less impressive, with fewer ornaments, but the general shape remained almost the same.

200. It refers to short jacket garnished with fur and sometimes with gallons or grommets.It was in the fashion of the late eighteenth century.

201. Like this in the text.

202. Ippolito Porcinari, already a lawyer, was at that time a Counselor of the Royal Sacred Council of Santa Chiara.

203. This could be Elisabetta Romanova Woronzow (1739–1792), commonly known as Vorontsova. She was the daughter of a Russian senator and the favourite of Peter III when he was still Grand Duke. She became Countess and was a favourite when the young man had ascended the throne. She accompanied Peter on all his trips and adventures, so much so that for- eign ambassadors and their governments had reported that the Emperor was going to banish his wife to a convent in order to marry Vorontsova. The presence of the young favorite was not appreciated by his wife Catherine II, who with the help of Elizabeth's sister, Princess Ekaterina Dashkova, staged a coup d'etat in July 1762 to remove her husband from power. Elizabeth was exiled and stripped of the title, which was immedi- ately assigned to Dahskova. She married a certain admiral Palenski and retired to the country, where she destined to spend the rest of her life, while her brothers Alessandro and Semyon became important diplomatic agents.

204. Luigi Capece Galeota (1742–1811) era stato brigadiere nell'esercito napoletano. Nel 1776 era stato inviato straordinario presso Torino. L'8 gennaio di quell'anno sposava donna Maria Caterina Lagni dei duchi di Marzano. In tale udienza si fa cenno della cognata del duca, Maria Vittoria Caracciolo, che era divenuta monaca "suor Giovanna Teresa" nel monas- tero dei Santi San Giovanni e Teresa a Napoli.

205. Here the diary mentionsthe Duke of Laurino, Vincenzo Spinelli (1759–1831), a descendant of the famous noble family of Naples. At this hearing, Maria Vittoria Caracciolo, the Duke's sister in law, was mentioned. She had become a nun, known as Sister Giovanna Teresa, in the monastery of St. John and St. Teresa in Naples.

206. The term *undressed* or *negligee* in this circumstance mean that the Queen did not wear official Court dress.

207. Italian in the text, (The astrologuer).
208. This probably refers to Donna Maria Beatrice de Mari (1771–1851), daughter of Don Carlo, Prince of Acquaviva, and of Donna Maria Rosa Gaetani of Aquila.
209. This is a reference to the wife of the judge Stefano Patrizi, already cited.
210. This is probably the brother of the judge and adviser to the Royal Kingdom, Giuseppe Crisconio.
211. This could be the noblewoman Angiola Pisanelli, from the Dukes of Pesche, who was married to Giuseppe Maria, Marquis of Petracatella, known for having restored and enlarged the family mansion.
212. Marianna Acciaioli was daughter of Antonio Francesco Acciaioli, Marquis of Novi and Count of Cassero, patrician of Florence and a noble Roman, and of Marquise Donna Teresa Serlupi Crescenzi. In June 1742 Marianna married Giacinto Emanuele Acciaioli, gentleman of the Chamberof the Grand Duke of Tuscany.
213. Like this in the text.
214. This could be Giuseppe Caracciolo, Prince of Torella (1747–1808), who was Grandee of Spain of the first class, a Neapolitan patrician, and a knight in the Order of San Gennaro.
215. Like this in the text.
216. The term *undressed* or *negligee* in this circumstance mean that the Queen did not wear official Court dress
217. Antonio Maresca (1750–1822), Duke of Serracapriola, was a Neapolitan minister to the Russian court from 1782 (see Journal, 1 de mars). The Duke negotiated many treaties between Russia and Naples and was also commissioned by Catherine II to conduct peace negotiations with Turkey (1790) and Sweden.
218. This could be Angelo Maria Bandini (1726–1803), religious scholar and bibliophile, in one of the canons of San Lorenzo. He was often contacted by Italian and European intellectuals, becoming one of the central figures of Florentine cultural life in the age of the House of Lorraine.
219. Antonio Anguissola of Podenzano was at the time General of the Royal Bodyguards.
220. Countess Vigoleno, Giuseppina Poulet, was the wife of Patrizio Scotti, General of the Neapolitan army. On 28 January of that year, the Queen appointed him superintendent of Capodimonte (see *Journal*, 28 January 1783).
221. Lady Bischi, Vittoria Sabucci, wife of Nicola Bischi, ordinary gentleman of Spain.
222. This is the wife of Antonio Mazzacane from the princes of Omignano, who was an officer in the Italian guards and the third master of ceremonies of the *La Victoria* lodge.

223. Italian in the text.
224. Italian in the text.
225. Like this in the text.
226. Count Nicola of Weissenwolf (1763–1825) was in those years Lieutenant Colonel of the Austrian Order of Grand Duke Leopold and patron of the Linz Philharmonic Institute.
227. Like this in the text.
228. Carlo di Tocco Cantelmo Stuart, Prince of Montemiletto, Duke of Popoli, was at the time gentleman of the King's chamber.
229. Vincenzo Pignatelli (1736–1795), Duke of Monteleone, was a member of "the Cassa Sacra" junta, which had been established with the aim of providing for the reconstruction of the province of Calabria.
230. Francesco Pignatelli of Strongoli, already cited.
231. In italian in the text.
232. After calling for the eternal rest of Carlo Tito (1775–1778) and Marianna (1775–1780), the Queen did the same for little Joseph, who died at the age of two.
233. This is a Sixteenth century mansion located on Mount San Leucio on the northern outskirts of Caserta, called *Lo Bello Vedere* (The Beautiful View).
234. This could be Carlo Marsigli or Marsili who was a Neapolitan painter.
235. Countess Charlotte Frendel (1751–1828) was the daughter of a Hungarian nobleman, Giorgio Cornelio Frendel, a wealthy businessman. After the untimely death of her father and then the wedding of one of her sisters, Charlotte moved to Vienna and soon became one of the most prominent women in Viennese society and enjoyed some consideration also from the Habsburg court. She had been called to Naples by the Queen to educate her second child, Princess Maria Luisa. In 1783 she married Gaetano Filangieri
236. This is a hint to the governess of Princess Maria Theresa.
237. This refers to the battalion of naval volunteers, also called the Liparoti (natives of the island of Lipari). Established in 1772, it formed – together with the cadets from the Royal Ferdinand regiment – the sovereign body-guard, and was similar to a small personal army.
238. The Duchess of andria, Margherita Pignatelli Aragona Cortés (1740–1810), was the daughter of Fabrizio Pignatelli, Prince of Noia, and of Costanza de' Medici, from the princes of Ottaiano.
239. Maria Teresa Salandra (1706–1803), Countess von Thürheim, was the mother of Giovanni Vincenzo II Revertera, Duke of Salandra. The Countess was in those years lady of the court of the Queen.
240. Like this in the text.
241. This could be Elisabetta Augusta of Baden-Baden (1726–1789), who in 1775 married the Austrian Count Michael Wenzel d'Althann (1743–1810), Lieutenant colonel and Chamberlain of the Imperial court.

242. This is probably a descendant of the noble Gepo family of Florence, as yet unidentified.
243. This is a reference to the palace Di Sangro di Casacalenda, which had been commissioned by Marianna Di Sangro, Duchess of Casacalenda.
244. Like this in the text, (Educational buildings).
245. This could be an ancestor of the French composer Gustave Bley, who died in 1887.
246. Italian in the text. It was a card game very much in vogue at the time, so called because it was played exactly in reversis, i.e. the person who won had the fewest points.
247. The xebec was a three-masted vessel, designed as a cargo ship, but which also had a dozen guns.
248. Italian in the text, (tuna-fishing nets).
249. Don Domenico Grillo I of Mondragone, third Duke of Mondragone, tenth Duke of Monterotondo, third Count of Carinola (1748–1801), was at the time in the King's service as Gentleman of the Chamber.
250. A card game already cited.
251. Antonio Micheroux (1755 – –1805) was the son of Giuseppe, Colonel of the Hainaut regiment. Like his brothers, he had a military career. At nine Micheroux entered as a cadet in his father's regiment. While he continued to serve in the battalion, thanks to his location, he was introduced at court, becoming one of the favorites of the young Queen. In these years we can trace the origin of his Masonic membership
252. This refers to the noblewoman Maria Antonia Firrao (1740–1836), who was the wife of Don Vincenzo Ruffo (1734–1804), Duke of Bagnara and Prince of Motta.
253. Anna Maria Suardo Guevara, Duchess of Bovino, was at the time a lady of the court.
254. Here the diary mentions Marianna Lanfranchi Aulla, a Poet from Pisa who was known in Arcadia by the pastoral name Euriclea Doriense, author of *Rime of Euriclea Doriense* in Volume XIII of the *Rime degli Arcadi* (Rime of the Arcadians).
255. This could be an ancestor of Judge Giovan Vincenzo Crispo, who from 1813 to 1824 held the position of prosecutor at the royal court in Catanzaro.
256. This could be Francisca de Paula de Benavides y Fernández de Córdoba (1763–1827), who was the wife of the Spanish nobleman Diego Pacheco Téllez-Girón y Velasco, thirteenth Duke of Frias (1754–1811), a politician who had supported the French during the Peninsular War, and who was known as an *afrancesado*.
257. Giuseppe Maria Carrara was at the time Bishop of Mileto.

258. This refers to Mortella, a place between the Torre del Greco and Torre Annunziata.

259. Donna Giovanna D'Evoli (1755–1785) was the wife of the Prince of Ardore, Don Giovanni Franco D'Aragona, perpetual Captain of the men-at – arms in the Kingdom of Naples, Gentleman of the Chamber. The princess was at the time lady of the court of the Queen.

260. Donna Maria Antonia Carafa Cantelmo Stuart (1763–1823) was the daughter of the Prince of Roccella, Don Gennaro I Cantelmo Stuart and of Donna Teresa Carafa, Duchess of Forli.

261. Here the diary mentions the wife of Pietro Pascale, who was at that time judge and governor of Solofra. The judge was a theatre lover. In 1779 his sacred tragicomedy, called *La Gerusalemme liberata. (Jerusalem Delivered)*, was published in Naples in the Neapolitan dialect.

262. This could be Joann Cristian Reil (1759–1813) who was a German doctor, psychiatrist, anatomist and physiologist.

263. Ignazio Gaetano Boncompagni (1743–1790) was Cardinal of the Holy Roman Church, Secretary of State of Pius VI.

264. This is Serafina Caracciolo, already cited.

265. Michele Imperiale, Prince of Francavilla, was in those years honorary Steward and Grand Chamberlain of the Kingdom. His wife was lady of the court.

266. This is Donna Anna Maria Galluccio, who in the previous year became the widow of Don Domenico Antonio Carafa (1756–1782), son of the Prince of San Lorenzo.

267. Here the diary mentionsMichelle Honoré Marie Delisle, who was the wife of the French consul in Naples, Charles-Cardin Amé of Saint-Didier.

268. The Elector of the Palatinate of Bavaria at that time was Carlo Teodoro of Wittelsbach (1724–1799).

269. It refers to the places where the nets for tuna fishing are set.

270. François Guillaume Le Vacher (1732–1816) was a descendant of a historical family of French doctors, Le Vacher. He was a former adviser to the Royal Academy of Surgery in Paris and was the first surgeon in the court of Parma.

271. This could be a descendant of Lorenzo Antonio Canuti (1727–1767), a Bolognese professor and an expert in anatomy.

272. In Italian in the text.

273. Vincenzo Cammarano (1720–1809), known as Giancola, was a well-known actor who is specialised in the Neapolitan dialect. From 1770 he worked at the San Carlino theater for over thirty years, acclaimed in the role of Pulcinella. Giancola's nickname, as his son Philip explains in a sonnet, comes from the name of a character, the Calabrian abbot Don

Pompilio Pecegreca, who was an interpreter of Francesco Cerlone's comedy, *Donzella maritata e vedova* (Donzella Married and Widowed). The nickname would accompany him for his entire career, even when he played the role of Pulcinella. Giancola's reputation as an interpreter of Pulcinella was not only known throughout Italy, but also in Europe.

274. Cecilia Carlotta Anna Mahony (1740–1789) was the daughter of Count James Joseph Mahony, Lieutenant General, who moved to Naples, and of Anne Clifford.

275. Maria Carolina does not specify what the King throw but it was probably a javelin.

276. Muzio Gaeta, Duke of San Nicola, was a diplomat at the court of St. Petersburg from 1777 to 1784. At the time he held the office of Regent of theVicaria.

277. Gaetano Latilla (1711–1788) was one of the most famous Italian composers of his time. Lucky in the theatrical genre, he composed about 60 works. Also noteworthy is his sacred and instrumental music. He was Kapellmeister and had taught in Rome, Naples and Venice, where among other things, he had a working relationship with Carlo Goldoni.

278. This refers to the news that on 11 June 1783 Carlos Domingo, the only son ofCarlo IV and Maria Louisa of Parma, was dead.

279. Gaetano Montalto (1729–1804), Duke of Fragnito, was at the time gentleman of the King's presence chamber.

280. On 27 July 1783, in the palace chapel in Naples, Charlotte Frendel married Gaetano Filangieri (the specifics relating to the matrimony are kept by ASN, *Cappellano Maggiore, Matrimoni*, fs. 921

281. On 18 July of that year, after taking part in both the Council of Finance and the Council of War, the Queen took to her bed, seized with violent pains and bleeding, after which she gave birth to a dead child. For the next two days, she was between life and death, renouncing all her commitments and political affairs. Owing to her strong malaise there is a change in the Queen's handwriting, which occurs from 18 until 27 July.

282. Jean Golo] Vincenzo Cammarano, known as Giancola, already cited.

283. Maria Carolina, in an improved physical condition, witnessed the marriage of Charlotte and Filangieri, which had been scheduled for 20 July, but was postponed owing to the unexpected illness of the Queen.

284. The Queen, now convalescent, resumed her court and political work, but did not recover completely until 11 August of that year.

285. At court a party was organized for the Queen's recovery.

286. On that date the Queen was born (13 August 1752).

287. This may be Maria Giuseppa Pignatelli, who was the widow of the Duke of Corigliano, Giacomo Saluzzo.

288. Marquis Saverio Simonetti was the primary lawyer in the capital and in Sicily. At the time he was a consultant to Viceroy Caracciolo.
289. Here the diary mentionsthe Spanish general Giuseppe Roca who, together with General Gioacchino Fons de Vela, was sent to Naples by Charles III with the intention of amending and suspending the innovations promoted by Minister Acton regarding the centralization of the Secretary of War and the Secretary of the Navy.
290. Like this in the text.
291. Donna Maria Antonia Oliva Grimaldi (1758–1822), Princess of Gerace, was a lady Queen's court.
292. Here the diary mentions the Frenchman Charles Abel de Loras, bailiff in the Order of Malta, who had been a representative in Piedmont, Sardinia, and in those years was in the service of Naples.
293. These are the Princes of San Lorenzo and their sister Anna Maria Galluccio, already cited.
294. It refers to Romualdo Braschi Onesti (1753–1817) who was the son of Count Girolamo, Marquis of Baldacchino, and of Giulia Braschi, sister of Cardinal Giovanni, the future Pope Pius VI. Thanks to the patronage of his powerful relative, he began an ecclesiastical career and became an apostolic delegate in France. In 1784 he was appointed Grand Prior of the Order of Malta in Rome.
295. Here the diary mentions Giuseppe de Saa y Pereira, who was at that time the Portuguese Minister Plenipotentiary in Naples.
296. This probably refers to the wife of Count Alessandro Delfino.
297. Maria Luisa of Parma (1751–1819) was the wife of Carlo IV of Bourbon, Prince of Asturie and then King in 1788.
298. There is limited biographical information on Francesco Farina. He was a merchant and businessman born in Chieti, in the second half of the 18th century.
299. Italian in the text, (kind of fish).
300. It refers to the sanctuary of Madonna della libera in Castellamare di Stabia.
301. This could be Melchior Antoine Monier (1746–1824), who was a parliamentary lawyer in Bourg and an adviser to the King of France.
302. This refers to Marianna Wollensfeld, wife of Vincenzo Goyzueta, son of Juan Ausenzio.
303. This is probably Carlo Tolomeo Gallio, Duke of Alvito (1741–1800). The early of Alvito was a fief of the Kingdom Terra di Lavoro
304. This could be Maria Maddalena Roffia Interminelli, daughter of knight commander Filippo Maria (1710–1783), who was Colonel of the Burgundy Regiment and Governor of Siracusa.

305. This refers to Teresa Spinelli (1759–1834), wife of Giulio Antonio Acquaviva (1741–1801), XXIII Duke of Nardo and XXVII Count of Conversano.

306. This refers to Vincenzo Goyzueta, son of Juan Asenzio, already cited.

307. This is Beatrice Correale, who on 4 October of that year married the national guard Antonio Mastrilli, Marquis of Schiava (1760–1834).

308. Here the diary mentions Giovanna Carrillo, widow of Judge Luigi Frontone (1720–1781).

309. Followed by two blank pages.

310. The Duke of Castelpagano, Ottavio Mormile (1761–1836), was at the time Minister of Foreign Affairs.

311. General Krottendorf was the name used by the Empress Maria Teresa and her daughters, Maria Carolina and Marie Antoinette, to indicate the arrival of their regular time of the month. It is interesting to highlight that to write names or mark with X for mestrual period in also reported in other personal diary such as in *The Journal of Claire Clairmont* edited by Marion Kingston Stocking, Cambridge : Harvard University Press, 1968, 91.

312. The German Theatine Joseph Sterzinger (1746–1821) belonged to an influential and aristocratic Tyrolean family. In 1778 he was appointed librarian of the Royal library in Palermo. The appointment of Sterzinger would have been, at the institutional level, a defeat for the Jesuits and the opening for the opposing Theatine deputation.

313. Maria Amelia of Habsburg-Lorraine (1746–1804) was the Queen's sister. She was married to Ferdinando of Bourbon, Duke of Parma.

314. This could be the Neapolitan physicist Tiberius Cavallo, also known as Tiberio (1749–1809), who, with his scientific contribution in that year had helped to fly the first air balloon. After a series of attempts, the first flight took place in Naples on September 13, 1789 in the presence of King Ferdinand and Queen Maria Carolina.

315. See above, Giovanni Giacomo Onorati.

316. Carlo Borromeo of Lichtenstein (1730–1789) was Emperor Joseph II's chamberlain as well as one of his confidants.

317. This refers to the visit by the statue of Benedict Labre, known as the *Tramp of God* (1748–1783), revered as a saint by the Catholic Church.

318. The Prince of Cutò, Alessandro Filingieri (1740–1806), was at the time Lieutenant General of the Bourbon army.

319. Here the diary mentions the Duke of Misilmeri, Emanuele Bonanno Filingieri (1734–1800), younger brother of Giuseppe Bonanno Filingeri, heir of the family and the protagonist of a brilliant career in Minister Bernardo Tanucci's entourage.

320. This is Giovanni Gioeni, Duke of Anjou (1740–1793), appointed Auditor General of the Court of Royal Patrimony. He had been superintendent general of the troops, and a pawnbroker in Palermo. At the time he was a member of Parliament.
321. This presumably refers to Maria Carolina's name day.
322. Here it mentons Commodore Roger Curtis, at the time the Commander of a vessel.
323. This could be Ferdinand M. Bayard de la Vingtrie (1763–1855), at the time Director of the Public Domain in Naples. King Ferdinand entrusted to his son Armand Joseph, together with other shareholders, the granting of the construction of the railway line from Naples to southern Nocera
324. This is a Royal site that was used for hunting wild game.
325. Emilia de Gennaro, Princess of Sirignano, already cited.
326. Francesco Antonio Bonanno e Borromeo, Prince of Cattolica (1744–1797), was First Horseman, gentleman of the Chamberand a Knight of Malta and San Gennaro.
327. Eloisa Malloy, of Irish origin. She was a descendant of a family of officers, the wife of Joseph Macdonald. At that time Joseph was adjutant of the King's regiment, a unit of the Spanish service whose cadres were composed mainly of Irish Catholics and Scottish exiles who had supported the efforts of the House of Stuart to regain the British throne.
328. Teresa Filangieri de Candida, wife of Judge Francesco Cicconi (1720–1792), Capo Ruota of the royal audience of Catanzaro and Governor of Reggio.
329. This refers to the widow of Francesco Vargas, who had been managing director of the Royal jurisdiction, a counselor in the Royal room of Santa Chiara.
330. This may be the wife of a son or a nephew of Giovanbattista Vico.
331. The Franciscan theologian and orator Giuseppe Maria Rugilo (1722–1789) was at the time Bishop of Lucera.
332. Giuseppe Sisto y Britto had been Bishop of Sora since 1768.
333. This could be the wife of Michele Maria Vecchioni, who was a lawyer and judge of the High Court of the civil Vicaria. In 1788, Vecchioni became a counselor in the Royal room of Santa Chiara.
334. This is probably the Marquess Costanza Scotti (1736–1794), a noblewoman who was the wife of Alessandro Sanvitale. In 1784, her son Stefano enlisted in the King Ferdinand's guard and later became gentleman of the chamber.
335. The French Count François-Henri of Virieu (1754–1793) was a general, belonging to the Martinist freemason lodge in Lyon.
336. Here the diary mentions Luigi Sanseverino (1758–1789), Prince of Bisignano, Spanish Grandee of the First Class who had abdicated in that year.

337. The comic opera was mainly performed by the Florentine singer Celeste Cottelini, who had moved to Naples with her sisters Anna, a singer and Constantine and Rosina, painters. Giovanni Morelli was at the time a singer at the Teatro dei Fiorentini and the Teatro San Carlo.

338. Here it most likely mentions Pietro Antonio Brentano (1735–1797), a descendant of a great mercantile family.

339. The Strina family was well-known in the seventeenth century. Beginning in 1616, the Ferrante brothers and Marco Angelo Strina started building the church of the Holy Spirit, which initially started as a the family's parish church. With a dispatch of 2 December 1765, the King had restored to the crown the Abbey of St. Salvatore Telese and gave it to the Father Ferdinand Strina, tutor to the royal princesses.

340. This is a reference to Vito Giuseppe Millico (1737–1802), who was known as "the Muscovite". He was an opera singer and teacher of the Neapolitan singing style.

341. Interrupted like so in the text.

342. Here the diary mentions Luigi Serio (1744–1799) who was a pupil of Antonio Genovesi. At the time he was a lawyer, taught language and rhetoric at the University of Naples. Serio also dabbled in poetry, becoming an improviser and writer of great repute.

343. Like this in the text.

344. The King of Sweden, Gustave III (1746–1792), son of the Crown Prince and later King, Adolph Frederick, ascended the throne in 1771. With the coup d'etat of 1772 he emasculated the party system of the so-called Era of Freedom and restored royal absolutism. In 1780 he became a Freemason and introduced the rite of strict observance. In that year he appointed his younger brother Charles, Duke of Sudermania and future King Charles XVIII, Grand Master of the Grand Lodge of Sweden. The Grand Lodge gave him the specific title of Vicarius Salomonis. From February to May 1784, Gustav III made a long trip to Italy, which took him, under the name of "Count of Haga", from Leghorn to Naples. The Swedish King had chosen to travel incognito as the best solution for political reasons.

345. This refers to General Pignatelli, who had been appointed to assist the inhabitants of the places affected by the earthquake in Calabria.

346. These are the Marcolini spouses: Camillo (1736–1814), who was a descendant of an influential noble family from Fano. As a young man he went to Dresden and Saxony, becoming a protégé of Frederick Augustus, Prince of Saxony and later King, who appointed him Privy Councillor, Grand Chamberlain, Head Equerry. In 1799 he became Minister of State. In June 1773 he married Maria Anna O'Kelly of Ireland (1749–1829), maid of honor of Maria Teresa of Habsburg. An orphan, she was raised in a convent under the direct supervision of the Empress.

347. Here the diary mentions Marquess Maria Maddalena Cavaselice, wife of the Marquis Matteo Angelo Ruggi of d'Aragon, who had been general superintendent of the castles of Naples and Sicily and the garrisons of Tuscany.
348. Cimitino] This is the Prince of Cimitile, already cited.
349. Here is a hint to Count Gustaf Mauritz Armfelt (1757–1814), Finnish soldier and statesman in the service of Gustav III, King of Sweden. At that time he held the office of Grand Chamberlain.
350. This may be Rose Marie Agathe Leonora Riecourt Vauzelle, wife of Jean Joseph Charles Richard Thscoudy (1764–1822), a Swiss general who in those years was in the service of the King of Naples
351. This is Carlo Vanvitelli (1739–1821), son of the famous architect Luigi Vanvitelli. During the last of his father's life, he resided in Caserta Royal Palace directing the works; when Luigi died (1773), Carlo Vanvitelli became direction of the construction.
352. The poet and librettist Simone Francesco Maria Ranieri de' Calzabigi (1714–1795) had studied Humanities in Leghorn and Science in Pisa, and under the name Liburno Drepanio, he became a member of the Etruscan Academy of Cortona and the Academy of Arcadia. In 1743 he served in a ministry in Naples, where he devoted himself to becoming a librettist. Because of his involvement in a trial for poisoning, he had to leave the city and travelled to Paris. Afterwards leaving France, in 1761 he went to Vienna to hold the office of the Chamber of Auditors in the Netherlands and later that of apostolic adviser to S.M.I.R. Subsequently, a scandal, on the orders of Empress Maria Teresa he left Vienna. In 1775 he stopped in Pisa and later settled in Naples, where until his death he devoted himself to the literary life of the city.
353. The Spanish ambassador Àlvaro de Nava, Viscount de la Herreria, was sent to the court of Naples from March 1784 to February 1785.
354. This is Ricciarda Catanti (–1787), who was the daughter of Count Giovanni Catanti and of Elisabetta Angeli. In 1740, Ricciarda married Minister Bernardo Tanucci.
355. Gennaro Capece Galeota, Duke of Regina, was at the time gentleman of the King's chamber.
356. This may be Pietro Antonio Poulet (1744–1793), son of Lieutenant general Amato Poulet and of Orosia of the Barbazzanni barons. In 1768 he was appointed Second Lieutenant of infantry, becoming Engineer of the armies of public squares and borders.
357. The Viscountess of Herreria, Francisca Javiera de Güemes, was the wife of the Spanish Ambassador, Álvaro de Navia, Viscount of Herreria, already cited.
358. The Queen does not mention what was printed.

359. This refers to the Episcopal suffragan seat in Capua, in Terra di Lavoro. It was a wooded area where the King used to go hunting.

360. Domenico Orsini d'Aragona (1719–1789), from the Dukes of Gravina, was the nephew of Benedict XIII. In 1743, Pope Benedict XIV appointed him Cardinal of the Roman Catholic Church. In addition to his long career in the Church, Domenico continued to act as head of the family, taking care of the administration of property.

361. This refers to the Duchess of Corigliano, Chiara De Marinis, who was the wife of Agostino Saluzzo. At the time the Duchess was lady of the court of the Queen.

362. This refers to the wife of the Marquis of Casabona, Donna Nicoletta Brunassi.

363. Here the diary mentions Donna Caterina Francone, daughter of Paul, Prince of Ripa Francone and of Donna Ippolita Ruffo, from the princes of Castelcicala. In 1757, Caterina married Don Nicola Mormile (1732–1810) second Duke of Castelpagano, older brother of Ottavio and Minister of Foreign Affairs.

364. Father Andrea Maria Labini (1735–1791) was a theatine of Bitonto.

365. Like this in the text.

366. This is probably Donna Bianca Doria del Carretto, Princess of Avella and Duchess of Tursi. She was the daughter of Don Francesco and of Donna Maria Giovanna Doria del Carretto (already cited). In 1781, Bianca married Fabrizio Colonna (1761–1813), a Neapolitan nobleman who later become Senator of the French Empire.

367. This refers to the arrest of Cataldo Rosso and Angelo Del Duca, known as Angiolello. The latter was a brigand chief famous for his exploits and for his generous spirit. An honest farmer, he was forced into hiding (probably in 1780) due to a quarrel with the Duke of Martina.

368. Here the diary mentions Filippo Capecelatro, at the time President of the province of Matera.

369. The Prince of Villafranca, Francesco Alliata (1754–1804), was at the time gentleman of the King's chamber.

370. Count Mérode of Westerloo, Guillaume Charles Ghislain (1762–1830), was at the time Ambassador of Emperor Joseph II in the United Provinces. Later, he became an officer under Napoleon.

371. Like this in the text.

372. Don Ferdinando Lucchesi was Knight of the Order of Malta, and had enlisted in the army holding the positions of Sergeant and Lieutenant colonel. In 1775, Lucchesi was appointed gentleman of the King's chamber. Later, in 1777, he was sent to Denmark as Minister Plenipotentiary, where he remained until 1784 when he moved to London.

373. This refers to Arkadyi Ivanovich Morkov (1747–1827), a Russian noble and diplomat at the court of France. He was a member of the Russian Collegium of Foreign Affairs and assistant to the Russian chancellor Alexander Bezborodko. At the time he was Ambassador to Sweden.

374. This could be the canon Domenico Ventapane, who was parish priest of Church of the Immaculate Conception in Materdei and later became Bishop of Teano.

375. François-Joachim de Pierre (1715–1794), Cardinal of Bernis, was a catholic Archi bishop and French politican. Bernis became one of the advisors of King Louis XV. Always assiduously followed by Pompadour, he headed the so-called "reversal of alliances" that led to, along with the Treaty of Versailles in 1756, the alliance of France with Austria to cope with the aggressive Prussian militarism and English imperialist expansionism. His action, which had maintained a peaceful balance in Europe, was however thwarted by the Prussian attack on Austria, consequently beginning the "Seven Years War". In 1757 he became Minister of State and shortly afterwards he joined the Ministry of Foreign Affairs. In 1764 he was appointed Ambassador to Rome. In February 1784, an edict from the court of Naples ordered bishops to grant dispensations before resorting to Rome. In May 1784, Cardinal de Bernis took a trip to Naples, taking advantage of the confidence which the Queen had in him to plead the cause of the Holy See, but he received nothing but vague promises.

376. This refers to a rock in the sea called Fiatamone, which was close to Castello dell'Uovo, where there were many caves.

377. This may refer to the new Queen's pregnancy.

378. Here it is possible thatthe lunch table was full.

379. Giuseppe and Baldassarre Hauss had come from Austria as tutors of Prince Francis. The two brothers were chosen by Emperor Joseph II and Minister Ignaz von Born, Worshipful Master of the Austrian Illuminati lodge.

380. This refers to Bishop Nicola Molinari (1707–1792), who had become Bishop of Ravello at the request of Pope Pius VI, but also on the explicit request of the King of Naples, Ferdinand IV.

381. Here the diary mentions the name day of the King.

382. This is José Nicolas of Azara, Marquis of Nibbiano (1730–1804), a Spanish diplomat who belonged to the Holy See in Rome. At the time he held the office of Attorney General. In 1785 he became Ambassador to Rome.

383. This may be Anna Beccadelli of Bologna (1757–1828), wife of Francesco Notarbatolo, Duke of Villarosa (1750–1814).

384. In those years Domenico Leonessa was a brigadier in the army of the Kingdom.

385. This could be Serafina Caracciolo, already cited.
386. The Duchess of San Clemente, Maria Teresa Arezzo, was interested in the literary salons of Naples and with Sanfelice was imprisoned, but Maria Teresa avoided the death sentence. She was a friend of Münter in the darkest hours of 1786. At 26 she was recognized as a "lady of great intellectual stature."
387. This is Ferdinando Maria Saluzzo (1744–1816), a priest in the Roman Catholic Church. On 4 July 1784 he was consecrated Archbishop. In 1801, Pope Pius VII elevated him to the rank of Cardinal.
388. Marquis Fuscaldo Giuseppe Spinelli (1743–1830), gentleman of the King's chamber. In 1768 he was nominated Chief Justiciar of the Kingdom. At the time he was regent in the High Court of the Vicar.
389. This is a reference to Alexander Lindsay, Count of Balcarres (1752–1825), who was an important commander in the 53rd Regiment of Light Infantry in the British Army under the command of General Burgoyne during the American Revolution. Along with the latter, he surrendered to American forces on 17 October 1777 at the Battle of Saratoga. In 1784 he became a Peer in Scotland, re–elected in 1807. On 27 August 1789 he was appointed Colonel of the 63rd Regiment of Foot. In 1793, he became Major General and Commander in Jamaica and Lieutenant Governor of that island in 1794.
390. This could be the Austrian baron Anton I Dobel Hoff-Dier (1733–1812), who in those years was Imperial Advisor to Joseph II.
391. Follow in the text: dine avec le Roi (lunched with the King), cancelled.
392. Like this in the text.
393. Here the diary mentions Gerardo Carafa, Count of Policastro (1748–1814), at the time gentleman of the King's chamber.
394. Vincenzo Tuttavilla, Duke of Calabritto, at that time was gentleman of the King's chamber.
395. This refers to the church of San Diego all'Ospedaletto situated in Naples.
396. Interrupted in this way in the text.
397. Scipione of Ricci (1740–1810) was a Catholic bishop educated in Rome by the Jesuits. He was Bishop of Pistoia from 1780 to 1791. He took part in the agreement between Pope Pius VI and King Ferdinand IV regarding the Freemasons, of which Naples was, at that time, the major centre.
398. Francesco Pignatelli of Strongoli, already cited.
399. This is a reference to Caterina Capasso, wife of the botanist and physician Innocenzo Cirillo. Her son Domenico had become a distinguished physician and professor of botany. Owing to his reputation he was called back to court and he became the personal physician of the Bourbons.
400. The Queen often opened her husband's letters and copied what she read with the intention of sending informations to her brothers.

401. This is the Royal house of the Torre del Greco.
402. Here the diary mentions the Neapolitan nobleman Don Domenico of Capua, Duke of San Cipriano (1745–1816).
403. This refers to the expedition to Algiers by Naples and Spain, which was under the command of Antonio Barceló, who left Naples 18 May 1784 and returned 2 September 1784.
404. This refers to the Royal Bourbon ships.
405. Nicola Vivenzio (1742–1816) had graduated in law from Naples and was soon to become a famous lawyer. He was a tax attorney in Sommaria and part of the Council of Correspondence which aimed to represent and defend the royal treasury.
406. This refers to the Herzan counts (husband and wife), specifically to Massimiliano Antonio Herzan of Harras (1736–1803) who was married to Marie Henriette of Bünau. Maximilian was the brother of Cardinal Francesco Herzan of Harras, Minister Plenipotentiary to the Austrian Emperor in Rome.
407. Maria Antonia Oliva Grimaldi (1758–1833), Princess of Gerace, was a Neapolitan noblewoman, lady of the court of the Two Sicilies.
408. This refers to Bishop Salvatore Spinelli (1746–1805), Marquis of Fuscaldo. Originally a Benedictine monk, on 18 June 1769 he became a priest. In the summer of 1779, he was elected Bishop of Catanzaro and consecrated in Rome by Cardinal Lazzaro Pallavicini. In 1797 he was promoted to the Archdiocese of Salerno.
409. This refers to the name day of the Queen's son, Francis.
410. Lisette was the governess of Princess Maria Theresa.
411. Giuseppe Rossi (1736–1797) was only twenty years old when he was made Reader of Theology at the archdiocesan seminary. In 1767 he was elected Canon of the cathedral by King Ferdinand IV of Naples. At the time he was appointed instructor and confessor to the princesses. In 1791, afterwards the death of Filippo Sanseverino, he became the King's confessor.
412. This is a reference to Count Michele Pignatelli, already cited.
413. Here the diary mentions Cardinal Francesco Carafa della Spina di Traetto (1747–1822), a native of one of the most noble Neapolitan families. On 27 January 1760 he was ordained a priest and the next day he was appointed tenured Archbishop of Patrasso. On 19 April 1773, Pope Clement XIV appointed him Cardinal of the Consistory. Afterwards having participated in the conclave of 1774–1775, which elected Pope Pius VI, on 29 March 1775 he was appointed Prefect of the Congregation for Bishops and Regulars. From 1778 to 1786 he was linked to the Archdiocese of Ferrara

414. Domenico Cotugno (1736–1822) was a famous Neapolitan anatomist and surgeon. Along with Domenico Cirillo, he had published scholarly works on medicine and botany. At the time he was court physician.
415. Like this in the text.
416. Donna Maddalena Montalto (1751–1828) was the daughter of Don Gaetano, Duke of Fragnito.
417. This refers to Maria Anna Albertini (1765–1858) who was the daughter of Prince Cimitile and had married Giovanni Antonio Muscettola, Prince of Leporano (1768–1845).
418. Like this in the text.
419. Like this in the text.
420. Don Nicola Brancaccio (1747–1822), Prince of Ruffano, who had married the daughter of the Prince of Butera, Teresa Branciforte.
421. Like this in the text.
422. Like this in the text.
423. Like this in the text.
424. This could be Francis Bray (1727–1804), an English surgeon, or Richard Bryan, who was also a surgeon.
425. Like this in the text.
426. The Queen gave birth to Princess Marie Antoinette (1784–1806).
427. Like this in the text.
428. Like this in the text.
429. Like this in the text.
430. Like this in the text.
431. Like this in the text.
432. Lord Hamilton made good use of his position as Envoy Extraordinary to the Court of Naples, in order to collect some of the antiquities of that time from that area. Many artifacts from Hamilton's collection ended up in the British Museum.
433. This is a reference to Princess Marie Antoinette.
434. This alludes to Shakespeare's tragedy, *Julius Caesar*, 1599.
435. This may be Amélie de Boufflers (1751–1794), the wife of the French general Armand Louis of Gontaut-Biron (1747–1793), Duke of Lauzan. He was the general of Gontaut, an ex-Mason, who had fought in the American Revolution. He was also the nephew of Choiseul and a friend of Duke Philip d'Orleans.
436. Ekaterina Vassilievna Engelhardt (1761–1829), was already lady of the Court of the Russian Empress. In 1781, she married Count Pavel Martynovich Skavronsky (1757–1793), the Russian ambassador to Naples, an important military commander and politician during the reign of Catherine.

437. This could be Isabella Pepoli, daughter of Marquis Francesco Pepoli, Count of Castiglione and patrician of Bologna. He was also Ambassador of the city of Ferrara to the Holy See and the old town of Bologna.
438. Spedale François] Theatre.
439. Peter von Biron, (1724–1800) was the last Duke of Courland and Semigallia, from 1769 to 1795, and Duke of Sagan in 1786. Peter was the eldest son of Ernest Johann von Biron, an aristocrat of Swabian origin, who had remained in exile with his family for twenty-five years, and was then reinstated in the government of the Duchy of Courland by Catherine II of Russia. Ernest Johann had died in 1769 and Peter was his successor. Peter ruled from 1769 to 1795 and obtained, most of time with the help of Russia, and some territories in Prussia, and eastern Bohemia. Peter was married three times. The third marriage took place in 1779 to Anna Charlotte Dorothea, Countess of Medem (1761–1821), known as the Dorothea of Courland. The Duchess promoted an aristocratic parlour in Berlin, taking care of the diplomatic interests of her husband. In 1784, the Dukes of Courland made a trip to Italy, visiting Venice, Bologna, and Rome, and in February 1785 they visited the court of Naples.
440. Marquis Federico Manfredini (1734–1821) was at the time Prime Minister of the Grand Duchy of Tuscany.
441. Vivenzio Nicola, already cited.
442. Here the diary mentions Muzio Gaeta, Duke of San Nicola, already cited.
443. Friedrich Münter (1761–1830) was a very learned man, an antiquarian and philologist. He became Bishop of Zealand in Denmark. In 1784 he obtained from the Danish Government a grant to carry out a study trip around Europe. He went to Italy and remained there from 1784 to 1787, thanks to Count Stolberg. Emissary of the Order of the Illuminati, he had been recomended by the "brothers" of Naples to visit Sicily in 1785. The action of Münter favoured the revival and expansion of a rationalist and Enlightened freemasonry, in contrast with the growth of the legitimist orientation of the 'national', with their elitist and occultist character and their loyalty to the tenets of Catholicism.
444. The *loto dauphin* was invented in 1775 by the toymaker Vaugeois was the favourite game of families of the aristocracy, and was practised until the early twentieth century before falling into oblivion. This is a more complicated game than the classic lotto, and it requires more hardware. See : ttp://expositions.bnf.fr/jeux/arret/01.htm
445. This may be Norbert Hadrawa, who was then Secretary of the Austrian Embassy in Naples. Between 1786 and 1790, Hadrawa undertook numerous excavations on the island of Capri and the mountain of Castiglione, where he found a large quantity of objects, including a floor in *opus sectile* that is kept in the Museum of Capodimonte.

446. This is the tragedy *The Widow of Malabar*, which the composer Gaetano Isola staged for the first time for the carnival that year in Genoa.

447. Simon de Las Casas was at the time Spanish Minister Plenipotentiary in Naples and followed the guidelines of his predecessor Herreria. The Spanish Minister, and the Marquis of Sambuca, were supporters of the Spanish cabal which plotted against the Queen and Acton in the spring of 1785.

448. Father Emanuele Maria Pignone of Carretto (1721–1796) was an Augustinian priest. In 1792 he became Bishop of Sessa Aurunca, a small town in province of Caserta.

449. The Queen had received news that on 27 Marchr 1785 her sister, Marie Antoinette, had given birth to Louis XVII.

450. This should be Rudolf Edling (1723–1804), who was Archbishop of Gorizia from 1774 to 1784. On 13 August 1784, the abbot left the arch-diocese as a result of a conflict with Emperor Joseph II, for refusing the edict of tolerance without permission from Rome.

451. On 30 April 1785, the Queen and King departed on a long journey to northern Italy, which ended five months later, on 7 September of the same year.

452. This alludes to the theatrical work inspired by a book written by the poet Rainieri of Calzabigi titled *Cook o sia gli inglesi in Othaiti*,(Cook or the British in Othaiti), published that year.

453. Here the text presents some codewords.

454. The Parisian playwright Charles Collé had produced the comedy *Dupui and Deronai* at the Opera in 1763.

455. Here we should mention the tragedy, *Gaston and Bayard*, written in 1773 by Pierre Laurent of Belloy.

456. Here we should mention the musical comedy entitled The Hunting King, also known as *The Hunting of Henry IV*, by the Neapolitan composer Angelo Tarchi, which was performed for the first time in Naples in 1780.

457. Monte Grane] Monte Grande.

458. This refers to two French comedy: *the Démocrite Amoureux*, which was written by Jean-François Regnard, and first performed on 12 January 1700; *Le procureur arbitre* was witten by Philippe Poisson in 1728.

459. Caserta Vecchia] Casertavecchia.

460. Here the diary mentions a descendant of the family of the Baratelli barons. This family was from Cesena and descended from the Porcelli Counts and from Marquis Romagnoli.

461. This is a reference to another comedy by Jean-François Regnard, *La Legataire Universel*, written in 1706.

462. Here we should mention the prose drama in four acts entitled *Montrose & Amélie* by Louis-F. Faur, performed for the first time in 1783.

463. This is a performance of the French drama *Eugenie*, written by Pierre Augustin Caron of Beaumarchais in 1767.
464. Lady Georgiana Spencer (1757–1806) was the eldest child of the Counts of Spencer, and was the sister of George Earl Spencer. A bright and intelligent woman, she was a patron of the arts. A dedicated writer, she participated in a surprising and lively correspondence in which she described with wit and acuity the facts of her era. In 1774, Georgiana married William Cavendish, Duke of Devonshire. The Queen of British parlours, she became famous for her beauty, charm and charisma. She was also active in politics. Both the Spencers and Cavendishs were staunch supporters of the Whigs, CJ Fox. Georgiana enjoyed enormous popularity. She travelled a lot. Lady Spencer, during one of her many stays in France, met and befriended Queen Marie Antoinette, the sister of Queen Maria Carolina. In 1785 Georgiana visited Naples.
465. Like this way in the manuscript.
466. Like this in the text.
467. This is a reference to the French comedy *Le Menechmes*, written by Jean-François Regnard in 1769.
468. Like this in the text.
469. This refers to Duchess Izabela Lubormiska (1736–1816), who was the wife of the President of the Polish Crown, Stanislaw Lubomirski. She was one of the most important women in eighteenth-century Poland. The Duchess took an active part in the politics of her country and sought to acquire both foreign courts and noble masses.

Author Index[1]

[1] Note: Page numbers with "n" denote notes.

© The Author(s) 2017   391
C. Recca, *The Diary of Queen Maria Carolina of Naples, 1781–1785*,
Queenship and Power, DOI 10.1007/978-3-319-31987-2

V
Vallecchi, F., 13n7
Verri, P., 17n46
Villa, P., 173, 237, 362n70,
  369n158
Viollet, C., 39n8
Viviani della Robbia, E., 14n14,
  15n25
von Helfert, J.A., 101, 104n10,
  105n25

W
Wandruska, A., 14n13
Washington, G., 22, 40n14
Weil, M.H., 16n39
Whitaker Scalia, T., 13n11
Woodacre, E., 17n52

Z
Zucco, A., 62n48

Name Index[1]

A
Acciaioli, Antonio Francesco, Marquis
  of Novi and Count of Cassero,
  373n212
Acciaioli, Giacinto Emanuele,
  gentleman of the Chamberof the
  Grand Duke of Tuscany, 373n212
Acciaioli, Marianna, daughter of
  Acciaioli, Antonio Francesco,
  373n212
Aci, Princess of. *See* Reggio,
  Ferdinanda, Princess of Aci
Acquaviva, Giulio Antonio, Duke of
  Nardò and XXVII Count of
  Conversano, 379n305
Acquaviva, Princess of. *See* de Mari,
  Carlo
Acton, John Francis Edward, 7,
  63–75, 76n3, 76n7, 77n17,
  77n26, 78n54, 79–83, 85–9,
  90n7, 93n11, 102, 117, 119,

127, 128, 130, 135, 139, 141,
142, 145–7, 151–3, 158, 162,
166, 174, 177, 178, 181, 182,
184–5, 187–90, 194–9, 201–3,
206–15, 217, 219–23, 225, 229,
233–6, 238, 241, 242, 244, 246,
249, 251, 254–6, 260, 261, 267,
268, 272, 274–7, 279–84, 287,
289, 292, 294, 296–300, 302,
304, 306, 307, 309, 312–17,
319, 320, 322, 324, 325, 329,
331, 332, 337–9, 341, 343–5,
348, 351, 353–6, 361n49,
365n110, 378n289, 389n447
Adolph Frederick, King, 381n344
Albertini, Fabio, Prince of Faggiano,
  360n28
Albertini, Giovan Battista, Prince of
  Cimitile, 71, 73, 370n173
Albertini, Maria Anna, Princess,
  387n417

[1] Note: Page numbers with "n" denote notes.

© The Author(s) 2017   395
C. Recca, *The Diary of Queen Maria Carolina of Naples, 1781–1785*,
Queenship and Power, DOI 10.1007/978-3-319-31987-2